Managing Organizational Change

A Multiple Perspectives Approach

Managing Organizational Change

A Multiple Perspectives Approach

Ian Palmer
University of Technology, Sydney

Richard Dunford
Macquarie University

Gib Akin
University of Virginia

McGraw-Hill Irwin

Boston Burr Ridge, IL Dubuque, IA Madison, WI New York
San Francisco St. Louis Bangkok Bogotá Caracas Kuala Lumpur
Lisbon London Madrid Mexico City Milan Montreal New Delhi
Santiago Seoul Singapore Sydney Taipei Toronto

The McGraw-Hill Companies

MANAGING ORGANIZATIONAL CHANGE: A MULTIPLE PERSPECTIVES APPROACH

Published by McGraw-Hill/Irwin, a business unit of The McGraw-Hill Companies, Inc., 1221 Avenue of the Americas, New York, NY, 10020.

Some ancillaries, including electronic and print components, may not be available to customers outside the United States.

This book is printed on acid-free paper.

4 5 6 7 8 9 0 DOC/DOC 0 9 8 7

ISBN-13: 978-0-07-249680-2
ISBN-10: 0-07-249680-0

Editorial director: *John E. Biernat*
Senior sponsoring editor: *Kelly H. Lowery*
Editorial assistant: *Kirsten L. Guidero*
Executive marketing manager: *Ellen Cleary*
Senior project manager: *Lori Koetters*
Production supervisor: *Debra R. Sylvester*
Design coordinator: *Cara David*
Lead media project manager: *Cathy L. Tepper*
Developer, Media technology: *Brian Nacik*
Cover design: *JoAnne Schopler*
Cover image: © *Geoff Manasse/Getty Images*
Typeface: *10/12 Times New Roman*
Compositor: *ICC*
Printer: *R. R. Donnelley*

Library of Congress Cataloging-in-Publication Data

Palmer, Ian, 1957–

Managing organizational change: a multiple perspectives approach / Ian Palmer, Richard Dunford, Gib Akin.
p. cm.
Includes index.
ISBN 0-07-249680-0 (alk. paper)
1. Organizational change. 2. Organizational change–Management. I. Dunford, Richard. II. Akin, Gib, III. Title.
HD58.8.P347 2006
658.4'06–dc22 2004065541

www.mhhe.com

To Dianne, Matthew, and Michelle—for making me laugh, often at myself.

Ian Palmer

To Jill, Nick, and Ally—for helping me keep it all in perspective.

Richard Dunford

To Liz—who truly knows the meaning of dedication.

Gib Akin

Brief Contents

Contents

Preface

Like the content of this book, the writing of it has been a change journey. The genesis of this journey was the teaching of organizational change at undergraduate, postgraduate, and executive levels over many years, and an increasing disquiet we each had about change texts. For example, organization development (OD) texts were readily available but somehow failed to capture for us the variety of approaches to managing change. Alternatively, the more popular recipe-driven, "here's how to do it" change books, while rich in examples, failed to capture the messiness of change that has been our experience—and that of many of those whom we have taught.

We started conversations with each other about these issues and out of them emerged our challenge to create a text that would fill what we saw as a gap in the material available to those teaching organizational change. We wished to write a text that stated upfront that organizational change is often messy and something that is not easily subject to control by those placed in charge of managing it. It seemed to us that conceiving of managing change as a shaping rather than as a controlling process was often a better way of approaching it. We also wanted a text that exposed readers to a variety of change approaches rather than presenting them with a single approach to all change situations. The text needed to be one that contained a wide variety of relevant teaching materials and exercises and was simple to use, but deep in its understandings of the underlying issues involved in managing change. It needed to connect with people's experience of change and help to highlight for them how to make sense of these experiences and identify options for future action.

The result of our conversations is a book that provides a multiple perspectives approach to managing organizational change. A backdrop to the chapters that follow is the ever-present theme that the images we hold of how organizational change should be managed affect the approaches we take to managing change. Adopting different perspectives and images helps to open up new ways of approaching the management of change. We hope that this approach will help to guide and inspire others in their own paths toward managing organizational change.

Acknowledgements

Many people have assisted us in the writing of this book. We could not have had a more supportive editor at McGraw-Hill/Irwin than Andy Winston. We are all grateful for his patience, guidance, flexibility, and continual encouragement. He deserves a medal for working with us. Others at McGraw-Hill/Irwin have assisted us along the way, including Amy Luck and Kirsten Guidero, who helped keep the production of the book on track. The background research and writing that went into the stories of change and many of the examples and case studies in the book was undertaken superbly by El Feletto. We owe her a special debt of gratitude for the thoughtful, speedy, and professional way that she contributed to the book. Kate Hughes' research was enormously helpful in identifying extra case studies that are referred to in each chapter. We are each fortunate to have many colleagues who have assisted us over the years in developing our ideas. Special mention is needed of the support from our families and friends who never tired of asking us, "Have you finished that book yet?" Well, yes, we have—thanks for asking! Finally, every effort has been made to trace references and quotations to their original source(s) in order to provide proper credits. We apologize for any inadvertent omission(s), and we welcome any corrections or changes.

Ian Palmer

Richard Dunford

Gib Akin

February 2005

Chapter One

Introduction: Stories of Change

> **Learning objectives**
>
> On completion of this chapter you should be able to:
>
> - Understand why change is both a creative and a rational process.
> - Identify why there are limits on what the manager of change can achieve.
> - Recognize how stories of change can illuminate key issues in managing change.
> - Appreciate the "roadmap" for this book and the multiple "images" approach that underlies it.

Changing organizations is as messy as it is exhilarating, as frustrating as it is satisfying, as muddling-through and creative a process as it is a rational one. This book recognizes these tensions for those involved in managing organizational change. Rather than pretend that they do not exist, it confronts them head on, identifying why they are there, how they can be managed, and the limits they create for what the manager of organizational change can achieve. It shows how the image(s) we hold about how change should be managed, and of what we think our role should be as a manager of change, affects the way we approach change and the outcomes that we think are possible.

As a way into these ideas, we commence this chapter by visiting four prominent companies to look at stories of recent changes. The Hewlett Packard story concerns Carly Fiorina's attempts to establish and then manage the merger with Compaq Computer; the IBM story shows how change to this organization has occurred both from the staff within as well as from management at the top; the Kodak story shows how pursuing changes to digitalize the company has provoked reactions from both staff and investors; and the McDonald's story points to the pressures on organizations to change in order to reestablish themselves in the marketplace. The stories contain both similar and different elements about managing organizational change and the broader tensions and choices this entails. In the last part of the chapter, we draw these out, identifying some key lessons that emerge and indicating where they are addressed in the chapters that follow. We also provide a "road map" that indicates the position taken by this book, that our understanding of the issues addressed in subsequent chapters is affected by our underlying images of managing change.

STORIES OF CHANGE

A Hewlett Packard Change Story: Managing a Merger

Around 7 a.m. on March 19, 2002, Hewlett Packard's CEO Carly Fiorina and CFO Bob Wayman were on the phone to Deutsche Bank trying to make one last ditch effort to convince them to vote yes.[1] The vote, scheduled for later that morning, was an important one. It would determine the future of the proposed Hewlett-Packard (HP) and Compaq Computer Corp. merger and the future of HP as a major player in the technology industry.[2] The months preceding the vote had been tumultuous. After the announcement of the proposed merger had taken place in September 2001, Walter Hewlett, the son of the co-founder of HP, had publicly opposed the proposition, which required shareholder approval.[3] Fiorina and her team faced serious and accumulating opposition to the merger, but there was also growing concern for HP's future if the deal was rejected. A Merrill Lynch portfolio manager said at the time, "If the deal is voted down, I don't know what I'm left with. I don't know if the board will stay, if management will walk out the door, or what the strategy will be. Sometimes the devil you know is better than the devil you don't."[4]

In the lead up to the vote, HP was confident that a yes vote by Deutsche Bank was a sure thing. Representatives of Deutsche Bank, such as George D. Elling, had been public supporters of the merger and had reportedly even given HP a $1 million contract to uncover the voting plans of other institutions.[5] Word of a change in Deutsche Bank's thinking reached Wayman and, despite reassurances from his contacts that the merger would be supported, talk strongly suggested that they had, in fact, reversed their decision. On the morning of the vote, Fiorina and Wayman were given their first and only opportunity to pitch the deal to the investment team at Deutsche Bank. Fiorina, using her innate ability to impress, gave a compelling and persuasive argument questioning the company's future if the merger did not go ahead. The Deutsche Bank team decided that a failure to continue with the merger would be more disastrous than the merger itself.[6] On March 19, 2002, the merger was approved by a shareholder vote[7]—a result that would have been more difficult had Deutsche Bank not supported the merger.[8]

Premerger

Back in 1999 when Fiorina joined HP, the company was in serious need of guidance. The personal computer division faced growing competition, the sales force needed better coordination, and the company was losing market share to rivals such as Dell and Sun Microsystems.[9] Fiorina joined the organization with aspirations, and external pressures, to change how it functioned. In her view, the culture of HP could be changed by "going back to the roots of the place."[10] One of the ways she set out to achieve this was by working with a local ad agency and the head of Human Resources to create a set of "Rules from the Garage" that outlined what she hoped the culture at HP would become. "The customer defines a job well done" and "Invent different ways of working" became signifiers of the company's direction and aspirations.[11]

She decided to restructure the company. Customers such as Ford and Boeing were frustrated by the separate sales teams from HP that were constantly marketing individual products to them. They wanted a complete package that addressed the needs they had in their entirety.[12] In light of these uncommunicative operational units within HP, Fiorina reorganized the company into "quadrants," creating two "front-end" sections that consisted of sales and marketing and two "back-end" functions where manufacturing and research occurred.[13] There was considerable, but subtle, employee resistance to the change. Fiorina's vision of HP creating a new interface with customers may have been sound, but, as a radical change, it was not widely welcomed by many who were part of the HP "system."[14]

Post-Merger

In the aftermath of the merger, and the ensuing lawsuit that opposed the merger and attempted to dissolve it,[15] Fiorina had a huge task ahead of her. The integration of the two corporate cultures was made more difficult by the strained relations Fiorina had with her own staff, many expressing serious concerns regarding the merits of the merger.[16] The transition was made slightly easier by the 65,000 new personnel who became a part of the HP community after the merger. They were more at ease with creating an organization in the way that Fiorina envisioned. According to Fiorina, the necessary cultural adjustment was simplified by this injection of "new DNA."[17]

Following the merger, Fiorina embarked on a series of technological symposiums and "coffee talks" with HP engineers.[18] Although the merger had already been undertaken by HP and Compaq, there were still many employees who were not convinced of the validity of HP's riskiest move, some of whom faced being victims of the job cuts resulting from the merger.[19] To win over the 147,000 employees worldwide, Fiorina used a range of methods of communicating including the "management by walking around" style that Packard and Hewlett had originally advocated within the organization. A company employee commented on her style and interaction with all members of the company by saying that her actions and down-to-earth nature "earned her a lot of points" with transferees from Compaq.[20]

The company faced challenges in the way of significant competition from both Dell in the PC business and IBM as a service provider.[21] Communicating a vision for the future of the company post-merger remained a key issue for Fiorina.[22] In February 2005 Fiorina was removed from her post as CEO of the company.[23]

An IBM Change Story: Transformational Change from Below and Above

Change from Below[24]

Before using the Internet became as commonplace as watching television, David Grossman and John Patrick from IBM took on the mammoth task of convincing their superiors and co-workers that the Internet was even worth looking at. Their subsequent actions helped to revolutionize Big Blue and drastically change its path into the future.[25]

When David Grossman, a computer programmer, stumbled across a rogue Olympic Internet site for the 1994 Winter Games in Lillehammer, Norway, he was troubled.

IBM had the official broadcast rights to the Games, but Sun Microsystems was taking the raw footage and making it available on the Internet under their logo. Although his position as a programmer did not require him to act on his findings, Grossman was deeply concerned about the implications of the branding of the Internet broadcast and the potential effects on IBM. He pursued the issue by contacting the IBM marketing team for the Olympics. The rogue site was eventually shut down, but the lesson had not been learned. IBM had not even begun to comprehend how the Internet could become an integral part of their business dealings.[26]

Grossman's persistence landed him a meeting with the head of marketing, Abby Kohnstamm, and some of her colleagues. It was here that Grossman was able to give a detailed explanation of the benefits of the Internet. He captivated one member of his audience wholeheartedly. John Patrick, a member of the strategy task force, attended the presentation that day and he immediately became Grossman's ally in the Internet Revolution and an important link to the world of senior management.[27]

As a team, Grossman and Patrick complemented each other. Grossman had the more developed technical know-how.[28] Patrick knew how to make the "boundaryless" culture at IBM work to his advantage.[29] Together they created an underground community of Web fans who shared technical information that ultimately helped IBM into the Internet era, albeit working, for the most part, unofficially.[30] The grassroots Web community infiltrated all corners of the company in a way that would have been difficult for an officially sanctioned, top-down created group. It was through the advocacy of the lower-level personnel that the Internet message was spread through IBM's culture.[31]

Of course, the downside of being an unofficial part of an organization is the potential lack of financial backing for a group's projects. However, when it came to finding money for IBM's first ever display at an Internet World trade convention in 1995, Patrick was not phased. By coordinating the funds and the Web technology from various business units and becoming a "relentless campaigner" for the project, he gained support and expertise from multiple parts of the organization.[32] By sharing experienced personnel and resources from many departments, Patrick and Grossman were able to provide departments with more expertise and highly trained personnel when they were "returned" to the area from which they came. This strategy reinforced internal support for the change.[33] Over the years, Patrick and Grossman succeeded in creating a system that revolutionized the way in which IBM does business. Coupled with the leadership of Lou Gerstner, the period from 1993 to 2002 was one of reinvention and change.[34] IBM transformed from a computer manufacturer to a global service provider, focusing on e-business and the Internet. By the late 1990s, IBM's trading in the e-business sector began to reflect in the bottom line, accounting for almost a quarter of its revenue.[35]

Change from Above

In 2002, Samuel Palmisano, a life-time IBMer, took over leadership of the company from Gerstner. Palmisano's focus changed to emphasize teamwork and collaboration. One of his first steps in demonstrating his new management style to investors and employees alike was a readjustment in executive compensation.[36] This involved a cut in the controversial CEO bonus that was redistributed within the top management team. Palmisano claimed that in order to function as a team, the gap between the CEO and his team must be reduced.[37] Insiders claim that the amount pooled was $3 to $5 million, approximately half Palmisano's personal bonus.[38] This was an effective way of communicating his intentions and commitment to his vision to the entire organization.

In an e-mail interview with *BusinessWeek*,[39] Palmisano wrote that in planning for change, "I kept thinking about an approach that would energize all the good of the past and throw out all the bad: hierarchy and bureaucracy." To this end, he disbanded the executive management committee and created three teams with which he would work directly. These management teams—in the areas of strategy, technology, and operations—were composed of people from all over the company, not exclusively top management.[40] The aim of the restructure is to make IBM a flatter, more creative organization striving to meet consumer needs.[41]

In addition to the restructure, Palmisano saw a lack of skills in IBM around the delivery of global services. In 2002, IBM acquired PwC Consulting as a way of bringing to it highly specific consulting skills and expertise to assist IBM in providing a full range of services to its clients, "from high-end technology consulting to low-end support."[42] It is as a result of these changes from the top that IBM hoped to meet the challenges of the future.

A Kodak Change Story: Provoking Reactions

Could this be the beginning of one of the biggest turnarounds in American corporate history or one of the most public and embarrassing busts? After more than a century of producing traditional film cameras, Kodak announced in September 2003 that it would cut this line of production. In Western countries, this involves a complete move away from traditional products within the film industry by the end of 2004 and a full-scale launch into digital technology.[43] The move is slated "to generate $16 billion in revenue by 2006 and $20 billion by 2010."[44] At an investor conference, CEO David A. Carp said:

> We are at the dawning of a new, more competitive Kodak, one that is growing, profitably, that has a more balanced earnings stream, and that will have a dramatically lower cost structure. . . To compete in digital markets, we must have a business model that lets us move even faster to take full advantage of the profitable growth that digital promises.[45]

Implementing this change would require Kodak to cut their dividend and to raise capital for new technology purchases.[46] Further elaboration of this strategy occurred in January 2004 when it was announced that to reach the proposed savings of between $800 million and $1 billion by 2007, Kodak needed to make two physical changes to the organization.[47] First, there would be a reduction in the square footage of Kodak facilities worldwide by consolidating current operations and divesting unnecessary assets. Second, Kodak intended to reduce employment worldwide with up to 15,000 jobs to be cut by 2007.[48]

Investor Reactions

The announcement in September 2003 took many external experts by surprise.[49] At a series of post-announcement meetings with investor groups, their reactions were not overly supportive,[50] particularly to the news that their dividends would be severely cut.[51] They were conscious of promises to increase the company's revenue which were not realized.[52] It was feared that this would become another "half-hearted transition"[53]—as with the $1 billion launch into APS cameras in 1996 that ended in failure.[54] They also pointed to the risk in moving in this direction given the competitive market with rivals such as Hewlett-Packard, Canon Inc., and Seiko Epson Corp., which were already ahead in digital technology research and product development.[55] Carp's response was to stand firmly by his decision to pursue digitalization of Kodak.[56]

Staff Reactions

For many of Kodak's employees, the future looked bleak regardless of the success of the company in moving into digital technology. Employees were rightly concerned about losing their jobs in light of the proposed 20 percent worldwide cutback in employment.[57] Downsizing is not new at Kodak. From 1997 to 2003, the company reduced its workforce by 30,000.[58] As argued in *The Wall Street Journal*,[59] this type of change "moves parallel [to] those at many companies whose comfortable business models have been threatened by rapid changes in information technology." As one union representative explained, the stress on workers in one Kodak production plant has been made worse than necessary because "management has not sought to reassure [Kodak employees] that they have got any long term future. When people have families to raise, financial commitments, that's a very difficult environment to work in."[60]

Hence, along with having to convince investors that the path of change is the right one for Kodak, Carp also had to manage the adverse effects of an ongoing program of downsizing and restructuring.

A McDonald's Change Story: Responding to Pressure

Imagine eating nothing but McDonald's for a month. Morgan Spurlock, independent filmmaker, did just that, restricting his diet with the following limitations:

- No food or drink other than McDonald's menu items.
- Meals supersized when given the option.
- Every item on the menu had to be eaten at least once.[61]

Spurlock spent one long month traveling across the United States interviewing various community groups about the implications of eating fast food and using himself as a guinea pig.[62] Before embarking on this journey, Spurlock underwent a full medical examination and was deemed to be a physically healthy man. One month later, the diagnosis was different.[63] After three square McDonald's meals a day for 30 days, Spurlock had gained 25 pounds and his cholesterol level had jumped from 168 to 230.[64] An alcoholic would have envied his liver given the state it was in after his month-long stint.[65]

The result of this personal experience was a documentary called *Super Size Me*, an entrant in the 2004 Sundance Film Festival. The aim? Spurlock claims that the reason for his exploration into the fast food habits of Americans is to uncover the link between foods like McDonald's and obesity,[66] a correlation that the company has long denied.[67] Nevertheless, the film's release coincided with the launch of McDonald's new Happy Meal for adults, comprising a salad, a bottle of water, and a "stepometer." Despite valiant attempts by McDonald's to counteract the claims of the film, *Super Size Me* became one of the five biggest-grossing documentaries in American history.[68]

Highlighting health issues related to fast food has only added to other worldwide pressures on McDonald's operations. Externally these include an epidemic of mad cow disease, foot-and-mouth disease, the SARS epidemic in the Asia-Pacific region, a fall in economies leading to weaker foreign currencies, and high commodity costs.[69] Internally these problems were compounded by McDonald's aggressive international expansion strategy that made future growth more difficult.[70] As the then CEO, James Cantalupo, admitted, "we took our eyes off our fries and paid a price."[71]

The problems that the company faced went beyond superficial fluctuations in sales and revenue. The year 1996 was a turning point, with McDonald's experiencing four consecutive quarters of declining sales and beginning to lose market share to competitors such as Wendy's and Burger King.[72] Jack Greenberg, the former CEO, implemented the highly unsuccessful "Made for You" kitchens with disastrous results.[73] The result was slower service in contrast to its aim, which was to add a welcome flexibility with new menu items.[74]

Franchisees became frustrated. Take Paul Saber. For 17 years, he was a McDonald's franchisee, but in 2000 he recognized the lack of fit between the product offerings at McDonald's and consumer tastes. "The McDonald's-type fast food isn't relevant to today's consumer,"[75] he commented as he sold his 14 stores back to the company. Others stuck it out with McDonald's. Richard Steinig remembers getting a 15 percent profit from the $80,000 sales at his two stores in the 1970s.[76] This was quite a comfortable income given that the minimum wage was less than $2 an hour. By 2003 he was struggling to make ends meet. Even the $1 menus advertised worldwide resulted in a loss for Steinig: as he said at the time, "we have become our own worse enemy."[77]

Getting Back to Basics

In 2003 Cantalupo was brought in to rectify the declining state of the organization.[78] He previously held the position of vice chairman and headed McDonald's international expansion. His return from retirement was controversial and analysts claimed that he lacked "the vision or stomach to make the necessary changes."[79] Nevertheless, his vision for the organization's future was in a "back to basics"[80] approach with organizational changes to refocus the organization on core values of quality and service.

Cantalupo began by cutting back new store openings. In 2004, 300 new stores were proposed, in comparison to 1995, when 1,100 new restaurants were opened.[81] There was also a complete overhaul of the advertising campaign. By introducing the "I'm lovin' it" slogan and commercials featuring pop singer Justin Timberlake,[82] the hope was to reinvent the company's image and connect with the younger generation.[83]

Another part of the revitalization of the McDonald's business was the introduction of the new salads menu.[84] McDonald's has long expressed little concern at the claims that its products are directly linked to obesity, but some critics see the launch into the "fresh salads" menus as a sign that the unhealthy reputation of fast foods may have been identified as a threat to the organization.[85] This new menu also has helped to draw in female customers who had previously been reluctant to dine at their restaurants[86] and increase the number of customers during the evening.[87] In the past, McDonald's had tried creating low-fat menu options for their patrons with the McShaker salads and McLean Deluxe burger, but their lack of commitment to the then-new menu saw its failure.[88] Now, responding to external pressures, customers are given healthier and tastier menu options.[89]

McDonald's also implemented an online training program for all U.S.-based employees to overcome customer service issues.[90] The aim was to bring the company back on the road to providing the basic, speedy service and quality products that it became famous for so many years ago.

DRAWING OUT THE CHANGE ISSUES AND WHERE THEY ARE FOUND IN THE CHAPTERS THAT FOLLOW

As outlined in Table 1.1, these four stories carry in them a wide variety of lessons and issues relating to managing organizational change. We now highlight the key issues and indicate how they are picked up in the chapters that follow.

TABLE 1.1 Managing Change: Some Lessons from the Four Stories

Hewlett Packard Change Story

- Different interests need to be recognized and addressed during an organizational change
- These interests are likely to provoke different reactions to change
- Organizational politics and lobbying are likely aspects of an organizational change that will need managing
- Negotiation and persuasion are key communication skills
- More successful communication strategies are likely to be those that "touch" the people to whom they are addressed
- Communicating change often entails providing a vision of the future that is compelling
- Pressures to change come from both outside and inside organizations
- Restructuring is a common organizational change when confronted with problems
- Any organizational change usually involves paying attention to organizational culture

IBM Change Story

- Innovative changes often emerge from below in organizations
- Making change stick requires persistence over time and actions that need to be taken on multiple fronts
- Change needs appropriately placed champions to gain support throughout the organization
- The informal network of the organization is an important part of mobilizing and communicating organizational change
- Change requires marshalling of appropriate resources
- Some changes are incremental, others transformational
- Some smaller change actions often convey powerful symbolic messages to help reinforce the sincerity and credibility that senior management attaches to the larger change

Kodak Change Story

- Organizational change involves handling reactions of both internal and external stakeholders
- Communication strategies need to be designed for internal and external groups
- Reactions to change are likely to be influenced by the success of previous changes and the extent to which there has been delivery on past promises
- Change involves risk and uncertainty
- The consequences of change cannot always be predicted
- Managers of change need to address the question for staff of "How will I be affected?"

TABLE 1.1 Managing Change: Some Lessons from the Four Stories—*(concluded)*

McDonald's Change Story	
• Organizational changes occur in a competitive, international business environment • This means that to prepare for the future, change may need to occur even when things still appear to be going well	• Organizations face external pressures to change such as providing socially responsible products and services • Some changes fail to deliver on their intended outcomes • Change in and of itself is not necessarily good for a company; careful assessment is needed of the relevance and likely success of a proposed change

Images of Managing Change . . . Chapter Two

One of the intriguing features of the IBM story is how David Grossman took on the role of manager of change without a formal mandate to do so. Many in his position would not have seen it as their responsibility to drive change through the organization in this way. They would more likely have experienced change as recipients rather than as initiators of change. Carly Fiorina's use of persuasion to get Deutsche Bank representatives to vote for the HP/Compaq merger indicates that she was aware that as CEO she couldn't simply order the merger to occur—she recognized that change involves different interests that need to be identified and managed. Kodak's David Carp, in the face of opposition from investors to digitalizing the company, stood steadfast in his resolve to move the company down this track.

Each person operates with an image or mental model of what they think is achievable. We can characterize David Grossman's image as being one of an *interpreter* of change—identifying for people in IBM what is going to be needed to keep the organization relevant in the future. For Carly Fiorina, an image of *navigator* might describe her change management style, figuring out how to steer HP towards a merger. David Carp's style might be characterized as a *director*, setting out where Kodak was headed and articulating why this redirection of the company was necessary.

Each image indicates a different approach to managing change and what might be achieved. The images with which we operate as individual change managers influence our actions. It is therefore important that we understand what these images are and how they impact our understandings and interpretations of organizational change. We need to appreciate how our images both illuminate certain aspects of change and take us away from paying attention to other aspects. Chapter 2 picks up the idea of images of change. It outlines six dominant images (change manager as *director*, *coach*, *navigator*, *interpreter*, *caretaker*, *nurturer*) and challenges managers of change to identify their own "in-use" images of change and assess their strengths and weaknesses. This is an important theme that acts as an undercurrent throughout the book and is therefore revisited at various points in subsequent chapters.

Why Organizations Change . . . Chapter Three

For McDonald's, fast international expansion coupled with increasing external pressures contribute to why it is now reorienting itself toward a fresh image. External pressures include changes in consumer preferences with more awareness by consumers of health issues related to fast foods; we also saw other external pressures in the form of currency fluctuations, the emergence of mad cow disease, and greater competition from other fast food chains. Fast-paced technological change acted as an external pressure on Kodak's traditional film cameras and pushed the company toward the digital era. Customer pressures for more streamlined and single-point-of-contact interactions were behind why, in 1999, Fiorina restructured HP "front-end" and "back-end" sections.

Chapter 3 picks up these issues of why organizations change. It elaborates a range of internal and external rationales for change. The premise of the chapter is that change is a risky business as change often fails to achieve its stated aims—witness, for example, Jack Greenberg's attempts to create flexibility at McDonald's through the "Made for You" kitchens. Given that change can be an expensive and traumatic event for any organization, managers of change need to be able to assess the pressures on them to engage in it. For example, the chapter alerts change managers to the way they are sometimes under pressure to change their organizations because of "fashion" pressures to do so—without an adequate assessment of the real need for the change—or without the change being likely to deliver economic or other beneficial returns to the organization.

What Changes in Organizations . . . Chapter Four

In the four stories of change, we witnessed multiple types of changes, often within the one organization and over time. For Carp, moving Kodak in new directions represents a strategic change, transforming the nature of the organization and the products it distributes. Nested inside this strategic redirection are a number of other changes including downsizing staff and decreasing plant size. At HP the merger with Compaq involves trying to establish a common culture—the new DNA—for the emergent enterprise. At IBM, technological changes in the form of new ways of doing business underpinned David Grossman's change efforts; Palmisano's recent creation of three core management teams represents an attempt to restructure the organization and to reduce hierarchical boundaries.

Chapter 4 focuses on these changes, in particular downsizing and restructuring changes, technological changes, and mergers and acquisitions. These are common types of changes that change managers are likely to experience—and Chapter 4 identifies key issues and challenges associated with them. It outlines how, for some organizations, these changes are strategic and proactive, whereas for others they are reactive. It also discusses the concept of scale of change, noting how what may appear to be incremental for some change managers may be experienced as transformational by the people affected by them.

Diagnosis for Change . . . Chapter Five

The question remains whether the changes implemented by Kodak, IBM, HP, and McDonald's represent the *right* changes for each organization. They were under pressure to change—but which particular changes should be made was not always clear-cut, nor agreed to, by different stakeholder groups such as in the cases of Kodak and HP. The need for change may be clear, but exactly what to change—and the impact of these changes on other parts of the organization—is an important question for the manager of change.

Chapter 5 addresses this dilemma by outlining a number of "macro" models and techniques for mapping and assessing where changes are needed in an organization. Common to these techniques are directing attention into areas such as an organization's structure, strategy, management skills and styles, communication patterns, reward mechanisms, decision-making procedures, and human resource and cultural modes of interaction. Other "micro" tools and techniques are outlined that enable more specific change actions to be identified in any one of these areas. Well-recognized tools include force-field analyses, gap analyses, stakeholder analyses, and news reporter techniques. Training change managers in such techniques provides them with greater appreciation of why they are conducting specific changes and the likely impact of these changes on other parts of their organization's operations.

Resistance to Change . . . Chapter Six

One of the first reactions to any change is likely to be "What's in it for me?" or "How will this affect me?" Certainly the reaction of staff to Kodak's announcement of more downsizing, or of its investors to the decree that dividends would be cut, attests to this, with resistance from both groups. Fiorina faced resistance to change both at a "family" level (Walter Hewlett) and at a staff level in her desire to press ahead with a merger with Compaq Computers.

Change managers need to pay attention to how people will react to change: whether they are likely to embrace it—even run away with it beyond initial expectations—or whether they are likely to display neutral or negative reactions to it. Resistance to announced changes may relate to their experience with previous changes, whether past promises were delivered or whether those announcing and enacting the changes are seen as sincere and credible. Chapter 6 delves in detail into understanding why people may resist change along with techniques that change managers can utilize to counteract such responses.

Implementing Change . . . Chapters Seven and Eight

How change occurs, and how it is managed in and through an organization, will vary. In the HP/Compaq change story, Fiorina employed two change styles: one to get the merger formalized; a second, later style to "sell" it to staff, albeit with varying degrees of success. In IBM, change emerged at different times both from below and above. The change from below occurred through exciting people, creating informal groups and teams and letting the ideas bubble up to the surface of the organization. This style of coaching and encouraging others and building momentum is a different style of producing change to simply announcing it and getting others to carry it out. The urgency, prevailing conditions, and attitudes toward the change are likely to influence how it is managed. What is clear is that a good idea for change may be badly implemented and fail—and the converse may be true.

Managers of organizational change therefore need to carefully assess the approach they will take to implementing change: how much they will involve people in what needs to be changed or how and when things will be changed. Whether the style of change will vary depending on the type and scale of change, the timing of the change and the stage of the change are other important questions to consider. Chapters 7 and 8 guide the manager of change through six central approaches to implementing change: organization development, appreciative inquiry, sensemaking, change management, contingency, and political/processual approaches. Reference is made to how adopting one or other of these change approaches is underpinned by different images of change, as discussed in Chapter 2.

Linking Vision and Change . . . Chapter Nine

The role of vision is embedded in each of the four stories of change. Carp's address to investors was underpinned by a vision of digital markets being the way of the future; Palmisano's vision is about rediscovering what was good about IBM in the past and taking these characteristics into the future; Fiorina had a similar vision for HP when she began in 1999, setting out to create the future culture of HP by molding it around the core roots of the organization. Conversely, bringing Cantalupo back into McDonald's to assist in turning around the company was criticized at the time on the grounds that he lacked vision.

Vision has apparently become core to managing organizational change. Yet vision is often one of those things to which lip service is paid without really addressing why some visions "take" and others do not in an organizational change. The latter situation can emerge because of the context in which the vision is presented (here we go again), because it fails to resonate or connect with the people for whom it is intended (what does it mean?), or because of the process through which it was developed (I don't know anything about this—who thought this one up?). These issues, which relate to the *content* of successful visions and the *process* through which visions are produced, are outlined in Chapter 9. This chapter provides the manager of change with three dilemmas associated with change visions: whether vision drives change or emerges during a change; whether vision helps or hinders change; and whether vision is an attribute of heroic, charismatic leaders or an attribute of heroic organizations. This chapter cautions the manager of change into accepting at face value that it is up to him or her to produce visions for organizational change—and to question whether vision is central to driving organizational change.

Strategies and Skills for Communicating Change . . . Chapters Ten and Eleven

An important part of managing change involves what, how, and to whom it is communicated. Some change communications are symbolic in nature, such as Palmisano's actions in cutting his bonus and redistributing it to his management team as a way of reinforcing the message that they are all in this together. Many communication strategies are directed to those *inside* an organization with the intention of winning the hearts and minds of staff in support of a change. Fiorina's internal communication strategy including "coffee talks," symposiums, and "management by walking around" provides examples of this and ones that appear to have gone down well with the Compaq people who were transferred into the newly merged organization. Other communication actions are directed to those *outside* the organization in an effort to keep them on board during a time of change. Given that changes do fail, it is clearly important to retain the support of external stakeholders during times of change. Carp's addresses to investors about Kodak's changes serves as an example of attempting to do this.

Having a strategy for communicating change is clearly important; having the skills to enact it is just as important. Chapters 10 and 11 address these two issues. Chapter 10 discusses the communication process—whether you can communicate too much and how to link the communication strategy to the type or phase of a change. It gets change managers to reflect on whether the strategy is intended to "get the word out" or to get "buy-in" about the change and what media will be used to assist them. Chapter 11 delves into the communication skills that change managers are likely to need, paying particular attention to the listening and language skills associated with "change conversations." The assumption adopted in this chapter is that these skills are needed to ensure that new ways of talking are produced (the outcome of change) and that change managers are not sending mixed or ambiguous messages about what they require or where they are trying to take things. This chapter widens this issue by outlining skills involved in managing change conversations with external stakeholders.

Consolidating Change . . . Chapter Twelve

David Grossman faced an issue in how to resource his "change from below" and teamed up with John Patrick, who developed some innovative ways of gathering resources opportunistically, especially at first. There are many other ways of supporting change aside from just the provision of resources. They may include putting in place a new mindset such as Palmisano did in disbanding the long-standing executive management committee at IBM. Other ways of supporting change may be at a human resource level, by realigning compensation systems or by implementing new training programs such as Cantalupo did at McDonald's in order to reemphasize customer service.

Consolidating change is necessary to ensure that sometime after they are implemented, things do not quietly drift back to how they used to be. Consolidating change is about how to make it stick, how to make it a core feature of how work will occur. As discussed earlier, Fiorina's restructuring of HP served as one way of consolidating change, creating a new interface between customers and the organization. Other ways include creating short-term wins so that people can see the benefits of the new approach and ensuring that senior management continue to reaffirm the changes and model them in their own behaviors. Chapter 12 concludes the book by elaborating on issues for resourcing and aligning change. It sets out how change is "powered"; that is, how powerful groups can be brought on side and retained in order to support the change process and how change can be measured—so that a shift can be demonstrated. At the same time, this chapter points out that, in practice, some changes are deliberately abandoned for a variety of reasons and that multiple changes may be introduced that need to be managed simultaneously. These present very specific challenges to managers when staff perceive them as replacing rather than complementing preexisting changes.

BRINGING IT ALL TOGETHER: A ROADMAP OF THE BOOK

Figure 1.1 provides us with a "roadmap" for the rest of the book. It outlines the approach we take to introducing you to managing organizational change from a multiple images perspective. As discussed above, and as will be outlined in more detail in the next chapter, the image(s) we have of ourselves as managers of change influence the approaches we take and the views we hold about how we should engage in change. This observation is central to this book. It is a theme that we weave throughout the chapters that follow. The image(s) we hold influence why we think change is needed

FIGURE 1.1 A Road Map of the Book
Image(s) we have of ourselves as managers of change influence how we do it and to what we pay attention

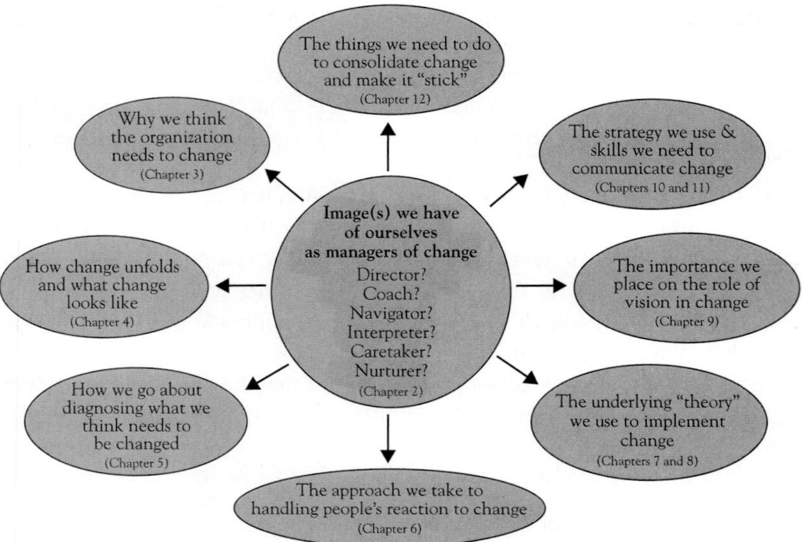

(Chapter 3), what change looks like and how it unfolds (Chapter 4), the techniques we use in going about diagnosing what needs to change (Chapter 5), the things we pay attention to in handling people's reaction to change (Chapter 6), the underlying "theory" we use in implementing organizational change (Chapters 7 and 8), the importance we attach to the role of vision in producing organizational change (Chapter 9), the communication strategies and skills we employ when we engage in change (Chapters 10 and 11), and the issues we need to address to consolidate change and make sure that it "takes" and endures over time (Chapter 12).

An assumption underlying Figure 1.1 is that our images affect our approaches to all of these issues. For that reason, the images are found in the center of the road map and their influence radiates out to all aspects of managing organizational change. Although the book follows an unfolding linear sequence of chapters, it should be appreciated that all issues of managing change are important—and that the sequence in which we address these issues is not necessarily the sequence in which change managers should take them into account when engaged in a change process. For example, although the last chapter, Chapter 12, addresses how to make change "stick," this does not mean that it is the last thing that needs to be addressed in a change process. Indeed, paying attention to the issues addressed in this chapter early on in a change process is likely to be needed in order to plan for how the consolidation of change might occur. Similarly, although issues of communication of change are not addressed until Chapters 10 and 11, the thoughtful change manager will be paying attention to these issues throughout a change process. The same logic applies to the other chapters.

EXERCISE 1.1

Creating Your Own Story of Change

Think back to a change that you have experienced, in either your personal or professional life.

Option One

Try writing it down in one page or less. Now, answer the following questions:

- What made it a "story"?
- Of the change "lessons" outlined in Table 1.1, which of these are present in your story? Which ones are absent? What are the implications of this?
- Are there other "lessons" embedded in your story for future changes in which you might be involved?
- Now, in small groups, compare and contrast your stories. What commonalities and differences emerge?
- What three key conclusions do you draw from these stories about managing change?

Option Two

In small groups (around five to six people), get each person to tell his or her story of change. This should take no more than three or four minutes each. Record key elements of the story on paper. Go around the group until each person has told his or her story. Put the sheets of paper on the wall so that you can observe them, and answer the following questions:

- What are the common issues across each story?
- What are the differences?
- Of the change "lessons" outlined in Table 1.1, which of these are present in these stories? Which ones are absent? What are the implications of this?
- Are there other "lessons" embedded in your story for future changes in which you might be involved?
- What three key conclusions do you draw from these stories about managing change?

A NOTE ON CHAPTER FORMATS

Each chapter adopts a common format. Learning objectives are provided at the start of each chapter and wide use is made of tables to provide vignettes to demonstrate the relevance of the material to the operations of well-known organizations. Each chapter has a section that provides a series of reflective questions for change managers, getting them to think how they will deal with the issues raised in the chapter, or how they have dealt with them in the past and what alternative ways of managing they might adopt for future changes. Further reading is provided to deepen knowledge of specific issues raised in each chapter should readers wish to delve further into particular areas. Each chapter addresses in different ways the implications of change managers' images of managing change, as outlined in Chapter 2, for the issues covered in each chapter. Learning exercises are available in each chapter to assist individuals in pursuing further the ideas in the chapter or to assist them in using the material in classroom situations. Each chapter has a case study to enable exploration of the material. This material often calls upon the reader to relate their experiences of change or of organizations with which they are familiar to the material covered in each chapter. Where experience of work organizations is minimal, we suggest that they apply this material to other organizations they have encountered, whether it be a sporting, religious, community, or other organization such as the family or other social institutions of which they are a part. In addition, they can call upon their own reading taken from press and business magazines in order to supplement the knowledge available to them. Each chapter also provides information about additional case studies that can be used to illustrate the material discussed.[91]

Conclusion

As proposed at the start of this chapter, engaging with organizational change and producing successful, intentional change outcomes cannot be guaranteed. It may not even be desirable, in retrospect, if the change idea turns out to be costly, marginal, irrelevant, or just plain wrong. This book does not set out to naively offer the manager of change a recipe book of "what to do." Such approaches, we believe, only compound the problem of maintaining an illusion that managers can control all change outcomes if only they utilize carefully planned steps. This is not a position that we accept. Rather, we suggest that most people's lived experiences of organizations are that they are complicated and messy arenas. Acknowledging this may be the first step to taking a more realistic view of what managers of change can expect to achieve. As discussed in the next chapter, *shaping* rather than *controlling* change may open up alternative images of what managing change actually means. Reflective change managers will accept that choices need to be made in order for change actions to proceed but these choices are informed ones, not ones naively adopted on the grounds that there is only "one best way" of approaching organizational change. We hope that you agree with this position!

TABLE 1.2 Additional Case Studies

Nestle's Globe Program (B): July Executive Board Meeting Killing, P. (2000) *IMD Lausanne*
Massport (A): The Aftermath of 9/11 Roberto, M. A., & Ferlins, E. M. (2004) *Harvard Business School*
Massport (B): Change at the Top Roberto, M. A., & Ferlins, E. M. (2004) *Harvard Business School*
Massport (C): A Revitalized Organization Roberto, M. A., & Ferlins, E. M. (2004) *Harvard Business School*
Massport (D): Looking to the Future Roberto, M. A., & Ferlins, E. M. (2004) *Harvard Business School*
Marks and Spencer's Turnaround Israni, J., & Ratha, C. S. V. (2004) *ICFAI University Press, Hyderabad, India*

Bibliography

Andres, G. 2003. *Perfect enough: Carly Fiorina and the reinvention of Hewlett-Packard.* Portfolio, cited in The Carly chronicles, *Fast Company*, no. 67 (February):66–72.

Anonymous. 2003a. Crunch time for IBM and HP: Can Palmisano and Fiorina deliver the goods? *Strategic Direction* 19(9):5–7.

Anonymous. 2003b. Q&A: We have reinvented ourselves many times. *BusinessWeek*, no. 3824 (March 17):88.

Anonymous. 2003c. Did somebody say a loss? McDonald's. *The Economist* 367(8319) (April 12):59

Anonymous. 2003d. Has McDonald's lost the plot? Troubled times under the golden arches. *Strategic Direction* 19(4):14–16.

Anonymous. 2004a. Has Kodak missed the moment? *The Economist* 370(8356) (January 3):46.

Anonymous. 2004b. Kodak's Australian workers concerned over job cuts: Union. *Asia Pulse*, January 23.

Ante, S. E. 2002. Shrewd move, Big Blue: Buying PwC Consulting gives it a full range of services. *BusinessWeek*, no. 3795 (August 12):39.

Ante, S. E. 2003. The New Blue Lou Gerstner saved Big Blue. Now it's up to new CEO Sam Palmisano to restore it to greatness. *BusinessWeek*, no. 3824 (March 17):80.

Arndt, M. 2004. McDonald's: Fries with that salad? *BusinessWeek*, no. 3890 (July 5):72–73.

Arndt, M., and Newman, A. 2003. James Cantalupo: Hotter McNumbers. *BusinessWeek*, no. 3845 (August 11):40.

Bandler, J. 2003. Kodak shifts focus from film, betting future on digital lines. *The Wall Street Journal (Eastern Edition)* 242(61) (September 25):A1.

Bandler, J. 2004. Ending era, Kodak will stop selling most film cameras. *The Wall Street Journal (Eastern Edition)* 243(9) (January 14):B1.

Burrows, P. 2001. Carly's last stand?: The inside story of the infighting at Hewlett-Packard. *BusinessWeek*, no. 3763 (December 24):43–50.

Burrows, P. 2003. *Backfire: Carly Fiorina's high-stakes battle for the soul of Hewlett-Packard.* New York: John Wiley & Sons. Cited in Showdown: How Hewlett Packard's Carly Fiorina prevailed in the most expensive proxy battle in the history of Corporate America. *BusinessWeek*, no. 3820 (February 17):58–60.

Doherty, J. 2004. New chef, old menu: McDonald's should stay course under new CEO. *Barron's* 84(17) (April 26):15.

Eisenberg, D. 2002. Can McDonald's shape up? *Time* 160(14) (September 30):52–57.

Garber, A. 2003. Lovin' it: McD sales soar; new ads, higher-tech gear on tap. *Nation's Restaurant News* 37(33) (August 18):3.

Gerstner, L. V., Jr. 2002. *Who says elephants can't dance?* New York: Harper Business.

Gogoi, P. 2003. Saving Mickey D's bacon: Salads are helping—but so are the gut-busting McGriddles. *BusinessWeek*, no. 3846 (August 25):46.

Gogoi, P., and Arndt, M. 2003. Hamburger hell:McDonald's aims to save itself by going back to basics. But the hamburger company needs more than a tastier burger to solve its problems. *BusinessWeek*, no. 3822 (March 3):104–108.

Gogoi, P., and Roman, M. 2003. Arch support. *BusinessWeek*, no. 3822 (April 21):52.

Gray, S. 2004. McDonald's net jumps as changes in menu pay off. *The Wall Street Journal (Eastern edition)*, July 23:A11.

Hamel, G. 2000. Waking up IBM: How a gang of unlikely rebels transformed Big Blue. *Harvard Business Review* 78(4):137–46.

Hernandez, E., and Brooks, B. 2004. The big "what if . . .": Spurlock eats McDonald's for a month, while Willmott imagines the South winning the Civil War. *indieWIRE*, http://www.indieswire.com.

Howard, T. 2002. McDonald's CEO Greenberg to retire. *USA Today*, December 5.

Jordan, M. 2003. A global journal report: McDonald's faces revolt in Brazil, declining sales abroad. *The Wall Street Journal (Eastern Edition)*, October 21:A17.

Kodak Press Release. 2003. Kodak digitally oriented strategy to accelerate growth. Kodak Web site, September 25. http://www.kodak.com.

Kodak Press Release. 2004a. Kodak to accelerate 35mm consumer film effort in emerging markets. Kodak Web site, January 13. http://www.kodak.com.

Kodak Press Release. 2004b. Kodak announces milestones in implementing growth strategy. Company plans three-year program to enhance competitive position. Kodak Web site, January 22. http://www.kodak.com.

Lashinsky, A. 2002a. The defiant ones. *Fortune* 145(1) (January 7):52–53.

Lashinsky, A. 2002b. Now for the hard part. *Fortune* 146(10) (November 18):66–73.

Morrison, S. 2002. Fiorina wins battle but now faces the war. *Financial Times*, May 9:18.

Rebort. 2004. Controversy attracts at Sundance. iofilm Web site, http://www.iofilm.co.uk.

Sieger, M. 2003. From Oz, shaking up a U.S. Icon. *Time* 162(22) (December 1): 80–81.

Stires, D. 2002. Fallen arches. *Fortune* 145(9) (April 29):74–76.

Stires, D. 2004. McDonald's keeps right on cookin'. *Fortune* 149(10) (May 17):174.

Super Size Me Web site. http://www.supersizeme.com (accessed March 3, 2004).

Symonds, W., with Arner, F. 2003. Not exactly a Kodak moment: Investors are split over CEO Carp's digital plan. And now Carl Ichan is in the picture. *BusinessWeek*, no. 3859 (November 24):44.

Tsao, A., and Black, J. 2003. Where will Carly Fiorina take HP? *BusinessWeek Online*, May 29. http://www.businessweek.com.

Vonder Haar, P. 2004. Super Size Me. *Film Threat*, February 13. http://www.filmthreat.com/Reviews.asp?Id=5496.

Zuckerman, G., and Bandler, J. 2003. Investors seek to rewind Kodak: Providence capital-led group wants company to roll back big plans for digital technology. *The Wall Street Journal (Eastern Edition)* 242(79) (October 21):C1.

Notes

1. Burrows, 2003:59.
2. Burrows, 2001.
3. Lashinsky, 2002a:52.
4. Burrows, 2003:59.
5. Burrows, 2003:59.
6. Burrows, 2003.
7. Morrison, 2002:18.
8. Burrows, 2003:60.
9. Andres, 2003:69.
10. Andres, 2003:69.
11. Andres, 2003:69.
12. Andres, 2003:70.
13. Andres, 2003:70.
14. Andres, 2003:70.
15. Morrison, 2002:18.
16. Morrison, 2002:18.
17. Andres, 2003:71–72.
18. Lashinsky, 2002:68.
19. Lashinsky, 2002:69.
20. Lashinsky, 2002:68–69.
21. Anonymous, 2003a.
22. Anonymous, 2003a.
23. Elgin, B. (2005) "Can anyone save HP?" *BusinessWeek*, Feb. 21, 36–43.
24. This section is adapted from Hamel, 2000.
25. Hamel, 2000:146.
26. Hamel, 2000:138.
27. Hamel, 2000:138–40.

28. Hamel, 2000:138.
29. Hamel, 2000:143.
30. Hamel, 2000:140.
31. Hamel, 2000:140.
32. Hamel, 2000:143.
33. Hamel, 2000:146.
34. Gerstner, 2002.
35. Hamel, 2000:138.
36. Anonymous, 2003b.
37. Anonymous, 2003b.
38. Ante, 2003.
39. Anonymous, 2003b.
40. Ante, 2003.
41. Anonymous, 2003b.
42. Ante, 2002.
43. Kodak Press Release, 2004a.
44. Kodak Press Release, 2003.
45. Kodak Press Release, 2004b.
46. Zuckerman & Bandler, 2003.
47. Kodak Press Release, 2004b.
48. Kodak Press Release, 2004b.
49. Bandler, 2004.
50. Anonymous, 2004a.
51. Zuckerman & Bandler, 2003.
52. Bandler, 2003.
53. Anonymous, 2004a.
54. Bandler, 2004.
55. Bandler, 2003.
56. Symonds with Arner, 2003.
57. Kodak Press Release, 2004b.
58. Bandler, 2003.
59. Bandler, 2003.
60. Anonymous, 2004b.
61. http://www.supersizeme.com
62. http://www.supersizeme.com
63. Rebort, 2004.
64. Vonder Haar, 2004.
65. Rebort, 2004.
66. Hernandez & Brooks, 2004.
67. Anonymous, 2003c.
68. Arndt, 2004.
69. Stires, 2002; Jordan, 2003.

70. Stires, 2002.
71. Gogoi & Roman, 2003.
72. Stires, 2002.
73. Anonymous, 2003d.
74. Eisenberg, 2002.
75. Gogoi & Arndt, 2003.
76. Gogoi & Arndt, 2003.
77. Gogoi & Arndt, 2003.
78. Howard, 2002.
79. Anonymous, 2003c.
80. Arndt & Newman, 2003.
81. Eisenberg, 2002.
82. Garber, 2003.
83. Sieger, 2003.
84. Gogoi, 2003.
85. Anonymous, 2003c.
86. Arndt, 2004.
87. Doherty, 2004.
88. Arndt, 2004.
89. Arndt, 2004.
90. Garber, 2003.
91. The additional case studies referred to in the chapters that follow can be obtained from Web sites such as http://harvardbusinessonline.hbsp.harvard.edu, www.ecch.cranfield.ac.uk, http://store.darden.virginia.edu, http://gobi.stanford.edu/cases/, http://www1.ivey.ca/cases/.

Images of Managing Change[1]

Learning objectives

On completion of this chapter you should be able to:

- Understand the importance of organizational images and mental models.
- Identify different images of managing and of change outcomes.
- Outline six different images of managing change.
- Identify the theoretical underpinnings of these six change management images.
- Understand the practical implications of the six images and how to use them.

Writers and practitioners such as Gareth Morgan, Lee Bolman, Terrence Deal, and Mary Jo Hatch have been telling us for some time that the images we hold of organizations affect our interpretations of what we think is going on, what we think needs to happen, and how we think things should happen.[2] These images, sometimes referred to as metaphors, frames, or perspectives, are held by us often without our being aware either of their existence or of how they affect our thinking, perceptions, and actions. They act as mental models, pointing us in certain directions in order to make sense of things going on around us. For example, if we think of organizations as if they are machines, then we are likely to be more aware of potential "breakdowns," seeing our role as maintaining them or fixing them. However, if we think of organizations as political arenas, we are likely to be constantly seeking out hidden agendas behind decisions and trying to identify who wins and who loses. We are also likely to see our role as building coalitions, gathering support for our causes, or even stimulating conflict in order to produce innovative outcomes. Alternatively, we may see our organizations as mini societies or cultures. In this case, we are likely to be constantly searching for "the way things get done around here" and thinking about how to encourage the organizational values that are best aligned to the type of work that we do. Providing vision and meaning to our staff so that their identity becomes closely associated with the organization are further activities we are likely to pursue. Each frame orients us to a set of issues and, like a child with a hammer who sees everything around him or her as if it is a nail,[3] if we only draw upon one particular frame, then this will take us away from thinking about what is going on from an alternative perspective.

In this book, we argue that the same situation applies to managers of change. The images, metaphors, or frames that we hold, both of managing and of change, influence our ideas of what we think managing change is all about. In this chapter, we outline six different images of managing change. We describe the underlying assumptions associated with each image and identify organization and change theories that support each image. Finally, we discuss how change managers are able to draw upon and utilize multiple perspectives and images of managing change.

IMAGES OF MANAGING CHANGE: WHERE THEY COME FROM

As outlined in Table 2.1, there are two key images of managing (*management as control* versus *management as shaping*) and three key images of change outcomes (*intended*, *partially intended*, and *unintended*). As we shall see, depending on the combination of these images, this leads to one of six different images of managing organizational change: *director*, *navigator*, *caretaker*, *coach*, *interpreter*, and *nurturer*.

Images of Managing

Table 2.1 identifies two dominant images of management: management as control and management as shaping.

Management as Control

This has been a dominant image historically. It underlies the classic Fayol[4] characterization of management as involving activities such as planning, organizing, commanding, coordinating, and controlling. It is one that has been present in a number of influential management writers[5] and continues to be in use today.[6] It is associated with

TABLE 2.1 Images of Managing Change

		Images of Managing	
		Controlling . . . (activities)	**Shaping . . .** (capabilities)
Images of Change Outcomes	Intended	Image of managing change: • DIRECTOR	Image of managing change: • COACH
	Partially intended	Image of managing change: • NAVIGATOR	Image of managing change: • INTERPRETER
	Unintended	Image of managing change: • CARETAKER	Image of managing change: • NURTURER

a top-down, hierarchical view of managing. Typically, the organization is treated as if it is a machine: It is up to managers to drive the machine in specific directions, people are told what their roles will be, and departments and business units are allocated resources (inputs) so that the machine can perform efficiently and produce the necessary products or services in which it is engaged (outputs).

Management as Shaping

This image, which has more recent origins, is one that sees managing as being about *shaping* an organization and what happens in it. It is an image often associated with a participative style of managing in which people are encouraged to be involved in decisions and to help identify how things can be done better: Being closer to the action, the assumption is that they are likely to have a better knowledge of how things can be improved. Managing people is therefore about shaping their behavior in ways that encourage them to take actions of most benefit to the organization. The image anthropomorphizes the organization, that is, it treats it like a living, breathing organism or person. While it is possible to shape the organism or person in various ways, whether through rewards, through inculcating a particular set of values, by providing certain types of resources or information, or by providing some types of opportunities rather than others, the final behavior of the organism or person can only be shaped, not controlled. It is through such shaping actions that organizational capabilities are enhanced. Capabilities provide the organization with operational requirements to assist in its effective functioning, even in times of high uncertainty or ambiguity. Typical of this approach is the following view:

> Corporate capabilities are embedded in the fabric of the organization—in its practices, processes, systems, structures, culture, values, know-how and technologies. Importantly this is as true for reshaping capabilities as it is for operational ones. While personal capabilities leave the organization when their owner does, corporate capabilities tend to endure, despite the comings and goings of individuals.[7]

In this approach, good management produces strong corporate capabilities that provide the organization with a firm platform from which to both respond to and shape the external changes and challenges it is likely to face.[8]

Images of Change Outcomes

Table 2.1 identifies three dominant images relating to whether intentional change outcomes can be achieved.

Intended Change Outcomes

In this image, the dominant assumption is that intended change outcomes can be achieved. This image of planned or intended outcomes is at the core of much of the change literature and is suggested to have dominated the practice of changing organizations for over 50 years.[9] Change is treated as the realization of prior intent through the action of change managers. One well-cited discussion of the planned, intentional approach is found in the work of Chin and Benne, who identify three broad strategies for producing intentional change.[10]

- *Empirical-rational strategies* assume that people are rational and follow their own self-interest. Effective change occurs when a change can be demonstrated as desirable and aligned with the interests of the group affected by the change. Once this has been done, then intentional change will be achieved.[11]

- *Normative–re-educative strategies* assume that changes occur when people dispense with their old, normative orientations and gain commitment to new ones.[12] Producing intentional change in this approach involves changes not just in their knowledge and information but in their attitudes and values.
- *Power-coercive strategies* rely upon achieving intentional change by those with greater power gaining compliance in behavior from those with lesser power. Power may be exercised by legitimate authority or through other less legitimate, coercive means.[13]

Common to each of these approaches is the view that intended change outcomes can be achieved, albeit through differing change strategies.

Partially Intended Change Outcomes

In this image, some, but not all, change intentions are achievable. Power, processes, interests, and the different skill levels of managers affect their ability to produce intentional change outcomes. As Mintzberg and Waters[14] note, the link between what is intended and what is the final outcome is not necessarily direct. This is due to the fact that both intended and unintended consequences may emerge from the actions of change managers; intended outcomes may be adapted along the way or externally imposed forces and factors may modify what was originally intended. For such reasons, systemwide change initiatives do not always achieve the many outcomes that were intended.[15]

Unintended Change Outcomes

Compared to the other two images of change outcomes, there is less attention paid to this image within the change literature although it is common to the mainstream organizational theory literature. This image implies that managers often have great difficulty in achieving intentional change outcomes. This is because there are a variety of forces that either lead to change outcomes that are not intended by managers (they are forced on to them) or inhibit the ability of managers to implement the changes that they desire. These forces may be internal or external to an organization.

- *Internally* they may include departmental or interunit politics, the drag of past practices and routines that are difficult to dislodge, or the presence of deep-seated values and perceptions that are at odds with the desired change and difficult to budge.
- *Externally* they may include a variety of factors such as a confrontational industrial relations environment (which brings desired management changes to a standstill), legislation that mandates various requirements if an organization is to continue to function (e.g., meeting taxation requirements or adhering to governance procedures), or even industrywide trends that impact all organizations operating in the same industry (e.g., imposition of trade sanctions, a run on the stock market, etc).

These forces are typically viewed as being much more powerful than the influence wielded by individual change managers: In such circumstances, change managers and their intentions are swamped by these other forces. Occasionally outcomes and intentions may collide, but this is the result of the serendipity of events rather than the outcome of planned, intentional actions by change managers.

SIX IMAGES OF MANAGING CHANGE

Arising from Table 2.1 are six differing images of managing change, each of which is dependent on the images held of managing and of whether intentional change outcomes can be achieved. In what follows, we outline each image and discuss various theories that underpin and support them.

Image 1: Change Manager as Director

The *director image* is based on an image of management as control and of change outcomes as being achievable. It is therefore up to the change manager to direct the organization in particular ways in order to produce the required change. The assumption is that change is a strategic choice that managers make and the survival and general well-being of the organization depends on them.[16] So, for example, if a change manager decides that it is important to realign the organization to changes in the environment by introducing a new information technology system throughout the organization, then it is assumed that this can be done, that it will work well, and that the outcome will be a better-performing, better-aligned organization.

Theoretical Underpinning of the Image

As we will see in Chapter 8, there are a variety of what are sometimes referred to as "*n*-step" models or theories of change that assume the image of the change manager as *director*. These *n*-step models outline a set of steps that change managers should use to implement whatever is the change. The models vary in the number of steps they propose and the order in which they should be taken. However, what unites them is an optimistic view that intentional change can be achieved—as long as the change manager follows the correct steps that need to be taken.

Even writers such as Kotter who acknowledge that "successful change efforts are messy and full of surprises,"[17] nevertheless remain optimistic and maintain that his eight-step change model will produce "a satisfying result"[18] as long as the change manager follows these steps. Similarly, Ghoshal and Bartlett[19] write that while change is often thought to be difficult and messy, there is nothing mystical about the process of achieving effective change as long as certain steps are followed.[20] As we will see in Chapter 8, *contingency* theories of change, such as found in Stace and Dunphy[21] and Huy[22] share with *n*-step theories the assumption that change can be directed; they part company with *n*-step theories in arguing that the nature of this direction depends (or is contingent upon) a range of organizational factors such as the scale of the change, the urgency of the change, and the receptivity of organizational members to engaging in the change. There will be different "best ways," that is, different types of steps that change managers should take, depending upon the confluence of such factors. However, as long as they align the type of change with the style best suited to it, then intended change outcomes can be produced.

Image 2: Change Manager as Navigator

In the *navigator image*, control is still seen as at the heart of management action, although a variety of factors external to managers mean that while they may achieve some intended change outcomes, others will occur over which they have little control. Outcomes are at least partly emergent rather than completely planned and result from a variety of influences, competing interests, and processes. For example, a change manager may wish to restructure his or her business unit by putting cross-functional teams in place in order to assist product development across the different business functions. While a change manager may be able to formally establish teams (an intentional outcome), his or her ability to get them to work effectively may be minimal where there is a history of distrust, hoarding of information, and boundary protection by functional units. In this situation, functional managers may appoint people to the cross-functional teams who they know will keep the interests of their department uppermost and block any decisions that might decrease their organizational power (an unintended outcome of putting the teams in place). As Pendlebury et al.[23] point out, "Any sort of change is a leap in the dark." For them, this does not mean that managing change is something that is not able to be controlled; rather "it is only *partially* controllable" with change managers navigating the process toward an outcome, not all of which will be intentional.[24]

Theoretical Underpinning of the Image

The *contextualist* or *processual* theories of change, which, Burnes[25] maintains, are associated with the work of writers such as Dawson[26] and Pettigrew and Whipp,[27] rely upon the *navigator* image. These theories share an assumption with contingency theory that change unfolds differently over time and according to the context in which the organization finds itself. However, they differ from contingency theory in assuming "that change should not be and cannot be solidified, or seen as a series of linear events within a given period of time; instead, it is viewed as a continuous process."[28] Change is therefore "a process that unfolds through the interplay of multiple variables (context, political processes and consultation) within an organization."[29] Directing is not an option as "there can be no simple prescription for managing transitions successfully."[30] It is up to change managers to navigate their way through this complexity by identifying the range of options open to them, gathering and monitoring information, and availing themselves of appropriate resources.[31]

Even so, change managers need to accept that there will be unanticipated disruptions so that even these options and resources will need to be reviewed and reevaluated. In so doing, change managers are urged to incorporate bottom-up involvement of staff in their approach to managing change so, for senior managers, "Instead of directing and controlling change, their role becomes one of ensuring the organization's members are receptive to, and have the necessary skills and motivation, to take charge of, the change process."[32] In this approach change managers are assumed to have "some scope for choice and maneuver."[33] In keeping with the metaphor of the change manager as *navigator*, change courses may need to be plotted, and then replotted as new information comes to light and variations are made. There is no guarantee that the final destination will be that which was initially envisaged (if there is, indeed, a final destination) and there is the ever-present likelihood that a variety of other, unanticipated destinations might eventuate, brought about by the shifting winds and currents underlying the change.

Image 3: Change Manager as Caretaker

In the *caretaker image*, the (ideal) image of management is still one of control, although the ability to exercise control is severely constrained by a variety of forces, both internally and externally driven, that propel change relatively independent of a manager's intentions. For example, despite the change manager's best intentions to implement activities to encourage entrepreneurial and innovative behavior, they may feel like this is a continually failing exercise as the organization grows, becomes more bureaucratic, and enacts strategic planning cycles, rules, regulations, and centralized practices. In this situation, inexorable growth and the issues associated with it are outside the control of any individual manager of change. In this rather pessimistic image, at best managers are *caretakers*, shepherding their organizations along as best they can.

Theoretical Underpinning of the Image

Three organizational theories reinforce this *caretaker* image of managers of change: life-cycle, population ecology, and institutional.

Life-Cycle Theory As in the example above, this theory views organizations as passing through well-defined stages from birth to growth, maturity, and then decline or death. These stages are part of the natural, developmental cycle of organizations. There is an underlying logic or trajectory and the stages through which it passes are sequential.[34] There is little change managers can do to stop this natural development; at best they are caretakers of the organization as it passes through the various stages (see Table 2.2). In all this, managers have a limited role, helping to smooth the various transitions rather than controlling whether or not they occur.

Population Ecology Theory Drawing on biology and neo-Darwinian logic, population ecologists focus on how the environment selects organizations for survival or extinction,[35] with whole populations of organizations changing as a result of ongoing cycles of variation, selection, and retention.

- Organizational *variation* can occur as the result of random chance.
- Organizational *selection* can occur when an environment selects organizations that are of best fit to its conditions.
- Organizational *retention* consists of forces that retain various organizational forms and thereby serve as a counterinfluence to the forces of variation and selection.[36]

Some population ecology theorists suggest that there are at least some limited actions that change managers may take to influence these forces. For example, some writers point to:

- The ability of some organizations, or their key stakeholders, to interact with other organizations to lessen the effect of the environment.
- The ability of an organization to reposition itself in a new market or environment.[37]

In general, however, the implication of population ecology theory is that managers have little sway over change where whole populations of organizations are impacted

TABLE 2.2 Life Cycle Stages and Change Management Issues

Source: Adapted from Harrison and Shirom, 1999:307–314.

Developmental Stage	Caretaker Activities
Entrepreneurial Stage	
Founder initiates an idea	• Making sure resources are available • Establishing market niche • Ensuring management procedures assist innovation and creativity • Ensuring founder generates commitment to vision
Collectivity Stage	
Coordination through informal means as group identity develops	• Ensuring coordination of communication and decision-making processes • Establishing cohesion and morale through guiding goals and culture • Ensuring skill development through appropriate reward systems
Formalization Stage	
Formalization of operations with emphasis on rules and procedures to promote efficiency and stability	• Facilitating shift to professional management • Providing mechanisms to monitor internal operations and scan external environment • Focusing procedures on efficiency and quality • Striking a balance between autonomy, coordination, and control
Elaboration Stage	
Change and renewal as structure becomes more complex and environmental domains change	• Adapting current products and developing new ones • Ensuring structure facilitates coordination among different units • Planning for turnaround, cutbacks, and renewal

upon by outside forces. One might point, for example, to how managers of many promising dot.com companies were unable to withstand the impact of the widespread dot.com crash in April 2000 that affected the whole population of dot.com organizations.

Institutional Theory Institutional theory argues that change managers take similar actions across whole populations of organizations. This similarity in the actions that they take occurs through pressures associated with the interconnectedness of organizations within an industry or environment.[38] DiMaggio and Powell[39] identify three such pressures:

- *Coercive* (including government-mandated changes).
- *Mimetic* (where organizations imitate the structures and practices of other organizations in their field, usually ones that they consider as legitimate or successful).

- *Normative* (where changes occur through the professionalizing of work such that managers in different organizations utilize similar values and modes of operating in their actions and decisions).

While not all organizations succumb to these pressures—there are "deviant peers"[40] — the assumption is that these external forces are inexorable and individual managers have only limited ability to implement change outcomes that are at odds with these forces. At best, change managers are *caretakers* having little influence over the direction of change.

Image 4: Change Manager as Coach

In the *coach image*, the assumption is that change managers (or change consultants) are able to intentionally shape the organization's capabilities in particular ways. Like a sports coach, the change manager shapes the organization or the team's capabilities to ensure that, in a competitive situation, it will be able to succeed. Rather than dictating the exact state of each play as the *director* might attempt to do, the *coach* relies upon building in the right set of values, skills, and "drills" that are deemed to be the best ones that organizational members, as players, will be able to draw on adeptly in order to achieve desired organizational outcomes.

Theoretical Underpinning of the Image

The traditional *organization development* (OD) theory reinforces the change manager as *coach* image. As we will see in more detail in Chapter 7, underlying the traditional OD focus is the implementation of change that stresses the importance of humanism, democracy, and individual development to organizational life.[41] Hence, in the same way that sports coaches have their own views on the best skills needed, so too does the OD approach. The traditional OD change consultant acts as a *coach* by helping to "*structure activities to help the organization members solve their own problems and learn to do that better.*"[42]

As we shall see, as the OD field grew and focused not just on small-scale but on larger-scale change, so was there a corresponding development of new techniques designed to get the whole organizational system into a room at one and the same time.[43] Retaining the value of drawing people into actions of their own making, proponents of these "coaching" techniques are glowing, sometimes almost evangelical, in outlining how they help to achieve their intended outcomes. For example, they are argued to produce results "with greater speed and increased commitment and greatly reduced resistance by the rest of the organization."[44]

Image 5: Change Manager as Interpreter

The *interpreter image* to managing change places the change manager in the position of creating meaning for other organizational members, helping them to make sense of various organizational events and actions. It is these events and actions that, in and of themselves, constitute a changed organization. It is up to change managers to represent to their staff (and others) what these changes actually mean. However, it is likely that there will be competing meanings within the organization of the same events and actions, especially given that there are differing groups in organizations not all of which share the same interests and understandings. This suggests that only some meanings—and therefore change intentions—are likely to be realized; other meanings are likely to emerge from alternative interpretations and understandings held by other people engaged in, or affected by, the particular change.

In this contested view of organizational change, managers as *interpreters* "need to be able to provide legitimate arguments and reasons for why their actions fit within the situation and should be viewed as legitimate."[45] For example, in an organizational downsizing, there may exist competing meanings about the change: While change managers may endeavor to portray it as way of strengthening the organization and so enable better protection of the jobs of those who remain, other organizational members may tell different stories, interpreting it as inevitable, given the changed environment of the organization; alternatively, they may present the fact of downsizing as evidence of management's incompetence, or as an underhanded way of getting rid of some politically troublesome individuals or even departments but in the name of making the organization more efficient. Better change managers, therefore, are those who see their role as *interpreters* and are able to dominate stories and understandings about the meaning of a specific change. In this sense, they are like strategists who, as argued by Linda Smircich and Charles Stubbart, enact a view of the world by creating "imaginary lines between events, objects and situations so that events, objects and situations become meaningful for the members of an organizational world."[46]

Theoretical Underpinning of the Image

The *interpreter image* is present in Karl Weick's[47] sense-making theory of organizational change. He suggests that a central focus is needed on the structuring processes and flows through which organizational work occurs. Adopting the latter perspective leads one to see organizations as being in an ongoing state of accomplishment and re-accomplishment with organizational routines constantly undergoing adjustments to better fit changing circumstances.[48] In this constant movement are four drivers of organizational change that shape how capabilities are produced:

- *Through animation* (whereby people remain in motion and may experiment, e.g., with job descriptions).
- *By direction* (including being able to implement in novel ways direct strategies).
- *By paying attention and updating* (such as updating knowledge of the environment and reviewing and rewriting organizational requirements).
- *Through respectful, candid interaction* (which occurs when people are encouraged to speak out, particularly when things are not working well).[49]

These sense-making drivers assist individuals in developing their capabilities for managing the ambiguity of organizational change.[50] At the same time, it is up to change managers to interpret how and why these adaptive emergent changes are occurring.[51] By providing meaning, and connecting the dots, the change manager as *interpreter* helps "to make sense of events that don't fit together."[52] From this perspective it is up to managers of change:

> to author interpretations and labels that capture the patterns in those adaptive choices. Within the framework of sensemaking, management sees what the front line says and tells the world what it means. In a newer code, management doesn't create change. It certifies change.[53]

Image 6: Change Manager as Nurturer

The *nurturing image* to managing change assumes that even small changes may have a large impact on organizations[54] and managers are not able to control the outcome of these changes. However, they may nurture their organizations, facilitating organizational qualities that enable positive self-organizing to occur. Like a parent's relationship with a child, future outcomes are nurtured or shaped, but the ability to produce intended outcomes at the end of the day is severely limited because of the impact of much wider, sometime chaotic forces and influences. Specific outcomes and directions of change cannot be intentionally produced but rather emerge and are shaped through the qualities and capabilities of the organization.

Theoretical Underpinning of the Image

Two organizational theories support the *nurturer* image: chaos and Confucian/Taoist.

Chaos Theory This theory assumes that organizational change is nonlinear, is fundamental rather than incremental, and does not necessarily entail growth.[55] Drawing on complexity theory, these theorists look at how "companies continuously regenerate themselves through adaptive learning and interactive structural change. These efforts periodically result in the spontaneous emergence of a whole new dynamic order, through a process called self-organization."[56] Self-organizing recognizes the chaotic nature of organizations that results from having to grapple simultaneously with both change and stability.[57] In this situation, the change manager nurtures the capacity for self-organization but has little ability to influence the direction of the spontaneous new orders that may emerge. This may all sound a little puzzling, but it could be argued that this is precisely the emergent strategy—of nurturing capabilities—that the highly successful Brazilian entrepreneur, Ricardo Semler, adopted in his manufacturing organization, Semco. It provides an explanation for how Semco moved successfully into other business areas, including electronic business (see Tables 2.3 and 2.4).

Confucian/Taoist Theory Marshak[58] points out that fundamentally different assumptions underlie a Confucian/Taoist approach—perhaps better regarded as a philosophy rather than a theory—to change compared to Western views of organizational change. Confucian/Taoist assumptions view change as cyclical (constant ebb and flow), processional (harmonious movement from one state to another), journey oriented (cyclical change, therefore no end state), based on maintaining equilibrium (achieving natural harmony), observed and followed by involved people (who constantly seek harmony with their universe), and normal rather than the exception. In this sense, organizational change outcomes are not intended so much as produced through the nurturing of a harmonious Yin–Yang philosophy in which each new order contains its own negation. Embedded in this philosophy is, therefore, an image of the change manager as nurturer.

USING THE SIX-IMAGES FRAMEWORK

Each of the images of managing change represents a Weberian "ideal type"; that is, they are ideal not in the sense of desirable but in the sense of a pure form that may not exist completely in reality. This situation is due to the fact that the images of managing and the images of change outcomes are not really separate categories but rather form a

TABLE 2.3 **Chaos Theory and Change Management Roles**

Source: Adapted from Tetenbaum, 1998.

Change Management Actions	Core Elements
Managing transitions	• Destabilize people • Get them involved in decision making and problem solving
Building resilience	• Provide people with the ability to absorb change
Destabilizing the system	• Create a state of tension • Seek disconfirmation of organizational beliefs • Act as a devil's advocate • Seek to nurture the creativity needed to cope with the chaotic environment in which organizations operate
Managing order and disorder, the present and the future	• Provide balance between a need for order and a need for change
Creating and maintaining a learning organization	• Facilitate ways in which continuous learning is available to everyone in the organization

TABLE 2.4 **Semco: A Chaotic Business?**

Semco is a well-known South American manufacturing business that has a flat hierarchy and emphasizes staff empowerment to engage in decisions about virtually all company issues, from strategy to setting their own salaries. Ricardo Semler, the Brazilian majority owner of Semco, has recently discussed how the company has moved away from being a manufacturing company, making industrial pumps and white goods, and into e-business and other services that now account for 75 percent of its business.[a] Many of the company practices and philosophies arguably illustrate principles of chaos theory at work. For example, Semler maintains that the company successfully "went digital without a strategy." He puts this down to what some might term a chaotic management style whereby, in his words:

> [R]ather than dictate Semco's identity from on high, I've let our employees shape it through their individual efforts, interests, and initiatives.
>
> That rather unusual management philosophy has drawn a good deal of attention over the years . . . The way we work—letting our employees choose what they do, where and when they do it, and even how they get paid—has seemed a little too radical for mainstream companies.
>
> . . . I do suggest that some of the principles that underlie the way we work will become increasingly common and even necessary in the new economy. In particular, I believe we have an organization that is able to transform itself continuously and organically—without formulating complicated mission statements and strategies, announcing a bunch of top-down directives, or bringing in an army of change-management consultants.[b]

[a]Semler, 2000:52.
[b]Semler, 2000:51–52.

continuum: in the case of managing, a continuum from controlling to shaping and, in the case of change outcomes, a continuum from intended to unintended change outcomes. For this reason, it is important to point out that the six images of managing change themselves have blurred boundaries and in practice elements of different images may overlap and intermingle.

These six images are enduring, each having, as we have seen, differing theoretical underpinnings that serve to legitimate them. Nevertheless, and as already noted, it is probably fair to say that the *caretaker* and *nurturer* images are less discussed in the change management literature—although they are quite accepted within the wider organizational theory literature, which has much less of a "practice" orientation than does the change management literature. This situation occurs for obvious reasons: the *director*, *navigator*, *coach*, and *interpreter* change images entail, to varying degrees, much more active, intentional, and directional assumptions about the ability of change managers to proactively produce organizational change (whether through control or shaping actions). In this sense, they are much more positive images than the *caretaker* and *nurturer* images, which entail a more reactive and possibly negative view of the effectiveness of the manager of change—in terms of both why specific changes are occurring and the extent to which these changes are related to the intentions held by change managers. Managers obviously do not like to feel that they are insignificant players in their organizational worlds. Rather, the assumption that they are able to produce positive and intentional change is an important part of Western change management lexicon.

We have seen this situation recently in relation to the six-images framework we have outlined in this chapter. A well-known change consultant based in Washington, DC, reported to us how he intended using the six-images framework in a major international organization to help in getting their staff to understand the impact of the culture of the organization and the multiple competing discourses about "organizational change" that existed within it. The organization agreed to use the framework and even requested and received copywrite reproduction permission to use it. However, at the last minute, some senior members of the organization argued against using it "because it might legitimate managers not assuming responsibility for initiating and managing change; it might give them an out." This was for two reasons: first, the possibility of seeing change as having unintended outcomes; second, the possibility that the change manager may have minimal impact where the organization is dominated by enforced change from the outside. In the end, the six-images framework was not used.

The implication of this example is instructive to us in the following terms. Some writers refer to certain topics as being "sacred" and to others as being "profane"; that is, respectively, some topics are not to be questioned (the sacred) and to do so is not seen as legitimate (the profane). The example just outlined suggests that sacred to the change field is the view that organizational change can be managed in the form of producing intentional outcomes; it is profane to suggest otherwise, that is, that managers of change might be dominated by forces much bigger than themselves. Our position in this book is that it is time to end this divide and recognize that, in the long run, such distinctions do not help managers of change; rather, it hinders them by stopping them from taking a reflective view of their actions—and what is achievable—in any particular change situation. It is to these wider implications to which we turn for the rest of this chapter.

Three Key Uses of the Six-Images Framework

In using the six-images framework, we draw attention to three interrelated issues for reflection by the manager of change: surfacing assumptions about change, assessing dominant images of change, and using multiple images and perspectives of change.

Surfacing Our Assumptions about Change

The six-images framework guides us in reflecting on the images and assumptions we hold about managing change. As we noted at the start of this chapter, we all have mental models and these help us to simplify and make sense of the complex organizational worlds in which we operate. At the same time as they simplify and illuminate, they turn our attention toward some things and away from others. Being aware of the mental models with which we work helps us to think more carefully about their relevance—and the extent to which the assumptions they entail are really ones that are going to be of assistance to us in approaching organizational change.

Being aware of these images enables change managers to assess the assumptions that are being made by *others* with whom they are working or interacting or from whom they are taking advice. Resulting from this assessment may be actions to reorient the images others have of the particular change in which they are involved by providing a new image through which the change can be seen.

For example, a change manager working with a *navigating* image may get others, who may view change through a *director* image, to acknowledge that unanticipated outcomes may occur as a change unfolds. He or she might get them to accept that one possibility of engaging in a change is that their current view of what is desired at the end of the change may shift as the change unfolds and new possibilities emerge. In this sense, awareness of differing change management images can lead to an educative process within a change team. It requires encouragement of conversations around images and assumptions about the anticipated change, testing these within a group and ensuring that all members of the team share common change image(s). This ensures that individual change managers are not talking past one another and making assumptions that are not shared by others.

Assessing Dominant Images of Change

The six-images framework encourages change managers to reflect on whether they are dominated, for all changes, by a particular view of change—and the limitations of such an image. For example, the *director* image turns our attention to the outcomes we want to achieve and the steps needed to get there; at the same time, it turns our attention away from whether the outcomes are really achievable (or even desirable) and whether unintentional outcomes also might occur should we pursue a particular change course.

The six-images framework directs attention to whether the organization in which the change is to occur is dominated by a particular view of what is achievable and how change should unfold. Indeed, Hamel & Prahalad[59] point out that some organizations are dominated by a particular view of how things should get done—almost to the point where the view is part of the "genetic coding" of the organization and is therefore seen as natural and not open for negotiation. In this instance, the change manager whose change image is at odds with a dominant organizational image may experience frustration and stress as he or she seeks to work with a change image that may be deemed by the wider organization to be less legitimate or relevant than another.

Using Multiple Images and Perspectives of Change

It is possible that a change manager's image-in-use may depend on his or her personal preference or it may be an unconscious decision based on the use of an approach with which the manager is familiar. One of the advantages of exposure to the range of images of managing change and associated techniques is that it reduces the likelihood of a change manager using a single image because of a lack of understanding of the range of options upon which he or she is able to draw. The six-images framework directs attention to the range of available options and how their use may vary.

- *Image-in-use depends on the type of change.* Change managers may assess some types of change as being more amenable to one image of change rather than another. An *interpreter* approach might be seen as possible for one but not another type of change. In this case, the change manager adjusts his or her image of change and the corresponding perception of what is possible depending on the change situation being confronted. For example, Anderson and Anderson[60] adopt a *coaching* image in arguing that developmental and transitional change, but not transformational change, can be managed. They draw on a *navigator* change image in relation to transformational changes, arguing that there are too many intangibles that can inhibit the arrival of predetermined outcomes; what is required is a mindset that accepts that organizations can be led into the unknown without the end point being predictable in advance.
- *Image-in-use depends on the context of the change.* As we will see in Chapter 6, the context of change may vary; in some situations, organizational members may be ready for a change and unhappy with the status quo. In this situation, the image-in-use might be *coach* or *interpreter*, involving people in particular ways in order to identify desired change outcomes. However, an alternative change context may be one where hostility and resistance may face the change manager in attempting to implement specific changes; in this case, the ability to achieve intended change outcomes may be deemed unlikely and a *caretaker* or at best *navigator* change management image might be assessed as the most feasible image with which to work.
- *Image-in-use depends on the phase of change.* Changes pass through different phases—to be explored in more detail in later chapters (e.g., Chapter 11). Change managers may choose to use different images depending upon the change phase—or their perception of the phase of the change. For example, in initiating a change imposed on them from outside—for example, the need to implement an ISO 9000 system in order to continue to be used as a supplier—the change manager may feel that the *caretaker* image is the most appropriate as the change was not intentionally produced from within but mandated from without. However, as the change progresses, they may feel that an *interpreter* role might be appropriate, conveying to staff new meanings associated with the implementation such as greater professionalism and the possibility for expanded business into new areas.
- *Image-in-use depends on simultaneous involvement in multiple changes.* In organizations, there are often multiple changes unfolding at one and the same time, either within various business units or across the organization as a whole. In this situation,

some changes might be imposed from outside the business unit and a *caretaker* image might apply to these; simultaneously, other change initiatives may be underway, initiated from within a business unit so that a *director* image is most applicable, that is, seeking intentional outcomes in a controlled manner. In this situation, multiple change images coexist, corresponding to different but simultaneous changes that are being concurrently managed. This implies that skilled change managers are able to swap images depending upon the change or the change situation—or manage multiple images simultaneously where they are related to different, concurrent changes.

EXERCISE 2.1

Assessing Change Managers' Images

Your task, either individually or in small groups, is to find and interview two people who have managed change in an organization. It is preferable to select people from different organizations and industries to provide a contrast. Compare and contrast the responses you receive and arrive at an assessment of the following issues:

- Which images of change did you come across?
- How did these images affect the actions they took as managers of change?
- Where they drew upon multiple images, to what extent were these different images related to
    - The type of change?
    - The context of the change?
    - The phase of the change?
    - Simultaneous involvement in multiple changes?
    - Were there any other factors that you identified?
    - What broad conclusions do you draw from your analysis about the impact of images and mental models on the way these change managers approached change?

Conclusion

In this chapter, we have explored six images of managing change: *director*, *navigator*, *caretaker*, *coach*, *interpreter*, and *nurturer*. Each of these images is based on differing assumptions about managing (controlling actions versus shaping capabilities) and change outcomes (intended, partly intended, unintended). Each is underpinned by theories drawn from the organizational theory and change literature—although we have kept to a minimum our discussion of these theories. We have identified three key uses of the six-images framework in order to assist the manager of change: surfacing assumptions, assessing dominant images, and using multiple perspectives and images of change.

We close this chapter by pointing out that there are a variety of other uses for this framework that will be noted in later chapters in the book. Two of these we will make mention of at this point. First, even assessing change as successful is often bound up with one rather than another image of change:

- Was it managed well?
- What went right?

- What went wrong?
- Did we get the outcome we were after?

Such questions are predicated on particular images of change and fail to appreciate that even judging the success of particular changes is open to interpretation depending upon who is doing the interpreting and what images they hold of managing change. As Pettigrew, Woodman, and Cameron note, "Judgments about success are also likely to be conditional on who is doing the assessment and when the judgments are made."[61] The six-images framework points to the need to raise conversations early about measurements of the success of a change (something we will visit in more detail in Chapter 12) and ensure that people within the organization adopt similar images and assumptions in relation to it.

Second, some writers argue that we need to think not of *managing change* but of *leading change*. For example, Kotter[62] differentiates between managing and leading change. Similarly, and as outlined above, Anderson and Anderson[63] suggest that transformational change cannot be managed, but it can be led as long as *leaders* have the right mindset. However, our six-images framework suggests that this distinction might be overstated. Rather, Anderson and Anderson are really referring to the distinction between a *coaching* image of managing change on the one hand (what they call *managing change*) and a *navigating* image of managing change on the other (what they refer to as *leading change*). In reality, both are aspects of managing change; it is the image and assumptions behind them that vary. Hence, we argue that the distinction between leading and managing change is too artificial a distinction to retain. Indeed, this is the position taken by other organizational change writers and practitioners who do not make such firm distinctions between managing and leading change. For example, Kanter, Stein, and Jick move freely between using the two terms, one being used interchangeably with the other, as in their statement: "The world does not stand still while leaders manage a change."[64] This is the position adopted in this book and one that we will visit again in Chapter 8.

TABLE 2.5 Chapter Reflections for the Practicing Change Manager

- To what extent are you more comfortable with one or other of the six images described in this chapter in terms of your own approach to managing change—or your anticipated approach to managing change?
- Why is this the case?
- What are the strengths and limitations of the images that you have identified as most relevant to you?
- What skills do you think are associated with each image in order to use it well?
- Are there areas of personal skill development that are needed in order for you to feel more comfortable in using other change management images?
- Have you been in an organization that was dominated by particular images or approaches to change?
- What barriers would you face in trying to bring consideration of alternative images in these organizations? What strategies could you use to assist you in overcoming these barriers?
- ***As a group exercise:*** In small groups, compare and contrast your responses to the above issues. Where do differences exist? Try and identify why this is the case.

Supplemental Reading

Anderson, L. A., and Anderson, D. 2001. Awake at the wheel: Moving beyond change management to conscious change leadership. *OD Practitioner* 33(3):4–10.

Beer, M., and Nohria, N., eds. 2000. *Breaking the code of change.* Boston: Harvard Business School Press.

Kanter, R. M., Stein, B. A., and Jick, T. D. 1992. *The challenge of organizational change: How companies experience it and leaders guide it.* Free Press: New York.

Kotter, J. P. 1996. *Leading change.* Boston: MA: Harvard Business School Press.

Lichtenstein, B.B. 2000. Self-organized transitions: A pattern amid the chaos of transformative change. *Academy of Management Executive* 14(4):128–41.

Mintzberg, H. 1975. The manager's job: Folklore and fact. *Harvard Business Review* 53(4):49–61.

Nader, D. A. 1998. *Champions of change: How CEOs and their companies are mastering the skills of radical change.* San Francisco: Jossey-Bass.

Semler, R. 2000. How we went digital without a strategy. *Harvard Business Review* 78(4):51–58.

Thietart, R. A., and Forgues, B. 1995. Chaos theory and organizations. *Organization Science* 6(1):19–31.

Van de Ven, A. H., and Poole, M. S. 1995. Explaining development and change in organizations. *Academy of Management Review* 20(3):510–40.

Green Mountain Resort was not expected to be in business for very long, not that anyone was making predictions. It was a small resort with golf, tennis, and, most notably, some skiing—on machine made snow for the most part—set in the Appalachians. It was a fair distance from major population centers and had none of the history of the famous southern spas of an older era, places like the Homestead.

But it didn't have to stand fully on its own: it was built as a draw for buyers of vacation homes at Green Mountain. The resort was the center of sales hospitality and an attractive amenity of home ownership. Being a property owner got you membership in the resort with ski passes, discount golf, and the like. Salespeople pointed to the resort as a symbol of their commitment to community: they were not just selling lots; they were offering a lifestyle.

Of course, the salespeople also knew that when the real estate sold out, the function of the resort as a sales tool would disappear along with the sales staff, and, if this were like other similar developments, the resort would lose its luster and perhaps even go out of business. The resort wasn't there for vacationers but for buyers. Soon, there would be no more buyers. And soon after that, the resort would have to make it on its own, as only a resort.

The top management of Green Mountain at this time came to the operation when the original developers failed. They were sent in by the investment bank that had financed the original operation to put the place in order and get it sold. But the bank's workout team fell in love with the rural beauty and lifestyle and bought it themselves. Actually, it was a very complex plan that structured eventual ownership for the homeowners, with part ownership by the remaining management company that would continue to run the operation. The former bankers were committed to building an actual community, one they wanted to stay in themselves, and to having the resort become a first-class operation on its own. They were explicit about their goal: make sure that Green Mountain, the community and the resort, didn't go to seed when the land sold out.

With the new structure, the resort manager was an owner. He decided to stay on, motivated by his ownership share as well as the opportunity to have his own show, no longer just an adjunct to sales. Gunter had been part of the original management and had expected to eventually leave for another resort job, enacting a pattern typical in the hospitality industry. But now he was an owner, not just an employee, and he had a vision of a first-class mountain resort.

The architecture of the lodge, and of most of the vacation homes, was more up-country than ski-country. In contrast to this uniquely American look was Gunter, in his Tyrolian hat, his accent recalling his native Austria. He didn't wear lederhosen but would have looked natural in them. His wife, Hilde, actually had blond braids, and when they were together, you could only imagine that they were off on a hike to an Alpine meadow. Their house was perfectly Teutonic, immaculate, and welcoming in a way that made you think you shouldn't touch anything. Gunter was nothing if not rational.

That is why Gunter was worried about the turnover of staff. Green Mountain Resort was in a beautiful rural county, but that county was also the poorest in the state. That meant that it was hard to find good employees locally, and those that were good, whether local or imported, didn't stay long. High turnover meant added training, plus the predominance of novice staff. And it was mainly the best service people who moved on, leaving behind the poorest performers. That, Gunter knew, undermined efforts to build a first-class operation. Turnover had to be reduced.

There weren't a lot of options. In such a small operation, the opportunities for promotion were few, and Gunter was faced with the irony that if he reduced turnover, there would be even fewer openings for advancement. Structural arrangements to keep people from leaving, such as term contracts, benefits that took time to vest, and the like, were seen as coercive and drove people away. Besides, such measures seemed out of character for Gunter and for Green Mountain.

The so-called hospitality industry, in its training and management development literature, saw turnover as a problem needing treatment, as well. One difference in the industry association view, however, was that turnover was defined as chronic, always there, something to be endured. All management could do, went the advice, was to minimize the debilitating effects: streamline training, simplify jobs, don't become dependent on individuals, make HR processes more efficient.

Gunter knew this perspective but didn't want to settle for a chronically sick organization. His efforts, though, had turned out to validate the industry view and even, sometimes, make things worse. Gunter also was beginning to see the paradox of his situation and recognize that he needed not just some new ideas but some new ways of thinking about his situation. So he called in a consultant.

The consultant was already working with the development company that was marketing the land and owned the resort but was not an expert in the hospitality industry. This was deliberate, as Gunter already knew the conventional industry take on turnover. Perhaps an outsider, someone with a fresh look, would see something new.

The consultant listened to Gunter's retelling of all he had done to reduce turnover, how it hadn't worked and had even driven away some of those he wanted to keep. After listening to the litany of failures, the consultant asked just what it was that Gunter really wanted, to which the reply was, reduce turnover, of course. It was said in a way that made the consultant think that Gunter believed he knew what to do and only needed help in the execution, help in finding a better tactic for reducing turnover.

The consultant told Gunter, with some embarrassment, that he couldn't really think of anything else to try. But he also was suspicious that, since nothing worked and some reasonable tactics just made things worse, they ought to try something different. The consultant suggested rephrasing the old aphorism, "If at first you don't succeed, try, try again," to say, "If at last you don't succeed, don't just try again, do something different." The issue now was how to break out of the set of failed solutions, all of which, even with their differences, left the situation essentially intact. What would be *really* different?

Since the so-called solutions continued to fail, perhaps a real difference would come from stopping attempts to solve the turnover problem. If turnover is so resistant to being changed, perhaps there is something functional about it. What if turnover were embraced, rather than scorned? The consultant suggested looking into what actually happened when good people left. Where did they go, and what did they do? In short, Gunter and the consultant went after the answer to a new question: What is good about turnover?

Things looked different from this perspective. The best employees, the ones Gunter most wanted to keep, usually left for better jobs, jobs that required the good training and variety of assignments they had at Green Mountain. And they tended to be high performers in their new jobs, which led to more promotions.

It began to look like turnover, an anathema to Green Mountain as an institution, was a good career development move for those who turned over. More investigation of those careers revealed—no surprise—that the best people, the ones Gunter wanted most to keep, did the best in their new jobs. But what was most interesting, they attributed their success, in large measure, to the training and early responsibility they had been given at Green Mountain. Their employers, usually other resorts, came to regard Green Mountain alumni as prime recruits.

The word got around: If you wanted great training, early responsibility, to get on the fast track, Green Mountain was the place to go. That meant that more smart, ambitious people began to apply for jobs at Green Mountain, expecting to work hard, learn a lot, and move on quickly. Gunter could now imagine the resort mainly staffed with these career builders, working hard and smart in order to learn and develop, and in doing so, providing exemplary levels of service. So what if turnover was high? The staff would always be highly motivated, and other potential top performers would be waiting at the gate.

Now with an explicit strategy for recruiting high-potential people, offering them the promise of rapid career development, turnover might actually increase, but it would mean something different: It would be a sign, given the reformulated strategy, of success rather than an organizational problem. The situation had been reframed, the facts given new meaning.

Was the problem solved? The answer is both yes and no. No, the facts of turnover remained, but, yes, that no longer was troublesome. It might be better to say the problem had been dis-solved, that is, it had been neutralized, and, by being given a new context, now had no effect. What had once been a liability was now transformed into an asset, and so there was no longer a need to engage in problem solving. The reframing of the situation rendered the failed first-order change efforts irrelevant, and so continuing efforts to reduce turnover could stop. Turnover had been a problem partly because of the efforts to get rid of it. (Problems are problems, in part, due to the ongoing efforts to fix them.) No more fix: no more problem.

This is an example of second-order change, one distinguishing feature of which is that change interventions are directed at the "solution." At Green Mountain, continuing efforts to reduce turnover were interrupted by the technique of reversal, that is, finding a plausible interpretation of the facts opposite in meaning to the generally accepted interpretation. (Turnover is bad, versus turnover is good.) With the new meaning, no fix was required, and when you aren't fixing something, there must not be a problem.

Green Mountain continues to fast-track new hires on to other resorts. Gunter has not moved to another resort but has expanded his own role to be a mentor.

Questions:

1. Which of the six change images discussed in this chapter can be identified in the assumptions about managing turnover that were held by
   - Gunter?
   - The hospitality literature?
   - The consultant?
2. How did these assumptions influence prescriptions for dealing with "the turnover problem"?
3. Choose another change image and apply it to "the turnover problem." To what new insights does it lead?
4. What conclusions do you draw from this about the statement at the start of the chapter that "if we only draw upon one particular frame, then this will take us away from thinking about what is going on from an alternative perspective"?

TABLE 2.6 Additional Case Studies

Yahoo!: Business on Internet Time Rivkin, J. W. & Girotto, J. (1999) *Harvard Business School*
Reviving Yahoo!: Strategies That Turned the Leading Internet Portal Gupta, V. (2003) *ICFAI Knowledge Centre, India*
The Rebirth of Air France (A), (B), (C), and (D) Trepo, G., & Autier, F. (2001) *HEC School of Management, France*
Ricardo Semler's Employee Empowerment Strategies at Semco Sumit, K. C., & Bala Kiran, V. (2004) *ICFAI Knowledge Centre, India*

Bibliography

Anderson, L. A., and Anderson, D. 2001. Awake at the wheel: Moving beyond change management to conscious change leadership. *OD Practitioner* 33(3):4–10.

Axelrod, D. 1992. Getting everyone involved: How one organization involved its employees, supervisors, and managers in redesigning the organization. *Journal of Applied Behavioral Science* 28(4):499–509.

Barge, J. K., and Oliver, C. 2003. Working with appreciation in managerial practice. *Academy of Management Review* 28(1):124–42.

Beer, M., and Nohria, N. 2000. Purpose of change: Economic value or organizational capability? In *Breaking the code of change*, ed. M. Beer and N. Nohria, 35–36. Boston: Harvard Business School Press.

Bunker, B. B., and Alban, B. T. 1992. Editors' introduction: The large group intervention—a new social innovation? *Journal of Applied Behavioral Science* 28(4):473–579.

Burnes, B. 1996. *Managing change: A strategic approach to organizational dynamics.* 2nd ed. London: Pitman.

Collins, D. 1998. *Organizational change: Sociological perspectives.* London: Routledge.

Cummings, T. G., and Worley, C. G. 1997. *Organization development and change.* 6th ed. Minneapolis/St. Paul: West Publishing Company.

Dawson, P. 1994. *Organizational change: A processual approach.* London: Chapman.

DiMaggio, P. J., and Powell, W. W. 1991. The iron cage revisited: Institutional isomorphism and collective rationality in organizational fields. In *The new institutionalism in organizational analysis*, ed. W. W. Powell and P. J. DiMaggio, 63–82. Chicago: University of Chicago Press.

Fayol, H. 1949. *General and industrial management.* London: Pitman. Original: *Administration Industrielle et Generale*, 1916.

French, W. L., and Bell, C. H. 1995. *Organization development: Behavioral science interventions for organization improvement.* Englewood Cliffs, NJ: Prentice Hall.

Fuller, C., Griffin, T., and Ludema, J. D. 2000. Appreciative future search: Involving the whole system in positive organization change. *Organization Development Journal* 18(2):29–41.

Gersick, C. J. G. 1994. Pacing strategic change: The case of a new venture. *Academy of Management Journal* 37(1):9–45.

Ghoshal, S., and Bartlett, C. A. 2000. Rebuilding behavioral context: A blueprint for corporate renewal. In *Breaking the code of change*, ed. M. Beer and N. Nohria, 195–222. Boston: Harvard Business School Press.

Hall, R. H. 1996. *Organizations: Structures, processes, and outcomes.* Englewood Cliffs: NJ: Prentice-Hall.

Hamel, G., and Prahalad, C. K. 1994. *Competing for the future*. Boston: Harvard Business School Press.

Higgins, J. M. 1994. *The management challenge: An introduction to management.* 2nd ed. New York: Macmillan.

Hoffman, A. J. 1999. Institutional evolution and change: Environmentalism and the U.S. chemical industry. *Academy of Management Journal* 42(4):351–71.

Huy, Q. N. 2001. Time, temporal capability, and planned change. *Academy of Management Review* 26(4):601–23.

Kanter, R. M., Stein, B. A., and Jick, T. D. 1992. *The challenge of organizational change: How companies experience it and leaders guide it*. New York: Free Press.

Kotter, J. P. 1996. *Leading change*. Boston: Harvard Business School Press.

Lichtenstein, B. B. 2000. Self-organized transitions: A pattern amid the chaos of transformative change. *Academy of Management Executive* 14(4):128–41.

Luthans, F. R., Hodgetts, M., and Rosenkrantz, S. A. 1988. *Real managers.* Cambridge, MA: Ballinger.

Manning, M. R., and Binzagr, G. F. 1996. Methods, values, and assumptions underlying large group interventions intended to change whole systems. *International Journal of Organizational Analysis* 4(3):268–84.

Marshak, R. J. 1993. Lewin meets Confucius: A re-view of the OD model of change. *Journal of Applied Behavioral Science* 29(4):393–415.

Mintzberg, H. 1975. The manager's job: Folklore and fact. *Harvard Business Review* 53(4):49–61.

Mintzberg, H., and Waters, J. A. 1985. Of strategies deliberate and emergent. *Strategic Management Journal* 6:257–72.

Nader, D. A. 1998. *Champions of change: How CEOs and their companies are mastering the skills of radical change.* San Francisco: Jossey-Bass.

Nicholl, D. 1998. From the editor: Is OD meant to be relevant? Part I. *OD Practitioner* 30(2).

Oliver, C. 1988. The collective strategy framework: An application to competing predictions of isomorphism. *Administrative Science Quarterly* 33(4):543–61.

Palmer, I., and Dunford, R. 2002. Who says change can be managed? Positions, perspectives and problematics. *Strategic Change* 11(5):243–51.

Pendlebury, J., Grouard, B., and Meston, F. 1998. *The ten keys to successful change management.* England: John Wiley & Sons Limited.

Pettigrew, A., and Whipp, R. 1993. Understanding the environment. In *Managing change*, ed. C. Mabey and B. Mayon-White. London: Open University/Chapman.

Pettigrew, A. M., Woodman, R. W., and Cameron, K. S. 2001. Studying organizational change and development: Challenges for future research. *Academy of Management Journal* 44(4):697–713.

Rajagopalan, N., and Spreitzer, G. M. 1997. Toward a theory of strategic change: A multi-lens perspective and integrating framework. *Academy of Management Review* 22(1):48–79.

Semler, R. 2000. How we went digital without a strategy. *Harvard Business Review*, September–October: 51–58.

Smircich, L. and Stubbart, C. 1985. Strategic management in an enacted world. *Academy of Management Review* 10(4):724–36.

Stace, D., and Dunphy, D. 2001. *Beyond the boundaries: Leading and recreating the successful enterprise.* 2nd ed. Sydney: McGraw-Hill.

Taffinder, P. 1998. *Big change: A route-map for corporate transformation.* Chichester: John Wiley & Sons Ltd.

Thietart, R. A., and Forgues, B. 1995. Chaos theory and organizations. *Organization Science* 6(1):19–31.

Turner, D., and Crawford, M. 1998. *Change power: Capabilities that drive corporate renewal.* Warriewood, NSW, Australia: Business & Professional Publishing.

Van de Ven, A. H., and Poole, M. S. 1995. Explaining development and change in organizations. *Academy of Management Review* 20(3):510–40.

Weick, K. E. 2000. Emergent change as a universal in organizations. In *Breaking the code of change*, ed. M. Beer and N. Nohria, 223–41. Boston: Harvard Business School Press.

Notes

1. An earlier and much shorter version of this chapter was published as "Images of managing change" by Palmer and Dunford in *Strategic Change*, 2002. Copyright © 2002 by John Wiley & Sons, Limited. Reproduced with permission of the publisher. We are grateful to the publishers of the journal for allowing us to incorporate and expand this article.
2. Morgan, 1997; Bolman & Deal, 1997, 2003; Hatch, 1997.
3. This idea is taken from Bolman and Deal, 1997:12–13.

4. Fayol, 1949.
5. E.g., see Luthans et al., 1988; Mintzberg, 1975.
6. E.g., see Higgins, 1994:5.
7. Turner & Crawford, 1998:15.
8. See Beer & Nohria, 2000:35–36.
9. Burnes, 1996:170.
10. Chin and Benne, 1976:22.
11. Chin and Benne, 1976:31.
12. Chin and Benne, 1976:23.
13. Chin and Benne, 1976:23–24.
14. Mintzberg & Waters, 1985.
15. Harrison & Shirom, 1999:31.
16. White et al., 1997:1384.
17. Kotter, 1995:67.
18. Kotter, 1995:59.
19. Ghoshal and Bartlett, 2000.
20. Ghoshal and Bartlett, 2000:220.
21. Stace & Dunphy, 2001.
22. Huy, 2001.
23. Pendlebury, Grouard, and Meston, 1998:39.
24. Pendlebury, Grouard, and Meston, 1998:39.
25. Burnes, 1996:187–88.
26. Dawson, 1994.
27. Pettigrew and Whipp, 1993.
28. Burnes, 1996:187.
29. Burnes, 1996:187.
30. Burnes, 1996:187.
31. Burnes, 1996:189–92.
32. Burnes, 1996:189.
33. Collins, 1998:70.
34. Van de Ven & Poole, 1995:512–20.
35. White et al., 1997:1384.
36. Van de Ven & Poole, 1995:512–20.
37. Hall, 1996:192–200.
38. Oliver, 1988:543.
39. DiMaggio & Powell, 1991:67–74.
40. DiMaggio & Powell, 1991:73.
41. Nicoll, 1998b.
42. French and Bell, 1995:4. (Italics in original.)
43. See Fuller, Griffin, and Ludema, 2000; Bunker and Alban, 1992.
44. Axelrod, 1992:507.

45. Barge & Oliver, 2003:138–39.
46. Smircich & Stubbart, 1985:726.
47. Weick, 2000.
48. Weick, 2000:229–32; see also Feldman, 2000.
49. Weick, 2000:235–36.
50. Weick, 2000:234–35.
51. Weick, 2000:236–37.
52. Weick, 2000:232.
53. Weick, 2000:238.
54. Thietart & Forgues, 1995:1.
55. Lichtenstein, 2000:131.
56. Lichtenstein, 2000:131.
57. See Thietart & Forgues, 1995:28.
58. Marshak, 1993.
59. Hamel & Prahalad, 1994.
60. Anderson and Anderson, 2001:9.
61. Pettigrew, Woodman, and Cameron, 2001:701.
62. Kotter, 1996:26.
63. Anderson and Anderson, 2001:9–10.
64. Kanter, Stein, and Jick, 1992:375.

Why Organizations Change

Learning objectives

On completion of this chapter you should be able to:

- Understand environmental pressures propelling organizations towards change.
- Articulate arguments about why not all organizations are affected equally by such pressures.
- Outline a range of issues internal to organizations that push them towards change.
- Gain an awareness of the interaction between forces for stability and forces for change.
- Relate differing images of managing change to pressures for change.

Managers are faced with a paradox. They are told to change their organizations or risk them perishing; at the same time, they are told that their organizations are at risk of perishing because of the disruptive impact of change.[1] Up to 84 percent of U.S. firms are involved in a major organizational change although many are deemed not successful.[2] Ghoshal and Bartlett[3] argue that for "every successful corporate transformation, there is at least one equally prominent failure." They contrast the successes of GE and ABB with the problems experienced by Westinghouse and Hitachi. Other writers estimate that up to 70 percent of large-scale changes fail and that "a conspiracy of silence"[4] accompanies these failures with most companies not being willing to discuss them publicly. Kotter[5] argues that the result has been "carnage . . . with wasted resources and burned-out, scared, or frustrated employees."

All this raises the question of why managers participate in change if it is such a risky activity. This issue has come under scrutiny in recent times.[6] One position is based on an *economic perspective* of organizational change. It is one that is closely aligned to images of organizational change that adopt a "management as control" assumption and assumes that:

- In competitive economies, firm survival depends on satisfying shareholders. Failure to do this will lead them either to move their capital to other companies or to use their influence to replace senior management with those better aligned with their interests. Therefore managers conduct change in order to produce better organizational performance in the form of better quarterly results with correspondingly better company share prices.

An alternative position, more aligned with change management images associated with the "management as shaping" assumption, is the *organizational learning perspective*, which assumes that:

- Organizations and human systems of all sorts are complex and evolving and therefore cannot be reduced to a single, linear objective of maximizing shareholder value. In this view, a better way of understanding the objectives of change management is the need to increase an organization's adaptive capacity, since how an organization might achieve shareholder value, and the knowledge needed for achieving this, is likely to change over time. Therefore, building in the capacity to both respond to, and shape, external changes is an alternative rationale for explaining why managers conduct change.[7]

Regardless of which position may be most appropriate to explaining why a specific organization change occurs, there are clearly a variety of pressures on managers to change. They come from many directions: the environment, the discovery of deviations from standards, new desires and visions of the future, or the fundamental nature of organizations themselves. The result of change is often supposed to be, paradoxically, stability. Managers are called upon to stabilize the unstable and destabilize the rigid; adapt to the present and anticipate the future; improve what is and invent what is to be; lead a renaissance while preserving tradition, the possibilities for which are grounded in the belief that progress is possible and that managers can make a difference. As Table 3.1 points out, how managers experience pressures for change—and which ones they attend to—will be influenced by their image of managing change.

This chapter picks up these issues by exploring why it is that managers change their organizations if it is such a risky activity. We start by considering the potential environmental pressures that managers face to participate in organizational change. Next, we consider why some managers apparently do not respond to such pressures. Finally, we discuss a number of internal organizational pressures that push managers toward changing their organizations. At the outset it should be noted that there are many pressures for change and that while the ones that we will discuss are particularly important, they by no means exhaust all possible pressures.

ENVIRONMENTAL PRESSURES FOR CHANGE

Environmental pressures are one focus for explaining change. These often occur where an organization's resource base decreases as a result of reduced demand for products and sales, decrease in market share, and bad investment decisions. In extreme circumstances, organizational change is designed to turn around negative cash flow and avoid bankruptcy and "organizational death."[8] In the following section, we focus on six types of environmental pressures for change that managers face: pressures to carry out fashionable management changes; pressures that are forced or mandated on the organization

TABLE 3.1 Images of Pressures for Change

Image of Managing Change	Pressures for Change
Director	Change occurs as a result of strategic pressures, driving the organization to new situations, entering new markets, or correcting an internal problem to create more efficient operations. Such pressures for change may exist, but they are seen as controllable with managers able to direct how the organization can respond to the pressures.
Navigator	Pressures for change seen as strategic and as a necessary response to internal and external pressures. There will always be some question about how well the organization will be able to respond to such pressures given the often-conflicting, multiple pressures facing managers and given the variety of influences and competing interests that need to be taken into account in responding to such pressures.
Caretaker	Most pressures to change come from a variety of inexorable influences upon the organization over which managers have little real control. Internal pressures may be due to organizational growth or external pressures due to new regulations or market conditions: in both cases, pressures are experienced as unable to be resisted by individual managers as they are overwhelmed by their enormity. Like caretakers, change managers in this image help to look after the organization as it is buffeted by such pressures for change—but they have little choice in the necessary actions that need to be taken by the organization in responding to the change pressures.
Coach	Pressures for change are constant and emerge from the need to better integrate the organization, especially in the form of better teamwork, common values, and mindsets to produce the collaboration and cooperation that are needed to better achieve better organizational outcomes. Pressures for change are more likely to be continual and developmental, shaping all parts of the organization's capabilities to enable better organizational outcomes.
Interpreter	Pressures for change emerge from internal and external forces; the key demand on managers is from staff to help provide them with meaning and understanding about "what is going on." Staff have a constant need to understand the importance of what it is that they are doing, what needs to happen, and where the organization is going. As new situations emerge, so is there pressure on change managers to make sense of these to staff. Sense-making changes assist in clarity and in turn in helping to align identity and commitment to the organization.
Nurturer	Pressures for change come from a variety of forces, both large and small. Such pressures are not necessarily rational or able to be coordinated beyond enhancing the organization's adaptive capacity in general to respond to the chaotic influences that buffet organizations. In this sense, pressures may appear to be small, but these also may have large consequences in terms of their impact on the organization. The ability of the organization to respond to such pressures will depend on how well it has been shaped in terms of its ongoing adaptive capacity.

from outside agencies; broad changes in geopolitical relationships necessitating changes in organizational operations; pressures associated with declining markets; hypercompetitive business pressures; and the pressure to maintain corporate reputation and credibility with stakeholders.

Fashion Pressures

In 2001 Boeing Co. initiated a series of changes under the direction of its CEO, Philip M. Condit. These changes were said to imitate those made by Jack Welch at GE, a company that is well recognized as having made a number of successful transformational changes over the past two decades. These mimetic changes included:

- Setting up a corporate learning and training unit (at St. Louis).
- Changing the culture.
- Restructuring the business into three key areas (commercial, military, and space).
- Giving CEOs of these units greater freedom in how to run their business.
- But at the same time, setting high performance standards and the need for them to compete for access to corporate funding.[9]

This is an example of what neo-institutional theorists refer to as *mimetic isomorphism.* This occurs when organizations imitate the structures and practices of other organizations in their field or industry, usually ones that they consider as legitimate or successful.

Organizational change can occur in response to the latest management fad or fashion: in order to be seen as professional, modern or progressive managers may change their organizations in line with the latest innovation in management practices. As outlined in Table 3.2, managers have been subjected to a steady stream of management fads and fashions over the years. Such pressures may lead them to adopt fashionable ideas but often with little critical assessment of the need for the change and without having clear information about the performance effects of making the change.[10] As argued by Eric Abrahamson,[11] the problem with management fads is that while the ideas seem to be novel, progressive, and rational, invariably they lack systematic research to legitimate their claims.[12] Although some fads may assist organizations,

TABLE 3.2 Management Fashions

Source: Taken from Carson et al., 2000:1144.

1950s	1960s	1970s	1980s	1990s
Management by objectives (MBO)	Sensitivity training and T-groups	Quality-of-work-life programs	Corporate culture	Employee empowerment
Program evaluation and review technique (PERT)		Quality circles	Total quality management	Horizontal corporations
Employee assistance programs (EAPs)			International Standards Organization 9000 (ISO 9000)	Vision
			Benchmarking	Reengineering
				Agile strategies
				Core competencies

others do not deliver their promise of better organizational performance; still others may have "devastating . . . effects on large numbers of organizations and their employees."[13] Some writers suggest that this is one way of understanding why large numbers of organizations have downsized—given that the performance effects of downsizing are, at best, unclear (see Chapter 4 for more on this issue).[14] Engaging in what is regarded as a progressive management innovation, like downsizing, does not need to be justified; it is accepted as professional and natural.

Nevertheless, it is unlikely that managers will succumb continually to pressures to conduct fashionable changes that do not have positive performance outcomes—other factors intervene such as market forces. This is clear from Heather Haveman's[15] study of why California savings and loan associations entered new markets. Her study points out that legitimization (or fad and fashion) processes help explain why companies enter new markets: the presence of successful incumbents legitimates the decisions of other potential entrants to do likewise. However, this only occurs up to the point where the competitive effects of the market take hold and entry becomes less attractive. At this point, the competitive effect dominates the legitimization effect, "making entry less attractive to other organizations."[16] On this basis, she claims that "The pull of imitation . . . is balanced by the brake of crowded markets."[17]

Mandated Pressures

In 1996 ChevronTexaco, then Texaco, settled a racial discrimination lawsuit against it for some $176 million. Filed by some of the company's African-American staff, it was alleged that the company was involved in acts of racism by the company's managers and employees. Racism was institutionalized in the company's culture and practices to such an extent that it "caused Texaco to be branded the worst of corporate rogues."[18] The ChevronTexaco settlement followed other companies such as Shoney's, which in 1992 paid nearly $133 million to settle a discrimination suit on behalf of 20,000 people, and Denny's, which in 1994 paid $54 million to settle two cases in which customers claimed the restaurant had not served or seated them.[19] In 2000 Coca-Cola also settled a case against it for $192 million.[20]

In the case of ChevronTexaco and Coca-Cola, part of the settlement agreement included organizational changes involving the establishment of external diversity task forces charged with monitoring the company's practices and ensuring fair treatment for minority staff.[21] Effectively, both companies were under court order to improve their record on diversity management.[22] This led to major company changes in policies and cultural practices. For example, in ChevronTexaco staff now attend diversity training, managers are provided with communication courses, minorities are targeted for new hires, and key executive appointments have been made to symbolize the shift in the culture. A range of new change programs were planned and implemented aimed at ridding racism from hiring, retention, and promotion decisions.[23] In September 2002, the fifth report of the *Equity and Fairness Task Force* outlined the changes made by the company since the 1996 settlement; while not every problem had been solved, the company's culture clearly had been changed.[24]

The same issues apply in the area of complying with mandates relating to the physical environment. As Dunphy et al. identify, compliance with environmental requirements is a "driver of change."[25] They note that "corporations which do not address social and environmental requirements face fines, workers' compensation cases, criminal convictions and payment of clean-up costs."[26] By way of example, they note that the total corporate liability in the United States for asbestos-related diseases has been estimated at $30 billion, which is "far more than the product ever earned its manufacturers."[27]

As with these examples, sometimes change is forced onto an organization through formally mandated requirements. This is referred to by neo-institutional theorists as *coercive isomorphism*, where organizations are forced to take on activities similar to those of other organizations because of outside demands placed on them to do so.[28] As outlined by DiMaggio and Powell,[29] these mandated pressures may be either formal or informal:

- *Formal coercive pressures* include government mandates, such as new laws and policies. In this instance, organizations are forced to change to meet new legal or other legislative requirements such as those having to do with pollution requirements, tax laws, or affirmative action programs. Alternatively, subsidiary organizations may be forced to adopt accounting standards, performance criteria, and other practices to suit the parent organization.
- *Informal coercive pressures* include commitment to certain types of organizational changes, such as empowerment, in order to get the support of other organizations also committed to such programs.

Geopolitical Pressures

These may be in the form of immediate crises or longer-term geographic realignments. September 11, 2001, and SARS are two global crises that have had immediate impacts on a range of businesses, in particular airlines and businesses closely connected to them. Often leading to a drop in sales and related activities, one common response of many companies has been cost control through layoffs. For example, Rockwell Collins, an avionics device company that sells radios and electrical equipment for airplanes, had a cutback in sales after September 11, 2001, from its customers, such as Boeing and Airbus. By the spring of 2002, it had reduced its workforce by 2,800 as one way of reducing costs associated with the reduced sales.[30] More immediate geopolitical crises leading to organizational change can be seen in Exxon's withdrawal in March 2001 from its Arun gas production facility in Indonesia. Faced with escalating violence against the company from separatist Aceh rebel soldiers, the company suspended production and evacuated its staff.[31] Similarly, Nike has been on the receiving end of negative publicity as a result of accusations about their management practices in developing countries.[32]

Longer-term geopolitical realignments in the 1990s forced 3M to initiate a series of organizational changes. 3M is a highly diversified company that operates throughout the world and has had subsidiaries in Europe for over 40 years. In 1989 the Berlin Wall collapsed and the following year saw the reunification of Germany. Concurrent with this was the market integration of many European countries, symbolized by the signing of the Treaty of European Union in Maastricht in 1991 and the establishment of a European Economic Area Treaty.[33] These moves opened up the borders of many European countries to freer trade and had the effect of integrating much of the European market. In this changing market environment, 3M found its old structure, mainly organized as independent, country-based operations, as being no longer suitable to the new context.[34] Many of its traditional European customers started working across Europe, which meant that the country-based 3M units had difficulty meeting their needs. For example, where a purchase order involved distribution to a variety of countries, this was difficult for 3M as each subsidiary had its own ordering system and cross-country ordering therefore needed to be done manually.[35] As Bill Monahan, the then product manager for Data Services in Europe, said:

> The business units were screaming that they could not respond to the marketplace the way they had to. Towards the end of the 1980s, you had the development of multinational buyers, companies like HP or Olivetti, who wanted to be treated the same in each country. Large distributors were popping up in Europe that were doing business in many countries and the pan-European distribution had really started to mature. Buyers would say to us, "Well, my price is 10 dollars in France, but in Italy, it is 15 dollars. Wait a minute, what is the deal?"[36]

As a result of such pressures, 3M reorganized its country-specific structure, creating regional organizations across Europe with responsibility for profit and loss across European product lines.[37]

In many ways, the 3M example illustrates what Kotter[38] identifies as four global environmental forces for change:

- *Technological*, which requires more globally connected people and faster communication and transportation.
- *Greater economic integration* of currencies and international capital flows.
- *Maturation and slowdown* of domestic markets, leading to greater emphasis on exports and deregulation.
- *Fall of socialist countries* and their reorientation toward capitalist economies. While the latter has led to new opportunities such as larger markets and fewer barriers to entry, it also has been associated with more competition and a demand for increased speed.

Kotter argues that all companies are affected by these forces for change.[39]

Market Decline Pressures

Declining markets for products and services place organizations under pressure to remain relevant. This situation has been recognized in relation to AOL Time Warner, where the introduction of broadband into U.S. households serves as a potential threat to AOL's continued growth. In the fourth quarter of 2002, subscriptions to AOL declined for the first time as broadband services grew by 59 percent. Wasserman[40] argues that broadband and its growth in penetration into American households represents a real threat to the continuing relevance of America Online: users paying around $50 per month to receive broadband are unlikely to continue to want to pay $15 per month to AOL for what becomes a redundant service. This situation points to the need for strategic changes by AOL, including partnering with cable companies and other options that move it away from over-reliance on dial-up services.[41]

In December 2002, telephone company Verizon Communications laid off 2,700 front-line repair and installation workers in New York and New Jersey. The company claimed that the layoffs were the result of an economic downturn in the telecommunications industry, including loss of sales and customers due to the changing nature of the industry. These changes included customers using communication technologies other than services based on traditional wire lines, such as mobile phones and cable services.[42] More generally, Verizon has been successful in producing strategic change during the 1990s, brought on as a result of the changing nature of the industry. Touted as a "doddering dinosaur," it faced competition from Internet carriers and other more nimble startup companies. However, the company has made strategic changes reflecting this changed environment, now controlling the largest mobile phone company, Verizon Wireless, as well as entering the long-distance telephone market to become the third-largest provider.[43]

Hypercompetition Pressures

In 1998 Gateway, the personal computer company, faced a fiercely competitive business and was becoming overshadowed by Dell, its direct-sales rival. Gateway founder and CEO Ted Waitt took the company through a major organizational change, hiring 10 new top managers and changing the way the company went about doing business, including its name, products, alliances, and business strategy.[44] Such changes reflect the new, some argue hypercompetitive,[45] business environments that confront many organizations. Labels such as "discontinuous,"[46] "postbureaucratic,"[47] and "chaotic"[48] have been applied to describe the current environment, which some writers associate with a "postmodern organizational paradigm."[49] Aligned with the rise of e-commerce and the use of the Internet, organizations are confronted with global changes in consumer preferences, industry boundaries, social values, and demographics.[50] Organizations are forced to deliver goods and services more quickly, more customized, and more flexibly.

Such pressures have required a variety of organizational changes, as in the case of Delphi Automotive Systems Corporations, now known as the Delphi Corporation. The Delphi plant in Oak Creek, Wisconsin, is an automotive supplier of catalytic converters. Its history dates back some 100 years, although it was spun off as a former division of General Motors in 1999. A number of dramatic changes were made to the plant in the subsequent two years, moving it from an old style assembly line to one based on small cells of workers. Each cell (of around four people) is organized in the form of a U or a circle and plastic conveyor systems that can be dismantled quickly and reformed to meet new orders are used to provide them with the necessary parts. The workers in each cell are involved in decision making with responsibility for work scheduling, quality, and productivity. The modular and portable nature of the work stations enables greater flexibility, speed, and customization in manufacturing converters. This was necessary to meet the demands of automakers who wanted converters customized to meet their specific needs—and who also were streamlining their suppliers in favor of a few, rather than many, vendors. These two business-environment pressures meant that the former delivery time of 21 days was no longer adequate—and neither was the inflexible assembly line, which was unable to deliver product variety. The end result of the changes is a system that can now deliver customized orders in five days and has increased productivity by 25 percent.[51]

Reputation and Credibility Pressures

For much of the 1990s, Walt Disney Company was cited by *BusinessWeek* as having one of the worst corporate boards in the United States. Issues included:

- Close ties between the CEO and the directors.
- Lack of management experience.
- Minimal oversight of the company.[52]

However, it was not until the corporate crises that confronted Enron, Tyco, and Worldcom that Walt Disney, like other companies, entered into a range of changes to rectify board structures and practices. For example, at Walt Disney now:

- Only independent directors are allowed on audit and compensation committees.
- Limits have been placed on the number of other boards of which directors can be members.
- Directors have to own a minimum of $100,000 in stock of the company.
- Board meetings are held separate to management.
- Ties between the company and directors have been severed.
- Consulting firms are not being used for financial auditing purposes.[53]

Similarly, at Citigroup, changes in management and business practices during 2002 occurred in a context in which Congress held hearings on its relationships with Enron, and federal and state investigations were being held into potential conflicts of interest at Salomon Smith Barney, its investment bank.[54]

As with these examples, change is associated with maintaining proper corporate governance mechanisms to ensure a positive corporate reputation. Corporate reputation, defined as "a collective representation of a firm's past actions and results that describes the firm's ability to deliver valued outcomes to multiple stakeholders,"[55] is an intangible[56] but important corporate asset, being positively correlated with organizational performance.[57] Maintaining and enhancing corporate reputation is therefore an important part of managing firm survival,[58] although, as in Walt Disney's case, the pressure to change to assist organizational reputation may vary from company to company; some may not respond as quickly as others.

Sometimes strategic changes are made to signal that an organization is taking steps to "put its house in order." One common change, meant to signal "a new era," is the symbolic exiting of a high-profile organizational person such as the CEO. For example, 2002 saw the departures of Gerald Levin, CEO of AOL Time Warner; Jean-Marie Messier, CEO of Vivendi Universal; and Thomas Middelhoff, CEO of Bertelsmann. As argued by Gunther and Wheat: "These executives, as it happened, had all bet too heavily on the Internet; their companies performed poorly, and they were held accountable. That's the way shareholder capitalism is supposed to work."[59] Such signaling changes seek to influence and change positively shareholders' sense-making processes[60] about the organization.

WHY ORGANIZATIONS MAY NOT CHANGE IN THE FACE OF EXTERNAL ENVIRONMENTAL PRESSURES

All organizations are not the same and not all managers respond to external pressures for change in the same way: Some resist them; some are slow to respond; some may simply not recognize them as a real threat in the same way that other managers do. In explaining why external pressures do not always lead directly to organizational change, we outline three debates about this issue: the organizational learning perspective compared to the threat-rigidity perspective, objective versus cognitive constructions of the environment, and the balance between forces for change and forces for stability. Each of these debates sheds light on this issue of why managers respond differently to external pressures for organizational change.

Organizational Learning versus Threat-Rigidity

Not all organizations adopt adaptive changes when faced with pressures from outside. As we saw above, Walt Disney did not move for some time to rectify images of poor corporate governance during the 1990s until other corporate scandals acted as triggers. Similarly, it took some time for Nike to respond in a positive way to public reports criticizing it for having its products manufactured offshore in poor, exploitative working conditions.[61] More generally, there is disagreement on whether environmental pressures facilitate or inhibit adaptation and innovative organizational change. Organizational learning theorists argue that environmental pressures such as market decline will lead to innovative organizational adaptation and change as managers learn from the problems and try to close the gap between performance and aspirations. However, threat-rigidity theorists argue that such pressures will inhibit innovative change as managers' cognitive and decision-making processes become restricted when confronted with threatening problems.[62]

Being trapped by success is another, related reason why organizations may fail to respond to pressures for change. Sull[63] argues that companies that have a winning business formula may become trapped by this when conditions change. Companies may become arrogant and assume that their market dominance will continue unchallenged into the future. This view is fueled by their cognitive frames, which become blinkered by success; by routines that become embedded in the organization as correct ways of operating; by relationships to stakeholders that act as shackles and inhibit them from exploring new business ventures, and by shared beliefs that become company dogmas that they are proceeding in the right direction. Such forces lead to organizations and their managers becoming "learning disabled" so that they do not respond appropriately to pressures for change. Some commentators, for example, argue that Nestlé was slow to respond to the impact of the Internet on its business because of the long-term market success of its brands, which had led to a risk-averse culture and an ingrained bureaucratic structure (see Chapter 4 for more on Nestlé).[64]

Environment as Objective Entity versus Environment as Cognitive Construction

The notion of the environment as an objective entity *per se* that pressures organizations to change has been brought into question. As Smircich and Stubbart[65] argue, some writers treat the environment as an objective, given entity but focus on whether managers' perceptions of it are accurate. However, misperceptions may occur. According to Boyd et al.:[66]

- A *Type 1 error* occurs when the environment is (objectively) stable, but managers perceive it as turbulent and take (unnecessary) actions accordingly.
- A *Type 2 error* occurs when managers threaten the survival of their firms by failing to take actions as they perceive their environment as stable when it is (objectively) turbulent.[67]

Smircich & Stubbart[68] identify a third view of the environment as not having an objective existence outside of individual views and perceptions of it. This *constructivist view*—that the outside world is brought into existence through individuals' perceptions of it—further questions the very status of the terms used in discussion about why organizations change—or don't take actions to change. Managers in different organizations (and sometimes in the same organization) see what is going on outside their organizations in very different ways and with different interpretations about change actions that are needed.

Bognor & Barr[69] take this position further by proposing that managers' sense-making activities contribute to the perpetuation of hypercompetitive environments. They suggest that the cognitive frameworks of managers influence how they make sense of events that occur around them, what they notice, how they interpret what they notice, and the resultant actions tied to these interpretations. Shared beliefs emerge over time within an industry that become taken for granted.[70] In hypercompetitive environments, they argue:

> a common cognitive framework emerges that suggests to managers that success is based on a series of rapid and anticipatory actions that move industry to the next round of competition. Institutional forces pressure firms to adopt the behaviors of those that are more successful, and process-dominated recipes emerge as the new industry recipe when it becomes apparent that the better-performing firms are those that utilize the adaptive sense-making processes.[71]

Their position is that hypercompetitive environments and the organizational changes associated with them are perpetuated by the cognitive interpretations of managers. In this sense, managers are trapped by their cognitive sense-making frames.

Forces for Change versus Forces for Stability

Mone et al.[72] claim that whether environmental pressures will lead to innovative change will be affected by three factors:

- The extent to which an organization's mission is institutionalized in stakeholders and the external environment: the less institutionalized it is, the more flexibility the organization will have to respond to innovative change.
- The extent of diffusion of power and resources throughout the organization: the more concentrated the power in the organization, the greater the ability to make decisions and allocate resources to achieve change.
- The rationale managers employ to explain decline: the more controllable or stable the causes, the more likely managers are to introduce innovative changes since the causes of decline are perceived to be permanent.[73]

What these arguments alert us to is the need to consider both *forces for stability* and *forces for change* and the interaction between these two. For example, it is argued that discussion of the hypercompetitive environment as a straightforward driver of organizational change has neglected the concurrent forces for stability.[74] This implies that greater recognition needs to be given to change and stability as simultaneous forces: "both are a necessary part of organizations' effective functioning in the long-term."[75] Table 3.3 outlines such forces.

TABLE 3.3 Forces for Change and Stability

Source: Derived from Leana & Barry, 2000.

Forces for Change	Forces for Stability
• *Adaptability* (of organizations to their environment) • *Cost containment* (especially making human resources a variable rather than fixed cost) • *Impatient capital markets* (demanding more immediate investment returns) • *Control* (less hierarchy but greater control and power through managerially imposed performance targets) • *Competitive advantage* (by being responsive to changing market conditions)	• *Institutionalism* (of current practices due to solidity of past practices and power structures) • *Transaction costs* (for example, stability in employment enables firms to invest rationally in employee development) • *Sustained advantage* (gained through stable organizational relationships not easily imitated or substituted) • *Organizational social capital* (the establishment of trust among co-workers becomes an organizational asset) • *Predictability and uncertainty reduction* (the need for these may inhibit change)

EXERCISE 3.1

Senior Management Team Role Play: Images of Pressures for Change

1. Form into groups of three.
2. Identify an organizational change that you are aware of, either through an organization in which you are working or an organization that you have read about recently. Alternatively, make up an organizational change.
3. Now, go to Table 3.1. Each person is to choose one of the images of managing change and adopt this role in the following activity.
4. You are now in a senior management board meeting. The agenda item you are dealing with is a question that has been referred to you from your chairman of the board. She has requested to know why the organization is going through the change that you have identified.
5. Debate how you will respond to this request, based upon the change management image that you have adopted.
6. At the conclusion of your team meeting, consider the following issues:
   (a) Did one image better explain the rationale for change? Why?
   (b) On reflection, what criteria did you use for making this judgment?
   (c) Is there an image with which you have the greatest affinity? Why? What would it take to change this?

ORGANIZATIONAL PRESSURES FOR CHANGE

In this section, we discuss five potential forces for change that are internal to organizations: pressures related to organizational growth, pressures related to the need for integration and collaboration, pressures around establishing or reestablishing organizational identities in new eras, "new broom" pressures associated with the appointment of new CEOs, and a variety of power and political pressures.

Growth Pressures

As companies age, change in the form of growth is brought about. In 1992 Kevin Sharer joined Amgen Inc., now the world's largest biotech company, as its president and chief operating officer. His aim was to turn it into a major pharmaceutical company. To enable business growth to occur, Amgen had to move beyond its startup days in which decisions were made based on hallway conversations. There was a lack of consideration of the market by its scientists, and salespeople were only loosely accountable for sales. When Sharer became CEO, he made organizational changes, including individual- (rather than regional-) based performance for sales representatives, monitoring the number of sales calls they made each week and the use of handheld computers to record details of their sales conversations so that their managers could identify poor sales tactics and take steps to change them.[76]

The same issues were present when Robert J. Herbold joined Microsoft from Procter & Gamble. He was astounded at the lack of discipline in Microsoft in terms of how decisions were made and how priorities were established. The hallmark corridor decision making of entrepreneurial companies was no longer up to the task of managing an organization as complex as Microsoft. Herbold set about establishing formalized decision-making processes and other protocols that sought to balance entrepreneurial creativity with the need for discipline in Microsoft given its size and scale of operations.[77] The organizational changes in both Amgen and Microsoft entail the routinization of work practices. These changes are often the outcome of company growth and they are implemented to handle the complexity of their business operations and to bring rigor to running them.

Of course, not all organizations continue to grow. One study of small business owners in Britain found that many of these managers actively resisted the growth of their businesses beyond the point at which they lost personal control of day-to-day operations. Beyond this point, they lost job satisfaction, which, at least for some, was why they had moved from large organizations in the first place and established their own company.[78] Other writers have pointed out that growth is not necessarily a linear, sequential movement from one stage to the next. As we saw in the previous chapter, chaos theory highlights that change may be nonlinear and fundamental rather than incremental and may not entail growth.[79] In addition younger, newer organizations may fail to grow because of the inexperience of their managers and through lack of organizational slack or resources to absorb bad business decisions.

Integration and Collaboration Pressures

Some changes are made in order to better integrate the organization or create economies of scale across different business units. In 1998 SunAmerica, a financial network of brokers, was acquired by the giant insurance company American International Group

(AIG). The resultant broker-dealer network consisted of six businesses: Advantage Capital, FSC Securities, Royal Alliance, Sentra Securities, Spelman, and SunAmerica Securities. Signaling greater integration of these businesses, the name was changed from the SunAmerica Financial Network to the AIG Advisory Group. At the same time, changes entailing consolidation across the different businesses included centralization in New York, San Diego, and Phoenix of recruitment, legal compliance, and advisory services. Other changes included the creation of uniform standards across the businesses, better profiling of the AIG brand, and leveraging buying power across the network.[80]

When Dick Brown became CEO of EDS in January 1999, he became head of a company that had pioneered IT services—but that was having its market share eaten away by faster, newer IT companies. Inside EDS Brown saw that coordination and information sharing were in need of attention. Early on he found that he could not even send an e-mail to all 140,000 people who worked at the company as there were 16 separate e-mail systems. The company had 48 different business units, which entailed duplication and often did not communicate well or have a consistent customer orientation. This meant that some parts of the organization were involved in activities that other parts had tried and rejected—but this information and learning was not transmitted throughout the organization. In relation to customers, this also meant that there was a lack of coordination across EDS's business units in collaborating to solve problems with clients. For example, EDS was in danger of losing Continental, a major client, for whom it handled reservation and accounting and payroll systems. Unfortunately these systems kept crashing and projects were delivered late and with poor-quality results. Brown commenced a series of cultural and structural changes within the company designed to produce better coordination across EDS and to provide a more overt customer orientation throughout the organization. The impetus for these changes was better coordination and collaboration across the multiple business units of the company in order to produce a customer-oriented culture.[81]

Identity Pressures

In January 1998, when Antoine Cau became CEO of the Forte Hotel, consisting of London Hotel, UK Hotels, and International Hotels, he found that they were often in market competition with each other and that hotel employees lacked cultural identity with Forte and its market name brand. In addition, their research found that service excellence was a key ingredient to achieving customer satisfaction and that this was linked to employee satisfaction. In order to address these issues, Cau created four distinct market segments—Le Meridien, Posthouse, Heritage, and Travelodge—and developed a major cultural change program across the various hotel groups. His aim was to enhance the identity and commitment of staff to the Forte brand as well as to achieve service excellence. Organizational changes to assist in achieving these ends included promoting people development and employee recognition schemes in order to enhance job satisfaction for hotel operators.[82]

Philip N. Diehl became head of the U.S. Mint in 1994. At that time, it was seen as slow, inefficient, and lacking in the performance standards operating in the business world. Its main goal was to produce coins—although it had no idea of the magnitude of its coin inventory. It also manufactured collectible and commemorative coins. However, the timing of the latter was often dictated to the Mint by Congress, sometimes five or six times a year. This meant that commemorative coins were no longer rare and so were of decreasing interest to coin collectors. The Mint faced what Muoio[83] describes as an identity crisis: Was it a passive organization manufacturing coins, including commemorative coins, simply following the dictates of the Federal Reserve and Congress? Or should it act more like a market-based organization, launching its own products and promotional campaigns? Establishing a new identity for the Mint through organizational changes such as making commemorative coins more collectable (by issuing fewer of them), using online marketing, portraying its role as a purveyor of history, and marketing innovations such as the 50 State Quarters Program helped move it toward a new, more modern, customer-focused identity.[84]

New Broom Pressures

The new broom phenomenon, when a new CEO (or manager) arrives, can act as a signal that the old ways are about to change. In April 2001, Kenneth D. Lewis took over as CEO of Bank of America. He then instituted what has since been called "a quiet revolution," moving the business away "from empire-building to value creation."[85] As opposed to following the growth strategy of his predecessor, he sought to grow profits by downscaling the bank's operations, getting rid of underperforming businesses such as auto leasing, and divesting unprofitable customer segments.[86] He also brought in new managers to infuse the organization with new ideas and sought to improve customer service through enhanced training programs for tellers, moving away from organizing around product lines in favor of customers and encouraging cross-selling of products by tying executive salaries to performance targets.[87]

Kate Betts took over as editor-in-chief at *Harper's Bazaar* in the summer of 1999. She was charged with changing the 130-year-old company, which had stagnated in terms of growth compared to other magazines such as *Vogue* and *Elle* and which was seen as stodgy and tedious—descriptions not best associated with fashion magazines. In "new broom" form in her first six months, she set out to change the magazine's logos, typeface, and staff in order to create a new mindset and better profile the magazine. This included replacing over half of the senior staff at *Bazaar* with her own "dream team" in order to regain market share related to more youthful readers.[88]

In September 1992, Arthur Martinez became head of the merchandising group at Sears. He joined at a time when Sears produced one of its worst sales records with a net loss in 1992 of $3.9 billion, the majority of which came from the merchandising group. In "new broom" tradition, in his first 100 days, Martinez started a turnaround plan for Sears, in part by reorienting its marketing away from being a "man's store" to appeal to women as well. At the same time as moving into cosmetics and other specialty store products, he set about closing down 113 stores, eliminated the 100-year-old Sears catalog, reengineered store operations, and—through training, incentives, and new staffing procedures—set about reorienting the company toward a service culture to include both men and women as customers.[89]

In Rosabeth Moss Kanter's analysis of recent organizational turnarounds at Gillette, the BBC, and Ivensys, she points out that each of these was led by a new CEO. She therefore asks the question: "Does this mean that only a new broom can sweep clean?"[90] She says that this is probably the case. New CEOs have advantages over their predecessors in a number of ways:

- They are likely to be able to create energy for change within the organization.
- They are unhampered by adherence to past organizational practices.
- They can focus on problems that may have been known but not able to be named in the past as they were organizational "sacred cows" that could not be brought into question.
- They are likely to be able to tackle customer problems with credibility since they are not associated with previous problems that may have been part of the relationship the company had with its clients.[91]

Power and Political Pressures

These can come in a variety of forms. Some are well documented and relate to internal political pressures associated with changes at board and CEO levels. The tussle between Philip Purcell and John Mack for the CEO position at Morgan Stanley after the company had been bought by Dean Witter & Discover Financial Services Inc. in 1997 is one example (Purcell became CEO).[92] As noted above, another was the ousting of Jean-Marie Messier, CEO of Vivendi, in mid-2002. *The Economist* claims that it was the Bronfman family, a major shareholder in the company, which had lost nearly €2 billion in share performance by the company over the previous year, that was behind the push to get rid of Messier. Removing Messier was also aligned with the interests of the French political right, who were concerned about ownership issues related to television and telephone companies.[93]

Some changes are made to alter traditional internal power relationships in order to speed up decision making and to allow others access to engaging in it. As outlined in Chapter 1, one example of this was at IBM when Sam Palmisano took over as CEO from Lou Gerstner. In January 2003, he abolished the 92-year-old, 12-person executive management team. Described as the "inner bastion of power and privilege" at IBM, this committee was the "inner sanctum" that made decisions concerning IBM's strategy and direction.[94] In disbanding the committee, Palmisano sent a message throughout IBM that power relationships were being restructured to avoid decisions being slowed down by waiting for the monthly meetings of this committee.[95]

Other power pressures leading to change relate to internal conflicts. For example, at Roche, the huge pharmaceutical company, a range of organizational changes has been put in place, including teamwork, in order to assist in the fast-developing field of genomics.[96] In 1999 Lee Babiss, head of preclinical research at Roche's headquarters at Nutley, noticed that there were an increasing number of corridor conversations between researchers working on genomics and researchers working on other areas such as oncology and cancer research. He sought to harness these interactions by creating interdisciplinary research teams that cut across traditional power and scientific departmental boundaries. For example, the Genomics Oncology (or GO) team brought together a diverse group of researchers united by the aim of using genomic innovations to assist the development of anticancer drugs. However, not all teams at Roche worked well. In earlier times, from the mid-1990s onwards, teams of research scientists were set up competitively, jostling with each other for access to scarce resources. Over time, these interactions took on the form of internal warfare, leading to the hoarding of technical expertise and knowledge within teams. It also led to a reluctance to abandon team projects, especially where the careers of research scientists had become caught up in their success. In 1998 this competitive approach was abandoned in favor of a collaborative approach that recognized the importance of establishing team structures that shared knowledge and information.

EXERCISE 3.2
Public Change Rationales

1. Choose up to three articles from the business section of a newspaper or from a business magazine about organizations going through change.
2. For each article, what is the rationale presented for the change? Which of the external and internal pressures considered in this chapter are referred to? Are there additional pressures not specifically considered in this chapter?
3. Now, compare and contrast the rationales in each article. Are there commonalities that emerge? Are some presented as more legitimate than others? In your opinion, why might this be the case?
4. To what extent are single versus multiple rationales utilized? What conclusions do you draw from this?

Conclusion

In this chapter, we have outlined a variety of pressures on organizations to change, both internal and external. Table 3.1 outlined how images of managing change impact what we perceive to be the pressures to engage in organizational change. Exercise 3.1 provided a forum for further exploring the impact of these images. We also have discussed debates related to why organizations and their managers do not always respond in the same way to external pressures. In concluding, we should point out that there are other destabilizing forces for change, including incoherence in organizational operations; experimentation;[97] pressures on organizations to behave like good corporate citizens, especially in relation to the natural environment;[98] and the existence of organizational tensions and paradoxes. The latter include managing for both the short and the long term, focusing on both product and process, being both a specialist and a generalist, leading and following, and managing both conflict and consensus.[99]

The issues outlined in this chapter suggest that more successful change managers are likely to be those who have a clear, personal understanding about the pressures on them to change their organizations and a well-developed rationale for what they are attempting to achieve and the likely effect of their actions.

TABLE 3.4 Chapter Reflections for the Practicing Change Manager

- As a change manager, to what extent can you identify environmental pressures propelling your organization toward change?
- To what extent do you have influence over whether and how to change?
- Do you relate better to one (or more) of the change management images outlined in Table 3.1 in relation to changes in which you are engaged as a change manager? Why?
- Which of the possible reasons for avoiding change presented in this chapter have you experienced or seen? On reflection, how might you have contributed to overcoming these? With what likely success?
- How easy is it to raise issues in your organization about the rationale for engaging in specific changes? Is there a dominant rationale? Why?
- What personal criteria might you adopt to ensure that you are initiating a specific change "for the right reasons"? Set out some questions that might help to guide you in the future to ensure that your rationale for change is clear.

Supplemental Reading

Abrahamson, E. 1996. Management fashion. *Academy of Management Review* 21(1):254–85.

Beer, M., and Nohria, N. 2000. Purpose of change: Economic value or organizational capability? In *Breaking the code of change*, ed. M. Beer and N. Nohria, 35–36. Boston: Harvard Business School Press.

Carson, P. P., Lanier, P. A., Carson, K. D., and Guidry, B. N. 2000. Clearing a pass through the management fashion jungle: Some preliminary trailblazing. *Academy of Management Journal* 43(6):1143–58.

DiMaggio, P. J., and Powell, W. W. 1991. The iron cage revisited: Institutional isomorphism and collective rationality in organizational fields. In *The new institutionalism in organizational analysis*, ed. W. W. Powell and P. J. DiMaggio, 63–82. Chicago: University of Chicago Press.

Dunphy, D., Griffiths, A., and Benn, S. 2003. *Organizational change for corporate sustainability*. New York: Routledge.

Fombrun, C., and Shanley, M. 1990. What's in a name? Reputation building and corporate strategy. *Academy of Management Journal* 33(2):233–58.

Herbold, R. J. 2002. Inside Microsoft: Balancing creativity and discipline. *Harvard Business Review* 80(1):72–79.

Leana, C. R., and Barry, B. 2000. Stability and change as simultaneous experiences in organizational life. *Academy of Management Review* 25(4):753–59.

Sull, D. N. 1999. Why good companies go bad. *Harvard Business Review* 77(4):42–52.

Weick, K. E. 1979. *Social psychology of organizing*. Reading, MA: Addison-Wesley.

Case Study Chipping Away at Intel[100]

Craig R. Barrett sat reflecting on the fact that he was halfway through his tenure as the fourth CEO of Intel—only another three more years to go until his mandatory retirement age would be reached. He had come into an organization that Andrew S. Grove, chairman of Intel, had shaped into a major global technology company. He had replaced Gordon E. More but retained his principle of doubling microprocessor performance every 18 months while at the same time making it progressively cheaper. In this context, what would be Barrett's legacy?

When Barrett came in three years ago, he took some bold moves, taking Intel beyond chip making for PCs into the production of information and communication appliances as well as services related to the Internet. Trouble is, the company was now in the worst shape that it had been for many years. Of course, every technology company had been affected by September 11, 2001, the slowing economy, and the potential threat of war with Iraq. But in Intel's case this had been compounded with problems such as product delays and shortages, recalls, overpricing, and even bugs in its systems. Analysts were predicting that by the end of the year, Intel's share of the PC chip market would be 9 percent worse than when Barrett had taken over three years earlier.

He had ploughed money into new markets—but then had to withdraw from these. For example, Intel withdrew from the production of network servers and routers after copping flak from Dell and Cisco, its biggest customers for its chips, for directly competing with them in these other markets. He also closed down iCat, which was an e-commerce service for small businesses, providing Web broadcasting of shareholder meetings, and cut back on Web-surfing applications except in Spain. In Barrett's mind, most of these withdrawals were a direct result of the downturn in economic conditions generally. There were also weak demand and overcapacity in the semiconductor industry with some researchers expecting a 34 percent fall in global sales of chips. Moreover, long-time rival Advanced Micro Devices had produced its Athlon processor chip, which turned out to be faster than Intel's Pentium III chip. At the same time, people seemed to be more interested in how fast their modem connection was than in the speed of their computer chip. And September 11, 2001, hadn't helped; before this catastrophe Intel's shares, at $26, were down 60 percent compared to their highest over the previous year. After September 11 they fell further—by October they were only $20.

Barrett felt that in this competitive—and segmented—market, Intel needed to be reorganized to make it more nimble. It also needed to be reorganized to avoid duplication and create better coordination. For example, the network operations group and the communications unit sometimes were in competition with each other, selling similar products to the same customers. Barrett engaged in a series of reorganizations during his first three years. In 1999 he created a new wireless unit that combined new acquisitions such as DSP Communications Inc. (a chipset supplier for digital communications) with Intel's flash memory operations. In his second year, Barrett created the Architecture Group, which combined development and manufacturing of core processors. In his third year, he reorganized the Architecture Group and created a new unit consisting of a merger of communications and networking operations. For Barrett, these reorganizations were needed to enable decentralization and delegation of decision making—all designed to make the company better coordinated and more nimble.

But there was so much reorganization over these years, trying to get the structure to work, that some commentators saw it as "shuffling execs like cards in a deck." Following the March 2001 restructuring, with up to 80 percent of the staff in the microprocessing unit being given new jobs, one customer thought that people seemed to be moved around a lot without them really knowing where they were going. A former general manager saw Intel as now "dabbling in everything and overwhelming nothing." Other commentators claimed that another problem was that chip managers were now being put in charge of new markets and products about which they knew very little—a charge denied by Barrett. There were also job cuts, with 5,000 jobs lost through attrition during 2001—and more expected.

At the same time, Barrett wanted to change the culture of Intel, drawing on outside consultants to assist him in the process. He wanted to move the mindset of Intel toward better customer relations and away from a perspective of being the only real competition in the marketplace. Strategically he decided to invest in research and development into new production technologies in order to cut chip-making costs. Reflecting on his time ahead, Barrett hoped that he would be able to increase sales and pull out in front of his competitors through these investments. But the jury was still out at this point: What would be his legacy by the time he retired?

Questions

1. What were the different changes at Intel over the first three years of Barrett's tenure?
2. Of the *environmental pressures for change* discussed in this chapter—fashion, mandates, geopolitical, declining markets, hypercompetition, and corporate reputation—which ones were experienced by Intel?
3. Of the *internal organizational pressures for change* discussed in this chapter that are associated with organizational change—growth, integration and collaboration, reestablishment of organizational identities, new broom, and power and political pressures—which ones were experienced within Intel?
4. Are there other external or internal pressures for change that you can identify?
5. What overall conclusions do you draw about why Barrett made the changes he did? Which issues were dominant? Why?
6. What pressures for change might face Barrett in the future? How do you arrive at this assessment?
7. What advice would you give Barrett for how to cope with these change pressures?

TABLE 3.5 Additional Case Studies

Peta's Kentucky Fried Cruelty, Inc. Campaign Seijts, G., & Sider, M. (2003) *Richard Ivey School of Business.*
The Transformation of BP Ghoshal, S.; Gratton, L.; & Rogan, M. (2002) *London Business School*

Bibliography

Abrahamson, E. 2000. Change without pain. *Harvard Business Review* 78(4):75–79.

Abrahamson, E. 1996. Management fashion. *Academy of Management Review* 21(1):254–85.

Abramson, M. A. 1996. Watch out for change busters. *Government Executive* 28(7) (July):56–58.

Ackenhusen, M., Muzyka, D., and Churchill, N. 1996. Restructuring 3M for an integrated Europe. Part 1: Initiating the change. *European Management Journal* 14(1):21–36.

Anders, G. 2002. Roche's new scientific method. *Fast Company*, no. 54 (January):60–68.

Anonymous. 2002. Maître dethroned. *Economist* 364(8280):58–59.

Ante, S. E. 2003. The New Blue. *BusinessWeek Online*, March 17.

Beer, M., and Nohria, N. 2000. Purpose of change: Economic value or organizational capability? In *Breaking the code of change*, ed. M. Beer and N. Nohria, 35–36. Boston: Harvard Business School Press.

Bogner, W. C., and Barr, P. S. 2000. Making sense in hypercompetitive environments: A cognitive explanation for the persistence of high velocity competition. *Organization Science* 11(2):212–26.

Bower, J. L. 2000. The purpose of change. In *Breaking the code of change*, ed. M. Beer and N. Nohria, 83–95. Boston: Harvard Business School Press.

Boyd, B. K., Dess, G. G., and Rasheed, A. M. A. 1993. Divergence between archival and perceptual measures of the environment: Causes and consequences. *Academy of Management Review* 210(2):204–26.

Breen, B. 2001a. Change is sweet. *Fast Company*, no. 47:168–77.

Breen, B. 2001b. How EDS got its groove back. *Fast Company*, no. 51 (October): 106–16.

Brooker, K. 2000. New blood for an old brand. *Fortune* 141(4) (February 21): 289–90.

Carson, P. P., Lanier, P. A., Carson, K. D., and Guidry, B. N. 2000. Clearing a pass through the management fashion jungle: Some preliminary trailblazing. *Academy of Management Journal* 43(6):1143–58.

Clegg, S. R. 1994. New organizational forms. In *Managing strategic action: Mobilizing change, concepts, readings and cases*, ed. C. Hardy, 109–23. London: Sage.

Cooper, E., and Kulkowski, L. 2002. AIG changes name of broker group; Consolidation next? *On Wall Street* 12(10):15–18.

D'Aveni, R. 1994. *Hypercompetition: Managing the dynamics of strategic maneuvering.* New York: Free Press.

Deephouse, D. L. 1997. The effect of financial and media reputations on performance. *Corporate Reputation Review* 1(1 & 2):68–72.

DiMaggio, P. J., and Powell, W. W. 1991. The iron cage revisited: Institutional isomorphism and collective rationality in organizational fields. In *The new institutionalism in organizational analysis*, ed. W. W. Powell and P. J. DiMaggio, 63–82. Chicago: University of Chicago Press.

Dorsey, D. 2000. Change factory. *Fast Company*, no. 35 (June):210.

Dunphy, D., Griffiths, A., and Benn, S. 2003. *Organizational change for corporate sustainability*. New York: Routledge.

Editorial. 2002. Disney gets the message. *BusinessWeek*, no. 3782 (May 13):132.

Edwards, C., and Sager, I. 2001. Can CEO Craig Barrett reverse the slide? *BusinessWeek*, no. 3753 (October 15):80.

Erstad, M. 2001. Commitment to excellence at the Forte Hotel Group. *International Journal of Contemporary Hospitality Management* 13(7):347–51.

EU Timeline, European Union Center Web site, http://www.eu-center.org/Resources/EU_timeline.html.

Faircloth, A. 1998. Guess who's coming to Denny's. *Fortune* 138(3) (August 3):108–10.

Faust, D. 2002. BofA: Whipping a Behemoth into Shape. *BusinessWeek Online*, January 21.

Fombrun, C., and Shanley, M. 1990. What's in a name? Reputation building and corporate strategy. *Academy of Management Journal* 33(2):233–58.

Fombrun, C., and van Riel, C. 1997. The reputational landscape. *Corporate Reputation Review* 1(1 & 2):5–13.

Ford, J. D., and Ford, L. W. 1994. Logics of identity, contradiction, and attraction in change. *Academy of Management Review* 19(4):756–85.

Ghoshal, S., and Bartlett, C. A. 2000. Rebuilding behavioral context: A blueprint for corporate renewal. In *Breaking the code of change*, ed. M. Beer and N. Nohria, 195–222. Boston: Harvard Business School Press.

Goodstein, L. D., and Butz, H. E. 1998. Customer value: The linchpin of organizational change. *Organizational Dynamics* 27(1) (Summer):21–34.

Gray, E. R., and Balmer, J. M. T. 1998. Managing corporate image and corporate reputation. *Long Range Planning* 31(5):695–702.

Gunther, M., and Wheat, A. 2002. The directors. *Fortune* 146(7) (October 14):130.

Haveman, H. A. 1993. Follow the leader: Mimetic isomorphism and entry into new markets. *Administrative Science Quarterly* 38(4):593–67.

Herbold, R. J. 2002. Inside Microsoft: Balancing creativity and discipline. *Harvard Business Review* 80(1):72–79.

Holmes, S., Matlack, C., Arndt, M., and Zellner, W. 2001. Boeing attempts a U-turn at high speed. *BusinessWeek*, no. 3728 (April 16):126–28.

Howe, P. J. 2003. Verizon able to make changes to remain successful in telecom market. *Boston Globe*, January 12.

Jenner, R. A. 1994. Changing patterns of power, chaotic dynamics and the emergence of a post-modern organizational paradigm. *Journal of Organizational Change Management* 7(3):8–21.

Jensen, M. C. 2000. Value maximization and the corporate objective function. In *Breaking the code of change*, ed. M. Beer and N. Nohria, 37–57. Boston: Harvard Business School Press.

Kanter, R. M. 2003. Leadership and the psychology of turnarounds. *Harvard Business Review* 81(6):58–67.

Kilgannon, C. 2002. Citing an economic slump, Verizon lays off 2,700 workers. *New York Times* 152(52338) (December 20):B10.

Kirkpatrick, D. 1999. New home. New CEO. Gateway is moo and improved. *Fortune* 140(12) (December 20):44–46.

Kotter, J. P. 1996. *Leading change*. Boston: Harvard Business School Press.

Kraatz, M. S. 1998. Learning by association? Interorganizational networks and adaptation to environmental change. *Academy of Management Journal* 41(6):621–43.

Kulikowski, L. 2002. AIG advisor rises as Sun sets. *Financial Planning* 32(10):27–28.

Labich, K. 1999. No more at Texaco. *Fortune* 140(5) (September 6):205–12.

Lavelle, L. 2002. The best and worst boards. *BusinessWeek*, no. 3802 (October 7): 104.

Leana, C. R., and Barry, B. 2000. Stability and change as simultaneous experiences in organizational life. *Academy of Management Review* 25(4):753–59.

Lee, L. 2000. Can Nike still do it? *BusinessWeek*, no. 3669 (February 21):120–28.

Lichtenstein, B. B. 2000. Self-organized transitions: A pattern amid the chaos of transformative change. *Academy of Management Executive* 14(4):128–41.

Markus, M. L., and Benjamin, R. I. 1997. The magic bullet theory in IT-enabled transformation. *MIT Sloan Management Review* 38(2):55–68.

McKinley, W., and Scherer, A. G. 2000. Some unanticipated consequences of organizational restructuring. *Academy of Management Review* 25(4):736–52.

McKinley, W., Zhao, J., and Rust, K. G. 2000. A sociocognitive interpretation of organizational downsizing. *Academy of Management Review* 25(1):227–43.

Mone, M. A., McKinley, W., and Barker, V. L. 1998. Organizational decline and innovation: A contingency framework. *Academy of Management Review* 23(1): 115–32.

Muoio, A. 1999. Mint condition. *Fast Company*, no. 30:330.

Nadler, D. A., Shaw, R. B., Walton, A. E., and Associates. 1995. *Discontinuous change: Leading organizational transformation*. San Francisco: Jossey-Bass.

Quinn, J. B. 1992. The intelligent enterprise: A new paradigm. *Academy of Management Executive* 6(4):48–63.

Reger, R. K., Mullane, J. V., Gustafson, L. T., and DeMarie, S. M. 1994. Creating earthquakes to change organizational mindsets. *Academy of Management Executive* 8(4):31–43.

Romano, C. 1995. Managing change, diversity and emotions. *Management Review* 84(7):6–7.

Rucci, A. J., Kirn, S. P., and Quinn, R. T. 1998. The employee-customer-profit chain at Sears. *Harvard Business Review* 76(1):82–97.

Salter, C. 2003. A reformer who means business. *Fast Company*, no. 69 (April):102. http://www.fastcompany.com/magazine/69/reformer.html.

Scase, R., and Goffee, R. 1987. *The real world of the small-business owner*. London: Croom Helm.

Schweizer, T. S., and Wijnberg, N. M. 1999. Transferring reputation to the corporation in different cultures: Individuals, collectives, systems and the strategic management of corporate reputation. *Corporate Reputation Review* 2(3):249–66.

Scott-Morgan, P. 1994. Ringing the changes. *International Management*, September: 59.

Senge, P. M. 2000. The puzzles and paradoxes of how living companies create wealth: Why single-valued objective functions are not quite enough. In *Breaking the code of change*, ed. M. Beer and N. Nohria, 59–81. Boston: Harvard Business School Press.

Siekman, P. 2002. A big maker of tiny batches. *Fortune* 145(11) (May 27):152–56.

Smircich, L., and Stubbart, C. 1985. Strategic management in an enacted world. *Academy of Management Review* 210(4):724–36.

Sull, D. N. 1999. Why good companies go bad. *Harvard Business Review* 77(4):42–52.

Tetenbaum, T. J. 1998. Shifting paradigms: From Newton to chaos. *Organizational Dynamics*, Spring:21–32.

Thietart, R. A., and Forgues, B. 1995. Chaos in the theory and organization. *Organization Science* 6(1) (January–February):19–31.

Thornton, E., and Reed, S. 2001. Morgan Stanley's midlife crisis. *BusinessWeek*, no. 3738 (June 25):90–94.

Timmons, H., Cohn, L., McNamee, M., and Rossant, J. 2002. Citi's sleepless nights. *BusinessWeek*, no. 3794 (August 5):42–43.

Timmons, H., and Holmes, S. 2002. Winds of change. *BusinessWeek*, no. 3814 (December 30):52.

Vergin, R. C., and Qoronfleh, M. W. 1998. Corporate reputation and the stock market. *Business Horizons* 41(1):19–26.

Wasserman, T. 2003. AOL's "first" (if not last) HURRAH. *Brandweek* 44(6) (February 10):20–24.

Weick, K. E. 1979. *Social psychology of organizing.* Reading, MA: Addison-Wesley.

Weintraub, A., and Barrett, A. 2002. Up from biotech. *BusinessWeek*, no. 3774 (March 18):70–74.

Notes

1. Abrahamson, 2000:75; Leana & Barry, 2000:753.
2. Romano, 1995; Reger et al., 1994:31; Markus et al., 1997.
3. Ghoshal & Bartlett, 2000:195.
4. Scott-Morgan, 1994:59.
5. Kotter, 1996:4; Ford & Ford, 1994:756.
6. See Jensen, 2000; Senge, 2000; Bower, 2000.
7. These arguments are summarized from Beer & Nohria, 2000:35–36.
8. Mone, McKinley & Barker, 1998:117.
9. Holmes, Matlack, Arndt & Zellner, 2001.
10. Carson et al., 2000:1143.
11. Abrahamson, 1996.
12. See also Carson et al., 2000:1143–44.
13. Abrahamson, 1996:279–80.
14. See McKinley, Zhao & Rust, 2000.
15. Haveman, 1993.
16. Haveman, 1993:622.
17. Haveman, 1993:624.
18. Labich, 1999:206.
19. Faircloth, 1998:108.
20. Salter, 2003:102.
21. Salter, 2003:102.
22. Labich, 1999:212.
23. Labich, 1999:208.
24. Salter, 2003:102.
25. Dunphy et al., 2003:49.
26. Dunphy et al., 2003:49.
27. Dunphy et al., 2003:49.
28. DiMaggio & Powell, 1991:67–74.

29. DiMaggio & Powell, 1991:67–74.
30. Information based upon Siekman, 2002.
31. Information from Bianco et al., 2001.
32. See, for example, Dunphy et al., 2003:43.
33. http://www.inta.gatech.edu/eucenter/resources/eu_timeline.html.
34. Ackenhusen, Muzyka & Churchill, 1996:21. This and subsequent quotes from the same article reprinted from *European Management Journal* 14(1) with permission from Elsevier.
35. Ackenhusen, Muzyka & Churchill, 1996:30.
36. Cited in Ackenhusen, Muzyka & Churchill, 1996:30.
37. Ackenhusen, Muzyka & Churchill, 1996:21.
38. Kotter, 1996:19.
39. Kotter, 1996:18.
40. Wasserman, 2003.
41. Wasserman, 2003.
42. Kilgannon, 2002.
43. Howe, 2003.
44. Information based on Kirkpatrick, 1999.
45. D'Aveni, 1994.
46. Nadler, Shaw, Walton & Associates, 1995.
47. Quinn, 1992; Thompson, 1993.
48. Jenner, 1994.
49. Jenner, 1994; Clegg, 1994.
50. Kratz, 2000:61.
51. This case study is based on Dorsey, 2000.
52. Lavell, 2002:104.
53. Editorial, 2002.
54. Timmons & Holmes, 2002; Timmons, Cohn, McNamee & Rossant, 2002.
55. Fombrun & van Riel, 1997:10.
56. Schweizer & Wijnberg, 1999.
57. Deephouse, 1997; Vergin & Qoronfleh, 1998.
58. Gray & Balmer, 1998.
59. Gunther & Wheat, 2002:130.
60. Weick, 1979.
61. Lee, 2000.
62. Mone et al., 1998:116.
63. Sull, 1999.
64. Breen, 2001a.
65. Smircich & Stubbart, 1985.
66. Boyd et al., 1993:213.
67. Boyd et al., 1993:213.
68. Smircich & Stubbart, 1985.
69. Bognor & Barr, 2000.

70. See also McKinley & Scherer, 2000; McKinley, Zhao & Rust (2000) for an application of this argument to explaining downsizing.
71. Bognor & Barr, 2000:221. Copyright © 2000, The Institute for Operations Research and the Management Sciences (INFORMS), 901 Elkridge Landing Road, Suite 400, Linthicum, Maryland 21090-2909 USA. Reprinted with permission.
72. Mone et al., 1998:116–26.
73. Mone et al., 1998:116–26.
74. Leana & Barry, 2000.
75. Leana & Barry, 2000:758.
76. Weintraub & Barrett, 2002.
77. Herbold, 2002.
78. Scase & Goffee, 1987.
79. Lichtenstein, 2000:131.
80. Cooper & Kulkowski, 2002; Kulikowski, 2002.
81. Information on EDS is based on Breen, 2001b.
82. Information based upon Erstad, 2001.
83. Muoio, 1999.
84. For more detail, see Muoio, 1999.
85. Faust, 2002.
86. Faust, 2002.
87. Faust, 2002.
88. Information based on Brooker, 2000.
89. Based on Rucci, Kirn & Quinn, 1998.
90. Kanter, 2003:64.
91. Kanter, 2003:64–65.
92. Thornton & Reed, 2001.
93. Anonymous, 2002.
94. Story as told by Ante, 2003.
95. Ante, 2003.
96. The following story on Roche is drawn from Anders, 2002.
97. Thietart & Forgues, 1995:28.
98. Goodstein & Butz, 1998:32.
99. Tetenbaum, 1998:44.
100. This case study is paraphrased from Edwards and Sager, 2001. Reprinted from October 15, 2001, issue of *BusinessWeek* by special permission, copyright © 2001 by the McGraw-Hill Companies, Inc.

What Changes in Organizations

Learning objectives

On completion of this chapter you should be able to:

- Understand the distinction between first-order and second-order change.
- Outline alternative concepts of change.
- Identify a range of common changes that confront organizations such as downsizing, introducing new technologies, and mergers and acquisitions.
- Be familiar with a variety of issues that emerge at the "front line" for those charged with managing these changes.
- Appraise your ability to engage with such changes in the future.

Some commentators suggest that, whereas change prior to the 1960s was more likely to be incremental and infrequent, the last two decades have been ones of significant and traumatic organizational change.[1] A study by Meyer, Brooks, and Goes[2] provides support to this position. Their study showed how changes in hospitals in the 1960s were evolutionary and related to a stable environment. During the 1970s and 1980s, the environment changed with mounting concern about health-care costs, which led to revolutionary strategic and structural changes in health-care corporations.

Other commentators take a different line, arguing that radical or discontinuous change is not new to the current period but is something that occurred between 1900 and 1950.[3] More generally, others suggest that too much attention has focused solely on large-scale transformational change without appropriate acknowledgment of the role of other changes in maintaining organizational survival.[4]

In this chapter, we pick up these issues in two ways. First, we distinguish between different types of change such as first-order and second-order change. We identify alternative ways of conceptualizing change that try to move beyond categorizing change as either first-order or second-order. Second, we identify three common organizational changes that are likely to confront change managers: downsizing, introduction of new technologies, and mergers and acquisitions. These common types are generally perceived as larger, second-order forms of change, but this is dependent on the perspective from which the change is interpreted. From these examples we identify various "frontline" experiences of these changes and the challenges they pose for people trying to manage them. These challenges form the context for the chapters that follow.

TYPES OF CHANGES

In this section we pursue the idea of there being different types of organizational change. We distinguish first-order from second-order change and then consider each of these in more detail. We complete this section by outlining two approaches that seek to move beyond seeing change as either first-order or second-order and draw out the implications of this discussion for the manager of organizational change.

Distinguishing between First-Order and Second-Order Changes

A common distinction in the change management literature is between first-order, incremental, continuous change and second-order, transformational/revolutionary, discontinuous change:

- *First-order, incremental change* "may involve adjustments in systems, processes, or structures, but it does not involve fundamental change in strategy, core values, or corporate identity."[5] First-order changes *maintain and develop* the organization: they are changes designed, almost paradoxically, to support organizational continuity and order.[6]
- *Second-order, discontinuous change* "is transformational, radical, and fundamentally alters the organization at its core."[7] Second-order change entails not developing but *transforming* the nature of the organization.[8]

Bate uses the metaphor of a floating boat to further understand this distinction. Given winds and tides, a boat has to remain in movement in the water if it is to remain at the same point in the sea. This is like first-order change: we have to change to stay the same. In second-order change, movement is directed toward taking the boat beyond the original spot in the sea at which it started: we have to move in order to arrive at a new position.[9] In terms of the scale of change, first-order change is seen as small-scale, incremental, and adaptive; second-order change is seen as large-scale and disruptive.

Nadler and Tushman[10] develop this distinction between incremental and discontinuous change by incorporating another dimension: whether the change is *reactive* to or *anticipatory* of changes in the external environment. This gives rise to four categories: tuning, reorientation, adaptation, and re-creation (see Table 4.1).

Fine-tuning occurs where incremental changes are made that anticipate changes to the external environment. These changes involve adjustment or modification to enable a better fit between the organization and the environment. Citibank's installation of automatic teller machines in New York in the late 1970s was an incremental change in which the bank attempted to gain a competitive edge on other New York banks by providing more flexible banking.[11]

TABLE 4.1 Types of Changes

Source: Adapted from Nadler and Tushman, 1995.

	Incremental	Discontinuous
Anticipatory	*Tuning* Improving, enhancing, developing: first-order change	*Reorientation* Of identity/values—frame bending
Reactive	*Adaptation* Internally initiated	*Re-creation* Fast change of all basic elements—frame breaking, second-order change

Adaptive changes are incremental but reactive to changes made by other organizations. An example of this is the catch-up response of other New York banks to install ATM machines following Citibank's lead.[12]

Reorientation is an anticipatory, discontinuous change, which involves "frame bending"; that is, major modification of the organization but by building on past strengths and history. An example of this is the changes made by CEO Bob Allen at AT&T. In the late 1980s, during a period of deregulation and international competitive pressures, AT&T was radically changed, restructuring its business units, making new acquisitions, installing a new management team, promulgating a new set of values, and changing the company's strategy to reorient it toward global markets.[13]

Re-creation is second-order change that is reactive and involves "frame breaking"; that is, major upheaval where the organization breaks with past practices and directions. The reactive changes in Chrysler under Lee Iacocca serve as an example of this type of change, where swift decisions were taken to re-create the company in order to survive, including redefining its scope, changing its past strategy of manufacturing full-sized cars, and changing its foreign operations.[14]

First-Order, Adaptive Changes

Some commentators contend that there is a preoccupation with second-order, transformational change without sufficient attention being paid to the importance of first-order adaptive changes.[15] In this section we identify two interrelated positions that point to how significant changes can be made to organizations by individuals at the local level. One argument focuses on individuals and the exercise of their initiative, the other on individuals and their impact on routines.

Change as the Taking of Individual Initiatives

Frohman[16] maintains that not enough attention has been paid to the overall impact on organizations of small-scale changes and the role of personal initiatives in identifying and implementing small-scale changes. He argues that large-scale changes such as restructuring and reengineering, often underpinned by the introduction of new technologies, are too mechanistic in their assumptions and ignore the importance of individual initiative in achieving lasting change. This is because organizations operate in a time where technology breakthroughs provide only a limited competitive advantage: "The only characteristic that is proprietary about technology is lead time, and that's a function of the individual's ability to create or exploit a technology for the purposes of the organization."[17]

EXERCISE 4.1

Weighing in on Types of Changes

Study Table 4.1. From your knowledge of different organizations, either from experience or from the business press, identify companies and their changes that fit:

- *Tuning* (anticipatory and incremental)
- *Adaptation* (reactive and incremental)
- *Reorientation* (anticipatory and discontinuous)
- *Re-creation* (reactive and discontinuous)

Now answer the following questions:

1. In your opinion, which of these changes were most successful? Why?
2. In your opinion, is one category more associated with successful changes than another? Why?
3. Do some organizations fit into more than one category?
4. How useful is the punctuated equilibrium theory (see below) for understanding why this might be?
5. What implications emerge from this for the practicing change manager?

He contends that what is most important to organizations is people who, at a local level, are able to identify relevant, innovative organizational changes. He maintains that, for too long, managers have ignored the bottom-line impact of smaller, local organizational changes and, in many organizations, do not foster the conditions that allow personal initiative to emerge. People who bring about local organizational changes are those who go beyond their jobs, strive to make a difference, are action-oriented, and focus less on teamwork and more on results. However, he points out that although such people are able to be easily identified by other staff in their organization, they are often not seen by managers as high-potential individuals in terms of progression through the company. He suggests that:

- *Autocratic* organizations discourage initiative by removing responsibility.
- *Meritocratic* organizations constrain individual initiative and action by tightly regulating controls and procedures throughout the company.
- *Social club* organizations discourage individual initiative by requiring conformity to the team rather than to the work itself. As an interviewee in one such organization said, "We spend more time prioritizing our meetings than we do meeting our priorities."[18]

Frohman[19] proposes that personal initiative directed toward local change is likely to occur when attributes from each of these three organizational types—strong leadership, bureaucratic systems, and teamwork—are balanced. Such organizations provide space for personal initiatives that are, at the same time, directed toward corporate objectives.

Change as the Development of Local Routines

Feldman[20] claims that mid-level and transformational changes are based on the assumption that routines are a source of stability in organizations and therefore need to be fundamentally disrupted to produce change. She presents a different view: that organizational routines can be the source of change in organizations when they are enacted by different people who place their own interpretations and actions on how the routines should occur. Two internal dynamics drive routines toward continuous change. One is where past outcomes fall short of what was intended; another is where achievement of outcomes opens up new possibilities.[21]

In support of this position, she cites the work of Burgelman,[22] who maintains that the product mix at Intel evolved as a result of changes in internal routines and decisions made by mid-level managers, rather than by these managers following the decisions of top managers. In her own study of organizational routines in the residential life section of a university, Feldman[23] found that actions associated with routines such as hiring, training, and budgeting evolved over time in response to the interpretations and actions of individuals involved in carrying them out. In this way, routines entail both stability and change. For example, in relation to the hiring routine, there was stability over time in the way in which people were screened and interviewed. However, the process of submitting applications became centralized over time: "In this case, the elements of the routine have not changed, but how they are accomplished has."[24]

EXERCISE 4.2

How Stable Are Your Routines?

Some argue that routines are a source of stability in organizations and therefore inhibit change and the ability of an organization to adapt to its environment. Others argue that routines do change and that these changes are an important, albeit relatively ignored, part of how organizations adapt to their environment over time. What's your experience?

- Identify an organizational routine with which you have had some familiarity over a period of time.
- To what extent has this routine changed over time?
- What was the source of the change?
- What aspects of it remained unchanged? Why?
- To what extent did the function of the routine remain stable but change in the way the function was accomplished?
- As a change manager, what are your conclusions about the above debate?

Second-Order, Transformational Change

Many organizational changes such as downsizing, restructuring, and reengineering are regarded as transformational, designed to fundamentally alter the basic nature of the organization.[25] In their study of 22 popular management books and 78 articles on current organizational changes, Palmer and Dunford[26] found eight commonly occurring recommendations for major organizational change in order to cope with hypercompetitive business environments:

- *Delayering* (reducing the number of vertical levels in the organization).
- *Networks/alliances* (involving internal and external strategic collaboration).
- *Outsourcing* (of activities in which the organization has no distinctive competence).
- *Disaggregation* (breaking up the organization into smaller business units).
- *Empowerment* (introduction of mechanisms to provide employees with the authority, resources, and encouragement to take actions).
- *Flexible work groups* (for specific purposes that are disbanded or reformed upon completion of the task).
- *Short-term staffing* (in which people are contracted to the organization for a short period of time to work on specific issues/tasks).
- *Reduction of internal and external boundaries* (to encourage communication and resource sharing).

In their survey of organizations in western Europe, Whittington et al.[27] identified a similar range of changes in which organizations are currently engaged, dividing these into changes in organizational structures, processes, and boundaries. These changes, and the rationales for entering into them, are summarized in Table 4.2.

Such changes are commonly seen as second-order, transformational changes, ones needed to produce a fundamental reorientation of an organization so that it can cope with highly competitive changes in the business environment (see Tables 4.3 and 4.4).

However, before rushing out to get rid of old organizational practices such as hierarchy, formalization, and centralization and replacing them with new, more flexible organizational practices, it is worth pointing out that a number of commentators are cautioning managers to be careful in taking such radical change actions. Rather than replacing the old with the new, the two should be integrated. The creation of boundaryless organizations does not mean dispensing with hierarchy.[28] Similarly, instituting empowerment and teamwork should be seen as assisting in the development of functional and divisional structures rather than replacing them.[29] Organizational environments may well be changing, but prescriptions for how organizations should be changed in order to meet these new environments need to move beyond evangelical pronouncements to careful consideration of current organizational strengths and future requirements.

Transformational Types

Not all transformational changes are of the same order of magnitude. As we saw above, Nadler and Tushman distinguished between frame-bending (reorientation) and frame-breaking (re-creation) transformations. Flamholtz and Randle[31] add to such distinctions by distinguishing among three types of transformational change:

- A *Type 1* transformation, which occurs when an organization moves from an entrepreneurial to a professional management structure; for example, the transformation of Apple Computers from an entrepreneurial company under its founder, Stephen Jobs, to a larger professional company under John Sculley.[32]

EXERCISE 4.3

Does the New Replace the Old—What's Your Experience?

Think back to the various changes that you have either witnessed or experienced over the *last three years* in organizations with which you are familiar. Answer the following survey.

Which of the new organizational changes identified by Palmer and Dunford[30] have you experienced and, in your opinion, to what extent did implementing them involve replacing past practices? Use the following 0-to-7-point scale where 0 = not experienced this practice; 1 = past practices remained intact; 7 = past practices completely replaced

(If you have no significant organizational experience on which to base your responses, consider the situation in the introductory stories and suggest to what extent new practices might replace old.)

New Organizational Change Practice	Scale
Delayering	=
Networks/alliances	=
Outsourcing	=
Disaggregation	=
Empowerment	=
Flexible workgroups	=
Short-term staffing	=
Reduction of internal boundaries	=
Reduction of all external boundaries	=

- How prevalent are these practices in your experience? Are some practices more prevalent than others?
- What conclusions do you draw about the relationship between new organizational change practices and past organizational practices? Does the old coexist with the new? Does the new replace the old? Is the old modified with the introduction of the new?
- Review Tables 4.2, 4.3, and 4.4. To what extent are the emerging characteristics replacing or coexisting with traditional characteristics?
- What implications does this have for change managers?

- A *Type 2* transformation, which involves the revitalization of already established companies. The organization remains in the same market but focuses on how to rebuild itself in order to operate more effectively.[33] An example of this is Compaq Computers. In the early 1990s, this company faced a changing environment, including changes in customer needs. The company reengineered its operational systems, downsized, lowered its purchase and production costs, and placed more emphasis on teamwork. The focus of this turnaround change was to enhance organizational effectiveness.[34]
- A *Type 3* transformation, which involves a visionary change in which the organization fundamentally changes the business in which it is involved. The change in Starbucks Coffee from a local roaster and importer of coffee beans (it did not initially sell coffee as a drink) to a string of national company-owned coffee retail

TABLE 4.2 Rationale for New Organizational Changes

Source: Adapted from Whittington et al., 1999:589.

New Organizational Changes	Rationale
Organizational Structures	
Delayering	Enhance information flows, speed of response, and removal of expensive middle management
Decentralization	Encourage cross-functional teams
Operational strategy	Harness knowledge, increase profit, improve response times
Project-based structures	Flexibility
Organizational Processes	
Information technologies	Intensify interactions in the new economy
Electronic data interchange	Enhance information flows, flexibility, and participation
HR practices	Enhance commitment and motivation to engage with new practices
Horizontal networking	Enhance communication exchanges and cross-boundary career paths
Organizational integration	Encourage corporate identity
Organizational Boundaries	
Downscoping	Increase strategic flexibility and enable greater focus
Outsourcing	Removal of low-value activities
Alliances	Increase access of organization to external skills and competencies

TABLE 4.3 Key Challenges in Destabilized Environments

Source: Adapted from Nadler and Shaw, 1995:6–8.

Key Challenge	Rationale
Increase quality and customer value	To increase customer expectations
Decrease costs of internal coordination	To decrease production costs
Enhance innovation	To meet customers' expectations
Reduce market response time	To respond quickly to shifts in the market
Motivate staff	To gain effective contributions
Create scale without mass	To compete globally but without adding costs associated with increased size
Change more quickly	To decrease periods of equilibrium
Enhance competitive advantage	To develop factors not easily replicated by competitors

TABLE 4.4 Emerging Organizational Characteristics of the 21st-Century Corporation

Source: Adapted from Wind and Main, 1999:4.

Traditional Characteristics	Emerging Characteristics
Goal-directed	Vision-directed
Price-focused	Value-focused
Product quality mindset	Total quality mindset
Product driven	Customer driven
Shareholder focused	Stakeholder focused
Finance oriented	Speed oriented
Efficient	Innovative
Hierarchical	Flat
Functional	Cross-functional
Rigid	Flexible
Domestic	Global
Vertically integrated	Networked

stores is an example of this type of change.[35] Compound transformations can occur when an organization simultaneously tackles multiple transformations, such as when Disney in the 1980s carried out both a professional and a visionary transformation.[36] Table 4.5 summarizes the factors associated with such transformations.

Beyond Either First-Order or Second-Order Change

Rather than retaining firm distinctions between categorizing changes as either evolutionary or transformational, two alternative approaches are being developed: midrange organizational change and punctuated equilibrium theory.

Midrange Organizational Change

Rather than pushing managers toward either incremental or revolutionary change, Reger et al.[37] point to a middle road that managers can take, one they describe as tectonic change that, they maintain, is suitable for "today's dynamic environments." Midrange changes are important where companies seek to modify the company without destroying employee loyalty and other positive company attributes.[38] For them, it is through mental models that individuals establish organizational identity and influence how announced changes are received:

- *High inertia* can result when the change is perceived as unnecessary, there being little gap between current identity and the one that is implied in the change.
- *High stress* can result when the change is perceived as unattainable and the gap is too wide between the current organizational identity and the one that will occur as a result of the change.[39]

A mid-road or "tectonic" change is one "that is large enough to overcome the inertia that plagues large organizations while avoiding the cataclysmic side effects of massive revolutions."[40] These "moderate earthquakes" are designed "to destroy outdated aspects of the organization's old identity while simultaneously building on other, still relevant,

TABLE 4.5 Types of Transformational Change

Source: Adapted from Flamholtz and Randle, 1998:39.

	Transformation Types		
Key Factors Influencing Design of Transformations	**Type 1: Entrepreneurial to Professional Management**	**Type 2: Revitalization**	**Type 3: Business Vision**
Organizational environment	Growth in markets and competition	Major change in environment	May or may not involve environmental change
Business concept	No transformation	No transformation	Major transformation
Building blocks of organizational success	Changing culture, management, and operational systems	Change needed in markets, services, resources, operational and measurement systems, and culture	Changes in markets, services, resources, operational and measurement systems, and culture
Organizational size	Associated with rapid growth	Usually change, including downsizing	May involve size change

elements."[41] Table 4.6 outlines steps they recommend tectonic change managers should follow in order to enact such change.

Change as Punctuated Equilibrium

Rather than focusing on either incremental or transformational change, an alternative position that has gained widespread currency is that more attention needs to be paid to the *interplay* between incremental and transformational change. In what is known as punctuated equilibrium theory, Romanelli and Tushman[42] portray organizations as evolving "through relatively long periods of stability (equilibrium periods) in their basic patterns of activity that are punctuated by relatively short bursts of fundamental change (revolutionary periods). Revolutionary periods substantially disrupt established activity patterns and install the basis for new equilibrium periods."[43] Their study of 25 minicomputer producers during 1967–1969 found support for this theory.[44] In developing this position, Nadler and Tushman[45] point to the way in which whole industries go through organizational change and often display periods of equilibrium in which change is relatively minor, "punctuated by intervals of major disequilibrium when the entire industry is shaken by some destabilizing event."

Implications for Change Managers

In assessing the issues and arguments outlined above, we suggest that they pose seven implications that need to be considered by the manager of change. Where relevant, we indicate how these relate to the various images of change outlined in Chapter 2.

1. Care needs to be taken in assuming that types of organizational changes can be neatly categorized as small, adaptive, and incremental compared to those that are large

TABLE 4.6 Prescriptions for Achieving Tectonic Change

Source: Adapted from Reger et al., 1994:38–41.

- Engage in an audit of the organization's identity prior to undergoing significant organizational change.
- Ensure that the change is aligned with the organization's different operations.
- Ensure that the change is seen as significant enough to overcome inertia but also seen as valuing relevant aspects of organizational identity.
- Make sure that the change occurs in the form of midrange steps so that the gap between the change and the current organizational identity is not seen as too significant.
- Take a path of least resistance by leveraging change in certain parts of the organization that are more receptive to the change and then using these parts to encourage others elsewhere in the organization.
- Identify the extent to which the organization can handle the specified changes—and whether to initiate it when the organization has problems or when it is performing well.

and transformational. Mental frameworks, individual perspectives, the extent to which a change is directly relevant to a person and his or her activities, and the degree to which he or she accepts the need for change (see Chapter 6 for more on this) will all influence how the change is viewed. A restructure in one section of an organization may be seen as small scale and adaptive by people elsewhere in the organization who are relatively unaffected by it. For those who are affected by it—including those who may lose their position—it may seem to be large scale in the sense that it is disruptive to current work practices and routines, entails large personal impacts, and requires different ways of approaching how to do things. The change manager as *interpreter* image reminds us that whether a change is adaptive, reactive, or transforming is not necessarily an objective "given" but will depend upon the perspective of the person doing the considering—and part of the role of the manager of change is to mold these perspectives or provide "sense making" for organizational participants about "what is going on here."

2. Much of the above discussion has been about single organizational changes without considering in detail the interactive effect of multiple types of changes simultaneously. In addition, some changes require other changes nested under them in order for another change to proceed. For example, putting in place mechanisms to empower staff may require multiple changes related to an organization's decision-making routines, reward systems, skill base, and work flow. Individually, each change may be seen to be achievable and relatively small scale (depending upon your perspective), but together they may be seen as transformational, even revolutionary. The *navigator* image reminds the managers of change that when they are implementing multiple changes, this is likely to bring them into contact with different groups, interests, and power relationships within their organization that will require negotiation and navigation through a range of issues—not all of which they will be able to control. The point here is that change managers need to avoid simply focusing on one change without an understanding of the way other related changes may impact upon their staff. They need to remember that they are likely to be placed in the position of navigating through multiple changes at one and the same time.[46]

3. The *nurturer* image reminds change managers about the need to remember the lesson from chaos theory that small changes, at an individual level, may have larger, unanticipated consequences throughout the organization.[47] Change managers can nurture and shape people's perceptions and reactions to change but not control them. What might seem to be a small, inconsequential change may have radical consequences that change managers may not be able to anticipate (see Table 4.7 for an example).

4. Adopting the *coach* image, the managers of change are likely to assume that, as long as people have been well "coached" in a variety of organizational and team skills, then, when organizational "problems" are triggered, they will take the initiative and make appropriate adaptive changes to alter organizational practices and routines. However, as we saw in Chapter 3, there are a number of inertial forces that act as a drag on individuals and organizations in adopting adaptive, first-order change. As Staudenmayer et al.[48] state, "[I]n organizations and in everyday life, problems do not always induce change. Many well-known cases exist where problems were ignored or silenced until organizations experienced full-blown disasters" such as NASA's *Challenger* explosion. As they note, the number of problems facing an organization is not associated with its propensity to engage in change.[49] Providing the conditions for the exercise of personal initiative becomes an important focus for change managers who wish to cultivate change through the exercise of frontline staff.

5. As in the example of the boat, change managers need to remember what might appear at first sight to be a paradox, that often change is needed in order to remain stable. This can be seen as another way of framing the fundamental paradox of stability and change where change may be needed to preserve or reestablish stability and stability must include change mechanisms to be adaptable. A more succinct expression of this paradox is in a saying often heard in talk about change: The more things change, the more they stay the same. Change managers who adopt a *directing* image of change also need to remember that they will need to provide directions about stability: telling people what will not be changing, or what will remain the same.

6. Change may mean adding on to, and integrating, rather than removing and replacing current practices. What this reminds the managers of change is that they need to assess how carrying out a change will impact upon current practices—and the extent

TABLE 4.7 Small Changes, Radical Consequences

Source: Hamel, 2001:152.

Gary Hamel provides this example to illustrate how small changes can have radical consequences:

A couple of years ago, an employee at Virgin Atlantic noticed a bit of empty curb space at Heathrow Airport. In a matter of days, he secured the rights to the space and laid out a plan for Virgin to build a curbside check-in kiosk. As a result, Virgin became the first airline at Heathrow to offer its business class passengers the luxury of getting a boarding pass without having to stand in a check-in line. Soon, check-in times were measured in seconds instead of minutes. Over the past decade, dozens upon dozens of similarly "radical" ideas have allowed Virgin Atlantic to differentiate its services from its large rivals. The point is this: radical innovation comes in all sizes . . . Enough "small" innovations can reorder competitive position in radical ways.

to which a change will create ripple effects on practices and routines that they need to retain.

7. There is often an implicit assumption that incremental, adaptive changes are less risky than large, second-order transformational changes. An alternative position is that staying the same is risky. For example, Hamel discusses how companies such as Xerox, Compaq, and Sears adopted a "steady as she goes" approach, which failed to match the fast-changing world around them.[50] He points out that radical change and the adoption of new assumptions may require organizational learning, but this is not necessarily a high-risk activity. The process of learning may entail "a series of low-cost, low-risk experiments and market incursions."[51] For the manager of change, this requires both assessing the *scale of change* (incremental/radical) from the perspective of the affected parties as well as *assessing the risk* involved (of changing rather than staying the same) and the different ways in which risk can be ameliorated.

TYPES OF CHANGES: LESSONS FROM THE FRONT LINE

In this section we outline briefly three common changes likely to face managers: downsizing as a form of organizational restructuring, implementation of new technology, and mergers and acquisitions. These are generally regarded as midrange or second-order changes, notwithstanding the arguments above about the scale of change being dependent upon the perspective of the person involved. For each change, we provide examples of companies that have confronted such changes and draw on their frontline experiences to identify the key issues and challenges that faced them. This helps to set further in context the chapters that follow and the way they assist in meeting these challenges.

Downsizing

Downsizing, or the intentional process of permanently reducing staff numbers in an organization, has been a widespread change practice since the 1970s and it is one that continues today. In 2001 alone, Fortune 500 companies reportedly cut a total of 1,040,466 jobs[52] and one prediction is that by 2015 a further 3.3 million U.S. jobs will be outsourced to countries such as India.[53] Recent companies to pursue downsizing include American Express, Alcoa, Motorola,[54] Hewlett-Packard, Dell, and Lucent[55]—to name a very few.

As can be seen in Table 4.8, there are a variety of approaches to downsizing, including retrenchment, downscaling, and downscoping. The reasons firms undertake this type of change are varied. As documented by Palmer et al.,[56] they include restructuring, closing or selling of a business unit, cost reduction and cost savings, increased productivity through greater efficiency and effectiveness, and coping with external pressures, including recessions and economic downturns, technological change, and increased competitive pressures through greater globalization of business.

Multiple strategies may be associated with downsizing beyond a simple cost-reduction approach. For example, after the tragic events of September 11, 2001, Praxair Inc., a supplier of specialty gases and coating in the United States, experienced a downturn in productivity.[57] They announced the need to reduce their worldwide workforce

TABLE 4.8 Types of Downsizing

Source: Adapted from DeWitt, 1998.

Type	Meaning
Retrenchment	This is done by centralizing or specializing a firm's operations to sustain or improve productivity. It is brought about by reengineering practices and the removal of unnecessary jobs and amenities. This form of downsizing may increase the economies of scale and help maintain a competitive advantage.
Downscaling	This is constituted by permanent alterations to employment and tangible resource capacity. This reduces the firm's economies of scale and competitive market share.
Downscoping	This is when the firm divests activities or markets in which it operates. This is done by reducing the vertical and/or horizontal differentiation.

by 900 employees[58] as well as the need to restructure their business to cater to products where demand was increasing. To this end they simultaneously downsized and invested in two new production plants.[59]

Companies may approach downsizing as one among a number of methods to achieve cost cutting, sometimes employing it as a last resort. For example, Charles Schwab & Company was hit with a major downturn in commission-based revenue at the end of the second quarter in 2001.[60] Schwab had hired people during the boom years and found itself with an overabundance of staff and a need to change its structure.[61] They implemented a system that would use downsizing as a last resort to restructuring the company and cutting costs.[62] By the end of 2003, Schwab had reduced its workforce by 25 percent and significantly decreased staff bonuses in a move to arrest the declining fortunes of the company.[63]

In part, this approach to downsizing—linking it with multiple, related changes—recognizes that by itself downsizing will not necessarily lead to gains in productivity where it is not associated with other changes in business strategy. For example, research in the early 1990s showed that expected increases in profits did not eventuate in two out of three cases through cost cutting by downsizing; this research showed that share prices may initially rise with the announcement of cost cutting through downsizing but then often fall, trading at or below the market over a two-year period.[64]

Downsizing can be a financially costly change process. For example, it has been calculated that the cost of retrenching a single employee who earns approximately $30,000 is around $7,000.[65] As outlined below, the process of downsizing can have significant social and psychological effects on employees—both those who remain and those who leave. For such reasons, "the smartest companies make sure they are addressing the right issues in the right ways before they jettison jobs"[66] and explore other alternatives before downsizing their operations. Where companies do go down the downsizing path, there are a number of challenges that confront them in the process of carrying out this change. A selection of these follow.

Change Challenges of Downsizing

- *Employee retention.* Downsizing may lead to the loss of important and skilled employees. When they see their peers leaving, they begin to doubt their future at the company. Without these valued members of the organization, the productivity of the company may be reduced.[67]
- *Survivor syndrome.*[68] The employees that remain with the organization following downsizing may suffer survivor syndrome, where they question why the change occurred, feel guilty that they remain while some of their valued work colleagues are unemployed, and may suffer from low morale wondering whether they are likely to lose their job in future downsizings. Particularly when they are not involved in the planning and goal setting for any subsequent organizational restructuring program, they feel disassociated from the organization. Managing survivors successfully is a major change challenge.[69]
- *Communication.*[70] Problems occur when companies are not open about the market situation they face and the future of their remaining employees is uncertain.[71] Communicating future vision and strategy to shareholders, employees, and other constituents becomes an important change concern.[72]
- *Due diligence.*[73] Unplanned and nonselective downsizing can lead to issues for companies such as whether the downsizing that occurred was really necessary and why it was that some people were retained and others let go. Lack of attention to such issues can lead to further deterioration in employer–employee relationships following downsizing.[74]
- *Cultural adjustment.* Restructuring an organization through any means, especially downsizing, requires significant cultural change. For example, subcultures may be broken up through downsizing and restructuring and informal networks, which were previously drawn upon to implement organizational work, may be disrupted. Paying attention to reintegration of culture with new strategic directions becomes a key postdownsizing challenge for change managers.[75]
- *Choice of restructuring technique.* As discussed, downsizing is not always the most appropriate and effective way to begin a restructuring program and many companies do not appear to seek initial alternatives to this method.[76] Deciding whether to use a substitute method is a key issue that needs to be assessed by change managers.

Technological Change

Introducing technological change into an organization has been the focus of change management activities for many years. Classic studies in the 1950s were made of technology changes in the mining industry in Britain. These gave rise to sociotechnical approaches to implementing change associated with people such as Fred Emery and Eric Trist of the London-based Tavistock Institute of Human Relations. These approaches highlighted the need to pay attention to the social aspects of implementing new technologies such as the way they can disrupt informal social patterns within organizations.[77] These same issues remain relevant today, where a variety of new technologies from e-commerce initiatives to customer relationship management (CRM) systems are introduced into organizations.[78] Table 4.9 outlines a sample of these.

There are numerous examples of companies implementing new technologies for varying reasons. Chase Manhattan Bank began a business process reengineering program to help facilitate a change to their operations.[79] Piper Aircraft sought to increase productivity by employing a CRM system to coordinate communications between its 17 suppliers and over 70,000 customers.[80] UPS wished to become more competitive within the package delivery market and made the decision to upgrade its technology system. To this end, they took on a new strategic platform that was a comprehensive package database that could service different parts of its operations.[81] Delta Airlines introduced a new technological platform because many of its business units had created their own systems and they needed a synthesized system. They created a platform named Delta Nervous System (DNS) to provide real-time information for flight operations and customer service. This was to correct previous confusions that led to incorrect information being given to customers.[82]

Implementing new technologies is not straightforward. One estimate is that, on average, 20 percent of a company's expenditures on corporate IT is used on products or services that fail to achieve their intended purpose.[83] Moreover the impact of new systems may not be manifested for a significant amount of time.[84] Conversely, managers often seek to use technologies for short-term solutions without paying

TABLE 4.9 Types of Technological Change

Type	Meaning
Enterprise resource planning (ERP)[a]	This system provides an organizationwide platform that consolidates the company's needs while still allowing particular departments to use the system for their specific needs
Customer relationship management (CRM)[b]	This system allows an organization to scrutinize their consumers' needs by tracking information relating to their sales and more effectively forecast their demand for the future
Wireless technology[c]	These devices transmit information from remote points back to a central point for collation or action
Business process reengineering (BPR)[d]	This is a way of managing change that requires a complete overhaul of business practices and can be implemented through technological changes
Six sigma[e]	This is a process of quality control that is monitored through the use of statistical information regarding defect occurrences

[a]Koch, 2004.
[b]Harris, 2003.
[c]Paul, 2001.
[d]Anonymous, 2003.
[e]Ettinger, 2001.

attention to longer-term advantages that IT might offer an organization.[85] Crises such as the Y2K bug forced many companies to rethink their information technology systems, but many did not take advantage of this opportunity to change their systems for the longer term.[86] The challenges that may be faced when implementing technological change are numerous. The following list outlines a number of the key issues that need to be considered.

Change Challenges of Introducing New Technologies

- *Goal synthesis*. A key problem when implementing a new technology is identifying its place within the organization.[87] IT frequently takes a secondary place to corporate operations; balancing this discrepancy is an issue for change managers.[88]
- *Choice of technology*.[89] As Table 4.9 indicates, there are a number of options offered for new technologies that can be introduced into an organization. An important challenge is to find technological platforms or applications that serve the company as a whole.[90]
- *The IT team*. The IT department may be treated as a division somewhat divorced from the main part of the organization.[91] Getting both the corporate and IT teams on board and working together is an issue that arises in initiating change.[92]
- *Communication*.[93] Communicating the direction of, and process for implementing, a technological change is an important element of the project and, if done ineffectively, can work against successful implementation.
- *Time frame*.[94] There is debate as to whether technological change should be implemented on a short-term or a long-term basis.[95] Either way, remaining within the given time frame for integration is often a difficult issue facing the change manager.[96]
- *Contingency planning*.[97] Overhauling a fundamental part of a firm's infrastructure can seriously damage its day-to-day operations. Change involves planning for the future as well as planning for how to keep day-to-day operations running. Contingency planning enables "what if" questions to be asked that can anticipate possible scenarios that might emerge and how they could be handled. Relaxing normal operating rules during the change process might be necessary for it to proceed smoothly without facing blockages.[98] Change managers need to give thought to both of these issues in implementing technological change.

Mergers and Acquisitions

Celebrated strategy writer Alfred Chandler argues that mergers have been a popular form of organizational growth at least since the 1890s.[99] Mergers and acquisitions enable organizational growth at accelerated rates[100] and they continue to be popular, albeit with "seasonal" variations. For example, 1998–2000 has been cited as one of the most hectic periods of mergers in U.S. economic history with almost $4 trillion being spent in merger and acquisition activities,[101] although this waned in 2002 with a decline by approximately 36 percent in the number of mergers and acquisitions.[102]

Despite such variation, it remains an entrenched change management activity with many companies undertaking this form of change. Johnson & Johnson (J&J) is an example of how acquisitions can be used to diversify an organization and increase research and development. By either licensing, partnerships, or acquisitions, Johnson & Johnson has created a drug and medical empire that is worth approximately $33 billion a year.[103] Well-known examples of mergers include Citicorp and Travelers Group; Conseco and Green Tree Financial; Daimler Benz and Chrysler Corp; and NationsBank and BankAmerica Corp.[104] Mergers and acquisitions are not without their challenges. This can be seen in very public and well-documented mergers such as that of America Online (AOL) and Time Warner in 2000.[105]

Mergers and acquisitions (whether forceful or friendly) can take many different forms, as outlined in Table 4.10. Outcomes also can vary. On the one extreme, an acquired company may be left to operate similar to the way it has done in the past, except for minimal governance or operational changes. At the other extreme, an acquired company may be subject to a complete overhaul in its governance structures, human resource systems, financial systems, and other operating systems, bringing these in line with the acquiring company. Between these two extremes is a range of other positions, including merging the two companies by integrating the best practices of both to form a new entity.

Producing successful mergers and acquisitions is clearly a change management challenge. A study of 21 merger-and-acquisition "winners" found that, in the long run, 17 of these were not in the best interests of their shareholders.[106] Other research in Canada in 2000 showed that, in the private sector, the success rate for corporate mergers is approximately 30 percent.[107] These findings make it clear that there are serious issues that are faced when undertaking mergers or acquisitions, including the pricing of merger-and-acquisition transactions, the consolidation of acquisitions and mergers, and cultural adjustments, to name a few. The following list identifies a number of related issues that confront the manager of change confronted with mergers or acquisitions.

Change Challenges of Mergers and Acquisitions

- *Cost savings*.[108] Estimated cost savings are typically overvalued initially. This leads to a focus on short-term returns to meet calculated goals.[109]
- *Cultural adjustment*.[110] The merging of different cultures and the adoption of new operating systems and procedures can often lead to conflict. The way in which this is managed can be a major determinant of the success or failure of a merger or acquisition.[111]
- *Due diligence*.[112] The lack of due diligence can lead to the incorrect pricing of the target company and integration of the two organizations. This affects shareholder wealth and is reflected in the market value of the stock.[113]
- *Employee retention*.[114] If people are an organization's best asset, then keeping key employees postmerger is another critical challenge facing merged organizations.[115]
- *Contingency planning*.[116] Many mergers do not begin with a compelling, well-thought-through strategy.[117] The ability to plan and set priorities and goals for the future is needed.[118]
- *Power structure*.[119] If there is a lack of commitment to the merger at all levels of the organization, especially the senior level,[120] then they may use their power to undermine the success of the merger; change managers therefore need to be aware of this potential issue and identify strategies for both detecting and dealing with it.

- *Communication.*[121] Communicating effectively to employees, customers, and shareholders is an important issue when undergoing a merger or acquisition. Failure to recognize the significance of this issue can be detrimental to success.

TABLE 4.10 Types of Mergers and Acquisitions

Source: Adapted from Bower, 2001:94.

Types	Meaning
Excessive capacity	In this situation, the acquiring firm has the opportunity to reduce excessive capacity and consolidate operations in more mature industries.
Neighboring market expansion	This is before industry maturity, when a strategically sound firm acquires operations in neighboring areas. This does not necessarily assume the centralization of operations but rather the increased benefits to the acquired firm through lower overhead costs and increased value for consumers.
New product or market investment	This is when two firms wish to explore the other's advantages in relation to extending product lines or global scope.
Research and development	This is used to increase market position at a more rapid rate. This is generally a preferred method when the product that is being developed has a shorter life cycle.
Leveraging to create new industries	This is when the resources of two firms are pooled and reconstructed to launch a new industry that the firms' boundaries did not cover previously. This involves leveraging the acquired firm's altered capabilities to be effective in a redefined industry.

EXERCISE 4.4

Identifying Frontline Change Experiences

Go back through the business press (*Fortune, The Economist, BusinessWeek*, etc.) and find at least three articles related to either downsizing, implementation of a new technology, or a merger or acquisition.

1. What were the key frontline experiences listed in relation to your chosen change?
2. How do they relate to those listed in this chapter? Did you identify new ones confronting change managers?
3. How would you prioritize these experiences? Do any stand out as "deal breakers"? Why?
4. What new insights into implementing this type of change emerge from this?

- *Speed of the transition.*[122] The pace at which integration is established between merging companies is another critical issue to assess. If the transition process becomes long and drawn out, it can become a crucial issue for the longevity of the merger.[123]

Conclusion

In this chapter we have seen how not all changes are of the same order of magnitude. Indeed, what constitutes magnitude of change depends on who is doing the assessing, how close they are to the change, and how much they are affected by it. It is in this sense that images of managing and change are relevant to this chapter. If change managers are unaware of the power of images and mental frames, then they will be continually surprised by the reactions of others in their organization to the introduction of change. What may appear to them to be a small, relatively inconsequential change may produce reactions from those affected by the change way beyond that anticipated by the change manager. It is the framing of change and peoples' *sense making* of it that come into play here (see Chapter 7 for more on this). Rather than adopting a *directive* change management image, being aware of the different *interpretive* processes at work in the organization will lead the change manager to engage in different change actions at different places in the organization in order to influence these differential understandings. What these actions might be will be addressed in more detail in the chapters that follow.

Finally, in the second part of this chapter, we have explored a variety of frontline experiences of three common, larger forms of organizational change. In reflecting on these frontline experiences despite their different foci, we can see that there are areas in which they overlap. Communicating where the change is headed and why, conducting due diligence about the need for the change, assessing its impact on the cultural imprint of the organization, ensuring that the appropriate people are on side and not disrupting the change, and both trying to plan the timeframe for the change as well as anticipating future problems that might eventuate were common to the three changes we considered. The challenge of the chapters that follow is identifying the change approaches and strategies available to managers of change upon which they can draw in order to address such issues.

TABLE 4.11 Chapter Reflections for the Practicing Change Manager

- How do you approach the paradox of change: in your view, is the risk of failing at change less risky than not changing? Is this a good assumption for all the changes that you undertake? What criteria can you develop to assist you in assessing this balance for future change decisions?
- When introducing new organizational changes, what assumptions do you make about traditional organizational practices: that they must be replaced? Retained? Modified?
- Where's your change focus? Are you open to both incremental and transformational changes? Do you tend to gravitate to one of these most often? Why? Are the changes you make more likely to be reactive or anticipatory? What influences this for you?
- What are your frontline experiences? Reflect upon the critical success factors. What were they? How well did you address them? What would you do differently in the future? What barriers might you face?
- How aware have you been as a change manager to the different sense-making routines that occur in organizations going through change? How might this knowledge assist you in the future?

Supplemental Reading

Feldman, M. S. 2000. Organizational routines as a source of continuous change. *Organization Science* 11(6):611–29.

Fox-Wolfgramm, S. J., Boal, K. B., and Hunt, J. G. 1998. Organizational adaptation to institutional change: A comparative study of first-order change in prospector and defender banks. *Administrative Science Quarterly* 43(1):87–126.

Frohman, A. L. 1997. Igniting organizational change from below: The power of personal initiative. *Organizational Dynamics* 25(3) (Winter):39–53.

Hamel, G. 2001. Revolution vs. evolution: You need both. *Harvard Business Review* 79(5):150–53.

Meyer, A., Brooks, G., and Goes, J. 1990. Environmental jolts and industry revolutions: Organizational responses to discontinuous change. *Strategic Management Journal* 11(5):93–110.

Mirvis, P., Ayas, K., and Roth, G. 2003. *To the desert and back: The story of the most dramatic business transformation on record.* San Francisco: Jossey-Bass.

Newman, K. L. 2000. Organizational transformation during institutional upheaval. *Academy of Management Review* 25(3):602–19.

Reger, R. K., Mullane, J. V., Gustafson, L. T., and DeMarie, S. M. 1994. Creating earthquakes to change organizational mindsets. *Academy of Management Executive* 8(4):31–43.

Romanelli, E., and Tushman, M. L. 1994. Organizational transformation as punctuated equilibrium: An empirical test. *Academy of Management Journal* 37(5):1141–66.

Staudenmayer, N., Tyre, M., and Perlow, L. 2002. Time to change: Temporal shifts as enablers of organizational change. *Organization Science* 13(5) (September–October):583–97.

By 2000 Nestlé was considered the world's biggest food company with 500 factories operating in 80 countries employing 224,000 people with annual sales of $47 billion.[124] A worldwide leader known for manufacturing products as diverse as chocolates and cosmetics, it is now a far cry from the company that was created by the underlying desire to help new mothers who could not breastfeed their newborn infants.[125] With a commitment to long-term outcomes that "will never be sacrificed for short-term performance,"[126] Nestlé has clearly been through many changes over the years.

CHANGING NESTLÉ

As a Swiss national organization, Nestlé only sold through sales agents to countries outside of its home market. By the 1900s it changed its approach to global expansion and began purchasing local subsidiaries in foreign markets.[127] Its launch into the American market was initiated when the First World War increased demand for dairy products. Nestlé took this opportunity to establish its presence in the United States by acquiring several existing factories.[128] During the Second World War, a feeling of isolation in Switzerland led to the transfer of many executive offices offshore to the United States.[129] These moves into offshore markets were part of Nestlé's commitment to changing the company in order to increase efficiency and productivity.

In 1974 Nestlé diversified for the first time outside the food industry in order to promote growth. It became a major shareholder in the cosmetic giant L'Oréal. This diversification has had significant consequences for the organization that continue today with investor concern that Nestlé may have overextended itself with its acquisition of debt-ridden L'Oréal.[130] To offset the instability of the risk involved in investing in developing markets,[131] Nestlé later made a second foray outside the food industry with the purchase of Alcon Laboratories Inc., a U.S. manufacturer of pharmaceutical and ophthalmic products.[132]

The CEO during the 1980s, Helmut Maucher, focused on financial improvement through divestitures and a continuation of strategic acquisitions. This resulted in the sale of many nonstrategic and nonprofitable businesses and more focused acquisitions such as the purchase of Carnation in 1984.[133] The restructuring that continued through this period into the 1990s created a company that was designed to be more flexible.[134]

NESTLÉ TODAY

> You can have slow and steady change, and that is nothing to be ashamed of [CEO Brabeck-Letmathe].[135]

Restructuring is a continual process at Nestlé, with restructuring charges of up to $300 million each year.[136] When he first began as CEO of Nestlé, Brabeck-Letmathe initiated a complete overhaul of the executive board, replacing it with 10 new executives.[137] Nevertheless, Brabeck-Letmathe views his focus as developing the strengths of the organization and holds the view that radical change is ideal for a crisis, but if a company is doing well, then unnecessary change should be questioned:

> Why should we manufacture dramatic change? Just for change's sake? To follow some sort of fad without logical thinking behind it? We are very skeptical of any kind of fad.[138]

The way in which change occurs at Nestlé is focused and conscious. Brabeck-Letmathe admits that

> My actions may sound slow in Silicon Valley, but they are fast for a company with factories in more than 80 countries and products that are sold in every country in the world.[139]

Nestlé relies on the commitment of its managers who have been "steeped in

Nestlé's corporate culture" and who would choose to maintain the longevity of the organization rather than improve its short-term operating profit.[140] In this culture, Nestlé has developed a list of "untouchables"—a number of the company's strengths such as how corporate growth should be handled[141] and the role of technology. In relation to technology, for example, Nestlé does not deny the importance of IT as a tool that can be used within the organization but rejects the implementation of new technology as being a central strategic direction in and of itself.[142] For Brabeck-Letmathe the focus is on how to reinforce and sustain strengths rather than changing them.

> You have to be clear about why the company has been successful in the past, and how you are going to keep those fundamentals from breaking down or disappearing.[143]

Questions

1. Did Nestlé undergo either first-order and/or second-order change according to the case? Answer, listing examples of types of change from the above story.
2. Brabeck-Letmathe emphasizes the need for an incremental approach to change. Do you agree that this is what he has done? Discuss the differences and similarities between his view and your view of what has occurred at Nestlé, both historically and in recent times.
3. What implications for change managers would apply specifically to Nestlé? Outline how the Nestlé management team may have reacted to each implication.
4. Find three examples of lessons from the front line that are evident in the Nestlé case. How could these issues be overcome?

TABLE 4.12 Additional Case Studies

PY and the Dome (A)
Voss, C.; Pullman, M.; & Gerbeau, P. (2000) London Business School
Managing Cultural Change at P&G
Gupta, V. (2004) *ICFAI Knowledge Centre, India*
Renault and Nissan—A Marriage of Reason
Lasserre, P.; Flament, A.-C.; Fujimura, S.; & Nilles, P. (2001) *INSEAD-EAC, Singapore*
Deloitte & Touche: Integrating Arthur Andersen
Seijts, G., & Mark, K. (2004) *Richard Ivey School of Business*

Bibliography

Anonymous. 2000. The great irony of AOL Time Warner. *BusinessWeek*, no. 3665 (January 24):188.

Anonymous. 2001a. Nestle finds mild recipe for success. *Human Resource Management International Digest* 9(6):4–5.

Anonymous. 2001b. Downsizing: Lessons learned. *Association Management* 53(4) (April):26.

Anonymous. 2001c. Peter Brabeck-Letmathe. *BusinessWeek Online*, June 11.

Anonymous. 2002. Mergers: Why most big deals don't pay off. *BusinessWeek*, no. 3803 (October 14):60.

Anonymous. 2003. How Chase Manhattan made BPR fit the bill. *Strategic Direction* 19(2):25–27.

Ashkenas, R., Ulrich, D., Jick, T., and Kerr, S. 1995. *The boundaryless organization: Breaking the chains of organizational structure.* San Francisco: Jossey-Bass.

Bate, P. 1994. *Strategies for cultural change*. Oxford: Butterworth-Heinemann.

Bower, J. 2001. Not all M&As are alike—and that matters. *Harvard Business Review* 7(3):93–101.

Burgelman, R. A. 1994. Fading memories: A process theory of strategic business exit in dynamic environments. *Administrative Science Quarterly* 39(1):44–56.

Cascio, W. F. 1993. Downsizing: What do we know? What have we learned? *Academy of Management Executive* 7(1):95–104.

Cascio, W. F. 2002. Strategies for responsible restructuring. *Academy of Management Executive* 16(3):80–91.

Chandler, A. 1987. Managerial hierarchies. In *Organization theory: Selected readings*, 3rd ed., ed. D. S. Pugh, 95–123. London: Penguin.

Creswell, J. 2001. When a merger fails: Lessons from Sprint. *Fortune* 143(9) (April 30):87.

DeWitt, R. 1998. Form, industry, and strategy influences on choice of downsizing approach. *Strategic Management Journal* 19(1):59–79.

Donaldson, L., and Hilmer, F. G. 1998. Management redeemed: The case against fads that harm management. *Organizational Dynamics* 26(4) (Spring):7–20. In *In defence of organization theory*, ed. L. Donaldson. Cambridge: CUP.

Echikson, W. 2001. Online extra: Nestlé: Getting fat and happy. *BusinessWeek Online*, June 11.

Ettinger, W. H. 2001. Six sigma: Adapting GE's lessons to health care. *Trustee* 54(8) (September):10–14.

Feld, C., and Stoddard, D. 2004. Getting IT right. *Harvard Business Review* 82(2):72–79.

Feldman, M. S. 2000. Organizational routines as a source of continuous change. *Organization Science* 11(6):611–29.

Flamholtz, E. G., and Randle, Y. 1998. *Changing the game: Organizational transformations of the first, second, and third kinds*. New York: Oxford University Press.

Florian, E. 2002. Layoff count. *Fortune* 145(1) (January 7):24.

Fox-Wolfgramm, S. J., Boal, K. B., and Hunt, J. G. 1998. Organizational adaptation to institutional change: A comparative study of first-order change in prospector and defender banks. *Administrative Science Quarterly* 43(1):87–126.

Frohman, A. L. 1997. Igniting organizational change from below: The power of personal initiative. *Organizational Dynamics* 25(3) (Winter):39–53.

Glanville, Y., and Belton, E. 1998. M&As are transforming the world. *Ivey Business Quarterly* 63(1) (Autumn):34–41.

Graetz, F., Rimmer, M., Lawrence, A., and Smith, A. 2002. *Managing organizational change.* Queensland, Australia: John Wiley & Sons.

Gumbel, P. 2003. Nestlé's Quick. *Time Canada* 161(5) (February 3):28.

Gurin, L. 1998. Bouncing back from downsizing. *Association for Quality and Participation*, September–October:24–29.

Hamel, G. 2001. Revolution vs. evolution: You need both. *Harvard Business Review* 79(5):150–53.

Harris, R. 2003. What is customer relationship management (CRM) system? *Darwin Magazine*, December.

Hilmer, F. G., and Donaldson, L. 1996. *Management redeemed: Debunking the fads that undermine our corporations*. New York: Free Press.

Jordan, M., and Stuart, N. 2000. Lessons learned. *CMA Management* 74(3) (April):35.

Kaye, B., and Greist, M. 2003. The New Survivors. *Executive Excellence* 20(10):16.

Kilcourse, T. 1995. Keep the small change. *Leadership & Organization Development Journal* 16(8):40–42.

Koch, C. 2004. The ABCs of ERP. *CIO Enterprise Resource Planning Research Center*, http://www.cio.com/research/erp.

Kotter, J. P. 1996. *Leading change*. Boston: Harvard Business School Press.

Large, M. 1996. The chaotic passages of developing companies: Tools for organizational transitions. *Leadership & Organization Development Journal* 17(7):44–47.

Lavelle, L. 2002. Swing that ax with care. *BusinessWeek*, no. 3769 (February 11):78.

Lynch, J. G., and Lind, B. 2002. Escaping merger and acquisition madness. *Strategy & Leadership* 30(2):5–12.

Masy, J. 2003. What have we learned? *E-Learning Age*, October:12–13.

McKinley, W., Sanchez, C. M., and Schick, A. G. 1995. Organizational downsizing: Constraining, cloning, learning. *Academy of Management Executive* 9(3):32–44.

Meyer, A., Brooks, G., and Goes, J. 1990. Environmental jolts and industry revolutions: Organizational responses to discontinuous change. *Strategic Management Journal* 11(5):93–110.

Morris, B., and Neering, P. 2003. When bad things happen to good companies. *Fortune* 148(12) (December 8):78.

Nadler, D. A., and Shaw, R. B. 1995. Change leadership: Core competency for the twenty-first century. In *Discontinuous change: Leading organizational transformation*, ed. D. A. Nadler, R. B. Shaw, A. E. Walton, and Associates, 3–14. San Francisco: Jossey-Bass.

Nadler, D. A., and Tushman, M. L. 1995. Types of organizational change: From incremental improvement to discontinuous transformation. In *Discontinuous change: Leading organizational transformation*, ed. D. A. Nadler, R. B. Shaw, A. E. Walton, and Associates, 15–34. San Francisco: Jossey-Bass.

Nestlé history. Nestlé Web site, http://www.nestle.com/html/about/history1.asp.

New York Capital Corporation. http://www.nycapital.com/merg.html.

Newman, K. L. 2000. Organizational transformation during institutional upheaval. *Academy of Management Review* 25(3):602–19.

Overby, S. 2001. Quick change artists. *CIO* 14(21) (August 15):90.

Palmer, I., and Dunford, R. 1997. Organising for hyper-competition. *New Zealand Strategic Management* 2(4) (Summer):38–45.

Palmer, I., Kabanoff, B., and Dunford, R. 1997. Managerial accounts of downsizing. *Journal of Organizational Behavior* 18:623–39.

Parks, C. M. 2002. Instill lean thinking. *Industrial Management* 44(5) (September–October):15–18.

Paul, L. G. 2001. Survival tips from the pioneers. *CIO* 14(11) (March 15):114.

Praxair news release. 2001. Praxair announces restructuring actions, third quarter charge. September 28. http://www.praxair.com/praxair.nsf/AllContent/831928146AD64F4685256AD50044DA90?OpenDocument.

Reger, R. K., Mullane, J. V., Gustafson, L. T., and DeMarie, S. M. 1994. Creating earthquakes to change organizational mindsets. *Academy of Management Executive* 8(4):31–43.

Rigby, D. 2002. Look before you lay off. *Harvard Business Review* 80(4):20–21.

Romanelli, E., and Tushman, M. L. 1994. Organizational transformation as punctuated equilibrium: An empirical test. *Academy of Management Journal* 37(5):1141–66.

Ross, J. W., and Weill, P. 2002. Six decisions your IT people shouldn't make. *Harvard Business Review* 80(11):84–91.

Staudenmayer, N., Tyre, M., and Perlow, L. 2002. Time to change: Temporal shifts as enablers of organizational change. *Organization Science* 13(5) (September–October):583–97.

Struckman, C. K., and Yammarinon, F. J. 2003. Managing through multiple change activities: A solution to the enigma of the 21st century. *Organizational Dynamics* 32(3):234–46.

Sullivan, M., Gustke, C., and Hutheesing, N. 2002. Case studies: Digital do-overs. *Forbes* 170(7) (October 7):2.

Taylor, A., III. 2002. Can J&J keep the magic going? *Fortune* 145(11) (May 27):117–20.

Thottam, J. 2003. Where the good jobs are going. *Time* 162(5) (August 4):36.

Voglestein, F., and Florian, E. 2001. Can Schwab get its mojo back? *Fortune* 144(5) (September 17):93–96.

Wallington, P. 2000. Technical difficulties. *CIO* 14(5) (December 1):66.

Wan, W. P. 2002. Interview: United Parcel Service's director of electronic commerce, Alan Amling, on the opportunities and challenges of global electronic commerce. *Thunderbird International Business Review* 44(4):445–54.

Wetlaufer, S. 2001. The business case against revolution. *Harvard Business Review* 79(2):113–19.

Whittington, R., Pettigrew, A., Peck, S., Fenton, E., and Conyon, M. 1999. Change and complementarities in the new competitive landscape: A European panel study, 1992–1996. *Organization Science* 10(5) (September–October):583–600.

Wind, J. W., and Main, J. 1999. *Driving change: How the best companies are preparing for the 21st century*. London: Kogan Page.

Notes

1. Kotter, 1996:3, 18.
2. Meyer, Brooks, and Goes, 1990, cited in Armenakis and Bedeian, 1999.
3. E.g., Kilcourse, 1995:40.
4. See Frohman, 1997:39; Fox-Wolfgramm et al., 1998:87–88.
5. Newman, 2000:604.
6. Bate, 1994:33.
7. Newman, 2000:604.
8. Bate, 1994:33.
9. Bate, 1994:33–34.
10. Nadler and Tushman, 1995:20.
11. Nadler and Tushman, 1995:15.
12. Nadler and Tushman, 1995:26.
13. Nadler and Tushman, 1995:16.
14. Nadler and Tushman, 1995:28.
15. Fox-Wolfgramm et al., 1998:87–88.
16. Frohman, 1997:39.
17. Frohman, 1997:52.
18. Frohman, 1997:49.
19. Frohman, 1997:50.
20. Feldman, 2000.

21. Feldman, 2000:613.
22. Burgelman, 1994.
23. Feldman, 2000.
24. Feldman, 2000:612.
25. Reger et al., 1994:32.
26. Palmer and Dunford, 1997.
27. Whittington et al., 1999.
28. Ashkenas et al., 1995.
29. Hilmer and Donaldson, 1996; see also Donaldson, 1985.
30. Palmer and Dunford, 1997.
31. Flamholtz and Randle, 1998:8–9.
32. Flamholtz and Randle, 1998:11.
33. Flamholtz and Randle, 1998:13.
34. Flamholtz and Randle, 1998:78–81.
35. Flamholtz and Randle, 1998:91–97.
36. Flamholtz and Randle, 1998:13.
37. Reger et al., 1994:32.
38. Reger et al., 1994:33.
39. Reger et al., 1994:36.
40. Reger et al., 1994:37.
41. Reger et al., 1994:37.
42. Romanelli and Tushman, 1994.
43. Romanelli and Tushman, 1994:1141.
44. Romanelli and Tushman, 1994:1159.
45. Nadler and Tushman, 1995:20.
46. See Struckman and Yammarino, 2003:244–45.
47. Large, 1996.
48. Staudenmayer et al., 2002:584.
49. Staudenmayer et al., 2002:584.
50. Hamel, 2001:150.
51. Hamel, 2001:152.
52. Florian, 2002.
53. Thottam, 2003.
54. Florian, 2002.
55. Cascio, 2002:80.
56. Palmer et al., 1997:629.
57. Lavelle, 2002.
58. Praxair news release, 2001.
59. Lavelle, 2002.
60. Voglestein and Florian, 2001.
61. Voglestein and Florian, 2001.
62. Cascio, 2002.

63. Morris and Neering, 2003.
64. Cascio, 1993:97–98.
65. McKinley et al., 1995:33.
66. Rigby, 2002:21.
67. McKinley et al., 1995:33.
68. McKinley et al., 1995:34.
69. Cascio, 2002:85.
70. Cascio, 2002:85.
71. Kaye and Greist, 2003.
72. Gurin, 1998:24.
73. Anonymous, 2001b.
74. Cascio, 2002:85.
75. Parks, 2002:15.
76. Cascio, 2002:85.
77. See Graaetz et al., 2002:100–102, for an overview of sociotechnical systems theory.
78. Wan, 2002.
79. Anonymous, 2003.
80. Adapted from Sullivan, Gustke, and Hutheesing, 2002.
81. Adapted from Ross and Weill, 2002.
82. Adapted from Ross and Weill, 2002.
83. Feld and Stoddard, 2004:73.
84. Masy, 2003:12.
85. Feld and Stoddard, 2004:75.
86. Feld and Stoddard, 2004:73.
87. Feld and Stoddard, 2004:73.
88. Wallington, 2000.
89. Feld and Stoddard, 2004:73.
90. Feld and Stoddard, 2004:73.
91. Feld and Stoddard, 2004:73.
92. Overby, 2001.
93. Wallington, 2000.
94. Wallington, 2000.
95. Overby, 2001.
96. Wallington, 2000.
97. Overby, 2001.
98. Overby, 2001.
99. Chandler, 1987.
100. Lynch and Lind, 2002:5.
101. Anonymous, 2002.
102. New York Capital Corporation, http://www.nycapital.com/merg.html
103. Taylor, 2002.
104. Anonymous, 2002.

105. Anonymous, 2000.
106. Anonymous, 2002.
107. Jordan and Stuart, 2000.
108. Anonymous, 2002.
109. Anonymous, 2002.
110. Glanville and Belton, 1998:37.
111. Lynch and Lind, 2002:6.
112. Lynch and Lind, 2002:6.
113. Anonymous, 2002.
114. Creswell, 2001.
115. Jordan and Stuart, 2000.
116. Creswell, 2001.
117. Lynch and Lind, 2002:6.
118. Creswell, 2001.
119. Glanville and Belton, 1998:37.
120. Jordan and Stuart, 2000.
121. Jordan and Stuart, 2000.
122. Jordan and Stuart, 2000.
123. Anonymous, 2002.
124. Echikson, 2001. This case was prepared by El Feletto.
125. Nestlé history, http://www.Nestlé.com
126. Nestlé history, http://www.Nestlé.com
127. Nestlé history, http://www.Nestlé.com
128. Nestlé history, http://www.Nestlé.com
129. Nestlé history, http://www.Nestlé.com
130. Nestlé history, http://www.Nestlé.com; Gumbel, 2003.
131. Nestlé history, http://www.Nestlé.com
132. Nestlé history, http://www.Nestlé.com
133. Nestlé history, http://www.Nestlé.com
134. Wetlaufer, 2001.
135. Wetlaufer, 2001.
136. Wetlaufer, 2001.
137. Wetlaufer, 2001.
138. Wetlaufer, 2001.
139. Anonymous, 2001c.
140. Wetlaufer, 2001.
141. Anonymous, 2001a.
142. Wetlaufer, 2001.
143. Wetlaufer, 2001.

Diagnosis for Change

Learning objectives

On completion of this chapter you should be able to

- Understand the role of diagnostic models.
- Apply a range of diagnostic instruments relevant to various aspects of the process of managing.
- Form a view on which instruments you find most attractive/helpful.

This chapter introduces a range of diagnostic instruments that can be applied to the management of change. Some are designed to highlight a particular aspect of the change process (e.g., the readiness of an organization for change), some deal with one aspect of an organization (e.g., its strategy or its structure), while others—"diagnostic models"—refer to the operation of the organization as a whole.

How a diagnostic device is used also relates to what sort of manager of change you are (in terms of the change manager images discussed in Chapter 2). One option consistent with the change manager as *director* is to use diagnostic tools to build up your own knowledge base and confidence about what needs to change by using models that specify relationships among variables and pinpoint where change is needed when things are not going well. This chapter provides a number of such models that depict the connections between organizational variables (through the use of boxes, lines, and arrows, etc). These models may be seen to engender a level of confidence about the desired outputs that will be produced following change interventions that focus on the identified variables and their interrelationships (see, e.g., Nadler and Tushman's *congruence model*).

The change manager as *navigator* also will find the diagnostic tools attractive; models are ways of "mapping" the environment they describe. The change manager as *caretaker* will be less convinced of the capacity of the diagnostic tools to support radical change, but several of the tools (see, e.g., *PESTEL* and *scenario analysis*) provide insights into the trends in the external environment that they will have to take into account.

The change manager as *coach* will focus on the diagnostic tools that highlight the goals being sought and the competencies needed to attain them (see, e.g., Table 5.5, "Testing the Quality of Your Strategy"), while the change manager as *interpreter* will be attracted to the diagnostic tools that emphasize images, framing, and cognitive maps (see, e.g., Table 5.2, "Diagnosis by Image"). However, the *nurturer* with an interest in emergent strategy may remain unconvinced as to the value of such diagnostic tools.

The issue of who does the diagnosing is also of relevance in the management of change. There are a range of views as to who is most appropriate. This will become clearer after Chapters 7 and 8, which deal with different "schools of thought" on how change should be managed. For example, in "change management" (see Chapter 8), the task of diagnosis is part of senior management and/or consultants employed as subject experts and advisers. In "organizational development" (see Chapter 7), consultants use diagnostic tools as part of their focus on helping the client by managing process (more than content). Organizational development and related approaches stress the importance of those who are to be affected by the change being involved in the diagnosis. The rationale is usually that such involvement produces greater commitment to the change process and, as a result, enhances prospects of success. Those organizational development consultants who subscribe to a future search approach (see Chapter 7) take a hard line on this, explicitly rejecting pressure to be thrust into the role of diagnostician.[1]

Directly connected to the "who diagnoses" is what Harrison calls "the political implications of diagnosis."[2] Diagnosis may be seen as "the thin edge of the wedge" for those fearing a particular change. No matter how nonaligned and objective the wielder of the diagnostic tools tries to be, it is almost impossible to avoid the situation where some party will see the "diagnostician" as firmly implicated in determining, or at least legitimating, a course of action that is not their preferred option.

MODELS: WHY BOTHER?

This discussion of models is based on some fundamental propositions:

- As managers—indeed as members of organizations in any capacity—we carry around in our heads our own views as to "how things work," "what causes what," and so forth, within our organizations. In this sense, diagnosis exists whether or not explicit diagnostic models are used.
- Although these views may not be explicitly stated, as implicit models they still have a powerful capacity to guide how we think about situations that we face in our organizations, how we talk about those situations, and what we deem to be appropriate courses of action.
- The apparent option of not using a model is not a real option; the choice is whether we use one that is explicit (such as those discussed in this section) or one that is implicit.
- While implicit models may provide valuable insights based on accumulated experience, they do have limitations. First, they are likely to be based on the limited experience of one or a few individuals; thus, their generalizability may be uncertain. Second, because they are implicit, it is difficult for other individuals to be aware of the framework/assumptions within which decisions are being made.

Burke identifies five ways in which organizational models can be useful:[3]

1. By making the complexity of a situation where thousands of different things are "going on" more manageable by reducing that situation to a manageable number of categories.
2. By helping identify which aspects of an organization's activities or properties are those most needing attention.

3. By highlighting the interconnectedness of various organizational properties (e.g., strategy and structure).
4. By providing a common "language" with which to discuss organizational characteristics.
5. By providing a guide to the sequence of actions to take in a change situation. Whether or not a specific model can do this depends on whether or not it includes differential weighting of its various component factors, as does, for example, the Burke-Litwin model.[4]

A range of models is available. Several are described in this chapter. No one model is "the truth"; each is simply a way of "getting a handle on" the complex reality that is an organization. The most important thing is to use (or even develop) a model that works for the specific situation that an organization confronts; that is, one that assists thought, discussion, and action in regard to the issue(s) affecting the organization. In some situations, this will involve identifying the aspect of an organization that is most in need of remedial action. In others, the model will assist in highlighting the systemic (flow-on) effect of a change in one part of the organization's operations.

MODELING ORGANIZATIONS

In this section, we provide a number of diagnostic models that can be applied to the functioning of organizations. These models commonly seek to capture the essential features of the determinants of organizational performance.

The Six-Box Organizational Model

Marvin Weisbord proposed one of the earliest diagnostic models, one that he describes as the result of "my efforts to combine bits of data, theories, research, and hunches into a working tool that anyone can use."[5] His model is based on six variables (see Figure 5.1):

1. Purposes: What business are we in?
2. Structure: How do we divide up the work?
3. Rewards: Do all tasks have incentives?
4. Helpful mechanisms: Have we adequate coordinating technologies?
5. Relationships: How do we manage conflict among people? With technologies?
6. Leadership: Does someone keep the boxes in balance?

He presents his visual representation of the model as akin to a radar screen: "Just as air controllers use radar to chart the course of aircraft—height, speed, distance apart and weather—those seeking to improve an organization must observe relationships among the boxes and not focus on any particular blip."[6] That is, while one variable might be identified as the site requiring the greatest attention, the systemic effect of any change must be noted.

The 7-S Framework

The 7-S Framework was developed by the McKinsey & Company consultants Robert Waterman Jr., Tom Peters, and Julien Phillips.[7] It is based on the propositions that (1) organizational effectiveness comes from the interaction of multiple factors and

FIGURE 5.1 The Six-Box Organizational Model

Source: Weisbord, 1976:431. Copyright © 1976 by Marvin R. Weisbord. Used by permission of the author.

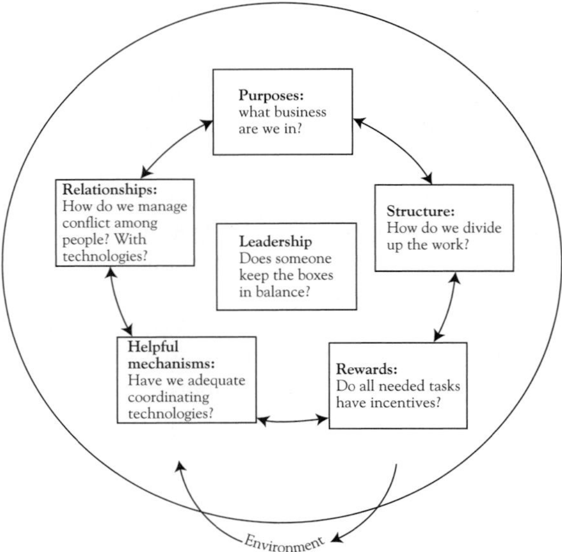

(2) successful change requires attention to the interconnectedness of the variables. They characterize the factors into seven categories: structure, strategy, systems, style, staff, skills, and superordinate goals (see Figure 5.2).

Structure refers to the formal organizational design. *Strategy* refers to "the company's chosen route to competitive success."[8] *Systems* are the various procedures in areas such as IT whereby an organization operates on a day-to-day basis. *Style* is a reference to patterns in the actions of managers and others in the organization; that is, how they actually behave (consultative? decisive?) when faced with the need to act. *Staff* refers to the processes for development of the human resources of the organization. *Skills* are described as the "crucial attributes"—the "dominating capabilities"—in areas such as customer service, quality control, and innovation that differentiate it from its competitors.[9] *Superordinate goals* refer to the organization's "vision" (see Chapter 9).

Waterman et al. stress that the visual representation of the model is intended to emphasize the interconnectedness of the variables. This aspect is central to their intention, which is to emphasize that those factors "that have been considered soft, informal, or beneath the purview of top management interest [e.g., style] . . . can be at least as important as strategy and structure in orchestrating major change."[10]

The Star Model

Jay Galbraith argues that an organization is at its most effective when what he labels "the five major components of organization design" are in alignment.[11] In this model, the five components are strategy, structure, processes and lateral capability, reward systems, and people practices (see Figure 5.3).

A preeminent role is given to *strategy*—"the cornerstone"—on the grounds that "if the strategy is not clear, . . . there are no criteria on which to base other design

FIGURE 5.2 **The 7-S Framework**

Source: Waterman et al., 1980:18.

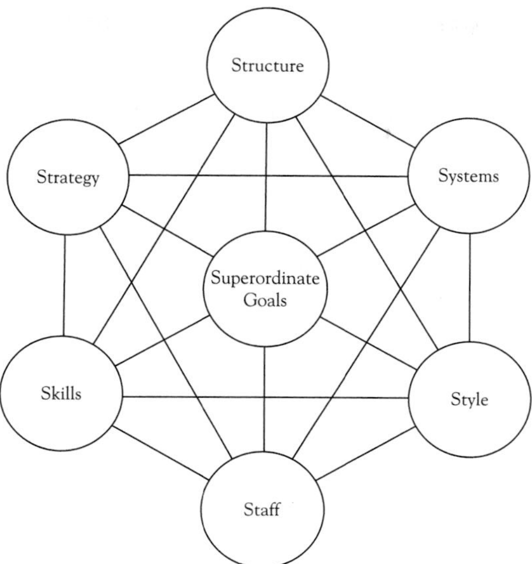

FIGURE 5.3 **The Star Model**

Source: Galbraith et al., 2002:2. Copyright © 2002. AMACON. Reproduced by permission through Copyright Clearance Center.

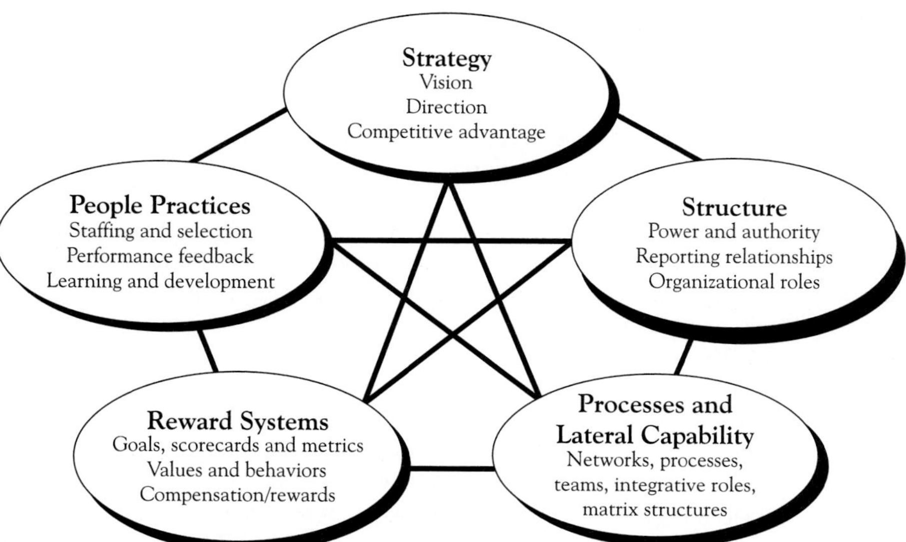

FIGURE 5.4 The Star Model: Effects of Misalignment

Source: Galbraith et al., 2002:5. Copyright © 2002 AMACON. Reproduced by permission through Copyright Clearance Center.

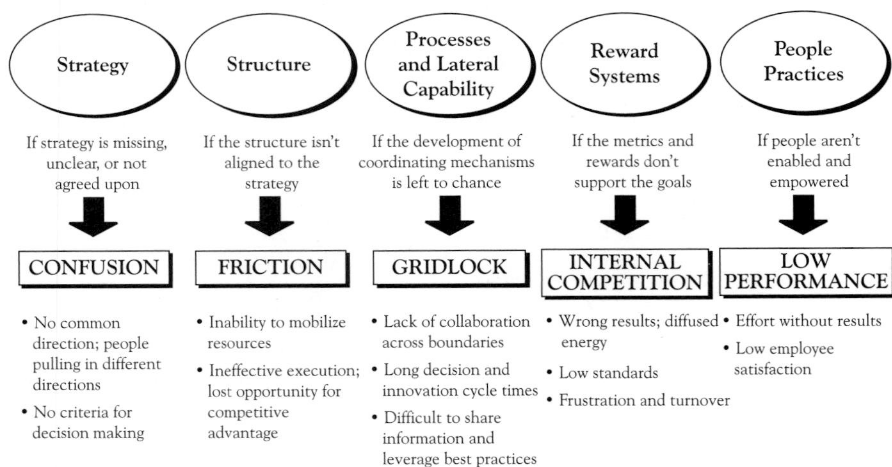

decisions."[12] *Structure* is defined as the formal authority relationships and grouping of activities as represented on an organization chart; *processes and lateral capability* refer to the processes, either formal or informal, that coordinate activities throughout the organization. *Reward systems* seek to align individual actions to organizational objectives, while *people practices* are the combined human resource practices (e.g., selection, development, performance management) of the organization. Misalignment of any of these five factors is considered to produce suboptimal performance (see Figure 5.4).

The Congruence Model

David Nadler and Michael Tushman have developed an open systems model of organizations based on the proposition that the effectiveness of an organization is determined by the consistency ("congruence") between the various elements that comprise the organization (see Figure 5.5).[13]

This model sees organizations as comprising four components: *task* (the specific work activities that have to be carried out), *individuals* (the knowledge, skills, needs, expectations) of the people in the organization, *formal organizational arrangements* (structure, processes, methods), and *informal organization* (implicit, unstated values, beliefs, and behaviors).

The model is based on the conceptualization of the organization as a transformation process. At the "front end" of the process is the *context* comprising the environment, resources, and history. *Environment* refers to factors outside the organization such as the economic, social, and technological conditions. *Resources* are the assets, tangible and intangible, internal to the organization. *History* refers to the organization's own history, which leaves an imprint on how the organization currently operates. Within this context, *strategy* is formulated. The organization then becomes the means for the attainment of strategy. The output of the transformation process is primarily the performance of the *organization*, but this is mediated via the performance of both *groups* and *individuals*.

Based on their experience of using the congruence model in organizational problem solving, Nadler and Tushman have identified a process for this activity (see Table 5.1).

FIGURE 5.5 Nadler and Tushman's Congruence Model

Source: Nadler and Tushman, 1988, Figure 2-6. Adapted by permission of Pearson Education, Inc., Upper Saddle River, NJ.

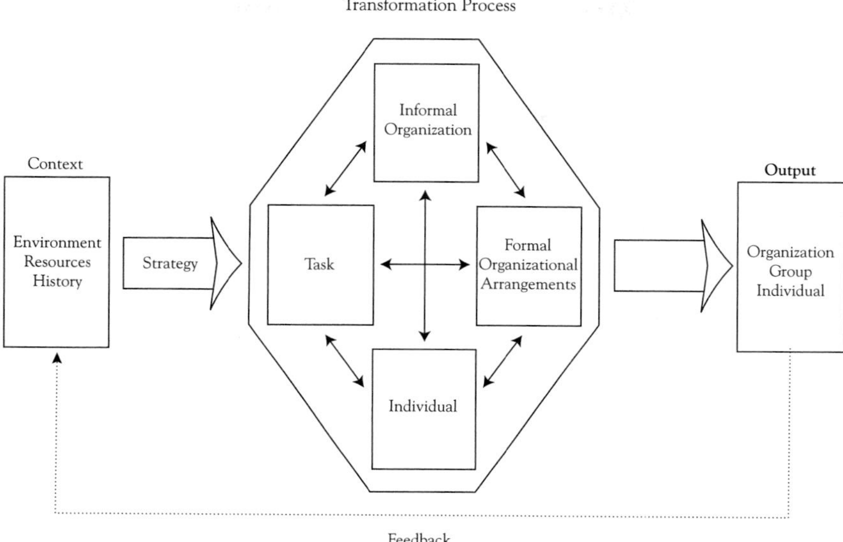

TABLE 5.1 Applying the Congruence Model to Organizational Problem Analysis

Source: Nadler and Tushman, 1988, Figure 2-7. Adapted by permission of Pearson Education, Inc., Upper Saddle River, NJ.

Step	Explanation
1. Identify symptoms	List the phenomena that suggest that there might be a problem.
2. Specify input	Identify key elements of the organization's environment, resources, history, and strategy.
3. Identify output	Collect information on both the intended organizational output and the output that is actually occurring.
4. Identify problems	Identify the gap between the intended and actual outputs, and the cost of this gap in terms of organizational performance.
5. Describe the organizational components	Collect data on the four organizational components, but in doing so recognize that not all problems have internal causes; the problem may be a strategy that is no longer appropriate.
6. Assess congruence	Evaluate congruence between the various components of the organization (as specified in the model).
7. Generate hypotheses	Link the congruence analysis to the problem identification to identify key factors needing attention.
8. Identify action steps	Indicate what actions might remove or reduce the problem.

FIGURE 5.6 The Burke-Litwin Model

Source: Burke, 2002, Figure 9-2. Copyright © 2002. Sage Publications, Inc. Reproduced with permission.

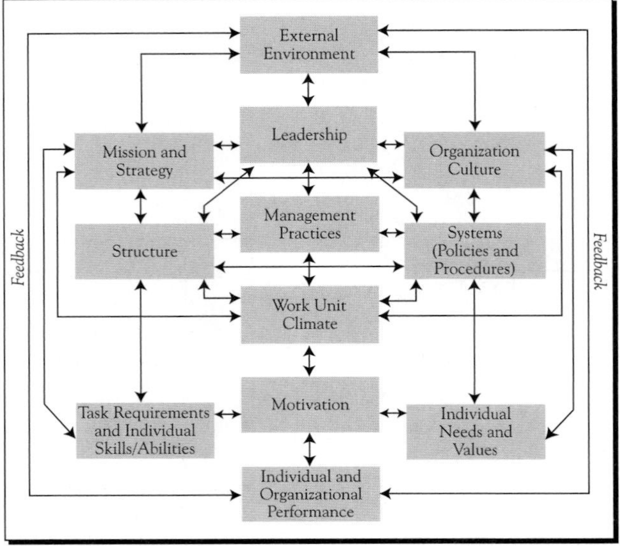

The Burke-Litwin Model

The main contribution of the 12-factor model developed by Warner Burke and George Litwin is that it differentiates between those elements of the model that are seen as likely to be the source of major ("transformational") change and those that are more likely to be the source of change that is experienced as incremental ("transactional"). The four transformational factors are *external environment*, *mission and strategy*, *leadership*, and *organizational culture*. These are intentionally located at the top of the diagram that represents the model (see Figure 5.6).

The fundamental premise of the model is that planned change should flow from the top of the diagram (environment) to the bottom (performance).[14] However, as indicated by the arrows, the feedback loops go in both directions, indicating that internal organizational factors can impact the environment and not just be on the receiving end of a one-way environmental determinism.

The Four-Frame Model

Lee Bolman and Terry Deal argue that managers benefit from being able to analyze organizations from the perspective of four different "frames" or "lenses," each of which provides a different "angle" on how organizations operate.[15] Without the capacity to use multiple frames, managers may become locked into their one favored way of seeing the world. Bolman and Deal comment:

> Organizations are filled with people who have their own interpretations of what is and what should be happening. Each version contains a glimmer of truth, but each is a product of the prejudices and blind spots of its maker.[16]

The four frames discussed by Bolman and Deal are the structural frame, the human resource frame, the political frame, and the symbolic frame. The *structural frame* presents organizations as akin to machines that are designed to efficiently turn inputs into outputs. From this perspective, the focus is on getting the correct formal design as one would find on an organization chart and rules and procedures manuals. The mantra for action is, "If there's a problem, restructure."

The *human resource frame* directs attention to the relationship between the organization and the people that comprise it. It is based on the proposition that a good fit between the needs of the organization and what people want out of work benefits both parties, and the reverse (where fit is lacking, both suffer).

The *political frame* suggests that we see organizations as sites where participants interact in pursuit of a range of objectives, some in common, some that differ; some that complement, some that conflict. One of the most important aspects of the political frame is that it does not present "political" as necessarily equating to "bad" or "underhand." Even where superordinate goals, such as the organization's mission, are shared, the means whereby that mission is to be operationalized may be fiercely contested between various individuals, each of whom may sincerely believe that his or her action is in the best interests of the organization.

The *symbolic frame* proposes that the essence of an organization may lie not in its formal structure and processes but in its culture—the realm of symbols, beliefs, values, rituals, and meanings. In Bolman and Deal's terms, "what is most important is not what happens but what it means."[17]

Diagnosis by Image

In many change situations, the initial diagnosis is enhanced by getting the perspective of various staff of the organization as to the current (as-is) situation. However, even where people are not intentionally "holding back," they will often find it difficult to encapsulate, in words, their sense of the current situation.

One technique that can often "cut through" this blockage—and that builds on the body of work of Gareth Morgan on the application of the notion of "images" to organizational analysis[18]—is to ask people to describe their organization and how it operates by providing an image in the form of either a simile ("my organization is like a well-oiled machine") or a metaphor ("my organization is a dinosaur") (see Table 5.2).

TABLE 5.2 Diagnosis by Image

Source: Adapted from Palmer and Dunford, 1996.

One way of describing an organization and how it operates is by using a metaphor or simile such as "my organization is like a well-oiled machine" (it runs very smoothly) or "my organization is a dinosaur" (it is big, slow-moving, unresponsive to change, and probably headed for extinction).

1. In relation to your organization (or an organization with which you are familiar), what metaphor or simile would you use to describe it?
   My organization is/is like...

2. What is it about your organization that you are trying to convey through this image?
   ....
   ....

Our experience using this approach shows that most people, when requested, can very quickly and very succinctly produce such an image. The images then become the focal point for discussion. Indeed, they generate discussion because a natural follow-on from the production of an image is that the producer is asked to "flesh out" the image; that is, to describe in more detail the situation that the image was intended to convey.

COMPONENT ANALYSIS

The approaches to diagnosis described in the previous section dealt with the organization as a whole in its relationship with the context/environment in which it operates. The approaches to diagnosis in this section deal with specific components within these models. Particular attention is given to the strategic context on the basis that this is a major—although, as noted in Chapter 3, by no means exclusive—driver of change.

The PESTEL Framework[19]

PESTEL characterizes the organizational environment in terms of six factors: political (e.g., the threat of terrorism), economic (e.g., unemployment levels), social (e.g., demographic changes), technological (e.g., development of new/substitute products), environmental (e.g., antipollution policies), and legal (e.g., antitrust law). Although this is a very broad-ranging framework, it can be a useful starting point for an organization that has not given much attention to the broad trends that might impact on the future operation of the business. To be able to assist in this role, it is important that the PESTEL framework incorporate trends—with the extrapolation into the future that this implies—rather than rigidly documenting the status quo. Applied in this way, it can form the basis for coarse-grained identification of necessary or desirable change initiatives.

Scenario Analysis

The pilots for major airlines routinely spend time in flight simulators as part of their training. One of the advantages of such simulators is that the pilots can be exposed to a range of different situations from the routine to the unexpected. While the pilots must become completely familiar with the former, as they constitute the everyday reality with which they will have to deal, the simulations extend to events that in all probability they will not encounter even once throughout their career. The rationale for exposure to the latter is clear enough: Although they are highly unlikely to be encountered, the consequences should they occur could be disastrous (literally) unless handled correctly and speedily.

Scenario analysis offers the same opportunity in the context of strategic change in organizations.[20] It received attention in the business world primarily through its extensive use by Royal Dutch Shell, who used it as a tool for addressing the possible futures that they would face as a result of uncertainties over oil supplies. A scenario is a description of some future state based on a set of assumptions about what is likely to happen in regard to a number of key factors believed to be key drivers of that future state. Scenarios may be constructed through the application of a specific methodology (see Table 5.3 and Exercise 5.1).[21]

TABLE 5.3 Scenario Methodology

1. "Brainstorm" the range of environmental factors with the potential to impact on the performance of your organization (in the spirit of brainstorming, accept all suggestions at this point; that is, suspend judgment as to the significance of any suggested factor).
2. Get individual participants to identify which factors from this list they believe to be the "key drivers" of performance over a specified time period (e.g., five years).
3. Aggregating these individual responses, identify the five most commonly cited key drivers (e.g., exchange rates, technological innovation, entry by new competitors, mergers, competition for key staff).
4. Using these key drivers as the core elements, construct multiple scenarios. One useful approach is to construct three scenarios: most likely, optimistic, and pessimistic. The most likely scenario is constructed on the basis of the "best guess" as to what will happen to each of the five key drivers over the specified timeframe. (Note: "Best guess" in no way implies a casual treatment of the exercise; the best guess can be based on highly sophisticated market intelligence). Optimistic and pessimistic scenarios focus attention on how the organization might respond should the situation develop other than as expected. The construction of the scenarios requires considerable skill and it is not uncommon for organizations to employ consultants who are experienced scenario writers. Scenarios need to be compelling and plausible (even if unlikely to eventuate) narratives. This is needed in order for them to work well as the basis of discussion as to what steps the organization should take in expectation of the situation developing as per one of the scenarios (see Exercise 5.1).

For a different and more detailed description of the scenario planning process see Schoemaker.[a]

[a]Schoemaker, 1993. See especially Table 2.

EXERCISE 5.1

Scenario Construction

In regard to an organization with which you are familiar:

1. What would your choice be of the five "key drivers" (see Table 5.3)?
2. Using these five factors as the building blocks of your scenarios, construct, in 100 words or less, the outline of a realistic, an optimistic, and a pessimistic scenario.

Gap Analysis

Gap analysis is a very basic tool for reviewing an organization's position. It is based on three questions:[22]

1. Where are we now?
2. Where do we want to get to?
3. How can we get there?

Although basic, these questions can be useful on a number of levels. First, their very generality means that most managers should be able to venture an opinion of some sort—at least in regard to the first two questions—which is likely to serve as a good basis for subsequent discussion.

Second, regardless of whether the responses indicate low or high degree of consensus, this can be put to good use. High consensus can generate two different courses of action. One option is to act immediately to close the gap, either by revising the objective or by taking the necessary action to meet the set objective. A second option is to suspend taking action until a direct challenge to the high consensus view can be arranged. The rationale for the second option is that—as long as immediate action to close the gap is not required—such a challenge can lead to either reinforcement of the wisdom of the preferred position or a timely revision of certain "taken-for-granted" positions.

Low consensus provides the perfect platform for further attention to the objectives and strategies of the organization on the grounds that commitment to specific courses of action should be based on a reasonably high degree of consensus on the answers to at least the first two questions. Agreement on the answer to the third question may be desirable, but it is not necessary as long as there is commitment to support the formal decision on the course of action to be taken.

The Elements of Strategy

Strategy is often conceived of as being at the heart of change in that it is about the most basic of issues with which an organization has to deal: what it is seeking to achieve and how it intends to do so. Strategy and change intersect because both strategies may change ("change of strategy") and change may be deemed necessary in order to realize a set strategy ("change for strategy").

TABLE 5.4 The Elements of Strategy

Source: Hambrick and Fredrickson, 2001, Figure 2. Copyright © 2001 Academy of Management Executive. Reproduced with permission of Academy of Management Executive through Copyright Clearance Center.

1. **Arenas: What business will we be in?**
   - Which product categories?
   - Which market segments?
   - Which geographic areas?
   - Which core technologies?
   - Which value-creation stages?
2. **Vehicles: How will we get there?**
   - Internal development?
   - Joint ventures?
   - Licensing/franchising?
   - Acquisitions?
3. **Differentiators: How will we win in the marketplace?**
   - Image?
   - Customization?
   - Price?
   - Styling?
   - Product reliability?
4. **Staging**
   - Speed of expansion?
   - Sequence of initiatives?
5. **Lowest costs through scale advantage?**
   - Lowest costs through scope and replication advantage?
   - Premium prices due to unmatchable service?
   - Premium prices due to proprietary product features?

Donald Hambrick and James Frederickson have developed a framework that characterizes the strategy of an organization in terms of five elements that should be mutually reinforcing (see Table 5.4). Any misalignment between elements identifies a need for action/change.

From this perspective, it is only after all five strategic elements have been determined that it is possible to appropriately assess the desirable characteristics of the various organizational structures and systems that facilitate the achievement of the strategy.[23] However, before moving to this stage, it is important to test the quality of the proposed strategy. Hambrick and Frederickson provide a list of "key evaluation criteria" to do this (see Table 5.5).

The Strategic Inventory

Strategy is about the future—committing resources to various activities based on "assumptions, premises and beliefs about an organization's environment (society and its structure, the market, the customer, and the competition), its mission, and the core competencies needed to accomplish that mission."[24] These assumptions, premises, and beliefs, often formed over time through experience, become a "mental grid" through

TABLE 5.5 **Testing the Quality of Your Strategy**

Source: Hambrick and Fredrickson, 2001, Table 1. Copyright © 2001 Academy of Management Executive. Reproduced with permission of Academy of Management Executive through Copyright Clearance Center.

Key Evaluation Criteria

1. Does your strategy fit with what's going on in the environment?

1.1 Is there a healthy profit potential where you're headed?

1.2 Does strategy align with the key success factors of your chosen environment.

2. Does your strategy exploit your key resources?

2.1 With your particular mix of resources, does this strategy give you a good head start on your competitors?

2.2 Can you pursue this strategy more economically than competitors?

3. Will your envisaged differentiators be sustainable?

3.1 Will competitors have difficulty matching you?

3.2 If not, does your strategy explicitly include a ceaseless regimen of innovation and opportunity creation?

4. Are the elements of your strategy internally consistent?

4.1 Have you made choices of arenas, vehicles, differentiators, staging, and economic logic?

4.2 Do they all fit and mutually reinforce each other?

5. Do you have enough resources to pursue this strategy?

5.1 Do you have the money, managerial time and talent, and other capabilities to do all you envision?

5.2 Are you sure you're not spreading your resources too thinly, only to be left with a collection of weak positions?

6. Is your strategy implementable?

6.1 Will your key constituencies allow you to pursue this strategy?

6.2 Can your organization make it through the transition?

6.3 Are you and your management team able and willing to lead the required changes?

TABLE 5.6 The Impact of Assumptions on Strategy: The Beech Starship Story

Source: Picken and Dess, 1998.

In the early 1980s, Raytheon Co. acquired Beech Aircraft, a light-aircraft company that had fallen on hard times. Raytheon-installed managers proposed to reinvigorate the Beech business by producing an advanced turboprop aircraft based on the latest carbon-fiber technology, which was expected to provide performance competitive with the lower end of the business jet market but be more fuel efficient and about 60 percent the price of the jets. An 85 percent scale model "Starship" was built and, on the basis of rave reviews, Beech announced that a new factory would be built to build the plane which would be ready for shipment within two years.

This initiative was based on several assumptions:

(i) That Beech could complete the design and get FAA certification for the new aircraft within two years.
(ii) That the fact that the existing regulations did not deal with the new carbon-fiber technology would not be a significant problem.
(iii) That sufficient aircraft would be built to justify the expenditure on a new factory.

However what happened was that the FAA had never certified an all-composite aircraft and insisted on compliance with the standards for metal aircraft. This led to redesign, which increased the weight, which produced a need for bigger engines, which required more fuel, which meant more weight, which necessitated redesign, and on and on. Eventually the Starship made it to market, but it was four years late, it carried only 60 percent of the planned passengers (6 versus 10), it cruised at 335 knots instead of the planned 400, and the price differential compared to jets had virtually disappeared. The expected demand failed to materialize; the production line was closed down.

which new information is sifted and interpreted. To the extent that this grid comprises assumptions, and so forth, that are an accurate reflection of the environment, it enhances the quality of strategic decision making. However, where assumptions fail to reflect accurately key elements of the business environment, they can lead to the adoption of inappropriate strategies (see Table 5.6), a phenomenon that has been labeled "strategic drift."[25]

Identifying the strategic assumptions of managers, and validating their accuracy, can be a useful way of assessing whether current strategy seems to be consistent with key elements of the business environment. It also assists in identifying whether the strategy of the organization may be a priority focal point for change.

Picken and Dess have developed a "Strategic Inventory" as a diagnostic tool for this purpose (see Table 5.7). Any given application of this tool may, or may not, reveal consensus on assumptions. Where consensus is found, the emphasis should move to its independent validation. Where significant divergence exists, attention should be directed to both which/whose assumptions are currently enshrined in strategy and which/whose assumptions can be independently validated.

The Strategic Inventory involves a much more sophisticated analysis than that provided by the ubiquitous SWOT analysis (strengths, weaknesses, opportunities, threats). The danger with SWOT analysis is that it very easily becomes a listing not of strengths but "believed strengths," not of weaknesses but "believed weaknesses," and so forth. That is, it captures existing beliefs—the current orthodoxy—which sometimes are precisely what need to be challenged if an organization is to improve its performance.

TABLE 5.7 The Strategic Inventory

Source: Picken and Dess, 1998, Exhibit 1.

Defining the boundaries of the competitive environment

- What are the boundaries of our industry? What is our served market? What products-services do we provide?
- Who are the customers? Who are the non-customers? What is the difference between them?
- Who are our competitors? Who are the non-competitors? What makes one firm a competitor and the other not?
- What are the key competencies required to compete in this industry? Where is the value added?

Defining the key assumptions

- Who is our customer? What kinds of things are important to that customer? How does he or she perceive us? What kind of relationships do we have?
- Who is the ultimate end user? What kinds of things are important to this end user? How does he or she perceive us? What kind of relationship do we have?
- Who are our competitors? What are their strengths and weaknesses? How do they perceive us? What can we learn from them?
- Who are the potential competitors? New entrants? What changes in the environment or their behavior would make them competitors?
- What is the industry's value chain? Where is value added? What is the cost structure? How does our firm compare? How about our competitors?
- What technologies are important in our industry? Product technologies? Production technologies? Delivery and service technologies? How does our firm compare? How about our competitors?
- What are the key factors of production? Who are the suppliers? Are we dependent on a limited number of sources? How critical are these relationships? How solid?
- What are the bases for competition in our industry? What are the key success factors? How do we measure up? How about our competitors?
- What trends and factors in the external environment are important to our industry? How are they likely to change? Over what time horizon?
- Are we able, in assessing our knowledge and assumptions, to clearly separate fact from assumption?

Is our assumption set internally consistent?

- For each pair of assumptions, can we answer "yes" to the question: "If assumption A is true, does assumption B logically follow?"

Do we understand the relative importance of each of our assumptions?

- In terms of its potential impact on performance?
- In terms of our level of confidence in its validity?
- In terms of the likelihood and expectation of near-term change?
- In terms of its strategic impact?

Are our key assumptions broadly understood?

- Have we documented and communicated our key assumptions? To our key managers? To the boundary-spanners? To other key employees?

Do we have a process for reviewing and validating our key assumptions and premises?

- Is there a process in place? Are responsibilities assigned? Are periodic reviews planned and scheduled?

Newsflash Exercise

Sometimes it is important to tackle the diagnostic issue by getting the management of an organization to focus in very specific terms on exactly what they are seeking to achieve. In such a situation, some diagnostic models can be too abstract; something that makes the issues very concrete achieves a clearer outcome. The Newsflash exercise is designed to meet this need (see Table 5.8).

TABLE 5.8 Newsflash

Fortune
A date five years in the future
YOURCORP Enters the List of America's Ten Most Admired Companies

Today we announce the results of our annual search for America's most admired companies. The list represents the results of a survey of the CEOs and CFOs of America's 1,000 largest companies. The big story this year is the appearance in the top ten, for the first time, of YOURCORP.

YOURCORP was judged to be the best performer in its industry according to three key indicators:
1...
2...
3...

How did YOURCORP achieve this remarkable position? When interviewed, CEO Jessie White said, "This is something that we have been working towards for the past five years. Just look at our achievements," she said. "These include:
1...
2...
3...

During this period, YOURCORP put particular emphasis on identifying the key changes in the business environment. These were used as a basis for generating a strategic dialogue within the company as to the implications for them. Key changes that were identified included
1...
2...
3...

Through this dialogue, YOURCORP had produced a clear sense of what its strategic objectives had to be over the five-year period. These objectives were
1...
2...
3...

We also spoke to customers. A spokesperson from one long-standing YOURCORP customer said, "We're with them for the long haul." He pointed to the aspects of the company's mode of operating that made it attractive to deal with, citing in particular
1...
2...
3...

CFO Alexandra Jean commented that she had worked in competitor companies. "However," she said, "as soon as I joined YOURCORP, I really noticed the difference. The place *felt* like a leading-edge company." When asked to nominate the adjectives she would use to describe the company, she suggested
1...
2...
3...

Fortune contacted three other senior managers in YOURCORP. Each was asked to identify the one thing that, more than anything else, made the company stand out from its competitors. All pointed to the same thing, which was

....

Finally, we interviewed several staff who had been with YOURCORP for five years or more. What was it that had made them stay? A consistent set of responses emerged that emphasized
1...
2...

FIGURE 5.7 **The Culture Web**

Source: Johnson, 1998, Figure 9-2. Copyright © 1998 Pearson Education. Reproduced with permission of the publisher.

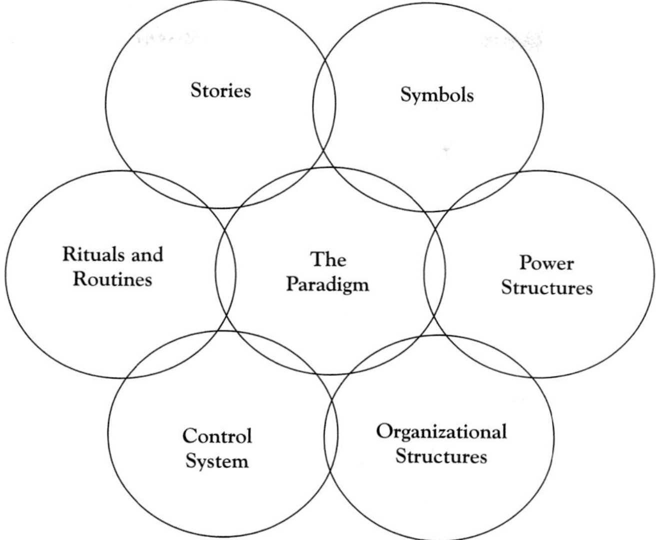

Cultural Web

Organizational culture appears as a component in several of the diagnostic models covered in this chapter (see, e.g., the Burke-Litwin model). There are also numerous typologies and tools that provide a characterization of organizational culture, including Robert Quinn's "competing values model"[26] and the Organizational Culture Inventory (OCI) developed by Robert Cooke and Clayton Rafferty.[27]

Gerry Johnson describes the culture of an organization using the concept of the "cultural web" (see Figure 5.7).

The web comprises seven elements:[28]

- The *paradigm* (the set of assumptions commonly held throughout the organization in regard to basic elements of the business such as what business we're in, how we compete, who our competitors are, etc.).
- The *rituals and routines* (in regard to how organizational members treat each other and, perhaps even more importantly, associated beliefs as to what is right and proper and valued in this regard).
- The *stories* told by organization members that, as a form of oral history, communicate and reinforce core elements of the culture.
- *Symbols* such as logos, office design, dress style, and language use that convey aspects of the culture.
- *Control systems*, which, through what they measure and reward, communicate what is valued by the organization.
- *Power structures*, which refer to the most influential management groupings in the organization.

- *Organizational structure*, which refers to the nature of the formal and informal differentiation and integration of tasks within the organization.

The specific value of "mapping" the culture of an organization is described by Johnson:[29]

1. Surfacing that which is taken for granted can be a useful way of questioning what is normally rarely questioned. If no one ever questions what is taken for granted then, inevitably, change will be difficult.
2. By mapping aspects of organizational culture it may be possible to see where barriers to change exist.
3. It may also be possible to see where there are linkages in the aspects of organizational culture which are especially resistant to change.
4. A map of organizational culture can also provide a basis for examining the changes that need to occur to deliver a new strategy.
5. This in turn can be used to consider whether such changes can be managed. In this way practical ideas for implementing strategic change can be developed.[30]

Structural Dilemmas

Many organizational change programs involve the organization's structure either directly or indirectly. One reason for this is that "getting the structure right" is a difficult challenge because managers "confront enduring structural dilemmas, tough trade-offs without easy answers."[31] Bolman and Deal identify six such dilemmas.[32]

1. *Differentiation versus integration*. As organizations grow or as tasks become more complex, there is value in specialization, but with each act of differentiation comes the need at some point to integrate the various parts into the coherent whole that is the product or service experienced by the customer.
2. *Gap versus overlap*. If all necessary tasks are not assigned to some position or department, key tasks may go undone to the detriment of the whole organization. However, if a task is assigned to more than one position or department, whether specifically or by default through ambiguity in instructions, the situation can easily become one where there is wasted effort and/or conflict.
3. *Underuse versus overload*. If staff have too little work, they are likely to be bored and/or get in the way in their efforts to find something to do. If staff are overloaded with work, their capacity to service fellow staff or customers/clients is impaired.
4. *Lack of clarity versus lack of creativity*. If the responsibilities of a position are left too vague, it is easy for the employee to undertake work that the employer did not intend or wish to be done (and perhaps at the expense of organizational performance). However, if job descriptions are very specific and either rigidly enforced or rigidly followed, a major source of organizational flexibility is lost and service is likely to suffer.
5. *Excessive autonomy versus excessive interdependence*. A high degree of autonomy can lead to a sense of isolation, but a high level of interdependence can stifle quick reaction to market opportunities.
6. *Too loose versus too tight*. Lack of accountability can lead to control failures but so can attempts at very close monitoring as it may be demotivating and/or encourage people to find ways to beat the system.

TABLE 5.9 Diagnosing Structural Dilemmas

Source: Created from Bolman and Deal, 2003:69–72.

Please respond to each of the following statements in regard to your organization.

1 represents very strong agreement with the statement on the left-hand side.
4 represents the view that the two aspects are well-balanced.
7 represents very strong agreement with the statement on the right-hand side.

Differentiation has not affected integration	*Differentiation has affected integration*
1..................2..................3..................4..................5..................6..................7	
Key tasks go unallocated	*There's too much overlap of tasks*
1..................2..................3..................4..................5..................6..................7	
Staff are underused	*Staff are overloaded*
1..................2..................3..................4..................5..................6..................7	
Roles are not clear enough	*Roles are too narrowly defined*
1..................2..................3..................4..................5..................6..................7	
We are left to work on our own too often	*We can't work on our own enough*
1..................2..................3..................4..................5..................6..................7	
Controls are too loose	*Controls are too tight*
1..................2..................3..................4..................5..................6..................7	

Changes may be needed where you have provided a 1 or 2, or a 6 or 7 response.

Table 5.9 provides a diagnostic instrument designed to address these issues.

The Boundaryless Organization

Ashkenas et al. have argued that organizations facing increasingly competitive environments will have to make significant shifts in key structural aspects if they wish themselves to remain competitive.[33] Specifically, they argue that organizations need to take into account a "shifting paradigm for organizational success" that positions speed, flexibility, integration, and innovation as the "new success factors."[34] *Speed* refers to speed in bringing products to market and in changing strategies; *flexibility* refers to the use of ad hoc teams and malleable job descriptions; *integration* refers to greater collaboration between specialists; and *innovation* refers to the encouragement of creativity.

The next step in their argument is that these new success factors will only be achieved if organizations reduce four types of organization boundary: vertical, horizontal, external, and international. *Vertical boundaries* are the layers in the internal vertical hierarchies of organizations; *horizontal boundaries* exist between organizational units (e.g., departments); *external boundaries* are those between the organization and the "outside world" (e.g., customers and suppliers); and *geographic boundaries* are those between different countries.

Table 5.10 provides a diagnostic instrument for testing the current state of "boundarylessness" of an organization across all four boundaries, while Table 5.11 looks specifically at the characteristics of an organization's vertical structure.

TABLE 5.10 How Boundaryless Is Your Organization?

Source: Ashkenas et al., 1995:28–29. Copyright © 1995 Jossey-Bass. Reprinted with permission of John Wiley & Sons, Inc.

Instructions: The following 16 statements describe the behavior of boundaryless organizations. Assess the extent to which each statement characterizes your current organization, circling a number from 1 (not true at all) to 5 (very true).

	Speed	Flexibility	Integration	Innovation	Total Score
Vertical Boundary	Most decisions are made on the spot by those closest to the work, and they are acted on in hours rather than weeks. 1 2 3 4 5	Managers at all levels routinely take on frontline responsibilities as well as broad strategic assignments. 1 2 3 4 5	Key problems are tackled by multilevel teams whose members operate with little regard to formal rank in the organization. 1 2 3 4 5	New ideas are screened and decided on without fancy overheads and multiple rounds of approvals. 1 2 3 4 5	
Horizontal Boundary	New products or services are getting to market at an increasingly fast pace. 1 2 3 4 5	Resources quickly, frequently, and effortlessly shift between centers of expertise and operating units. 1 2 3 4 5	Routine work gets done through end-to-end process teams; other work is handled by project teams drawn from shared centers of experience. 1 2 3 4 5	Ad hoc teams representing various stakeholders spontaneously form to explore new ideas. 1 2 3 4 5	
External Boundary	Customer requests, complaints, and needs are anticipated and responded to in real time. 1 2 3 4 5	Strategic resources and key managers are often "on loan" to customers and suppliers. 1 2 3 4 5	Supplier and customer reps are key players in teams tackling strategic initiatives. 1 2 3 4 5	Suppliers and customers are regular prolific contributors of new product and process ideas. 1 2 3 4 5	
Geographic Boundary	Best practices are disseminated and leveraged quickly across country operations. 1 2 3 4 5	Business leaders rotate regularly between country operations. 1 2 3 4 5	There are standard product platforms, common practices, and shared centers of experience across countries. 1 2 3 4 5	New product ideas are evaluated for viability beyond the country where they emerged. 1 2 3 4 5	
Total Score					

Questionnaire Scoring

1. Rate each statement.
2. Total your scores for each row and column.
3. According to Ashkenas et al., a score of 12 or less for any "success factor" or boundary measurement suggests that that particular factor needs attention; a score of 16 + indicates an already existing strength in that factor.

TABLE 5.11 How Healthy Is Your Organization's Hierarchy?

Source: Ashkenas et al., 1995:59–60. Copyright © 1995 Jossey-Bass. Reprinted with permission of John Wiley & Sons, Inc.

Part 1: Success Factors

Instructions: Determine how critical the four new paradigm success factors are in your organization, circling High, Medium, or Low for each factor.

1. Speed	High	Medium	Low
2. Flexibility	High	Medium	Low
3. Integration	High	Medium	Low
4. Innovation	High	Medium	Low

Part 2: Red Flags

Instructions: Evaluate how often the following five danger signs appear in your organization, circling a number from 1 (too often) to 10 (seldom).

	Too often				Sometimes				Seldom	
1. Slow response time	1	2	3	4	5	6	7	8	9	10
2. Rigidity to change	1	2	3	4	5	6	7	8	9	10
3. Underground activity	1	2	3	4	5	6	7	8	9	10
4. Internal employee frustration	1	2	3	4	5	6	7	8	9	10
5. Customer alienation	1	2	3	4	5	6	7	8	9	10

Part 3: Profile of Vertical Boundaries

Instructions: Assess where your company stands today on the four dimensions of information, authority, competence, and rewards, circling a number from 1 (traditional) to 10 (healthy).

Traditional Hierarchy											**Healthy Hierarchy**
Information closely held at top.	1	2	3	4	5	6	7	8	9	10	Information widely shared.
Authority to make decisions centralized at top.	1	2	3	4	5	6	7	8	9	10	Authority to make decisions distributed to wherever appropriate.
Competence specialized and focused; people do one job.	1	2	3	4	5	6	7	8	9	10	Competence widespread; people do multiple tasks as needed.
Rewards based on position.	1	2	3	4	5	6	7	8	9	10	Rewards based on skills and accomplishments.

Questionnaire Follow-up

Ashkenas et al. suggest that once a company's managers complete the questionnaire (individually), they should hold a group forum to discuss the following questions:

1. How important is it to our organization's success that we loosen our vertical boundaries? In other words, do we really need to operate faster and more flexibly?
2. Are the red flags serious and recurrent? Which ones are most worrisome?
3. To what extent is our current vertical profile dragging us down and causing us problems?
4. In the current profile of our hierarchy, which dimensions are strongest? Where do we most need to change in order to be more successful?
5. What is our desired profile of vertical boundaries? Where would we like to be on each of the four dimensions in the next year or two; that is, what profile do we need to compete successfully now and into the future?[a]

[a]Ashkenas et al., 1995:61.

DIAGNOSING READINESS TO CHANGE

Knowing what needs changing is only part of the story. The degree of attention to the process of managing change is a reflection of the fraught nature of the process. Change initiatives often fail. Knowing this, a prechange audit of the readiness of an organization for change can provide an indication of the likely outcome of a change initiative at a particular point in time. It also may identify key areas where further action could significantly enhance the prospects of success. The instrument provided in Table 5.12 is an adapted version of one designed by Andrea Sodano as published in *Fortune*.[35]

TABLE 5.12 Readiness for Change

Source: Stewart, 1994:8–10.

The left-hand column lists 17 key elements of change readiness. Rate your organization on each item. Give three points for a high ranking ("We're good at this; I'm confident of our skills here."); two for a medium score ("We're spotty here; we could use improvement or more experience."); and one point for a low score ("We've had problems with this; this is new to our organization."). Be honest. Don't trust only your own perspective; ask others in the organization, at all levels.

Readiness Scoring

How to score: High = 3
Medium = 2
Low = 1

Category	Score
Sponsorship. The sponsor of change is not necessarily its day-to-day leader; he or she is the visionary, chief cheerleader, and bill payer—the person with the power to help the team change when it meets resistance. Give three points—change will be easier—if sponsorship comes at a senior level; for example, CEO, COO, or the head of an autonomous business unit. Weakest sponsors: midlevel executives or staff officers.	☐
Leadership. This means the day-to-day leadership—the people who call the meetings, set the goals, work until midnight. Successful change is more likely if leadership is high level, has "ownership" (that is, direct responsibility for what's to be changed), and has clear business results in mind. Low-level leadership, or leadership that is not well-connected throughout the organization (across departments) or that comes from the staff, is less likely to succeed and should be scored low.	☐
Motivation. High points for a strong sense of urgency from senior management, which is shared by the rest of the company, and for a corporate culture that already emphasizes continuous improvement. Negative: tradition-bound managers and workers, many of whom have been in their jobs for more than 15 years; a conservative culture that discourages risk taking.	☐
Direction. Does senior management strongly believe that the future should look different from the present? How clear is management's picture of the future? Can management mobilize all relevant	☐

parties—employees, the board, customers, etc.—for action? High points for positive answers to those questions. If senior management thinks only minor change is needed, the likely outcome is no change at all; score yourself low.

Measurements. Or in consultant-speak, "metrics." Three points if you already use performance measures of the sort encouraged by total quality management (defect rates, time to market, etc.) and if these express the economics of the business. Two points if some measures exist, but compensation and reward systems do not explicitly reinforce them. If you don't have measures in place or don't know what we're talking about, one point.

Organizational context. How does the change effort connect to other major goings-on in the organization? (For example: Does it dovetail with a continuing total quality management process? Does it fit with strategic actions such as acquisitions or new product lines?) Trouble lies ahead for a change effort that is isolated or if there are multiple change efforts whose relationships are not linked strategically.

Processes/functions. Major changes almost invariably require redesigning business processes that cut across functions such as purchasing, accounts payable, or marketing. If functional executives are rigidly turf conscious, change will be difficult. Give yourself more points the more willing they—and the organization as a whole—are to change critical processes and sacrifice perks or power for the good of the group.

Competitor benchmarking. Whether you are a leader in your industry or a laggard, give yourself points for a continuing program that objectively compares your company's performance with that of competitors and systematically examines changes in your market. Give yourself one point if knowledge of competitors' abilities is primarily anecdotal—what salespeople say at the bar.

Customer focus. The more everyone in the company is imbued with knowledge of customers, the more likely that the organization can agree to change to serve them better. Three points if everyone in the workforce knows who his or her customers are, knows their needs, and has had direct contact with them. Take away points if that knowledge is confined to pockets of the organization (sales and marketing, senior executives).

Rewards. Change is easier if managers and employees are rewarded for taking risks, being innovative, and looking for new solutions. Team-based rewards are better than rewards based solely on individual achievement. Reduce points if your company, like most, rewards continuity over change. If managers become heroes for making budget, they won't take risks even if you say you want them to. Also, if employees believe failure will be punished, reduce points.

Organizational structure. The best situation is a flexible churn—that is, organizations are rare and well received. Score yourself lower if you have a rigid structure that has been unchanged for more than five years or has undergone frequent reorganization with little success; that may signal a cynical company culture that fights change by waiting it out.

Communication. A company will adapt to change most readily if it has many means of two-way communication that reach all levels of the organization and that all employees use and understand. If communications media are few, often trashed unread, and almost exclusively one-way and top-down, change will be more difficult.

Organizational hierarchy. The fewer levels of hierarchy and the fewer employee grade levels, the more likely an effort to change will succeed. A thick impasto of middle management and staff not only slows decision making but also creates large numbers of people with the power to block change.

Prior experience with change. Score three if the organization has successfully implemented major changes in the recent past. Score one if there is no prior experience with major change or if change efforts failed or left a legacy of anger or resentment. Most companies will score two, acknowledging equivocal success in previous attempts to change.

Morale. Change is easier if employees enjoy working in the organization and the level of individual responsibility is high. Signs of unreadiness to change: low team spirit, little voluntary extra effort, and mistrust. Look for two types of mistrust: between management and employees and between or among departments.

Innovation. Best situation: The company is always experimenting; new ideas are implemented with seemingly little effort; employees work across internal boundaries without much trouble. Bad signs: lots of red tape, multiple signoffs required before new ideas are tried; employees must go through channels and are discouraged from working with colleagues from other departments or divisions.

Decision making. Rate yourself high if decisions are made quickly, taking into account a wide variety of suggestions; it is clear where decisions are made. Give yourself a low grade if decisions come slowly and are made by a mysterious "them"; there is a lot of conflict during the process, and confusion and finger pointing after decisions are announced.

Total Score

If Your Score Is

41–51: Implementing change is most likely to succeed. Focus resources on lagging factors (your ones and twos) to accelerate the process.

28–40: Change is possible but may be difficult, especially if you have low scores in the first seven readiness dimensions. Bring those up to speed before attempting to implement large-scale change.

17–27: Implementing change will be virtually impossible without a precipitating catastrophe. Focus instead on (1) building change readiness in the dimensions above and (2) effecting change through pilot programs separate from the organization at large.

An alternative means for assessing change readiness, the Support for Change instrument, designed by Rick Maurer, focuses on eight factors: values and vision, history of change, cooperation and trust, culture, resilience, rewards, respect and face, and status quo (see Tables 5.13 and 5.14).[36]

TABLE 5.13 Support for Change Questionnaire

Source: Maurer, 1996:104–105.

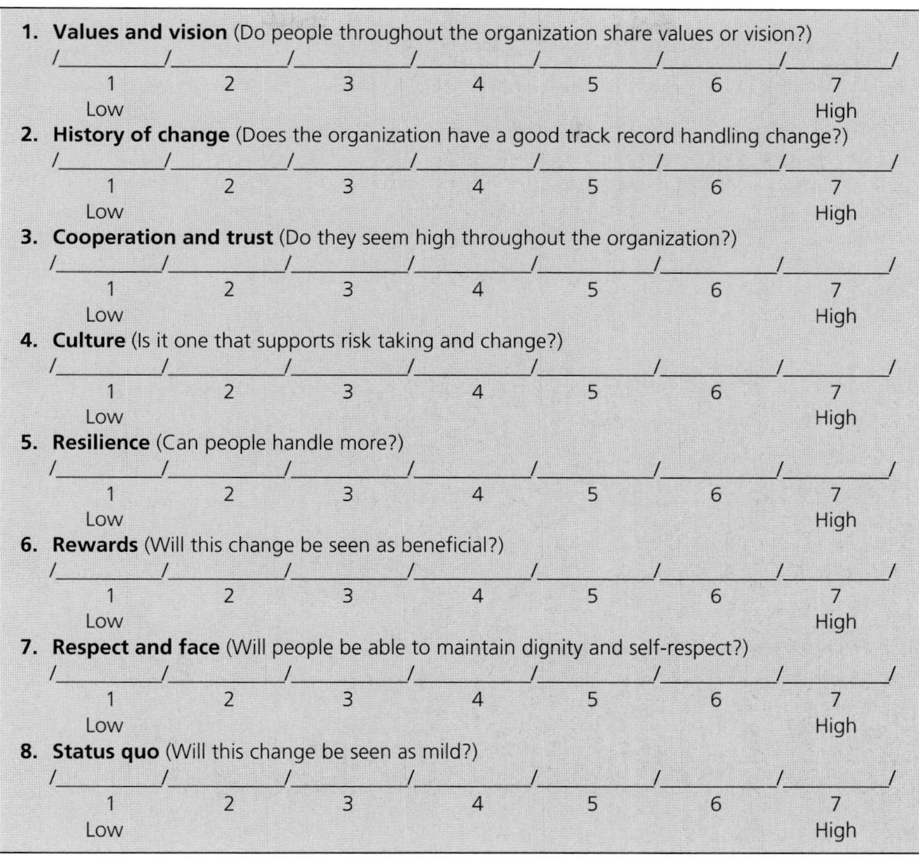

1. **Values and vision** (Do people throughout the organization share values or vision?)
/______/______/______/______/______/______/______/
1 2 3 4 5 6 7
Low High
2. **History of change** (Does the organization have a good track record handling change?)
/______/______/______/______/______/______/______/
1 2 3 4 5 6 7
Low High
3. **Cooperation and trust** (Do they seem high throughout the organization?)
/______/______/______/______/______/______/______/
1 2 3 4 5 6 7
Low High
4. **Culture** (Is it one that supports risk taking and change?)
/______/______/______/______/______/______/______/
1 2 3 4 5 6 7
Low High
5. **Resilience** (Can people handle more?)
/______/______/______/______/______/______/______/
1 2 3 4 5 6 7
Low High
6. **Rewards** (Will this change be seen as beneficial?)
/______/______/______/______/______/______/______/
1 2 3 4 5 6 7
Low High
7. **Respect and face** (Will people be able to maintain dignity and self-respect?)
/______/______/______/______/______/______/______/
1 2 3 4 5 6 7
Low High
8. **Status quo** (Will this change be seen as mild?)
/______/______/______/______/______/______/______/
1 2 3 4 5 6 7
Low High

TABLE 5.14 Working with the Support for Change Questionnaire

Source: Maurer, 1996.

1. Use the Support for Change questionnaire to begin discussion within the organization about the degree of support that exists for the change.
2. Give the questionnaire to a cross section of people in the organization.
3. Aggregate scores to ensure anonymity for individuals but publicize the different scores for different groups (e.g., middle c.f. senior management, marketing department c.f. production department).
4. Hold a meeting of all interested parties to discuss the results. Discuss where the greatest agreement exists and why, and where the greatest divergence exists and why. Conduct the meeting in a nonthreatening atmosphere and encourage people to explain why they scored the way they did.
5. On the basis of the information that you receive from the questionnaire and the subsequent discussion, consider the implications for the proposed change; for example, do you need to do more (and if so what?) to improve the prospects of successful implementation?

Galbraith et al. provide a diagnostic tool for change readiness but couch it in terms of an organization's "reconfigurability" (see Table 5.15).[37]

TABLE 5.15 How Reconfigurable Is Your Organization?

Source: Galbraith et al., 2002. Copyright © 2002 AMACON. Reproduced by permission through Copyright Clearance Center.

Use this tool to gain a preliminary perspective on how your organization responds to change. This tool is for use with an executive team.

Instructions: A reconfigurable organization is one that is characterized by active leadership, knowledge management, learning, flexibility, integration, employee commitment, and change readiness. Each of these characteristics is defined by three statements below. For each one, rate your organization by how strongly you agree ("5") or disagree ("1") with the statement. Then, total your scores.

	Strongly Disagree				Strongly Agree
Item	**1**	**2**	**3**	**4**	**5**
Active Leadership					
The executive team believes that organization design is a source of competitive advantage.					
When strategy discussions are held, organization design is considered one of your strategic elements.					
The executive team can articulate how each of the organization's components is aligned with the strategy.					
Knowledge Management					
People have easy access to all the information they need to make decisions on behalf of customers.					
Technology and HR practices allow for rapid collection and dissemination of information.					
The organization has mechanisms in place for converting information into useable knowledge for innovation, best practices, and organizational learning.					
Learning					
People are selected for their learning aptitude.					
Performance metrics and feedback allow employees to measure their performance against internal and external standards and share in the responsibility for increasing their own capabilities.					
The organization uses a wide variety of methods in addition to training to support learning.					
Flexibility					
Employees are skilled at working in teams.					
Networks across organizational boundaries are actively fostered, not left up to individual initiative or chance.					
People expect and accept being frequently reassigned into new roles and responsibilities.					

Item	Strongly Disagree 1	2	3	4	Strongly Agree 5
Integration Assignments and career paths for high performers are designed to promote cross-functional skills, broaden interpersonal networks, and provide exposure to senior management.					
Specialists are available to the entire organization through either special assignment or career paths.					
Managers are moved between organizational units, not just upward in their own unit, for promotions and development.					
Employee Commitment Employees are provided with the opportunity to develop job-related skills and are rewarded for developing skills that increase their value to the organization.					
Employees have the tools, systems, information, and skills to deliver excellence to internal and external customers.					
Employees actively recommend the company as a good place to work.					
Change Readiness Employees understand the strategy and goals of the organization.					
Employees understand the rationale for the current organization design.					
Your overall organizational culture, vision, and values support organizational change and innovation.					

Now, enter your totals for each area below (your scores should all be between 3 and 15):

Active Leadership ____________

Knowledge Management ____________

Learning ____________

Flexibility ____________

Integration ____________

Employee Commitment ____________

Change Readiness ____________

Lower numbers indicate areas of greater concern as you proceed through the organization design process. Similarly, higher numbers are strengths you can build on going forward. Continue to use this tool when questions arise as to how flexibly your organization can respond to changing strategic imperatives. Return to it to diagnose your progress as you implement change.

Stakeholder Analysis

Stakeholder analysis focuses on one specific aspect of change readiness: the position of key stakeholders in regard to the proposed change. In the context of a planned change, stakeholders are those individuals or groups, inside or outside the organization, who have the capacity to influence, directly or indirectly, the success or otherwise of the change. It is usually helpful to add some reference to "interest in the issue" to the definition to make it clear that bodies with the capacity to influence such as the armed forces or police need not be included.

Stakeholder analysis involves the following process:[38]

1. Identify stakeholders, who may comprise both groups with a formal connection to the organization (e.g., owners, suppliers, customers, employees) and other groups who can exert influence over the organization.
2. Assess each stakeholder's capacity to influence the particular change being proposed (e.g., rate as high, medium, low).
3. Check each stakeholder's "track record," particularly in regard to comparable issues.
4. Assess each stakeholder's interest in the particular change being proposed (e.g., rate as high, medium, low).
5. On the basis of the above, identify the stakeholders most likely to be interested and able to be influential in regard to the change in question.
6. Try to find out what position, if any, each of these stakeholders is taking on the change. Be cautious if only attitudes, not actions, are reported. While attitudes are worth knowing—and may alert the change team to a potential problem—those expressing support may not "come through" if the going gets tough, just as those expressing opposition may "fall into line" if they believe that the change is going to happen.

One approach involves plotting level of stakeholder interest against stakeholder power (see Figure 5.8). In this model, specific action is advocated based on the categorization of specific stakeholders.

FIGURE 5.8 The Power-Interest Matrix

Source: Scholes, 1998, Figure 10-1. Reprinted with permission of Pearson Education.

POWER \ LEVEL OF INTEREST	Low	High
Low	A Minimal effort	B Keep informed
High	C Keep satisfied	D Key players

Grundy suggests that the following questions be addressed:[39]

- Can new stakeholders be added to the situation to change the balance?
- Can any oppositional stakeholders be encouraged to leave?
- Can the influence of pro-change stakeholders be increased?
- Can the influence of antagonistic stakeholders be decreased?
- Can the change be modified in away that meets concerns without undermining the change?
- If the stakeholder resistance is strong, should the proposal be revisited?

Stakeholder analysis allows the change manager to be much better informed as to the likely reception to the change among key stakeholders and, on this basis, steps can be taken to try to improve the prospects of the change initiative receiving a good reception.

Force-Field Analysis

Force-field analysis is another model for looking at the factors that can assist or hinder the implementation of change. The forces pushing for change are *driving forces*; those working against the change are *restraining forces*.

To do a force-field analysis:[40]

1. Define the problem. Get individuals to do this first, then share these definitions. Write the problem in the center of the main force-field arrow on a force-field figure (see Figure 5.9).

FIGURE 5.9 **Force Field Diagram**

Source: McWhinney, 1997:165. Copyright © 1997 Sage Publications, Inc. Reprinted with permission.

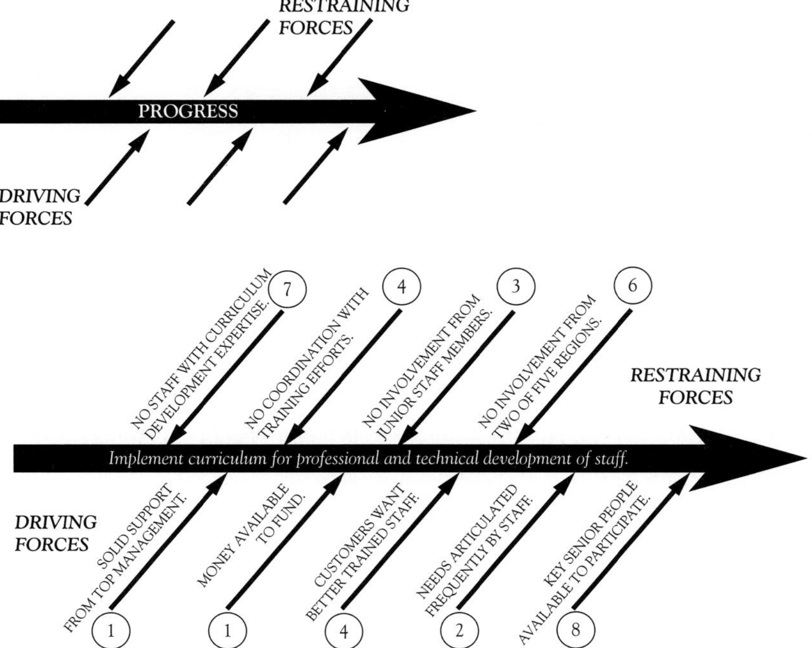

2. Determine the restraining forces and add them to the figure (one arrow per force). Put all the restraining factors on one side of the central stem. Indicate the relative strength of each factor by using a consistent format (e.g., numbers, as in Figure 5.9, or thickness of the arrow).
3. Repeat step 2, except this time for driving forces.
4. If the identity and strength of the restraining and driving forces have been accurately assessed, this will clarify both the likely outcome (will the change be able to be successfully implemented?) and the sources of greatest restraint (useful to know if on balance the change looks like it is not succeeding). It also suggests change actions that can be taken, such as decreasing restraining forces and increasing or adding to the driving forces. This enables disruption of the status quo, resulting in change.

Conclusion

In this chapter we introduced a range of diagnostic instruments that can contribute to the management of change by providing a perspective on a range of organizational situations. Explicit models of "how organizations work" provide a complement to the implicit models that managers and others have in their heads. No one model is "the truth," but each offers its user the opportunity to view the operation of an organization from a particular perspective. It is up to those who use a diagnostic tool to determine the value of the perspective and to make decisions accordingly. As suggested at the start of this chapter, this assessment will be influenced by the image(s) of managing change that are adopted.

TABLE 5.16 Chapter Reflections for the Practicing Change Manager

- As a manager, do you feel that you now have knowledge of a number of diagnostic tools/models?
- Do you feel that you could apply them when necessary?
- If you were to select two or three favorite tools/models, which would they be and why?
- Is there a key area of organizational activity where you'd like a diagnostic tool that is not provided in this chapter? Where might you go to find such a tool?
- To what extent do your image(s) of change influence which diagnostic tools you are most comfortable using or see as most relevant?

Supplemental Reading

Ambrosini, V., Johnson, G., and Scholes, K. 1998. *Exploring techniques of analysis and evaluation in strategic management*. New York: London.

Burke, W. W. 2002. *Organization change: Theory and practice*, chapters 8–10. Thousand Oaks, CA: Sage.

Harrison, M. I. 1994. *Diagnosing organizations: Methods, models and processes*. 2nd ed.,Thousand Oaks, CA: Sage.

Harrison, M. I. and Shirom, A. 1999. *Organizational diagnosis and assessment*. Thousand Oaks, CA: Sage.

Howard, A., and Associates. 1994. *Diagnosis for organizational change: Methods and models*. New York: Guildford Press.

Johnson, G. 1998. Mapping and re-mapping organizational culture. In *Exploring techniques of analysis and evaluation in strategic management*, ed. V. Ambrosini, G. Johnson, and K. Scholes, 137–51. New York: London.

Mante-Meijer, E., van der Duin, P., and Abeln, M. 1998. Fun with scenarios. *Long Range Planning* 31:628–37.

Manzini, A. O. 1988. *Organizational diagnosis*. New York: AMACOM.

McWhinney, W. 1997. *Creating paths of change*. 2nd ed. Thousand Oaks, CA: Sage.

Scholes, K. 1998. Stakeholder mapping: A practical tool for managers. In *Exploring techniques of analysis and evaluation in strategic management*, ed. V. Ambrosini, G. Johnson, and K. Scholes, 152–68. New York: London.

The long list of Boeing's woes seems to have reached its pinnacle in late 2003 with the scandal surrounding the Pentagon deal that alleged inappropriate behavior and the loss of documents by Boeing officials. After his seven-year reign at the head of the organization, December 2003 saw the eventual resignation of Phil Condit. Many breathed a sigh of relief at the news. The problems at Boeing were reportedly endless. From a stock price that had decreased by 6.5 percent while the company was under his leadership to increasing competitive pressures, the future for Boeing was in doubt and changes were needed.

For many years Boeing graced American corporate news for their prowess as the leading manufacturer of aircraft. However, in 1994 Airbus—their main rival—booked more orders. This shocked the management executives and began a series of changes that were implemented to overcome the bureaucratic structure, outdated technological systems, and unnecessary processes in a company that had reportedly changed little since World War II.

THE BEGINNING OF CHANGE AT BOEING

In 1997 market demand increased dramatically and Boeing attempted to meet this surplus of orders by doubling their production capabilities instantaneously. A manufacturing crisis ensued and Boeing's reputation took a dramatic turn for the worse when they were required to halt production of the 747 aircraft for 20 days. The company had "stubbed its toe," according to the then-president of the Commercial Airplane Group, Ron Woodward, who was dismissed not long after the crisis. The "win at all costs" approach that Boeing supposedly had to its business dealings and a lack of communication within the organization appeared to have been the source of this problem.

After experiencing these manufacturing difficulties an attempt was made to revitalize Boeing's operations by streamlining aircraft assembly and increasing the efficiency of the company. This was to be done by focusing on production and costs, not on "airy vision statements."[42] Their overall strategy was to update their technology systems, downsize their operations and reestablish relationships with their suppliers—the only feasible way costs could be cut.

Perhaps the first step in recognizing that the cycle of demand for their products caused massive fluctuations in revenue each year and the company needed more stability occurred when Boeing acquired McDonnell Douglas in 1997 to increase its defense contracts. This merger, however, brought with it difficulties in the way of cultural synthesis. McDonnell Douglas had a very strong culture that focused on their dealings with government officials for defense contracts. Combined with Boeing's family-orientated culture, the merger was not without integration issues. The merger also had financial implications when investors accused the organization of trickery in regard to the merger with McDonnell Douglas and a payout of $92.5 million was made to shareholders.

WHEN TECHNOLOGY BECAME AN ISSUE

In 2001 Boeing adopted the principles of lean manufacturing and aimed to rejuvenate their reputation by making their production more efficient. The object of the project was to implement an automated system of assembly lines. They also hoped to coordinate and facilitate easier channels of communication between Boeing staff and suppliers. They implemented a Web-based procurement system that allowed suppliers to monitor stock levels and replenish supplies when they dipped below a predetermined minimum.

The process of automating the production line was a struggle for Boeing. Information technology within the organization was decentralized and over 400 systems were being used to meet the needs of various departments. The lack of collaboration in regard to product procurement meant that the same product could be manufactured by Boeing for one aircraft but subcontracted for another. Boeing had recently chosen to implement a technological platform to regulate product lifecycles. This was hoped to cut costs and facilitate the more rapid production of the 7E7. It would do this by standardizing the "use of specifications, engineering rules, operational parameters and simulation results across its extended enterprise."[43] It was hoped that this new system "will improve collaboration, innovation, product quality, time-to-market and return-on-investment."[44]

THE CULTURAL IMPLICATIONS OF DIVERSIFICATION

The decision was made to diversify from the traditional commercial airline industry and the many acquisitions that were made created integration issues for the company. The aim again was to add more stability to the business by diversifying into information services and the space industry—providing services with elevated margins that would reflect on Boeing's bottom line. Condit later admitted that entry into the space industry was an erroneous move. According to the CEO of Airbus, Noel Forgeard, the process of diversification was "extremely demoralizing for Boeing employees," but Boeing's vice president of marketing, Randy Baseler, claimed that "what affects morale right now is that we are in a down cycle."[45] Regardless of the reasoning behind it, Boeing's employee morale was at a low and this issue needed to be addressed.

According to a *BusinessWeek* reporter, Boeing was in dire need of "a strong board and a rejuvenated corporate culture based on innovation and competitiveness, not crony capitalism."[46] Boeing's past had left its culture in pieces. After the merger with McDonnell Douglas and many other organisations, the decision was made in 2001 to move the headquarters of their operations from their historical home in Seattle to Chicago. The relocation was said to be the factor that most significantly disturbed the culture of Boeing. The move was instigated to provide a neutral location for the diversified Boeing. Having acquired many different organizations, the past connections to the Seattle site were to be severed. The strategic reason for this move was to help refocus attentions on international growth prospects.

Harry Stonecipher, the past head of McDonnell Douglas who had come in as the new chief operating officer of Boeing after the company was acquired, was announced as the new CEO after Condit's resignation. His first important decision was regarding the new 7E7 planes, which would be Boeing's first new plane in a decade. On December 16, 2003, Stonecipher announced that Boeing was to go ahead with the production of the 7E7 jets. Stonecipher has promised to work closely with unions to see that the low morale is reversed and that the planes are produced at a quicker pace and for less money. Despite Stonecipher's best efforts, critics are calling for an outside leader to come in and take Boeing back to basics.

A researcher of a shareholding firm claimed that Boeing's problems lay in the fact that they had "overpromised and underdelivered."[47] The past has shown that Boeing's inability to react to external pressures has increased their demise. The future of the industry will now depend on the ability of either Airbus or Boeing to predict the way the market will go. Boeing has bet its future on the market developing a partiality for smaller aircraft, like their new 7E7. Airbus, on the other hand, projects that the airlines will purchase larger aircrafts in the future.

Questions

1. Select one or more diagnostic models that you believe provide a framework that succinctly identifies the key factors at the center of the Boeing situation. Explain your choice of model.
2. Explain the Boeing situation in the terms of your selected model.

TABLE 5.17 Additional Case Studies

VITAL Workflow Management in the Insurance Industry (Multimedia Case)
Haaken, S., & Christensen, G. (2000) *Norwegian School of Economics & Business Administration*
Manufacturing Strategy at Sico
Tchokogue, A., & Duguay, C. R. (2002) *HEC Montreal*
Organisational Alignment Exercise (Case/Assessment Exercise)
Beer, M., & Gabarro, J. J. (2003) *Harvard Business School*

Bibliography

Anonymous. 2001. Inside Boeing's big move. *Harvard Business Review*, April 22–23.

Anonymous. 2003. Pulling Boeing out of a tailspin. *BusinessWeek*, December 15.

Anonymous. 2004a. The fallen managers: Phil Condit: Boeing. *BusinessWeek*, January 12.

Anonymous. 2004b. IBM: Boeing signs long-term contract with IBM and Dassault Systemes to standardize Product Lifecycle Management platform on version 5. *M2 Presswire*, February 12.

Ashkanasy, N. M., Wilderom, C. P. M., and Peterson, M. F. 2000. *Handbook of organizational climate and culture*. Newbury Park, CA: Sage.

Ashkenas, R., Ulrich, D., Jick, T., and Kerr, S. 1995. *The boundaryless organization*. San Francisco: Jossey-Bass.

Billsberry, J. 1998. Gap analysis. In *Exploring techniques of analysis and evaluation in strategic management*, ed. V. Ambrosini, G. Johnson, and K. Scholes, 219–28. New York: London.

Bolman, L. G., and Deal, T. E. 2003. *Reframing organizations*. 3rd ed. San Francisco: Jossey-Bass.

Burke, W. W. 2002. *Organization change: Theory and practice*. Thousand Oaks, CA: Sage.

Cooke, R. A., and Lafferty, J. C. 1983. *Level V: Organizational culture inventory (form 1)*. Plymouth: Human Synergistics.

Donlan, T. D. 2003. Decline of a giant. *Barron's*, December 8:46.

Emery, M., and Purser, R. E. 1996. *The search conference*. San Francisco: Jossey-Bass.

Galbraith, J., Downey, D., and Kates, A. 2002. *Designing dynamic organizations*. New York: AMACOM.

Grundy, T. 1997. Accelerating strategic change: The internal stakeholder dimension. *Strategic Change* 6:49–56.

Hambrick, D. C., and Fredrickson, J. W. 2001. Are you sure you have a strategy? *Academy of Management Executive* 15(4):48–59.

Harrison, M. I., and Shirom, A. 1999. *Organizational diagnosis and assessment.* Thousand Oaks, CA: Sage.

Holman, W. J., Jr. 1998. Business world: Boeing's trouble: Not enough monopolistic arrogance. *The Wall Street Journal* (Eastern Edition), December 16.

Holmes, S. 2001. Boeing goes lean. *BusinessWeek*, June 4.

Holmes, S. 2003a. Boeing: What really happened. *BusinessWeek*, December 15.

Holmes, S. 2003b. Boeing: Putting out the labor fires. *BusinessWeek*, December 29.

Johnson, G. 1998. Mapping and re-mapping organizational culture. In *Exploring techniques of analysis and evaluation in strategic management*, ed. V. Ambrosini, G. Johnson, and K. Scholes, 137–51. New York: London.

Johnson, G., and Scholes, K. 2002. *Exploring corporate strategy*. 6th ed. Harlow: Pearson Education.

Laing, J. R. 2003. Above the clouds. *Barron's*, December 8:17.

Mante-Meijer, E., van der Duin, P., and Abeln, M. 1998. Fun with scenarios. *Long Range Planning* 31:628–37.

Martin, J. 2001. *Organizational culture: Mapping the terrain*. Newbury Park, CA: Sage.

Maurer, R. 1996. *Beyond the wall of resistance*. Austin: Bard Books.

McWhinney, W. 1997. *Creating paths of change*. 2nd ed. Thousand Oaks, CA: Sage.

Morgan, G. 1993. *Imaginization*. Newbury Park, CA: Sage.

Morgan, G. 1997. *Images of organization*. Thousand Oaks, CA: Sage.

Nadler, D., and Tushman, M. 1988. *Strategic organization design: Concepts, tools, & processes*. Glenview, IL: Scott, Foresman.

Palmer, I., and Dunford, R. 1996. Understanding organizations through metaphor. In *Organizational development: Metaphorical explorations*, ed. C. Oswick and D. Grant, 7–19. London: Pitman.

Pickens, J. C., and Dess, G. G. 1998. Right strategy—wrong problem. *Organizational Dynamics* 27(1):35–48.

Prahalad, C. K., and Hamel, G. 1990. The core competence of the corporation. *Harvard Business Review* 70 (May–June):79–91.

Quinn, R. E. 1988. *Beyond rational management: Mastering the paradoxes of competing demands and high performance*. San Francisco, CA: Jossey-Bass.

Reinhardt, A., and Browder, S. 1998. Fly, damn it, fly. *BusinessWeek*, November 9.

Schoemaker, P. J. H. 1993. Multiple scenario development: Its conceptual and behavioural foundation. *Strategic Management Journal* 14:193–213.

Schoemaker, P. J. H. 1995. Scenario planning: A tool for strategic thinking. *Sloan Management Review*, (Winter): 25-40.

Scholes, K. 1998. Stakeholder mapping: A practical tool for managers. In *Exploring techniques of analysis and evaluation in strategic management*, ed. V. Ambrosini, G. Johnson, and K. Scholes, 152–68. New York: London.

Stauffer, D. 2002. Five reasons why you still need scenario planning. *Harvard Management Update*, June:3–5.

Stewart, T. A. 1996. Rate your readiness for change. *Fortune*, April 23:8–10.

Taylor, A., III. 2003. Lord of the air. *Fortune*, November 10.

Verity, J. 2003. Scenario planning as a strategy technique. *European Business Journal*, 185–95.

Wallace, J. 1998. How Boeing blew it. *Sales & Marketing Management*, February:52–57.

Waterman, R. H., Jr., Peters, T. J., and Phillips, J. R. 1980. Structure is not organization. *Business Horizons*, June:14–26.

Weisbord, M. R. 1976. Organizational diagnosis: Six places to look for trouble with or without a theory. *Group and Organization Studies* 1:430–47.

Notes

1. Emery and Purser, 1996.
2. Harrison and Shirom, 1999.
3. Burke, 2002.
4. Burke, 2002. This model is discussed later in this chapter.
5. Weisbord, 1976.
6. Weisbord, 1976:431.
7. Waterman et al., 1980.
8. Waterman et al., 1980:20.
9. Waterman et al., 1980:24. The characteristics to which "skills" refer have become mainstream in management thinking in the form of the concept "core competencies" (Prahalad and Hamel, 1990).
10. Waterman et al., 1980:26.
11. Galbraith et al., 2002:3.
12. Galbraith et al., 2002:3.
13. Nadler and Tushman, 1988.
14. Burke, 2002.
15. Bolman and Deal, 2003.
16. Bolman and Deal, 2003:17.
17. Bolman and Deal, 2003:242.
18. Morgan, 1993, 1997.
19. Johnson and Scholes, 2002.
20. Verity, 2003.
21. See also Stauffer, 2002; Mante-Meijer et al., 1998; and Schoemaker, 1995.
22. This treatment of gap analysis is derived from Billsberry, 1998.

23. Hambrick and Frederickson, 2001.
24. Picken and Dess, 1998:35.
25. Johnson and Scholes, 2002.
26. Quinn, 1988.
27. Cooke and Lafferty, 1983. The OCI instrument is marketed by Human Synergistics, who claim that it is the most widely used of all organizational culture measures. For details on the OCI, see http://www.human-synergistics.com.au/content/products/diagnostics/p_oci.html.
28. Johnson, 1998:141.
29. Johnson, 1998:139.
30. For detailed treatments of the concept of organizational culture and associated measurement issues, see Ashkanasy et al., 2000, and Martin, 2001. The former is the more mainstream treatment of the two; the latter, a more critical perspective.
31. Bolman and Deal, 2003:69.
32. Bolman and Deal, 2003.
33. Ashkenas et al., 1995.
34. Ashkenas et al., 1995:7.
35. Stewart, 1996.
36. Maurer, 1996.
37. Galbraith et al., 2002.
38. This discussion is drawn from Grundy, 1997; Harrison and Shirom, 1999; and Scholes, 1998.
39. Grundy, 1997.
40. This treatment of force-field is based on McWhinney, 1997, and Harrison and Shirom, 1999.
41. This case was prepared by El Feletto and is based on material provided in Anonymous, 2001, 2003, 2004a, 2004b; Donlan, 2003; Holmes, 2001, 2003a, 2003b; Holman, 1998; Laing, 2003; Reinhardt and Browder, 1998; Taylor, 2003; Wallace, 1998.
42. Reinhardt and Browder, 1998.
43. Anonymous, 2004b.
44. Anonymous, 2004b.
45. Taylor, 2003.
46. Anonymous, 2003.
47. Anonymous, 2004a.

Resistance to Change

Learning objectives

On completion of this chapter you should be able to:

- Identify signs of resistance to change.
- Understand reasons for resistance to change.
- Be alert to resistance from within the ranks of management.
- Recognize the strengths and weaknesses of various approaches to the management of resistance to change.

One of the commonly cited causes for the lack of success of organizational change is "resistance to change." As such, it is not surprising that it is a phenomenon that encourages some strong responses. Maurer asserts, bluntly, that "resistance kills change,"[1] while Foote colorfully describes resistance as "one of the nastiest, most debilitating workplace cancers [and claims that] there isn't a more potent, paradoxical or equal-opportunity killer of progress and good intentions."[2] In a similar vein, Geisler describes those with a pattern of resisting change as "bottom-feeders" who resist change because of its potential to remove the "waste" (infighting, inefficient processes) on which they "feed."[3]

At the same time, other commentators have a more sympathetic "take" on resistance to change. A stark example in popular culture is the treatment of change in the *Dilbert* cartoons.[4] (See Table 6.1.)

Similarly, the image that one has of managing change is likely to be associated with a different perspective on the meaning of resistance (see Table 6.2).

This chapter investigates the phenomenon of resistance to change and what it might mean to manage it.

SUPPORT FOR CHANGE

Although "resistance to change" is a deeply embedded concept in the field of change, attention to this phenomenon should be placed in the context of recognition that people do not always resist change. Instead, they will often "embrace change"[5] and work enthusiastically in support of change. There are many reasons why people are likely to

TABLE 6.1 The Dilbert Principle on Change

Source: Adams, 1996:198.

People hate change, and with good reason. Change makes us stupider, relatively speaking. Change adds new information to the universe, information that we don't know. . . . On the other hand, change is good for people who are causing the change. They understand the new information that is being added to the universe. They grow smarter in comparison to the rest of us. This is reason enough to sabotage their efforts. I recommend sarcasm with a faint suggestion of threat.

Changer: "I hope that I can count on your support."

You: "No problem. I'll be delighted to jeopardize my short-term career goals to help you accomplish your career objectives."

Changer: "That's not exactly—"

You: "I don't mind feeling like a confused rodent and working long hours, especially if the payoff is a new system that I vigorously argued against."

The goal of change management is to dupe slow-witted employees into thinking change is good for them by appealing to their sense of adventure and love of challenge. This is like convincing a trout to leap out of a stream to experience the adventure of getting deboned.

TABLE 6.2 Images of Resistance to Change

Image of Managing Change	Perspective on Resistance to Change
Director	Resistance is a sign that not everybody is on board in terms of making the change. Resistance can and must be overcome in order to move change forward. Change managers need specific skills to ensure that they can deal with resistance to change.
Navigator	Resistance is expected. It is not necessarily a sign of people being outside of their comfort zone so much as the fact that there are different interests within the organization and some of these may be undermined by the change. Resistance, therefore, will not always be able to be overcome although this should be achieved as much as possible.
Caretaker	Resistance is possible but likely to be short-lived and ultimately futile. This is because, ultimately, changes will occur regardless of the attempts of individual actors within the organization to halt them. At best resistance might temporarily delay change but not be able to halt its inexorable impact.
Coach	Resistance is something that needs to be recognized and expected as change takes people out of their comfort zone. Change managers need to work with resistance in a way that reveals to the resistor that such actions are not in accord with good teamwork within the organization.
Interpreter	Resistance is likely where people lack understanding of "what is going on," where the change is taking the organization, and what impact it will have on specific individuals. Making sense of the change, helping to clarify what it means, and reestablishing individual identity with the process and the expected outcome of the change will assist in addressing the underlying problems that led to the emergence of resistance.
Nurturer	Resistance is largely irrelevant to whether or not change will occur. Changes will occur but not always in predictable ways. Therefore, resisting change will be largely a matter of guesswork by the resistor since change often emerges from the clash of chaotic forces and it is usually not possible to identify, predict, or control the direction of change.

be supportive of change. Kirkpatrick identifies the following as possible outcomes that are likely to cause people to react positively to change:[6]

- *Security*. The change may increase demand for an individual's skills and/or may put the organization on a more secure footing with subsequent impact on employment prospects.
- *Money*. The change may involve salary increases.
- *Authority*. The change may involve promotion and/or the allocation of additional decision-making discretion.
- *Status/prestige*. There may be changes in titles, work assignments, office allocations, and so forth.
- *Responsibility*. Job changes may occur.
- *Better working conditions*. The physical environment may change; new equipment may be provided.
- *Self-satisfaction*. Individuals may feel a greater sense of achievement and challenge.
- *Better personal contacts*. The change may provide an individual with enhanced contact with influential people.
- *Less time and effort*. The change may improve operational efficiencies.

SIGNS OF RESISTANCE TO CHANGE

Resistance to change may take many forms. Hultman draws a distinction between active and passive resistance and identifies a range of "symptoms" associated with each.[7] The symptoms of active resistance are identified as:

- Being critical.
- Finding fault.
- Ridiculing.
- Appealing to fear.
- Using facts selectively.
- Blaming or accusing.
- Sabotaging (see Table 6.3, "Merger in Adland").
- Intimidating or threatening.
- Manipulating.
- Distorting facts.
- Blocking.
- Undermining.
- Starting rumors.
- Arguing.

Those symptoms identified with passive resistance are:

- Agreeing verbally but not following through ("malicious compliance"[8]).
- Failing to implement change.

TABLE 6.3 Merger in Adland

Source: Coombs, 1990.

When the advertising agencies Mojo and MDA merged, a decision was made to house all staff in the same building. However, as an interim step, all creative staff (copywriters, art directors, and production staff) would move to the existing Mojo offices and all management staff (the "suits") to MDA's offices.

One of the Mojo people required to move was its finance director, Mike Thorley. Mike was one of the original Mojo employees and had come to think of himself more as a partner in the business than as an employee. However, the merger quickly disabused him of this when, the same as all other Mojo employees, he had no warning of the merger. When the announcement came, he reacted with both shock and anger. To add insult to injury, he was now required to move to the MDA offices—a move that felt to him like a banishment—where he would report to MDA's finance director, who had been put in charge of finance for the merged entity.

The Mojo culture had been considerably less formal than that of MDA. It was custom for Mojo staff to have a few drinks together after work seated around an old, solid-white bench in the office. In an attempt to make Thorley and his Mojo colleagues feel more at home, a modern black laminate bar had been installed in the MDA offices. One morning, Mike Thorley arrived at work with a chainsaw and cut the bar in two.

- Procrastinating or dragging one's feet.
- Feigning ignorance.
- Withholding information, suggestions, help, or support.
- Standing by and allowing change to fail.

This list is not exhaustive and there can clearly be some debate about whether the various symptoms are mutually exclusive (e.g., "ridiculing" and "being critical"). However, this does not reduce its value, which is primarily to alert us to the diverse range of phenomena through which resistance to change can be manifest.

WHY DO PEOPLE RESIST CHANGE?

Dislike of Change

It is very common to hear it said that the major impediment that managers face in introducing change is that people dislike change and will resist it. However, the difficulty with the blanket statement that "people dislike change" is that, if this is so, how do we explain that people sometimes welcome change? This suggests that it is unwise to assume an innate dislike of change, independent of context. Karp provides a possible explanation when he argues that people don't resist change; they resist pain and one of the most painful things is boredom, which is the opposite of change (see Table 6.4).

Discomfort with Uncertainty

As individuals we tend to vary in terms of how comfortable we are with ambiguity. Some of us revel in—or at least are not particularly perturbed by—"mystery flights" where the destination is unknown. However, others of us are uncomfortable in this situation, leading us to be resistant to change unless significant details of the journey

TABLE 6.4 **A Personal View on Change**

Source: Maurer, 1996:23.

John Cage, the U.S. composer, pianist, and writer provides an interesting perspective on the notion of innate dislike of change when he states, *"I can't understand why people are frightened of new ideas. I'm frightened of the old ones."*

and destination are revealed. For some, the uncertainty is magnified by a lack of confidence that they have the skills/capabilities needed in the postchange situation.

To the extent that the strategic intent is not complemented by clarity as to expected actions, the chances increase that employees will fail to convert a change initiative into supporting action at their level of the organization. The key point here is that the lack of supporting action is not due to overt resistance or even apathy; it is due to the lack of a clear understanding of what such supportive action would "look like."

Perceived Negative Effect on Interests

The readiness for change will also be affected by people's perceptions of the likely effect of the change on their "interests," a term that can cover a wide range of factors including their authority, status, rewards (including salary), opportunity to apply expertise, membership of friendship networks, autonomy, and security. People find it easier to be supportive of changes that they see as not threatening such interests and may resist those that are seen as damaging to these interests.[9]

Attachment to the Established Culture/Ways of Doing Things

As noted previously, one valuable "image of organizations" is of them as cultural systems that comprise beliefs, values, and artifacts, or, put simply, "the way we do things around here."[10] Readiness for change can be significantly affected by the degree of attachment to the existing culture. Reger et al.[11] argue that organizational members interpret change proposals from management through their existing mental models. In this regard they note:

> A particularly powerful mental model is the set of beliefs members hold about the organization's identity . . . Identity beliefs are critical to consider when implementing fundamental change because organizational identity is what individuals believe is central, distinctive, and enduring about their organization. These beliefs are especially resistant to change because they are embedded within members' most basic assumptions about the organization's character.[12]

Reger et al.[13] argue that two specific mental barriers tend to undermine the acceptance of change initiatives that are interpreted as inconsistent with the existing organizational identity. First, passive resistance (for example, apathy or anxiety) occurs when managers exhort subordinates to implement a change without first clarifying the connection between the change and some aspect of the organizational identity. According to Reger et al., such a connection is necessary "for deep comprehension and action."[14] Second, active resistance occurs when a change is interpreted as directly in conflict with key elements of the organizational identity. Greenwood and Hinings make a similar point when they argue that ways of organizing "become infused with a taken-for-granted quality, in which actors unwittingly accept the prevailing template as appropriate, right, and the proper way of doing things."[15]

Perceived Breach of Psychological Contract

Employees form beliefs as to the nature of the reciprocal relationship between them and their employer, that is, a "psychological contract."[16] A breach or violation of this contract occurs when employees believe that the employer is no longer honoring its "part of the deal." In a variant on this theme, Strebel argues that employees and the organization for which they work can be seen as involved in a "personal compact" that defines their relationship.[17] This compact may be explicit or implicit (or a mix of both) and involves three dimensions: *formal*, *psychological*, and *social*. The formal dimension covers such things as the specific task that a person is employed to do, how this relates to tasks carried out by others in the organization, how performance is assessed, and the associated level of remuneration. The psychological dimension—largely unwritten—relates to expectations in terms of trust, loyalty, and recognition. The social dimension refers to the espoused values of the organization. According to Strebel, where the proposed change conflicts with key elements of personal compacts, the outcome is likely to be resistance to change.[18]

Lack of Conviction That Change Is Needed

It helps change advocates if the belief that change is needed is widespread within the organization. However, what seems obvious to some ("We must change!") is not necessarily seen this way by others ("What's the problem?"). There are many reasons that may account for complacency, including a track record of success and the lack of any visible crisis. People are likely to react negatively to change when they feel that there is no need for the change.[19]

Lack of Clarity as to What Is Expected

Sometimes proposed changes, particularly of a strategic nature, are not complemented by clear information as to the specific implications at the level of action by individuals. Where this is the case, the chances increase that employees will fail to convert a change initiative into supporting action at their level of the organization. "A brilliant business strategy . . . is of little use unless people understand it well enough to apply it."[20] The key point here is that that lack of supporting action is not due to antagonism toward the proposed change; it is due to the lack of a clear understanding of what such supportive action would "look like." Taking this as their starting point, Gadiesh and Gilbert argue the virtue of organizations having a "strategic principle"; that is, "a memorable and actionable phase that distils a company's corporate strategy into its unique essence and communicates it throughout the organization."[21]

Belief That the Specific Change Being Proposed Is Inappropriate

Those affected by a proposed change are likely to form a view that it is either a good idea ("We needed to do something like this") or a bad idea ("Whose crazy idea is this?" or "It's a fad"). In turn, this view is likely to affect their readiness for change. As an advocate of a particular change, it is very easy to see those who support the change as perspicacious and to lament as myopic those who do not support the change. In this regard, it is not uncommon for those who are unsupportive to be given the pejorative label "resistant to change." This is not necessarily an appropriate label given that the stance being judged is not a reaction to a proposal for change in a generic sense but to a proposal for a specific change.

In this regard, it is also worth considering that in some cases the "resistors" might be right; the proposed change may not be the great idea that its proposers assume. That is, sometimes "the voice of resistance can keep us from taking untimely or foolish actions."[22] The change also may be seen as inappropriate because of a fundamental difference of "vision." Strategies are means to achieve objectives that flow from an organization's vision. Change, as a part of the enactment of strategy, is therefore highly likely to be an arena of organizational life where divergent views over appropriate strategic direction will be manifest.

Belief That the Timing Is Wrong

People may resist, not because they think that the proposed change is wrong—they may, in fact, like the idea—but because they believe the timing to be wrong.[23] This may be due to change fatigue (as noted above) or it may be due to a completely different matter such as the view that the proposed change, if it were to occur at the proposed time, would have undesirable effects on key customers or employees or alliance partners—effects that would not eventuate if the timing were to be altered.

Excessive Change

Stensaker et al.[24] note the phenomenon of "excessive change," which they characterize as having two forms. The first form occurs where an organization is pursuing several change initiatives at once and these are perceived by people in the organization as unrelated or, even worse, in conflict. The second form occurs where an organization introduces a series of changes and people in the organization feel that resources (including their time) are being reassigned to new initiatives before the earlier ones have been given sufficient attention for them to be effectively implemented. These "waves of changes" may produce "initiative fatigue" and "burnout," which inhibit readiness for further change.[25] Similarly, Maurer refers to this as a matter of "resilience," arguing that people will resist further change when they are "just plain beat,"[26] while Abrahamson refers to "permafrost" organizations where change-fatigued managers react to "initiative overload" by resisting further change and voicing "an aggressive cynicism."[27] (For more detail on "excessive change," see Table 6.5.)

Cumulative Effect of Other Changes in One's Life

Individuals' readiness for change at work is affected by what else is going on in their lives. Indexes of stress comprise elements from diverse aspects of one's life, not just those associated with the employment relationship.

Perceived Clash with Ethics

Piderit[28] notes that research on obedience to authority indicates that resistance might be motivated by individuals' desires to act in accordance with their ethical principles.[29] However, this need not mean that the resistance is overt because, as Piderit also notes,

TABLE 6.5 The Organizational Effects of Excessive Change

Source: Stensaker et al., 2002.

In their research into the phenomenon of "excessive change," Stensaker et al. identified three common organizational consequences of excessive change that they characterized as "musical chairs," "orchestrating without a conductor," and "shaky foundations."

Musical chairs—a reference to the children's game—is the phenomenon whereby managers move frequently between a declining number of positions in a regularly changing organization structure. Unless carefully managed, this can have detrimental effects. For example, those managers who are the most capable—and therefore likely to be the most attractive on the job market—may be the ones who leave the organization rather than the lesser performers. Another detrimental effect that was observed was that with the "churn" in management positions, fewer people in positions with implementation responsibilities had a grasp of the overall strategic intent that lay behind the various change initiatives.

Orchestrating without a conductor refers to the related situation where lower-level employees felt that they had been abandoned to their own devices because their middle managers seemed incapable of managing the change process. Sometimes this took the form of the incapacity of middle managers to translate the change initiatives into terms relevant to the daily work of the lower-level employees, because, due to restructuring at middle management level, those managers were not sufficiently familiar with the employees' work.

Shaky foundations refers to the sense by employees that the organization is in a chaotic state, in an uncomfortable limbo between partially abandoned past practices and partially introduced new practices. Where waves of change are involved, the new practices are in various stages of implementation from just introduced to nearly complete.

threats to advancement or security can lead middle managers to not speak up about such ethical concerns.[30]

Reaction to the Experience of Previous Changes

The most reliable predictor of how people will interpret the implications of an announcement of change is their experience of previous organizational changes.[31] Based on such experiences people develop "scripts" for "how change works" which become the "lens" through which they view subsequent change initiatives.[32] (See Exercise 6.1.)

EXERCISE 6.1

Identify Your Change Script

People's previous experiences of change provide them with a "script"—a set of assumptions/beliefs as to what happens in a situation of organizational change.

Based on your previous experiences of organizational change, what are your expectations in terms of what events/actions/outcomes will follow the announcement of a program of change in an organization?

Note: Choose the format that suits you; for example, one option is bullet points; another is a narrative (story-like) approach.

The significance of this is that managers, when seeking to implement change in an organization, are likely to be the unfortunate victims, or fortunate beneficiaries, of

TABLE 6.6 Change Scripts: Implications for Managing Change

Source: Geigle, 1997:8.

1. Begin change initiatives with a systematic inquiry into organizational members' memories of past organizational changes.
2. Don't tell organizational members to leave their past behind as this is unlikely to occur. Because they are experience-based, scripts have a credibility that cannot be removed by edict. Suppressing them means that they "may go underground but they won't go away."
3. If existing scripts are an impediment to successful change, their effect will only be challenged if the script-holders are subject to "direct, fully-engaged, rich-with-stimuli experiences" through which they learn that the change experience can be different/positive.

scripts that were generated in contexts in which they had no part and of which they are quite likely to be unaware. Where key elements of this script come from experiences in the same organization and maybe also the same managers, the impact on reactions to change is likely to be even more significant. Scripts are influential because they are based on real-life experiences and, as such, are likely to be given greater credibility than the words/assurances of current managers (see Table 6.6).

Where the past experience has been negative, cynicism is likely to result, which in turn reduces willingness to engage in future change efforts.[33] Stensaker et al. argue that the cynical, often-cited BOHICA ("Bend over, here it comes again.") response is a strategy based on learning by experience.[34]

Disagreement with the Way the Change Is Being Managed

Dent and Goldberg describe this notion that people resist change as "a mental model that . . . is almost universally accepted in organizational life."[35] However, they argue, despite its acceptance, the concept "resistance to change" is severely compromised by its association with the idea that this resistance is a fundamental psychological syndrome.[36] According to Dent and Goldberg, the use of this concept ultimately impacts negatively on the quality of change implementation because it focuses management attention on the supposedly innate reactions of employees to change and away from the quality of the management of the change process. Rather than framing situations as ones in which management must "overcome resistance to change," they argue that they could often equally validly be labeled "overcoming perfectly natural reactions to poor management" or "common management mistakes in implementing change."[37]

In a similar vein, Kahn advises:

> In considering obstacles to change, we must keep in mind the deceptive nature of our concepts. When we want change, we speak of those who do not as presenting obstacles and resistance. When we want stability, we speak of perseverance and commitment among those who share our views. Behavior of people in the two situations might be identical; it is their stance relative to our own that dictates the choice of language.[38]

Piderit argues that the construction of the situation as one of "resistance to change" may be a manifestation of a fundamental attribution error; that is, those managing the change initiative attribute negative outcomes to the actions ("resistance") of others rather than to inadequacies in their change management.[39] (Note: This blaming is not one-sided; Piderit notes that employees are also likely to blame management for failed change rather than themselves.)[40]

It is easy to understand how a manager can be attracted to the proposition that the lack of success of a change program in which he or she is deeply involved is due to "resistance to change," as this explanation displaces attention from the actions (specifically, the change management skills) of the manager to the actions of the recipients. It is also an explanation that is likely to seem very plausible to many people because of the "almost universal acceptance" of the view that people resist change.

EXERCISE 6.2

Preventing Resistance

Listed below are a numbers of reasons why people may be resistant to a change. For each of the reasons, identify *at least one action* that could be taken by management to reduce the prospect that it will be a significant source of resistance.

Reason for Resistance	Proposed Action
Dislike of change	
Discomfort with uncertainty	
Perceived negative effects on interests	
Attachment to established culture/ways of doing things	
Perceived breach of psychological contract	
Lack of conviction that change is needed	
Lack of clarity as to what is expected	
Belief that the specific change being proposed is inappropriate	
Belief that the timing is wrong	
Excessive change	
Cumulative effect of other changes in one's life	
Perceived clash with ethics	
Reaction to the experience of previous changes	
Disagreement with the way the change is being managed	

However, while this explanation may be comforting to the manager concerned, it might not be the wisest course of action in an organization seeking to enhance the quality of its management practice. The latter is more likely to be served through a reflection on the contribution to the lack of success made by the way the change was managed. If a change is felt by those affected to be managed in a manner that is inappropriate—for example, insufficiently consultative—they may resist the change.[41] This can occur even where they are supportive of the idea that the proposed change is needed.

MANAGERS AS CHANGE RESISTORS

Most discussions of resistance to change present managers as the advocates of change with lower-level employees cast in the role of resistors. However, it is important not to assume that the only ones who may not respond positively to proposals for change are "the managed" and not the managers. This requires a shift in the way in which we normally think of change; that is, as something that managers have to manage in the face of varying degrees of resistance from nonmanagement employees. While the latter certainly occurs in many instances, it is important to recognize that the managers in an organization are not necessarily always passionate advocates of change.[42]

One reason why it makes sense to recognize that managers may resist change is that while it sometimes makes sense to refer to managers collectively—that is, as one group—on other occasions it is the differences within the ranks of management that are of more significance. Change represents a situation where differences are often to the fore; for example, where a particular change initiative is proposed by some managers in a company (perhaps those within a particular department) but opposed by others (those in a different department). Managers, at least as much as any other category of employee, are likely to have within their ranks a range of opinions as to whether a proposed change is "a good idea." Even where there is absolutely no question as to the dedication of all managers to the long-term interests of their company, different views are likely to form as to which initiatives/changes represent the best ways to achieve that outcome.

Even when we treat managers as one group, they may act in ways that, albeit unconsciously and unintentionally, resist change. Managers are likely to have particular beliefs as to the nature of the business that they're in, who the key competitors are, and where future "threats" are most likely to come from, and these beliefs become "cognitive maps" that act as filters through which the plausibility/desirability of possible changes are assessed.[43] Whereas lower-level employees may resist a change once it is in the process of being implemented, the resistance by senior managers is likely to occur at the stage of conceptualization of strategic options (see Table 6.7).

In some instances, managers may feel themselves ready for change but "miss" the signs that it is needed. The process whereby this can occur has been called the "boiled frog" phenomenon, as it is seen as analogous to a classic experiment involving the physiological response of frogs.[44] In the experiment, a frog is put in a pan of water, which is then slowly heated. As long as the water temperature increases slowly, the frog will stay in the pan until it boils to death even though there is nothing preventing it from jumping out at any point. However, if a frog is put into a pan of already boiling water, it will quickly jump out and survive. Organizations become the equivalent of the boiled frog if they fail to respond to a series of changes, each of which may be small but that cumulatively comprise a situation where the organization is placed in peril.

It is often when organizations are at their most successful that they are most vulnerable to this phenomenon, because success—interpreted as the "proof" that they are doing "the right thing"—predisposes them to be less receptive to cues that change is needed. The very characteristics that have led to success become, over time, the basis for an organization's downfall. Information that should set off warning bells—such as radical environmental change—is either ignored or interpreted in such a way that it is

TABLE 6.7 Liz Claiborne

Source: Siggelkow, 2001.

Founded in 1976, Liz Claiborne went public in 1981 and five years later was on the *Fortune* 500 list. During the 1980s, it achieved the highest average return on year-end equity of all *Fortune* 500 industrial companies. In May 1991, shares that cost $10,000 at the time of the initial offering now had a market value of $610,000.

The company's success began in the late 1970s when designer Liz Claiborne identified professional women as a growing market segment. Her approach was to design clothes that provided an option between the classic dark-blue suit and haute couture. The collections were designed to allow mixing and matching of items; by pioneering clothes production overseas, Liz Claiborne was able to add very competitive pricing to its attractions.

Liz Claiborne sold its clothing in large up-market department stores. Although such stores were traditionally organized around classifications (such as blouses and pants), Liz Claiborne required a dedicated space to present its collection and rejected orders from stores not willing to do this. This developed into the idea of dedicated Liz Claiborne concept shops within department stores. Because of the popularity of its brand, Liz Claiborne was able to talk the stores into covering the costs of adding these shops. Also, stores were unable to purchase individual components of a "concept group" of clothes; they were required to purchase the full group (matching blouses, shirts, skirts, and pants). The company also had a policy of manufacturing about 5 percent less merchandise than was ordered by stores and had a no-reorder policy.

However, by the early 1990s, some changes in the environment began to work against the Liz Claiborne approach. A trend toward more casualization in the workplace was initially underestimated by the company and, as a result, it did not produce clothing responsive to this need. Subsequently (1992), it did acquire Russ Togs, a manufacturer of moderately priced women's sportswear, as a basis for its move into national and regional chain department stores; however, this move took the company head-on with competitors who offered reordering.

At the same time, traditional department stores were under extreme pressure, many filing for bankruptcy and all seeking to cut costs. They cut down the retail support that they provided to their suppliers, a change that directly and significantly affected Liz Claiborne given its in-store strategy. Department stores also demanded larger discounts from their suppliers. However, the company refused to pay for retailing support or to cut prices. Liz Claiborne, with declining sales and lower margins for its retailers than other brands provided, became less attractive to department stores. Liz Claiborne's net income went into decline and, from 1992 to 1994, its market capitalization fell from $3.5 billion to $1.3 billion.

But why was this situation allowed to occur? Why was the management team resistant to change? According to Nicolaj Siggelkow, past success had created in the minds of Liz Claiborne executives a "mental map" as to the basis of the company's success, which, although it may have been an accurate reflection of past performance, was not helpful as a guide to necessary action in the changed environment. He suggests that this situation was also contributed to by a sense of infallibility and "a tinge of hubris," characteristics sometimes found in companies that have been very successful. A senior executive of Liz Claiborne is quoted as proudly stating: "We like to think of ourselves as the IBM of the garment district."[a]

P.S. In 1995, a new CEO, Paul Charron, was appointed who initiated a series of operational and marketing changes that reversed the decline in the company's fortunes and, by May 1997, Liz Claiborne's market capitalization was up to $3.2 billion.

[a]Deveny, 1989, cited in Siggelkow, 2001.

seen as confirming rather than requiring a questioning of existing strategy.[45] This phenomenon—"the paradox of success"[46]—has been popularized by Danny Miller as "The Icarus Paradox."[47] This is an allusion to the Icarus of Greek mythology whose wax wings gave him the power to fly high, so high that he got too close to the sun, whereupon his wings melted and he fell to his death. Several high-profile international firms, including IBM, General Motors, Laura Ashley, Polaroid, Apple, McDonald's, and Xerox, have been identified as being affected by this phenomenon at some point in their history.[48]

MANAGING RESISTANCE

In this section, we present a range of different approaches to the management of resistance. Each takes a different angle on how to deal with resistance. Collectively, they provide an array of options for managers to consider.

A "Situational" Approach

A *Harvard Business Review* article by Kotter and Schlesinger provides the "classic" prescription on managing resistance to change.[49] They propose six methods for managing resistance:

1. Education and communication.
2. Participation and involvement.
3. Facilitation and support.
4. Negotiation and agreement.
5. Manipulation and cooptation.
6. Explicit and implicit coercion.

This approach is "situational" in that they argue that the selection of method by managers should be determined by contextual factors (see Table 6.8). However, according to Kotter and Schlesinger, "the most common mistake managers make is to use only one approach or a limited set of them regardless of the situation."[50]

The Resistance Cycle, aka "Let Nature Take Its Course"

One approach to the management of change presents the reactions of people to change as involving a progression through a series of psychological stages. For Jick and Peiperl, these stages are shock (manifest as immobilization), defensive retreat (anger), acknowledgment (mourning), and adaptation and change (acceptance).[51] For Scott and Jaffe, the cycle has four phases, beginning with *denial*, then moving through *resistance* to *exploration* to *commitment*.[52]

Denial involves a refusal to recognize the situation being faced. This may variously involve outright denial ("this can't be happening), ignoring what is happening on the grounds that there is no need to act any differently because "it'll all blow over," not being receptive to new information, or minimizing the necessary change in action ("all that's needed are a few minor changes to what we do"). *Resistance* begins with the recognition that the situation is not going to go away; the past is mourned, stress levels rise, and both passive and active forms of resistance emerge (see previous discussion of signs of resistance).

However, within the Scott and Jaffe model, resistance is a phase that ends as individuals begin to separate from the past and become more confident of their capacity to

TABLE 6.8 Kotter and Schlesinger's Methods for Managing Resistance to Change

Source: Adapted from Kotter and Schlesinger, 1979.

Method	Characteristic	Context (where to use)	Concern (possible difficulties)
Education and communication	Informing people as to the rationale for the change; providing information	Where resistance is due to lack of information or misinformation	May be very time-consuming, which, in some change situations, may be a significant problem
Participation and involvement	Involving people in the change process as active participants	Where resistance is a reaction to a sense of exclusion from the process	May slow the process and may introduce an element of compromise in decisions that could reduce the optimality of the change
Facilitation and support	Providing resources—both technical and emotional	Where resistance is due to anxiety and uncertainty	Requires financial, time, and interpersonal support that managers might not feel able or prepared to give
Negotiation and agreement	Offering incentives to actual or potential resistors	Where resistors are in a strong position to undermine the change if their concerns are not addressed	May lead to a "watering down" of key elements of the change
Manipulation and cooptation	Selective use of information; "buying" the support of certain individuals by giving them key roles in the change process	Where participation, facilitation, or negotiation is too time-consuming or resource-demanding	This approach runs the risk of creating a backlash if it is seen as a crude and unethical attempt to trick or bribe them into compliance
Explicit and implicit coercion	Threatening people with undesirable consequences (e.g., firing) if they resist	Where the change recipients have little capacity to effectively resist; where survival of the organization is at risk if change does not occur quickly	The desired change may occur; however, "support" achieved in this manner is likely to be superficial and a threat to the enduring nature of the change. Underlying resentment may come back to "haunt" the manager(s)

play a role in the future that they face. The third phase, *exploration*, involves a reenergizing and a preparedness to explore the possibilities involved in the new situation. Finally, the individual enters the *commitment* stage, where attention is focused on the new course of action.[53]

If the response of individuals conforms to this pattern, it opens up the possibility that a viable approach to managing resistance is to "let nature take its course"; that is, to minimize intervention on the grounds that resistance is a phase that is both "natural"—perhaps even necessary (as a coping mechanism)—and one from which individuals will emerge.[54] However, Scott and Jaffe also argue that moving through the phases can take several months and that an individual can become "stuck" in a phase.[55] Even if such situations are not the norm, they are sufficient to indicate that a laissez-faire response by management is likely to be unwise given that intervention may at least reduce some of the negative effects of resistance to change.

"Creative Counters" to Expressions of Resistance

Karp deals with a micro-level phenomenon: specific statements made in response to suggestions for change and that may be a surface manifestation of resistance. He identifies specific verbal replies to these statements that he argues constitute "creative counters" to the statements of resistance (see Table 6.9).[56]

Thought Self-Leadership

Thought self-leadership (TSL) is "a process of influencing or leading through the purposeful control of one's thoughts."[57] This approach to the management of change is based on a series of linked propositions and the application of associated techniques. These propositions are:[58]

1. People's perceptions are a primary determinant of how they respond to change.
2. TSL can influence these perceptions through the use of the three processes: *beliefs and assumptions*, *self-talk*, and *mental imagery*.
   a. Some of the problems that individuals encounter result from dysfunctional thinking. Individuals are able to identify the *beliefs and assumptions* that constrain their ability to view change positively and replace them with ones that make them more positive.
   b. What we covertly tell ourselves (*self-talk*) corresponds to emotional states that in turn affect cognitions and behavior. Individuals who become aware of their "self-defeating internal verbalizations" and who are able to reformulate these in a positive manner are able to develop more positive perceptions of change.[59]
   c. *Mental imagery* refers to the imagining of the performance of a task before it is undertaken. Mental visualization of the successful accomplishment of a task can enhance an individual's perception that the task be successfully undertaken.
3. Together, these three processes contribute to the creation of habitual ways of thinking (aka *thought patterns*). Thought patterns that are likely to impact a person's response to change include "opportunity thinking" and "obstacle thinking."[60] Opportunity thinking involves framing a new situation positively; that is, as an opportunity to learn new things and expand one's capabilities and experiences. On the other hand, obstacle thinking involves framing the same situation negatively, that is, as a threat. Individuals who perceive challenging situations (such as change) as opportunities make more effort to deal constructively with the challenges that they present, whereas those who focus on the threat aspect are more likely to resist the change.

TABLE 6.9 Expressions of Resistance and Management Responses

Source: Adapted from Karp, 1996:120–22.

Expression 1: "I don't want to." (aka "the block")

Comment: This is a direct/authentic response; relatively unambiguous and therefore most straightforward to handle.

Response/Counter: "Why?"/"What's your concern?"

Expression 2: "Tell me *exactly* what you want me to do." (aka "the rollover")

Comment: This response is ambiguous as it may be a genuine request for more specific information, but it also may be a form of passive resistance (i.e., the subtext may be "If you do not communicate absolutely clearly and precisely what you want me to do, I cannot be held accountable for what may or may not be done."

Response/Counter: "In what respects are you unclear as to what you are being asked to do?"

Expression 3: "I'll get on it first thing next week." (aka "the stall")

Comment: It may be that this is a response to a genuine lack of awareness of the urgency of action but it also may be an indication of a desire to avoid complying.

Response/Counter: "Is there anything of a serious nature that would prevent you from starting tomorrow?"

Expression 4: "Wow, what a great deal!" (aka "the reverse")

Comment: While it may be a genuine comment, it is also something that a resistor may say; that is, telling you what you want to hear to "get you off her back" and with no intention of actually doing anything supportive of the change.

Response/Counter: "I am really pleased that you feel this way. What exactly can I count on you to deliver and by when?"

Expression 5: "I think that the change would be better if it were first implemented in X's division/department." (aka "the sidestep")

Comment: There may be some truth in such a comment, but it is also a ploy that a resistor may use to shift the pressure to change to someone/anyone else in the organization.

Response/Counter: "I appreciate your concern and I do have plans for X. What I specifically want you to do is . . ."

Expression 6: "X isn't going to like this." (aka "the projected threat")

Comment: The resistance involves an implied threat that someone important—probably someone senior to you—will not be happy with the proposed change.

Response/Counter: Either (if true) "X has been part of the change process and is fully supportive" or "I'll be talking to X about the change. But what I'm most interested in at the moment is what *your* views are."

Expression 7: "You owe me one." (aka "the press")

Comment: This involves asking to be exempt from having to change as reciprocity for some previous favor done.

Response/Counter: "I haven't forgotten that I owe you one, but I need your support right now on this change."

Expression 8: "See what you're making me do." (aka "the guilt trip")

Comment: The resistor is attempting to deflect attention from his or her reactions by changing the focus of the discussion to the actions of the manager.

TABLE 6.9 Expressions of Resistance and Management Responses—*(concluded)*

Response/Counter: "I'm sorry that there is a problem for you—and we can talk about what we might be able to do to help—but we've given the matter a lot of thought and it is important for the organization that the change go ahead."

Expression 9: "But we've always done it the other way." (aka "the tradition")

Comment: New ways are not always better ways. However, if traditional ways are maintained, it should be because they are still the best ways, not just because they are how things have always been done in the past. Unfortunately, the attraction of established ways is sometimes (often?) because they are "safe," that is, less threatening than the unknown new ways.

Response/Counter: "The other way has served us well for a long time, but it was designed for a situation that has now changed." or "What could we do to make sure that the new way incorporates the best of our traditional approach?"

Neck and Manz report the results of a training program in which employees of America West Airlines received instruction on the application of techniques in regard to beliefs and assumptions, self-talk, mental imagery, and thought patterns. To this was added a final stage involving a process designed to prevent relapse into pre-TSL responses. From this study they conclude that "the effective self-regulation of cognitions can be learned/developed in an organizational setting—e.g., an individual's pattern of negative thinking can be altered."[61]

Thus, TSL focuses attention on the reactions of the recipients of change.[62] The strengths in this approach are that (1) it draws attention to the way in which the framing of the situation by the recipients can directly impact on their actions in regard to the change and (2) there are associated techniques that can be used to help people reframe a change situation more positively. However, in light of the many possible bases for resistance to change, it would be unwise for managers to assume that resistance to change is purely an artifact of misconception by the recipients of change.

Tinkering, Kludging, and Pacing

Because Abrahamson places a lot of emphasis on the detrimental effects of change fatigue (see above), his prescription for managing resistance centers on dealing with this phenomenon. He argues that in order to change successfully, organizations should make use of processes that he labels *tinkering* and *kludging*.

Both processes involve "the reconfiguration of existing practices and business models rather than the creation of new ones."[63] The difference between tinkering and kludging is a matter of scale, with tinkering being the more modest. As an example of *tinkering*, Abrahamson cites a company that produced military helicopters that was under intense market pressure to improve its development and production processes. Employees were burnt out and cynical due to the company's history of failed large-scale change initiatives. However, by adapting a very good product development model from the company's software division and making use of the mass-production expertise of employees who had previously worked in the automobile industry, resistance was minimal and a successful change to the helicopter development and production process was achieved.

Kludging is tinkering on a larger scale, such as where the leveraging of existing capabilities results in the development of a new business or division. Abrahamson cites

TABLE 6.10 **The Value of Pacing**

Source: Abrahamson, 2000:77–78.

One business leader who understands the value of pacing is Lou Gerstner. At IBM and, before that, at American Express Travel Related Services (TRS) and RJR Nabisco, his initial impact was pure creative destruction. In his first nine months at TRS, for example, Gerstner launched a massive reorganization of the card and traveler's check businesses, which was accompanied by a widespread shift of managers across those units. A rash of new product introductions followed quickly. . . .

But Gerstner had a genius for knowing when it was time to rest. He was alert to early signs of change fatigue: cynicism and burnout. He recognized that the success of the overall change campaign depended on the stability of the units involved and he was very thoughtful about how and when to intersperse the small changes among the big. At TRS, no new products were launched and no new executives were brought in from the outside for 18months after Gerstner's initial blitz. But he didn't sit back and do nothing. He tinkered constantly to prevent the company from drifting into inertia; he played with the structure, with the compensation system, with TRS product offerings. But the unthreatening nature of the interim changes allowed the company to better absorb a second wave of product launches and restructurings when it came.

the example of Barnes and Noble developing its Internet business based on its already-existing brand and its capabilities in areas such as procurement and inventory management. As with tinkering, it is presented by Abrahamson as much less likely to induce change fatigue and resistance. *Pacing* refers to the ability to mix major change initiatives, the ones most likely to be destabilizing and disruptive, with tinkering and kludging (see Table 6.10).

The "Power of Resistance"

Rather than treating resistance to change as something that must be overcome, Maurer argues for an approach that uses the power of resistance to build support for change." This approach is based on the view that showing respect toward resistors builds stronger relationships and thereby improves the prospects of success of the change.[64] He identifies five "fundamental touchstones":[65]

1. *Maintain clear focus.* Keep focused on the objective; persevere and don't be diverted or demotivated if the immediate reaction of others is to resist.
2. *Embrace resistance.* Find out more about the resistance. Who are the resistors? What is the basis for their resistance? Recognize that there may be a further level of reason below the stated reasons.
3. *Respect those who resist.* Assume that those who are resistant to your initiative are doing so in good faith (even if you believe them to be misguided). Treat them, and their views, with respect.

4. *Relax.* Resist the temptation to "push back" if attacked. Tension limits your ability to keep the broader picture in mind. Listening will enable you to learn more about their hopes and fears and the actions that they might take.
5. *Join with the resistance.* Listen for points of commonality (e.g., fears, interests) to establish some common ground.

Jick and Peiperl take a similar position, arguing that managers should "rethink resistance" by recognizing it as a natural part of the adaptation to change process, a form of energy that may be able to be tapped and a form of feedback about the change process.[66] However, for these potential benefits to be gained, the resistance needs to be active. In some instances, passive resistance may take the form of silence, that is, the withholding of feedback/information.[67]

As noted earlier in this chapter, attributing problems in the change process to "resistance" has the potential to cause managers to direct insufficient attention to the extent to which the quality of their own management practices is contributing to the problems.

Although Maurer espouses the approach (above) as one to apply in most situations, he also acknowledges that there are likely to be times when it is not appropriate and when focusing a lot of attention on dissenters can be counterproductive:

> Sometimes it is best just to let resistance be. Woody Allen spoke of ruining his stand-up comedy by focusing on people who heckled him. By doing so, he lost his timing and the laughter of those who thought he was funny.[68]

Maurer identifies several "default options" for dealing with resistance (see Table 6.11).

EXERCISE 6.3

Responding to Resistance: Assessing Your Personal Style[69]

Consider a past change in which you were involved that was seriously affected by resistance.

1. When did you first become aware of resistance?
2. What form did the resistance take?
3. What were your first thoughts (e.g., anger, betrayal, confusion, relief)?
4. What made you decide that you had to do something?
5. What actions did you take?
6. What was the impact in the (a) short term and (b) long term?
7. If you could "rewind the tape," would you do anything differently? If so, what approach would you use?

TABLE 6.11 Dealing with Resistance: Default Options

Source: Adapted from Maurer, 1996.

Default Position	Characteristic	Limitations
Use power	. . . use of power may be subtle: a gentle reminder that lets people know who the boss is; a joke during a meeting just so that no one forgets who conducts their performance reviews; a recollection of what happened to others who opposed similar initiatives. Or it may be blatant: ranting, raving and striking fear into the hearts of those who dare to go against their wishes.[a]	• Possibly well-founded concerns may be suppressed. • Resistance is pushed underground. • Compliance rather than commitment is received. • There may be a "tit-for-tat" response.
Manipulate those who oppose	For example, use selective release of information so that opponents only have "part of the story."	• There may be destruction of trust if "trickery" is revealed, with resulting escalation of resistance.
Apply force of reason	Try to overwhelm opponents with "facts."	• This may "close-off" rather than enable needed dialogue.
Ignore resistance	Assume that resistance will be ineffective or disappear.	• Resistance may not disappear; by being ignored it may escalate.
Play off relationships	Call on opponents' sense of obligation to reciprocate support that has been previously provided to them.	• The [possibly well-founded] reasons for the original resistance remain unaddressed. • It is unlikely to be effective where concern is deep.
Make deals	"If you do this [for me], I'll do that [for you]."	• This does not work if resistance is high.
Kill the messenger	Get rid of the people who dare to question the wisdom of the change.	• Messengers will quickly learn only to bring "good news," ultimately destroying the capacity of top management to make informed decisions.
Give in	Give up on the initiative before the strength or validity of the resistance has been determined.	• This may mean a premature suspension of a necessary initiative.

[a]Maurer, 1996:36.

EXERCISE 6.4

Jack's Dilemma

Jack White is the newly appointed general manager of the pet food division of Strickland Corporation. He has completed a strategic review that has convinced him that the division needs to undergo substantial change in a number of areas and to do so relatively swiftly given the recent strategic moves of key competitors.

Although he is new, he is familiar enough with the company to know that there will be significant resistance to the changes from a number of quarters. He also suspects that some of this resistance will come from people with the capacity to act in ways that could seriously impede successful change.

Jack reflects on the situation. He believes that it is important to introduce the proposed changes soon, but he also recognizes that if he acts speedily in this regard, he'll have virtually no time to have a dialogue with staff about the proposed changes, much less involve them in any significant way.

One option is to act speedily and to make it clear that "consequences" will follow for anyone not cooperating. He certainly has the power to act on such a threat. The risk, Jack knows, is that even if no one outright resists, there's a big difference between not cooperating and acting in a manner that reflects commitment. He knows that he needs the cooperation of key groups of employees and that sometimes "minimum-level compliance" can be as unhelpful as outright resistance when it comes to implementing change. "But maybe I'm exaggerating this problem," he thinks to himself. "Maybe I should just go ahead with the change. If people don't like it, they can leave; if they stay, they'll come around."

But Jack's not sure. He reflects on another option: Maybe he should spend more time on building up support at least among key groups of managers and employees, if not more broadly within the organization. "Maybe," he thinks, "the need to change is not quite as immediate as I think." "I just know that I'd feel a whole lot better if this consultation could happen quickly."

Your Task

Jack respects your opinion on business matters and has asked you for your views on his situation. What factors would you suggest to Jack that he take into account in deciding what course of action to take?

EXERCISE 6.5

Ajax Minerals[70]

Ajax Minerals is a U.S. mining company. Recently, it was operating at full capacity but there were problems on the horizon. Within the next three or four years, Pacific Rim companies will be able to mine and ship the same minerals to the U.S. for less than Ajax can get them out of the ground. The leadership team saw this challenge and wanted to do something immediately. However, no one else in the company saw the threat. Supervisors and hourly workers could only see that work was going on around the clock and that they were earning a lot of overtime pay.

Although the current group of senior managers was fairly well respected, there was a history within Ajax of poorly run changes and even poorer management-labor relations. The latter had got so bad that if management asked for something, workers were immediately suspicious that management was up to something that would have unpleasant outcomes for the workers (e.g., layoffs, paycuts). In light of this, the leadership team was aware that, at the very least, the workers' reaction to any current initiative was likely to be a resigned "here we go again." Similarly, they were concerned that the union was likely to view any reference by management to "problems on the horizon" as a ploy to gain concessions during the next contract talks.

Given the history of their relationship, the leadership team expected workers to drag their feet on implementing any new approaches and by so doing undermine the prospects of success. History suggested that both supervisors and workers would do just enough to "get by," that is, they would provide minimum compliance.

Ajax management responded to the situation by establishing interactive sessions involving both managers and supervisors. They decided that they needed to make a compelling case for change before they began thinking about specific strategies. In the past, they had done the planning before ever getting others involved in any way, and suspected that that had contributed to the subsequent resistance. During the interactive sessions, the general manager and the managers made the case for change. As part of this process they used stories about various companies that had faced similar situations and had suffered badly as a result of their inability to respond to competitive forces. They also, for the first time, adopted an "open-book" approach in which employees were given unprecedented access to data on Ajax's financial performance, particularly "the numbers that drive the business." Following on from this, a practice was established whereby workers, supervisors and managers met weekly to share key performance numbers.

In the view of the Ajax management, they are already seeing a new level of cooperation between management and labor and are hopeful that it will help turn around the situation that has applied in the past in terms of management-labor relations.

Your Task:

1. Comment on the Ajax managers' approach to the situation that they faced. Do you think that it will work long-term? Provide supporting arguments for your view.
2. If you were dealing with the situation that the Ajax managers faced, what approach would you have taken? Provide supporting arguments for your approach.

Conclusion

In this chapter, we have focused on resistance to change. While it is understandably a key concern for those involved in the management of change, it is also important for the manager of change not to ignore the very many reasons that people can have for supporting change.

Resistance to change can be indicated by one or more of a wide range of active and passive signs ranging from willful acts of sabotage through to procrastination. It is also a phenomenon from which managers are not exempt. A wide range of different actions are available to managers as a means of trying to manage the resistance.

Specific implications flow from knowing that in most organizational change situations, there will be those who are resistant to the change. Prior to a proposed change, those managing the process should carry out a "resistance profile" that identifies:

1. The likely resistors and the likely reasons for the resistance.
2. The likely strength of the resistance.
3. The likely manifestations of the resistance.
4. The potential for the resistance to undermine the change initiative.

On the basis of the results of such a profile, managers should be able to identify, ahead of time, the likely situation that they will face and, on that basis, make informed decisions in regard to the actions that need to be taken to manage the resistance.

TABLE 6.12 Chapter Reflections for the Practicing Manager

- What symptoms of resistance to change have you experienced? Have you experienced both active and passive forms? Have you experienced them as a resistor yourself (as a recipient of change)? Have you experienced them as someone responsible for the management of change (as an initiator of change)?
- Which of the various reasons for resisting change do you believe to be the most common? What are your "top three" in this regard?
- Which of the various reasons for resisting change do you believe to be the most difficult to deal with (as a manager)? What are your "top three" in this regard?
- When senior managers resist change at the strategic level, they are in a position to cause more damage than employees resisting changes at the operational level. Have you worked in a company where you believe that management resistance to change may have existed? As a manager yourself, what would you try to do to prevent this happening?
- Which approach to the management of resistance attracts you? What is the reason for your choice? For example, is it because you think it to be the most effective or does it also relate to a view that you have about how people should be managed?

Supplemental Reading

Dent, E. B., and Goldberg, S. G. 1999. Challenging "resistance to change." *Journal of Applied Behavioral Science* 35:25–41.

Dym, B. 1999. Resistance in organizations: How to recognise, understand & respond to it. *OD Practitioner* 31(1):6–19.

Ford, J. D., Ford, L. W., and McNamara, R. T. 2001. Resistance and the background conversation of change. *Journal of Organizational Change Management* 15(2):105–21.

Jick, T. D., and Peiperl, M. A. 2003. The recipients of change. In *Managing change: Cases and concepts*. 2nd ed., 299–311. New York: McGraw-Hill/Irwin.

Kotter, J. P., and Schlesinger, L. A. 1979. Choosing strategies for change. *Harvard Business Review*, March–April:106–14.

Maurer, R. 1996. *Beyond the walls of resistance*. Austin, TX: Bard Books.

Piderit, S. K. 2000. Rethinking resistance and recognizing ambivalence: A multidimensional view of attitudes toward an organizational change. *Academy of Management Review* 25:783–94.

Reichers, A. E., Wanous, J. P., and Austin, J. A. 1997. Understanding and managing cynicism about organizational change. *Academy of Management Executive* 11(1):48–59.

Reger, R. K., Mullane, J. V., Gustafson, L. T., and DeMarie, S. M. 1994. Creating earthquakes to change organizational mindsets. *Academy of Management Executive* 8(4):31–43.

Strebel, P. 1996. Why do employees resist change? *Harvard Business Review*, May–June:86–92.

Case Study Problems at Perrier[71]

Perrier may well be the iconic brand in the world of mineral waters. However, regardless of the profile of the brand, the company that produces the bottled sparkling mineral water is having a tough time. It is the focus of what one commentator describes as "a vicious struggle underway for the soul of the business."[72]

The origins of the Perrier company can be traced to 1898 when a local doctor, Louis-Eugène Perrier, bought the mineral water source near Vergèze, France. The company grew steadily but demand really escalated in the late 1980s when it became highly fashionable and championed by a range of admirers including Wall Street yuppies. At its peak (1989), Perrier sold 1.2 billion bottles (830 million in 2003), almost half to consumers in the United States.

The boom years were good for the Perrier workers. Buoyant profits were associated with regular pay rises, social benefits, and extra holidays. However, in 1990, the finding of a minute trace of benzene in a bottle led to the collapse of U.S. sales.[73] By 1992, annual output had halved and the company was close to bankruptcy. At this point it was bought for $2.7 billion by Nestlé, the world's largest food company. Attracted by the combination of bottled water as a fast-growing business and the world's best known mineral water brand, Nestlé identified Perrier as an attractive takeover target.

However, Perrier struggles to turn a profit. In 2003 its pretax profit margin on $300 million sales was only 0.6% compared with 10.4% for the Nestlé Waters division overall. In 2004 it again recorded a loss.[74]

The Perrier factory is on a 234-acre site on the Mediterranean coastal plain near Nimes. The factory itself is rather nondescript, so much so that "from a distance it could be mistaken for a power station or auto plant."[75] Perrier employees work a 35-hour week and earn an average annual salary of $32,000 which is good for this part of France and relatively high for this industry. However, the average Perrier worker produces only 600,000 bottles a year, compared with 1.1 million bottles at Nestlé's two other international French mineral-water brands (Vittel and Contrex).

Relations between management and workers are not good. Almost all (93 percent) of Perrier's 1,650 workers belong to the CGT, a union that is viewed by the management as consistently resisting Nestlé's attempts to improve Perrier's financial performance. According to Nestlé CEO Peter Brabeck-Letmathe, "We have come to the point where the development of the Perrier brand is endangered by the stubbornness of the CGT."[76]

Jean-Paul Franc, head of the CGT at Perrier, sees the situation differently. In regard to the company's plan to cut 15 percent of its workforce he protests, "Nestlé can't do whatever it likes." He says, "There are men and women who work here... Morally speaking the water and the gas stored below this ground belong to the whole region."[77]

When, in 2004, Danone launched a new product (Badoit Rouge) that was designed to directly compete with Perrier's new super-bubbly brand, Eau de Perrier, Perrier's management put bottles of Badoit Rouge in the factory cafeteria. This had been done to emphasize the point to Perrier employees that they were involved in a head-to-head battle for that niche in the market. However, this act was not well received.

"It was a provocation," recalls one Perrier truck driver. "We took the bottles and dumped them in front of the factory director's door, so he couldn't get into his office."[78]

QUESTIONS

1. Identify the key elements of the resistance to change described in this situation.
2. Construct a change management strategy for dealing with this situation. In so doing, identify what approach(es) to managing resistance you recommend and provide a clear justification for your choice.

TABLE 6.13 Additional Case Studies

Triangle Community Foundation
Dees, J. G., & Anderson, B. (2001) *Stanford University*
Ballarpur Industries Limited (A) & (B) (Video & Case)
Killing, P. (2003) *IMD Lausanne*
Taking Charge at Dogus Holding (A)
Khurana, R.; Carioggia, G. M., & Simon, J. (2001) *Harvard Business School*
Taking Charge at Dogus Holding (B)
Khurana, R., & Carioggia, G. M. (2002) *Harvard Business School*—Supports (A)
Donna Dubinsky and Apple Computer, Inc (A)
Gentile, M., under direction of Jick, T. (1986) *Harvard Business School*

Bibliography

Abrahamson, E. 2000. Change without pain. *Harvard Business Review*, July–August:75–79.

Adams, S. 1996. *The Dilbert principle*. NewYork: Harper Collins.

Agocs, C. 1999. Institutional resistance to organizational change: Denial, inaction and repression. *Journal of Business Ethics* 16:917–31.

Audia, P. G., Locke, E. A., and Smith, K. S. 2000. The paradox of success: An archival and a laboratory study of strategic persistence following radical environmental change. *Academy of Management Journal* 43:837–53.

Bartunek, J. M. 1984. Changing interpretive schemes and organizational restructuring: The example of a religious order. *Administrative Science Quarterly* 23(3):355–72.

Buchanan, D. A., Claydon, T., and Doyle, M. 1999. Organization development and change: The legacy of the nineties. *Human Resource Management Journal* 9(2):20–37.

Clinard, M. B. 1983. *Corporate ethics and crime: The role of middle management*. Beverley Hills, CA: Sage.

Coombs, A. 1990. *Adland: A true story of corporate drama*. Melbourne: Heinemann.

Deal, T. E., and Kennedy, A. A. 1992. *Corporate cultures*. Reading, MA: Addison-Wesley.

Dent, E .B., and Goldberg, S. G. 1999. Challenging "resistance to change." *Journal of Applied Behavioral Science* 35:25–41.

Dent, E. B., and Goldberg, S. G. 1999. "Resistance to change": A limiting perspective. *Journal of Applied Behavioral Science* 35:45–47.

Deveny, K. 1989. Can Ms. Fashion bounce back. *BusinessWeek*, January 16:64.

Doyle, M., Claydon, T., and Buchanan, D. A. 1999. Mixed result, lousy process: Contrasts and contradictions in the management experience of change. *British Journal of Management* 11:59–80.

Drucker, P. 1994. The theory of the business. *Harvard Business Review*, September–October:95–110.

Dunford, R. 1992. *Organizational behavior: An organizational analysis perspective*. Sydney: Addison-Wesley.

Dym, B. 1999. Resistance in organizations: How to recognise, understand & respond to it. *OD Practitioner* 31(1):6–19.

Eisenhardt, K. M., Kahwajy, J. L., and Bourgeoise, L. J. 1997. How management teams can have a good fight. *Harvard Business Review*, July–August:77–85.

Foote, D. 2001. The futility of resistance (to change). *Computerworld*, January 15.

Ford, J. D., Ford, L. W., and McNamara, R. T. 2001. Resistance and the background conversation of change. *Journal of Organizational Change Management* 15(2):105–21.

Fossum, L. B. 1989. *Understanding organizational change*. Menlo Park, CA: Crisp.

Gadiesh, O., and Gilbert, J. L. 2001. Transforming corner-office strategy into frontline action. *Harvard Business Review*, May:73–79.

Geigle, S. 1998. Organizational memory and scripts: Resistance to change or lessons from the past. Paper presented at the Annual Conference of the Academy of Human Resource Development, Chicago, March.

Geisler, D. 2001. Bottom-feeders: People who reject change. *Executive Excellence* 18(12):19.

Gioia, D. A., and Chittipeddi, K. 1991. Sensemaking and sensegiving in strategic change initiation. *Strategic Management Journal* 12(6):433–88.

Hamel, G 1996. Strategy as revolution. *Harvard Business Review*, July–August:69–82.

Hultman, K. E. 1995. Scaling the wall of resistance. *Training and Development*, October:15–18.

Jackson, S., and Dutton, J. 1988. Discerning threats and opportunities. *Administrative Science Quarterly* 33:370–82.

Jick, T. D., and Peiperl, M. A. 2003. *Managing change: Cases and concepts*. 2nd ed. New York: McGraw-Hill/Irwin.

Jones, E. E., and Harris, V. A. 1967. The attribution of attitudes. *Journal of Experimental Social Psychology* 3:1–24.

Kahn, E. F. 1982. Conclusion: Critical themes in the study of change. In *Change in organizations*, ed. P. S. Goodman and Associates, 409–29. San Francisco: Jossey-Bass.

Karp, H. B. 1996. *The change leader*. San Francisco: Pfeiffer.

Kirkpatrick, D. L. 2001. *Managing change effectively*. Boston: Butterworth-Heinemann.

Kotter, J. P., and Schlesinger, L. A. 1979. Choosing strategies for change. *Harvard Business Review*, March–April:106–14.

Krantz, J. 1999. Comment on "Challenging resistance to change." *Journal of Applied Behavioral Science* 35:42–4.

Kubler-Ross, E. 1969. *On death and dying*. Toronto: Macmillan.

Manz, C. C., and Neck, C. P. 1991. Inner-leadership: Creating productive thought patterns. *Academy of Management Executive* 5:87–95.

Marks, M. L., and Shaw, R. B. 1995. Sustaining change: Creating the resilient organization. In *Discontinuous change: Leading organizational transformation*, ed. D. A. Nadler, R. B. Shaw, A. E. Walton, and Associates, 97–117. San Francisco: Jossey-Bass.

Maurer, R. 1996. *Beyond the walls of resistance*. Austin, TX: Bard Books.

Milgram, S. 1965. Some conditions of obedience and disobedience to authority. *Human Relations* 18:57–76.

Miller, D. 1990. *The Icarus paradox*. New York: Harper Collins.

Modigliani, A., and Rochat, F. 1995. The role of interaction sequences and the timing of resistance in shaping obedience and defiance to authority. *Journal of Social Issues* 51(3):107–23.

Morrison, E. W., and Milliken, F. J. 2000. Organizational silence: a barrier to change and development in a pluralistic world. *Academy of Management Review* 25:706–25.

Neck, C. P. 1996. Thought self-leadership: A self-regulatory approach towards overcoming resistance to organizational change. *International Journal of Organizational Analysis* 4(2):202–16.

Neck, C. P., and Manz, C. C. 1996. Thought self leadership: The impact of mental strategies training on employee cognition, behavior, and affect. *Journal of Organizational Behavior* 17:445–67.

Pate, J., Martin, G., and Staines, H. 2000. Exploring the relationship between psychological contracts and organizational change: A process model and case study evidence. *Strategic Change* 9:481–93.

Pickens, J. C., and Dess, G. G. 1998. Right strategy—wrong problem. *Organizational Dynamics*, Summer:35–49.

Piderit, S. K. 2000. Rethinking resistance and recognizing ambivalence: A multidimensional view of attitudes toward an organizational change. *Academy of Management Review* 25:783–94.

Reger, R. K., Mullane, J. V., Gustafson, L. T., and DeMarie, S. M. 1994. Creating earthquakes to change organizational mindsets. *Academy of Management Executive* 8(4):31–43.

Reichers, A. E., Wanous, J. P., and Austin, J. A. 1997. Understanding and managing cynicism about organizational change. *Academy of Management Executive* 11(1):48–59.

Robinson, S. L., and Rousseau, D. M. 1994. Violating the psychological contract: Not the exception but the norm. *Journal of Organizational Behavior* 15:245–59.

Rousseau, D. M. 1995. *Psychological contracts in organizations: Understanding written and unwritten agreements*. Thousand Oaks, CA: Sage.

Scott, C. D., and Jaffe, D. T. 1989. *Managing personal change*. Menlo Park, CA: Crisp.

Siggelkow, N. 2001. Change in the presence of fit: The rise, the fall, and the renaissance of Liz Claiborne. *Academy of Management Journal* 44(4):838–57.

Stensaker, I., Meyer, C. B., Falkenberg, J., and Haueng, A. C. 2002. Excessive change: Coping mechanisms and consequences. *Organizational Dynamics* 31(3):296–312.

Strebel, P. 1996. Why do employees resist change? *Harvard Business Review*, May–June:86–92.

Sull, D. N. 1999. Why good companies go bad. *Harvard Business Review*, July–August:42–52.

Tichy, N., and Devanna, M. 1990. *The transformational leader*. New York: John Wiley & Sons.

Waddell, D., and Sohal, A. 1998. Resistance: A constructive tool for change management. *Management Decision* 36(8):543–48.

Notes

1. Maurer, 1996:17.
2. Foote, 2001.
3. Geisler, 2001.
4. See, for example, Adams, 1996.
5. Stensaker et al., 2002:305.
6. Kirkpatrick, 2001.
7. Hultman, 1995.
8. Maurer, 1996, refers to "malicious compliance"; Fisher, 1995, refers to "vicious compliance" (a term she attributes to Michael Hammer).
9. Dym, 1999:12.
10. Deal and Kennedy, 1982.
11. Reger et al., 1994.
12. Reger et al., 1994:33–34. Reproduced with permission of Academy of Management Executive through Copyright Clearance Center.
13. Reger et al., 1994.
14. Reger et al., 1994:34.

15. Greenwood and Hinings, 1996:1027.
16. Robinson and Rousseau, 1994; Rousseau, 1995.
17. Strebel, 1996.
18. See also Pate, Martin, and Staines, 2000.
19. Kirkpatrick, 2001; Ford et al., 2001.
20. Gadiesh and Gilbert, 2001:74.
21. Gadiesh and Gilbert, 2001:74.
22. Maurer, 1996:21.
23. Maurer, 1996.
24. Stensaker et al., 2002.
25. Buchanan et al., 1999; Doyle et al., 2000; Marks and Shaw, 1995.
26. Maurer, 1996:94.
27. Abrahamson, 2000:76.
28. Piderit, 2000:785.
29. Milgram, 1965; Modigliani and Rochat, 1995.
30. Piderit, 2000, citing Clinard, 1983.
31. Bartunek, 1984; Geigle, 1998; Gioia and Chipeddi, 1991; Reichers et al., 1997.
32. Geigle (1998). Ford et al. (2001) make a similar argument using the concept of "conversation" rather than "script."
33. Reichers et al., 1997.
34. Stensaker et al., 2002:304.
35. Dent and Goldberg, 1999:25.
36. On the basis of this position, Dent and Goldberg (1999:27) refer to resistance to change as "a bankrupt mental model." We do not subscribe to as extreme a position. We take the view that, given the entrenched nature of the concept "resistance to change," more is to be gained by encouraging a much more critical (and, as a result, a more realistic and useful) approach to the use of the term.
37. Dent and Goldberg, 1999:38.
38. Kahn, 1982:416.
39. Piderit, 2000.
40. Piderit, 2000.
41. Hultman, 1995; Kirkpatrick, 2001.
42. The idea that managers, not just other employees, resist change is also a well-established perspective of those who see themselves as advocating change on behalf of "the powerless and disadvantaged" (see, e.g., Agocs, 1997:16).
43. Drucker, 1994; Pickens and Dess, 1998; Gadiesh and Gilbert, 2001; Jackson and Dutton, 1988.
44. Tichy and Devanna, 1990.
45. Sull, 1999; Audia et al., 2000.
46. Audia et al., 2000. Because of this phenomenon, a number of high-profile commentators on strategic change, including Gary Hamel (1997) and Kathleen Eisenhardt (1997), argue strongly for heterogeneous, top-management teams so that there would be a greater "diversity of voices" in the "strategy conversations" within organizations.

47. Miller, 1990.
48. Sull, 1999.
49. Kotter and Schlesinger, 1979.
50. Kotter and Schlesinger, 1979:112.
51. Jick and Peiperl, 2003.
52. Scott and Jaffe, 1989.
53. Scott and Jaffe, 1989.
54. Jick and Peiperl (2003:301) argue that "to speed up the process is to risk carrying unfinished psychological 'baggage' from one phase to the next."
55. Scott and Jaffe, 1989. Jick and Peiperl (2003) similarly argue that some people may get stuck in the cycle and not move through to acceptance.
56. Karp, 1996; see also Manz and Neck, 1991.
57. Neck, 1996:204.
58. Neck, 1996.
59. Neck, 1996:205.
60. Neck, 1996.
61. Neck and Manz, 1996:460.
62. Abrahamson, 2000.
63. Abrahamson, 2000:76.
64. See also Dym, 1999; Waddell and Sohal, 1998.
65. Maurer, 1996.
66. Jick and Peiperl, 2003:306.
67. Morrison and Milliken, 2000.
68. Maurer, 1996:64.
69. Adapted from Maurer, 1996.
70. This case is provided by Rick Maurer. Ajax is a pseudonym.
71. This case is based on Tomlinson, R. (2004) "Bubble, bubble, toil and trouble," *Fortune*, November 29, 65–67.
72. Tomlinson (2004:65).
73. Eating or drinking foods containing high levels of the chemical benzene can cause a range of symptoms including vomiting, dizziness, convulsions and in some instances, death.
74. Although this loss is significant for Perrier, it is much less so for Nestlé as a whole as the Perrier brand contributes less than 0.5% of Nestlé total revenue.
75. Tomlinson (2004:66).
76. Tomlinson (2004: 65–66).
77. Tomlinson (2004:66).
78. Tomlinson (2004:65).

Implementing Change: Organization Development, Appreciative Inquiry, and Sense-Making Approaches

Learning objectives

On completion of this chapter you should be able to:

- Appreciate more clearly the organizational change approaches underpinning the *coach* and *interpreter* images of managing change.
- Understand the organization development (OD) approach to change.
- Outline recent extensions of the OD approach such as appreciative inquiry.
- Be familiar with a sense-making approach to change.
- Articulate a range of strengths and weaknesses among these approaches.
- Reflect upon your own approach to managing change.

Of the six images of managing change, the *caretaker* and *nurturer* images have their foundations in the field of organization theory; the other four images—*director, coach, navigator*, and *interpreter*—have stronger foundations in the organizational change field. This chapter and the one that follows delve further into the foundations of the four that are rooted in the organizational change field and explore their implications for how to manage organizational change. They are also the four that, in various ways, assume that the change manager has an important influence on the way change occurs in organizations. In contrast, the first two images, *caretaker* and *nurturer*, have in common an assumption that change managers *receive rather than initiate* change. This chapter, and the one that follows, therefore explore the four images that assume that change managers have an active role in the initiation, support, and outcomes of organizational change. This chapter considers the foundational approaches associated with the *coach* and *interpreter* images, and the following chapter considers the foundational approaches associated with the *director* and *navigator* images.

Underpinned by the *coach* image, the organization development (OD) approach has dominated the organizational change field for over half a century. Adherents to the approach present their developmental prescriptions for achieving change as being based, at least traditionally, upon a core set of values. These values emphasize that change should benefit not just organizations but the people who staff them. However, some writers are grappling with the question of whether OD is "in crisis"[1] while others claim that OD's "salad days are clearly over"[2] and that it has been sidelined from the concerns of the business community with its preoccupation with humanistic values rather than with other issues such as business strategy.[3] This has led to the development of the OD field in terms of new approaches to managing change such as large-scale, systemwide intervention techniques and appreciative inquiry.

However, other approaches to managing change also have emerged. Underpinned by the *interpreter* image, the sense-making approach maintains that change emerges over time and consists of a series of interpretive activities that help to create in people new meanings about their organizations and about the ways in which they can operate differently in the future. We commence this chapter considering the approaches underpinned by the *coach* image and then move on to the *interpreter* image.

COACH IMAGE OF IMPLEMENTING CHANGE: THE ORGANIZATION DEVELOPMENT (OD) AND APPRECIATIVE INQUIRY (AI) APPROACHES

In this section, we consider the underlying tenets of the OD approach to managing change along with the role of the OD practitioner. We then review a number of challenges that have been directed to OD including the continuing relevance of the values underlying the OD approach, the universal applicability of these values, the relevance of OD to large-scale change, and the emergence of appreciative inquiry.

Traditional OD Approach: Fundamental Values

As set out in Table 7.1, OD as a change intervention technique has developed over time, being influenced by a number of different trajectories. As such there is no single, underlying theory that unifies the field as a whole. Rather, it is informed by a variety of differing perspectives, drawing on theorists such as Herzberg, Maslow, Argyris, and Lewin.[4]

TABLE 7.1 Evolution of Organization Development

Source: Developed from Cummings and Worley, 1997:6–18.

Period	Background	Developers	Focus
1940s/1950s+	National Training Laboratories (NTL) and T-groups	Kurt Lewin, Douglas McGregor, Robert Blake, Richard Beckhard	Interpersonal relations, leadership, and group dynamics; use of team building to facilitate personal and task achievement
1940s/1950s+	Action research and survey feedback	Kurt Lewin, John Collier, William Whyte, Rensis Likert	Involvement of organizational members in researching themselves to help create new knowledge and guide change actions
1950s/1960s+	Participative management	Likert	Assumption that a human relations approach with its emphasis on participation is the best way to manage an organization
1950s/1960s+	Productivity and quality of work-life	Eric Trist and Tavistock Institute, W. Edward Deming, and Joseph Juran	Better integration of people and technology through joint participation of unions and management; quality circles; use of self-managing workgroups; creation of more challenging jobs; total quality management
1970s/1980s+	Strategic change	Richard Beckhard, Christopher Worley	Need for change to be strategic, aligning organization with technical, political, cultural, and environmental influences upon it

In drawing together the common threads of these perspectives, Richard Beckhard[5] depicts the classic OD approach as one that has the following characteristics:

- *It is planned* and involves a systematic diagnosis of the whole organizational system, a plan for its improvement, and provision of adequate resources.

- *The top of the organization* is committed to the change process.
- *It aims at improving the effectiveness* of the organization in order to help it achieve its mission.
- *It is long-term*, typically taking two or three years to achieve effective change.
- *It is action-oriented.*
- *Changing attitudes and behavior* is a focus of the change effort.
- *Experiential-based learning* is important as it helps to identify current behaviors and modifications that are needed.
- *Groups and teams* form the key focus for change.

Though it is commonly presented as being aimed at incremental, developmental, first-order change, other writers claim that what unifies the OD field, at least traditionally, is an emphasis on a core set of values. These values build upon humanistic psychology and emphasize the importance of developing people in work organizations and helping them to achieve satisfaction.[6] Three value sets are involved:

- *Humanistic values* relate to openness, honesty, and integrity.
- *Democratic values* relate to social justice, freedom of choice, and involvement.
- *Developmental values* relate to authenticity, growth, and self-realization.[7]

Human development, fairness, openness, choice, and the balance between autonomy and constraint are fundamental to these values.[8] It is said that these values were radical and "a gutsy set of beliefs" in relation to the time in which they were developed; that is, in the 1940s and 1950s when organizational hierarchy was dominant, emphasizing authority, rationality, and efficiency rather than humanism and individuality.[9] In this sense, the traditional practice of OD has as its focus people and is not necessarily meant to be solely focused on the interests of management or the profitability of the firm.[10]

The OD Practitioner

Central to the traditional OD approach is the role of the OD practitioner, who may be either internal or external to the organization. A typical OD consultant helps to "structure activities to help the organization members solve their own problems and learn to do that better."[11] Where this is based upon *action research*, it involves a variety of steps such as:

1. *Problem identification.* Someone in the organization becomes aware of what they think is a problem that needs to be addressed.
2. *Consultation with an OD practitioner.* The client and the practitioner come together with the latter endeavoring to create a collaborative dialogue.
3. *Data gathering and problem diagnosis.* Interviews, observations, surveys, and analysis of performance data occur to assist in problem diagnosis. Each of these techniques is recognized as an intervention in itself in the sense that it involves an interaction with people.
4. *Feedback.* The consultant provides the client with relevant data, at the same time protecting the identity of people from whom information was obtained.

5. *Joint problem diagnosis*. As part of the action research process, people are involved in consideration of information and discuss what it means in terms of required changes.
6. *Joint action planning*. The specific actions that need to be taken are identified.
7. *Change actions*. The introduction of and transition to new techniques and behaviors occur.
8. *Further data gathering*. Outcomes of change are determined and further actions identified.[12]

In coaching people through such change processes, Cummings and Worley[13] argue that OD practitioners need a variety of skills, including:

1. *Intrapersonal skills*: having a well-developed set of values and personal integrity including the ability to retain their own health in high-stress organizational situations.
2. *Interpersonal skills*: which are needed in order to work with groups and gain their trust in order to "provide them with counseling and coaching necessary to develop and change."[14]
3. *General consultation skills*: including knowledge about intervention techniques (such as those discussed in Chapter 5) to assist them in diagnosing problems and designing change interventions.
4. *Organization development theory*: to ensure that they have a current understanding of the specialist field of which they are a part.

Underpinning these OD practitioner interventions is the classic 1947 change process model developed by Kurt Lewin.[15] He developed a three-stage model of how change occurs: *unfreezing* how the organization operates, *changing* the organization in specific ways, and then *refreezing* the changes into the operations of the organization. How Lewin's model of change relates to the actions of the OD practitioner is set out in Table 7.2.

TABLE 7.2 Classic OD Change Intervention Processes

Sources: Adapted from French and Bell, 1995:81–83; Cummings and Worley, 1997:28–29.

Lewin's Change Process	OD Action Research Change Process
Unfreezing: establishing the need for change	• Identification of problems • Consultation with OD practitioner • Gathering of data and initial diagnosis
Movement: to new behavior through cognitive restructuring	• Client group feedback • Joint problem diagnosis • Joint planning of change actions • Engagement in change actions
Refreezing: integration of new behaviors into social and organizational relationships	• Post-action data gathering and evaluation

Criticisms of OD

Advocates of the OD approach acknowledge that there are problems in the field. For example, French and Bell[16] identify six of these:

1. *OD definitions and concepts*. OD may consist of single or multiple interventions over different periods of time, so establishing the relationship between "OD" and its ability to enhance "organizational effectiveness" is difficult, especially given that the latter term itself also lacks precise definitions.
2. *Internal validity problems*. This relates to whether the change that occurred was caused by the change intervention or a range of other factors.
3. *External validity problems*. This is the generalizability question and relates to whether OD and its techniques are appropriate to all organizational settings.
4. *Lack of theory*. There is no comprehensive theory of change to assist researchers in knowing what to look for in what they study.
5. *Problems with measuring attitude changes*. Using prechange and then postchange surveys to measure attitudinal changes are problematic as people may view the scale differently when they answer it a second time.
6. *Problems with normal science approaches to research*. The ability to use these techniques (hypothesis testing, assessing cause–effect relationships, etc.) is questioned in relation to OD being a process based on action research.

French and Bell adopt an optimistic view of this situation, arguing that "These do not appear to be insurmountable problems at this time, although they continue to plague research efforts."[17] However, other writers are critical of such optimism, pointing out that the approach is largely descriptive and prescriptive, often failing to adequately consider the inherent limitations and underlying assumptions of its own techniques.[18] OD has been presented with a range of other criticisms relating to the extent to which it deals adequately with issues such as leadership, strategic change, power, and reward systems.[19] Three further criticisms relate to the current relevance of OD's traditional values, the universality of those values, and the ability of OD to engage in large-scale change. Each of these issues is addressed below.

Current Relevance of OD's Traditional Values

Prominent OD thought leader Warner Burke argues that, for many experienced OD practitioners, "the profession has lost its way—that its values are no longer sufficiently honored, much less practiced, and that the unrelenting emphasis on the bottom line has taken over."[20] This has occurred particularly as practitioners have been placed in a position of advising on and implementing management strategies such as downsizing and reengineering despite their potential to hurt individuals and therefore go against the fundamental values of OD. As a result, "OD has lost some of its power, its presence, and perhaps its perspective."[21] An editor of *OD Practitioner*, Dave Nicholl, agrees with Burke's general assessment. He points to how many of the values of OD are confrontational to many of the values held in our organizations. This has led to "stark contrasts" between being relevant and value-neutral, or being value-laden and marginal. He urges the OD field to move beyond such either/or distinctions by reassessing the values that OD should espouse in the 21st century.[22]

Some OD supporters have started to take up this reassessment. Nicholl, for example, argues that OD practitioners need to remind themselves of the dilemma they face, of assisting both individual development and organizational performance—which he characterizes as "contradictory elements." By delving back into OD's heritage, he suggests that they regain their humility and present to clients not certainty but educated conjecture. Finally, he proposes the need for a paradigm shift in how the corporation is viewed and rebuilt, allowing space to recognize that corporations are not necessarily just institutions for profit but social institutions.[23]

Other OD writers challenge managers to make their organizations more inclusive (multiple levels of involvement in decision making), to create mutual accountability (linking performance remuneration to adherence to core values, stakeholders, and corporate sustainability), to reinforce interdependence (between individuals, organizations, and the wider society), to expand notions of time and space (such as considering the impact of decisions for future generations), to ensure the wise use of natural resources (such as consideration of renewable and nonrenewable resources), and to redefine the purpose of the organization in terms of multiple stakeholders (including customers, stockholders, community, planet, descendants, organizational leaders, employees, and directors).[24]

Are OD Values Universal?

One challenge leveled at OD is whether the approach and the values underpinning it are relevant outside of the United States where it was predominantly developed. Some advocates portray OD change values as being universal, with cultural differences serving as "a veneer which covers common fundamental human existence."[25] For example, Blake et al. claim that the *Managerial (or Leadership) Grid* developed by Robert Blake and Jane Mouton in the 1960s "is probably the first systematic, comprehensive approach to organizational change."[26] and has played a central role in the development of OD. The grid maps seven leadership styles that vary in terms of their emphasis on people versus results: controlling, accommodating, status quo, indifferent, paternalist, opportunist, and sound—the latter style being preferred insofar as it portrays a leadership style that is concerned for both results and people.[27] The grid is used as the basis for change leadership seminars, helping to establish both individual awareness and skills. How applicable is this grid outside of the United States? They claim that the grid has been used extensively in a variety of countries (including Asia), in part because of "its ability to effectively employ a universal model of effective management and organizational development within diverse cultures."[28] Application of the grid is assisted by country-based "translators" who help to adapt it to the local culture.[29] They argue that the grid sustains and extends core OD values in seeking greater candor, openness, and trust in organizations.[30]

However, other advocates are more circumspect about how far the OD approach is relevant across cultural boundaries. For example, Marshak[31] contends that there are fundamentally different assumptions underlying eastern (Confusian/Taoist) and western (Lewinian/OD) views of organizational change. These differences are outlined in Table 7.3. Certainly Marshak's cogent and challenging arguments indicate that OD practitioners need to view with care any assumptions they hold that OD change practices have universal applicability. Similarly, Fagenson-Eland, Ensher and Burke[32]

TABLE 7.3 Is OD Change Culture-Bound?

Source: Adapted from Marshak, 1993.

Lewinian/OD Assumptions	Confucian/Taoist Assumptions
• Linear (movement from past to present to future)	• Cyclical (constant ebb and flow)
• Progressive (new state more desirable)	• Processional (harmonious movement from one state to another)
• Goal oriented (specific end state in mind)	• Journey oriented (cyclical change, therefore no end state)
• Based on creating disequilibrium (by altering current field of forces)	• Based on maintaining equilibrium (achieve natural harmony)
• Planned and managed by people separate from change itself (application of techniques to achieve desired ends)	• Observed and followed by involved people (who constantly seek harmony with their universe)
• Unusual (assumption of static or semistatic state outside of a change process)	• Usual (assumption of constant change as, in the yin-yang philosophy, each new order contains its own negation)

EXERCISE 7.1

OD Reports from the Front Line

This exercise requires you to interview two organization development practitioners about how they go about doing their work. Compare and contrast them in terms of the following issues:

- Their background.
- The values they espouse.
- The steps that they say they use in approaching a consulting assignment.
- The tensions they identify in working as an OD practitioner.
- Their perceptions of the way the OD field has changed and likely changes into the future.

What general conclusions do you draw about the practice of OD?

based on a seven-nation study argue that "OD practitioners should carefully consider dimensions of national culture when recommending specific OD interventions."

Engaging in Large-Scale Change

One of the biggest challenges to the traditional OD field was the criticism that it was ill-suited to handle second-order, large-scale organizational change. Traditional OD techniques focused on working with individuals and group dynamics through processes such as survey feedback and team building. Such methods came under attack as being insufficient to deal with the large-scale changes needed by organizations to cope with the hypercompetitive business world that confronts them.[33] As a result of

TABLE 7.4 Example of a Search Conference Format

Source: Adapted from Baburoglu and Garr, 1992.

Phase 1	Identifying relevant world trends = shared understanding of global environment
Phase 2	Identifying how trends affect specific issue, organization, institution = how global trends impact on operations of the system
Phase 3	Evolution of issue, organization, institution = creation of its history including its chronology (timeline)
Phase 4	Future design of issue, organization, institution = use of small-group creativity and innovation to design a consensus scenario for the way forward
Phase 5	Strategy formulation = generation of agreed action plans

Note: For a comprehensive treatment of the search conference approach, see Emery and Purser, 1996.

such criticisms, organization development is said to have moved its focus from micro-organizational issues to macro, large-system issues, including aligning change to the strategic needs of the organization.[34]

This has led to the development of a range of techniques designed to get the whole organizational system, or at least representatives of different stakeholders of the whole system, into a room at one and the same time. The techniques themselves come in a variety of forms and include search conference (see Table 7.4), future search, real-time strategic change, Simu-Real, whole-system design, open-space technology, ICA strategic planning process, participative design, fast-cycle full participation, large-scale interactive process, and appreciative future search.[35] Such techniques are typically designed to work with large groups of people simultaneously, ranging from 32 people up to 2,500 or more at a time.[36] The various techniques do entail differences. Some techniques assume that organizational participants can shape and enact both their organization and its surrounding environment; others are based on the assumption that the environment is given (although its defining characteristics may need to be actively agreed upon) and that organizations and their participants join together democratically to identify appropriate adaptation processes.[37] Other differences relate to the extent to which the technique includes a majority of organizational members and stakeholders. Some techniques are highly structured and use a consultant who manages the process, whereas others utilize a more flexible self-design approach.[38]

What unites these techniques is an underlying assumption that "the few are no longer left in the position of deciding for the many" as a result of the inclusion of "new and different voices"[39] in the change process. These techniques are designed to assist organizations in being responsive to their current business conditions by providing the means "for getting the message to the total system by enhancing everyone's understanding of the organization's situation and its context. This reframing leads to a common recognition of the changes required and becomes the impetus for concerted actions."[40] These techniques are presented as producing results "with greater speed and increased commitment and greatly reduced resistance by the rest of the organization,"[41] enhancing "innovation, adaptation, and learning."[42] An example of this technique in a large setting, involving over 4,000 people who came together to identify how the World Trade Center 9/11 site should be developed, is outlined in Table 7.5.

TABLE 7.5 Large-Scale Interventions: "Listening to the City": Town Hall Meeting on Rebuilding the World Trade Center after 9/11

Source: Sources drawn on for this story were Lukensmeyer and Brigham, 2002; *New York Daily News*, http://www.nydailynews.com, July 21, 2002; http://www.americaspeaks.org.

In New York City on July 20, 2002, over 4,300 New York citizens came together for what has been billed as the largest town hall meeting ever held. The meeting was organized by *Americaspeaks*, a nonprofit organization headed by Carolyn Lukensmeyer that uses 21st century town meetings to design and facilitate large-scale dialogues on public issues. Up to 5,000 people are grouped into one room and profiled in such a way that they represent the various interests and stakeholders associated with the issues for discussion and debate. They are arranged into small groups of around a dozen people, each having a facilitator. Each group has a networked computer that records the ideas of participants and a wireless network within the room transfers these data to a central computer. This enables a "theme team" to read the data from each group, identify key themes in real time, distill them, and present them back to the whole room via large overhead video screens. Each participant in the room has a wireless keypad that he or she can then use to vote in relation to the distilled themes. This provides instant feedback to the entire group, which, at the conclusion of the day, receives a summary of the major issues and outcomes. Involving key decision makers in the meeting is an important way of trying to ensure that the outcomes of the day have a meaningful input into public policy.

In the case of the World Trade Center, the town meeting was held after five months of organizing, sponsored in part by the Lower Manhattan Development Corporation (LMDC) and the Port Authorities of New York and New Jersey. During this period, a representative sample of New Yorkers was identified and invited to the July 20 meeting, which was titled "Listening to the City." The room contained 500 tables, each with a facilitator. Theme team members provided feedback throughout the day and issue experts were on hand to answer specific questions from participants. Representatives from various federal, state, and city agencies also were present. A key outcome of the meeting was an expression of dissatisfaction with the six memorial site options being considered and a demand for one having more open space; the meeting also made recommendations regarding expansion of the transit service and more affordable housing. The outcome was that the LMDC began a new planning process for the World Trade Center and the Port Authority agreed to reduce the amount of commercial development planned for the site in order to enable more space for hotel and retail. As reported by the *New York Daily News* (July 21, 2002), "the process was an exercise in democracy."

Appreciative Inquiry: From Problem Solving to (Building on) What Works Well

Techniques of "inclusion" appropriate to large-scale or large-group intervention techniques have led to them being labeled as part of a new "engagement paradigm,"[43] a "new type of social innovation,"[44] a "paradigm shift,"[45] and "an evolution in human thought, vision and values uniquely suited to our awesome 21st Century technical, economic, and social dilemmas."[46] They represent a shift from an emphasis on problem solving and conflict management, common to earlier OD programs, to a focus on joint envisioning of the future.[47] For example, Fuller, Griffin, and Ledma[48] maintain that with a problem-solving approach comes the assumption that "organizing-is-a-problem-to-be-solved" and entails steps such as problem identification, analysis of causes and solutions, and the development of action plans. Contrary to this logic, they point to the assumptions underlying the appreciative inquiry approach to large-scale change, which seeks to identify what is currently working best and to build on this knowledge to help develop and design what might be achieved in the future. They depict the technique as involving four steps:

- *Discovering* or appreciating the best of what is currently practiced.
- *Building* on this knowledge to help envision (or dream) about what the future could be.
- *Designing* or co-constructing (through collective dialogue) what should be.
- *Sustaining* the organization's destiny or future.

In these techniques the act of participation or inclusion of a wide variety of voices itself constitutes a change in the organization: the "what" to change and the "how" to change cannot be easily separated.

Proponents of these techniques are glowing, sometimes almost evangelical, in expounding their benefits. Weisbord claims that future search conference outcomes "can be quite startling"[49] and produce restructured bureaucratic hierarchies in which "People previously in opposition often act together across historic barriers in less than 48 hours."[50] In their outline of the benefits of appreciative inquiry, Fuller, Griffin, and Ludema[51] claim that it "releases an outpouring of new constructive conversations," "unleashes a self-sustaining learning capacity within the organization," "creates the conditions necessary for self-organizing to flourish," and "provides a reservoir of strength for positive change." These are not minor claims. Certainly, the techniques have been reportedly used successfully in a variety of organizational settings.[52] However, it is probably fair to say that whether these approaches are successful in achieving their outcomes is difficult to establish, being based most often on the assertions of their proponents rather than on rigorous research evidence.

Some disagreement exists in the field regarding both the origin of large-scale, whole-system change techniques and their likely effectiveness in the future. Some writers disagree with the version of "OD history" that depicts the field as having moved over time from a micro to a macro focus. They maintain that large-scale techniques have always been part of the OD approach[53] and that "O.D.ers have a strong tendency to neglect their past."[54] Others maintain that because of the need for more rapid responses, systemwide culture change programs that rely on 5- to 15-year time frames are less relevant today than more specific, situational interventions such as virtual team building and management of merger processes.[55] Aligned with this critique is the issue of the feasibility of systemwide changes in an era when "The old model of the organization as the center of its universe, with its customers, share-owners, suppliers, etc. rotating around it, is no longer applicable in 'new-era' organizations."[56] As one OD practitioner argues, "I'm not sure that 'system wide' change is really possible, since the real system often include[s] a number of strategic partners who may never buy into changes that fit one company but not another."[57]

INTERPRETER IMAGE OF IMPLEMENTING CHANGE: SENSE-MAKING APPROACHES

Drawing on the *interpreter* image of managing organizational change, Karl Weick's[58] sense-making model provides an alternative approach to the OD school. Weick's[59] point of departure is to argue against three common change assumptions.

EXERCISE 7.2

Designing a Large-Scale Change Intervention

Choose a current issue in your local neighborhood. This exercise gets you to figure out how you would design a large-scale change intervention program in relation to this issue. Give consideration to the following issues:

- How many people would it make sense to involve?
- Where and when would you hold it?
- How would you ensure that you have a representative cross sample of relevant people in the room at the same time? What data sources would you need to achieve this?
- Who are the key decision makers in relation to this issue? What arguments will you use to get them to attend the meeting?
- How will you structure the agenda of the meeting? What would be the best way of doing this so that people who attend on that day have appropriate buy-in to it?
- How would you run the actual meeting?
- What technology would you need to make it work well?
- What would people take away from the meeting?
- What follow-up actions would you plan to ensure that actions and decisions flowed from it?
- What possible funding sources might you draw on to finance the meeting?
- As a result of considering such questions what new issues emerge for you, as a large-scale change intervention agent, to consider? What specific skills would you need to make such an event work well? Which of these skills would you need to develop more?

The first is the *assumption of inertia*. Under this assumption, planned, intended change is necessary in order to disrupt the forces that contribute to a lack of change in an organization so that there is a lag between environmental change and organizational adaptation.[60] He suggests that the central role given to inertia is misplaced and results from a focus on structure rather than a focus on the structuring flows and processes through which organizational work occurs. Adopting the latter perspective leads one to see organizations as being in an ongoing state of accomplishment and re-accomplishment with organizational routines constantly undergoing adjustments to better fit changing circumstances.[61]

The second *assumption is that a standardized change program is needed*. However, he says that this assumption is of limited value since it fails to activate what he regards as the four drivers of organizational change. As outlined in Chapter 2, these drivers are:

- *Animation* (whereby people remain in motion and may experiment, e.g., with job descriptions).
- *Direction* (including being unable to implement, in novel ways, directed strategies).
- *Paying attention and updating* (such as updating knowledge of the environment and reviewing and rewriting organizational requirements).

- *Respectful, candid interaction* (which occurs when people are encouraged to speak out and engage in dialogue, particularly when things are not working well).[62]

These drivers emerge from a sense-making perspective that assumes "that change engages efforts to make sense of events that don't fit together."[63] For him, most programmed or intentional changes fail to activate one or more of these sense-making forces that assist individuals in managing ambiguity.[64]

The third *assumption is that of unfreezing*, most often associated with Kurt Lewin's unfreezing–changing–refreezing change formula. Unfreezing is based on the view that organizations suffer from inertia and need to be "unfrozen." However, "if change is continuous and emergent, then the system is already unfrozen. Further efforts at unfreezing could disrupt what is essentially a complex adaptive system that is already working."[65] If there is deemed to be ineffectiveness in the system, then his position is that the best change sequence is as follows:

- *Freeze* (to show what is occurring in the way things are currently adapting).
- *Rebalance* (to remove blockages in the adaptive processes).
- *Unfreeze* (in order to enable further emergent and improvisational changes to occur).[66]

In this view of organizational change, change agents are those who are best able to identify how adaptive emergent changes are currently occurring, much of which often is dismissed as noise in the system.[67] (See Table 7.6.)

TABLE 7.6 More Than Noise in the System? Change as Ongoing Patching

An alternative to large-scale structural change is what Eisenhardt and Brown[a] term "patching." They argue that this is a strategic process of small-scale changes that enable constant realignment of organizational processes to external changes. Patchers have distinct mindsets that involve making many small organizational changes in relation to target markets, including additions, splits, exits, transfers and combinations. Change managers with patching mindsets create organizational routines to support the process:

For instance, Cisco's pattern for adding businesses includes routines for selecting acquisition targets (the preference is for new companies about to launch their first product), for mobilizing special integration teams, for handling stock options, and for tracking employee retention rates. The routines also cover mundane details like when and how to change the contents of the vending machines at the acquired company.[b]

Similar patching processes are also found, the authors argue, in high-performance companies such as Hewlett-Packard, 3M, and Johnson & Johnson. They suggest that patching decisions should be made quickly, the direction of the patching should emerge from consideration of three or four alternative ways of proceeding, in some cases part of the organization should experiment with it to reduce major errors and problems, and scripts need to be developed to help with the ongoing coordination of tasks, work, and people as the new patch is applied. The authors argue that patching helps organizations "to stay poised on the edge of chaos"[c] and underpins shareholder value by helping to drive business growth.[d]

[a]Eisenhardt and Brown, 1999. "Patching: Restitching Business Portfolios in Dynamic Markets." *Harvard Business Review* 77(3): 72–82. Selections reproduced with permission of Harvard Business School Publishing.
[b]Eisenhardt and Brown, 1999:76.
[c]Eisenhardt and Brown, 1999:80.
[d]Eisenhardt and Brown, 1999:77.

As noted in Chapter 2, from a sense-making perspective, it is up to managers of change:

> to author interpretations and labels that capture the patterns in those adaptive choices. Within the framework of sensemaking, management sees what the front line says and tells the world what it means. In a newer code, management doesn't create change. It certifies change.[68]

In what is likely to become a landmark study in using and extending the sense-making framework to the management of organizational change, Jean Helms Mills[69] conducted a study of Nova Scotia Power, a large electrical utility company based on the eastern shore of Canada. From 1982 to 2002, Nova Scotia Power went through a variety of major organizational changes including:

- The introduction of a cultural change program.
- Privatization.
- Downsizing.
- Reengineering.
- Strategic business units.
- Balanced scorecard.[70]

She found that there were a variety of interpretations within the organization about these change programs. Drawing on the work of Karl Weick, Helms Mills argues that these differing "sensemaking" activities across the organization are indicative of the importance of understanding change as the accomplishment of ongoing processes for making sense of organizational events. She used eight features of a sense-making framework to show how they impacted on understandings of organizational changes in the company. She drew out from each feature their implications for change managers.[71] These features are outlined in Table 7.7.

In reviewing the sense-making framework, it is clear that it provides less a set of prescriptions for managers of change and more a set of understandings about how to proceed. It acknowledges the messiness of change and accepts that competing voices mean that not all intended outcomes are likely to be achieved. However, critical to engaging these competing voices is the ability to shape and influence how they make sense of organizational events. The sense-making approach alerts change managers to the different facets that influence these interpretations. At the same time, it is clear that these influences are often deeply embedded and less tangible than a clear set of steps that can be followed. Intangible does not mean less important or helpful—but they do require change managers to be what Bolman and Deal call more artistic than rational: managing change as artistry "is neither exact not precise. Artists interpret experience and express it in forms that can be felt, understood, and appreciated by others."[72] Change managers who are comfortable with these concepts are likely to find the sense-making framework of assistance to them in exploring the "tangled underbrush"[73] of organizational change. At the same time they need to be mindful of organizational limitations on their sense-making abilities. This point is made by Balogun and Johnson[74] in their study of sense-making by middle managers when they "question the extent to which leaders can manage the development of change recipients' schemata—particularly in the larger, geographically dispersed, modularized organizations we are increasingly seeing."

TABLE 7.7 Eight Features of a Sense-Making Framework

Source: Developed from Helms Mills, 2003.

Sense-Making Framework Feature	Definition	Implications for Change Managers
Sense-making and identity construction	The different ways in which people make sense of the same organizational change events and how it is related to their understanding of the way their identities are constructed within organizations.[a]	The "top-down initiatives requiring dramatic changes of self (i.e., from humanist to efficiency focused) are highly problematic and need either to be avoided or handled with great skill."[b]
Social sense-making	The need that people have to make sense of their situations not just as individuals but as social individuals is connected to a variety of influences on them such as supervisors, management, trade unions, and so forth.	An understanding of social sense-making highlights the need for managers to identify the social factors that influence sense-making in their organizational contexts.
Extracted cues of sense-making	The need for managers of change to be aware of the way people draw on a variety of "cues" or ideas and actions, perhaps taken from the external environment, in order to make sense of various decisions.[c]	Change managers need to identify appropriate cues and match them to intended change programs. The way in which these cues are interpreted, however, may inadvertently create problems for staff in accepting the legitimacy of the change program and its intended purposes.
Ongoing sense-making	Sense-making changes over time as new cues are experienced and events addressed.	Change managers need to understand "that on-going sensemaking stabilizes a situation and how change acts as a shock, generating emotional response and new acts of sensemaking."[d]
Retrospection	Reference to Karl Weick's argument that people make sense of their actions retrospectively.	Change managers need to understand that different groups will apply their own retrospective sense-making in order to understand emerging organizational events.
Plausibility	The way that change management programs need to be sold so that the "story" about the change is plausible rather than necessarily accurate.	Change managers need to understand the way the context and power relations impact on their ability to provide plausible stories that gain widespread acceptance of the need for change.[e]

TABLE 7.7 Eight Features of a Sense-Making Framework—*(concluded)*

Enactment	Whereas the above aspects of sense-making act as influences on sense-making, "enactment is about imposing that sense on action."[f]	Enactment alerts change managers to the need to connect sense-making to actions.
Projective sense-making	The ability of a powerful actor to project sense-making onto a situation, shaping the interpretations of others.	The implication of this is that using legitimate power to impose sense-making on parts of the organization may be an important aspect of understanding the implementation of change.

[a]Helms Mills 2003:126.
[b]Helms Mills 2003:145.
[c]Helms Mills 2003:153.
[d]Helms Mills 2003:164.
[e]Helms Mills 2003:173.
[f]Helms Mills 2003:173–74.

EXERCISE 7.3

Making Sense of Sense-Making

Identify a current change in an organization with which you are familiar. Alternatively, identify a current public issue about which "something must be done." In relation to the change issue, think about what sense-making changes might need to be enacted and how you would go about doing this. Assess this in terms of the eight elements of the sense-making framework suggested by Helms Mills and as set out in Table 7.7:

- *Identity construction*
- *Social sense-making*
- *Extracted cues*
- *Ongoing sense-making*
- *Retrospection*
- *Plausibility*
- *Enactment*
- *Projection*

What ones did you feel that you might have most/least control over? Why? What implications does this have for adopting a sense-making approach to organizational change?

Conclusion

In Chapter 2 we suggested that the *coach* image is a metaphor for thinking about the organization development approach. OD practitioners coach organizations and the people in them toward intentional outcomes. These outcomes are shaped by a set of values that emphasize humanistic, democratic, and developmental aspirations. In recent times, these values have been placed under the microscope—in terms of their universal applicability, their applicability in an environment that appears to demand radical, not developmental change and in an era where the bottom line rather than democratic values appears to have a higher priority for engaging in change. Of course, there does not necessarily have to be a dichotomous choice between a focus on people and a focus on the bottom line: one may lead to the other. Nevertheless, adherents to the OD approach have had to reassess how their approach to managing change can be adapted to the changing times.

The next chapter will pick up this theme in more detail; suffice it to say that we expect that the OD approach is likely to remain a strong contender for managing change in the future. However, it is also likely that it will lose its distinctive, traditional character as it is molded in different ways to take into account the demands placed on it to deliver tangible, measurable outputs. Some of the ways it is being molded have been outlined in this chapter such as its reorientation to large-scale change interventions and the development of the appreciative inquiry approach.

In Chapter 2 we depicted the sense-making approach to organizational change as drawing upon an image of the change manager as *interpreter*. In this chapter we have been able to delve deeper into the different elements of this image. As Helms Mills' study of Nova Scotia Power showed, there are a number of different levels on which the change manager as *interpreter* operates, each of which requires attention. At the same time, this approach does not imply that mastering each of these levels will always enable intended outcomes to be achieved. Wider forces, both inside and outside the organization, will ensure that there will always be competing forces vying for a privileged place in providing for organizational members an interpretation of "what's going on here" as well as "what needs to go on here." The interpreter image therefore points out to change agents the need to have a realistic view of what can be achieved in undergoing organizational change. While managers of change may find the sense-making approach to be more difficult given that it is less tangible in terms of "what needs to be done," it is also likely to give other managers comfort in reaffirming their experience of the messiness of change and identification of new ways of approaching it.

TABLE 7.8 Chapter Reflections for the Practicing Change Manager

- Do you model the change behavior you desire?
- Whose interests do you serve when you engage in change?
- Is your approach value-laden or value-neutral? If value-laden, can you articulate what these are? Are you comfortable with them?
- What do you mean when you talk about a change being successful? What criteria do you use? Do they relate to organizational performance? How can you determine this?
- Are there other people, inside or outside your organization, who have differing perspectives on such questions? What would you say are the criteria that they use to evaluate change? Is your organization open to having conversations around this issue?
- If you manage across different countries, to what extent have you observed the necessity for different ways of engaging in organizational change in those countries? Why is this the case?
- Can you identify different sense-making activities going on during organizational change? What ability do you have to influence these? Do you exercise power in your attempts to influence the interpretations others have of change situations? With what success? What are the implications of this?

Supplemental Reading

Bazigos, M. N., and Burke, W. W. 1997. Theory orientations of organization development (OD) practitioners. *Group & Organization Management* 22(3):384–408.

Bunker, B. B., and Alban, B. T. 1997. *Large group interventions: Engaging the whole system for rapid change.* San Francisco: Jossey-Bass.

Cummings, T. G., and Worley, C. G. 1997. *Organization development and change.* 6th ed. Minneapolis/St. Paul: West Publishing.

French, W. L., and Bell, C. H. 1995. *Organization development: Behavioral science interventions for organization improvement.* Englewood Cliffs, NJ: Prentice Hall.

Helms Mills, J. M. 2003. *Making sense of organizational change*. London: Routledge.

Holman, P. and Devane, T. 1999 (eds) *The change handbook: Group methods for shaping the future.* San Francisco: Berrett-Koehler.

Ludema, J. D., Whitney, D., Mohr, B. J., and Griffin, T. J. 2003. *The appreciative inquiry summit: A practitioner's guide for leading large-group change.* San Francisco: Berrett-Koehler.

Manning, M. R., and Binzagr, G. F. 1996. Methods, values, and assumptions underlying large group interventions intended to change whole systems. *International Journal of Organizational Analysis* 4(3):268–84.

Marshak, R. J. 1993. Lewin meets Confucius: A re-view of the OD model of change. *Journal of Applied Behavioral Science* 29(4):393–415.

Weick, K. E. 2000. Emergent change as a universal in organizations. In *Breaking the code of change*, ed. M. Beer and N. Nohria, 223–24. Boston: Harvard Business School Press.

As we walked through the manufacturing areas of Dupont, the plant manager, Tom Harris, greeted each worker by name. The plant was on a site that stretched over 10 acres beside the South River on the edge of town and it was the major employer in the community.

The plant seemed to be a permanent fixture, or at least more permanent than most things. There had been changes, big ones, but the plant was still the plant. The Orlon manufacturing operation had been shut down, the equipment dismantled and sent to China. As far as I could find out early in my work there, these changes, despite their magnitude, were seen as doing the regular business of the enterprise. No one framed the changes as needing unusual attention, so there was no change management design. The projects—getting rid of one operation and installing another—were planned and executed just like any project. Change management was not a rubric used to either accomplish or explain what was going on. More changes were coming, whether there was any formal practice of change management or not. The plant would soon enough look very different from what I saw on that first tour with Tom.

I first met Tom when he came to the University of Virginia seeking to make contact with the academic community in order to bring some of the latest thinking in business to his operation. His interest lay in introducing his managers to new ideas, and in applying those ideas to improving the plant. He was not, he said, looking for solutions to specific problems, but rather in improving overall organization effectiveness. This was important because he was under increasing pressure to do more with less.

In February this general bulletin was sent to all employees, and I began the field-work from which a portrayal of the work culture would be built.

> Gib Akin, a professor from the University of Virginia, will be spending time at the plant. He has been asked to give us some new perspectives on our work and our organization that we might use to help us develop people and continually improve. Most importantly, he is here to help us appreciate and develop what goes right, assist us in building on our strengths, to make the plant work better for everybody. His presence is not due to any particular problem, but is a result of our desire to continuously improve.

Over the next six months I conducted interviews with workers and managers, spending time in the workplace, learning about everyday life there. This yielded a thick description of the shared stock of knowledge that organizational members used to interpret events and generate behavior. What we made explicit with this process was the local, widely used, everyday, common-sense model of work performance, unique to this scene. In a sense this was the local organization theory that people used for getting along at work.

Of course this theory was more important than any imported academic theory of organization, because it had to work well or the users would not be successful in their work. This was the practical theory in use every day and by everyone. Such culturally embedded theory also tends to create what it is intended to explain, thus making it even more powerful and generative. For example, in this plant the local model of teamwork was organized around a southern stock-car racing metaphor, which was not only used to explain teamwork but was also the pattern for accomplishing it. And since everyone knew the metaphor, and used it, it became so.

Tom and the other managers were surprised to learn of the NASCAR (the premier stock-car racing organization) metaphor, but it explained why they had not recognized existing teamwork in the workplace (they had a different metaphor for teamwork) and gave them a language in which to introduce change for improvement. Similarly, illumination of the local meaning of effective supervision, high performance, and what constituted a good day at work gave those with leadership roles constructs to work with for making improvements, and the language for introducing change.

Managers, and particularly first-line supervisors, were asked to use this new understanding gained from the findings of the study. Their new understanding could be used to interpret the local meaning of effective work to capitalize on strengths, to expand and develop existing good practices in order to swamp problems, that is, to render problems less troublesome even if unsolved.

The findings of the study could also be used as the basis for experiments. Members of the so-called Leadership Core Team were instructed to introduce change as an experiment—something to be tried and watched closely, and after a designated time, if it is not working as hoped, it can be stopped. Framing changes as experiments requires thinking through what is expected, and how and when to measure the results. And by interpreting the possible results before they happen, all outcomes can be positive. Even if things don't go as hoped, what does happen can yield learning. All experiments are successes at one level or another.

Tom embraced the framing of change as experiment, and it was probably his most pervasive concept regarding change. "A notion I use all the time is that everything is an experiment. If you describe every change as an experiment, the ability of people to digest it goes up an order of magnitude. And that goes for officers as well as people on the shop floor. As a matter of fact, nothing is forever anyway."

Questions

1. To what extent are the following approaches to change embedded in the Dupont story (justify your answer, providing specific examples):
   a. OD
   b. Appreciative inquiry
   c. Sense-making
2. In your opinion, how compatible are these three approaches? Why? What evidence is there in the Dupont story for your answer? As a change manager, to what extent could you utilize insights from each approach?
3. Imagine you are an OD practitioner brought into Dupont at the time of the Orlon manufacturing operation closure. Describe the steps that you would take to help manage this change based upon action research.
4. As a class, decide on a fictional large-scale change that could affect Dupont. Divide the class into three groups (and role-play the situation in two acts). In Act 1, one group will take a problem-solving approach and introduce the change with the second group (Dupont staff affected by the change). In Act 2 a third group (the appreciative inquiry group) will introduce the change with the second group (Dupont staff affected by the change). After the exercise, compare and contrast the steps taken in each approach. From the point of view of group two (Dupont staff), which approach seemed to work best? Why? From the point of view of groups one and two, how easy/difficult was it adopting this approach? What broad conclusions can be drawn?

TABLE 7.9 **Additional Case Studies**

SMA: Micro-Electronic Products Division (A), (B), & (C)
Beer, M., & Tushman, M. L. (2000) *Harvard Business School*
Avon Products (A) & (B)
Paine, L. S., & Rogers, G. C. (2000) *Harvard Business School*
Sony Europa (A)
Kashani, K., & Kassarjian, J. B. M. (1999) *IMD, Lausanne*
Peter Browning and Continental White Cap (A, B, C)
Gentile, M., under direction of Jick, T. (1986) *Harvard Business School*

Bibliography

Axelrod, D. 1992. Getting everyone involved: How one organization involved its employees, supervisors, and managers in redesigning the organization. *Journal of Applied Behavioral Science* 28(4):499–509.

Axelrod, R. H. 2001. Terms of engagement: Changing the way we change organizations. *Journal for Quality & Participation*, Spring:22–27.

Baburoglu, O. N., and Garr, M. A. 1992. Search conference methodologies for practitioners: An introduction. In *Discovering common ground*, ed. M. R. Weisbord, 72–81. San Francisco: Berrett-Koehler.

Balogun, J., and Johnson, G. 2004. Organizational restructuring and middle manager sensemaking. *Academy of Management Journal* 47(4):523–49.

Bazigos, M. N., and Burke, W. W. 1997. Theory orientations of organization development (OD) practitioners. *Group & Organization Management* 22(3):384–408.

Beckhard, R. 1969. *Organization development: Strategies and models*. Reading, MA: Addison-Wesley.

Blake, R., Carlson, B., McKee, R., Sorenson, P., and Yaeger, T. F. 2000. Contemporary issues of grid international: Sustaining and extending the core values of O.D. *Organizational Development Journal* 18(2):54–61.

Bolman, L. G., and Deal, T. E. 2003. *Reframing organizations: Artistry, choice, and leadership*. San Francisco: Jossey-Bass.

Bunker, B. B., and Alban, B. T. 1992. Editors' introduction: The large group intervention—A new social innovation? *Journal of Applied Behavioral Science* 28(4):473–579.

Bunker, B. B., and Alban, B. T. 1997. *Large group interventions: Engaging the whole system for rapid change*. San Francisco: Jossey-Bass.

Burke, W. W. 1997. The new agenda for organization development. *Organizational Dynamics* 26(1):7–20.

Cummings, T. G., and Worley, C. G. 1997. *Organization development and change*. 6th ed. Minneapolis/St. Paul: West Publishing.

Dannemiller, K. D., and Jacobs, R. W. 1992. Changing the way organizations change: A revolution of common sense. *Journal of Applied Behavioral Science* 28(4):480–98.

Eisenhardt, K. M., and Brown, S. L. 1999. Patching: Restitching business portfolios in dynamic markets. *Harvard Business Review* 77(3):72–82.

Emory, M., and Purser, R. E. 1996. *The search conference*. San Francisco: Jossey-Bass.

Fagenson-Eland, E., Ensher, E.A., and Burke, W. Warner (2004) Organization development and change interventions: A seven-nation comparison. *Journal of Applied Behavioral Science* 40 (4): 432-464.

French, W. L., and Bell, C. H. 1995. *Organization development: Behavioral science interventions for organization improvement*. Englewood Cliffs, NJ: Prentice Hall.

Fuller, C., Griffin, T., and Ludema, J. D. 2000. Appreciative future search: Involving the whole system in positive organization change. *Organization Development Journal* 18(2):29–41.

Gelinas, M. V., and James, R. G. 1999. Organizational purpose: Foundation for the future. *OD Practitioner* 31(2):10–22.

Golembiewski, R. T. 1998. Process observer: Where did that goodwill go and what can we do about it? OD and macro-trends II. *Organization Development Journal* 16(3):5–9.

Golembiewski, R. 1999a. Process observer: Large-system interventions, I: Reflections on a second-time around (or is it the sixth or seventh?). *Organization Development Journal* 17(2):5–9.

Golembiewski, R. 1999b. Process observer: Large-system interventions, II: Two sources of evidence that O.D.ers have been there, been doing that. *Organization Development Journal* 17(3):5–8.

Helms Mills, J. 2003. *Making sense of organizational change*. London: Routledge.

Herman, S. 2000. Counterpoints: Notes on O.D. for the 21st century, Part 1. *Organization Development Journal* 18(2):108–10.

Holman, P., and Devane, T. 1999 (eds) *The change handbook: Group methods for shaping the future*. San Francisco: Berrett-Koehler.

Hornstein, H. 2001. Organizational development and change management: Don't throw the baby out with the bath water. *Journal of Applied Behavioral Science* 37(2):223–26.

Kanter, R. M., Stein, B. A., and Jick, T. D. 1992. *The challenge of organizational change: How companies experience it and leaders guide it*. New York: Free Press.

Klein, D. C. 1992. Simu-Real: A simulation approach to organizational change. *Journal of Applied Behavioral Science* 28(4):566–78.

Levine, L., and Mohr, B. J. 1992. Whole system design (WSD): The shifting focus of attention and the threshold challenge. *Journal of Applied Behavioral Science* 28(4):305–26.

Lewin, K. 1947. Frontiers in group dynamics. *Human Relations* 1:5–41.

Lukensmeyer, C. J., and Brigham, S. 2002. Taking democracy to scale: Creating a town hall meeting for the twenty-first century. *National Civic Review* 91(4) (Winter):351–66.

Manning, M. R., and Binzagr, G. F. 1996. Methods, values, and assumptions underlying large group interventions intended to change whole systems. *International Journal of Organizational Analysis* 4(3):268–84.

Marshak, R. J. 1993. Lewin meets Confucius: A re-view of the OD model of change. *Journal of Applied Behavioral Science* 29(4):393–415.

Nicholl, D. 1998a. From the editor: Is OD meant to be relevant? Part I. *OD Practitioner* 30(2).

Nicholl, D. 1998b. From the editor: Is OD meant to be relevant? Part II. *OD Practitioner* 30(3).

Nicholl, D. 1998c. From the editor: Is OD meant to be relevant? Part III. *OD Practitioner* 30(4).

Nicholl, D. 1999. From the editor: A new profession for the next millennium. *OD Practitioner* 31(4).

Oswick, C., and Grant, D. 1996. Organization development and metaphor—Mapping the territory. In *Organization development: Metaphorical exploration*, ed. C. Oswick and D. Grant, 1–3. London: Pitman.

Weick, K. E. 2000. Emergent change as a universal in organizations. In *Breaking the code of change*, ed. M. Beer and N. Nohria, 223–41. Boston: Harvard Business School Press.

Weisbord, M. R. 1992a. Preface. In *Discovering common ground*, ed. M. R. Weisbord, xi–xvi. San Francisco: Berrett-Koehler.

Weisbord, M. R. 1992b. Applied common sense. In *Discovering common ground*, ed. M. R. Weisbord, 3–17. San Francisco: Berrett-Koehler.

Notes

1. See Special Issue of *Journal of Applied Behavioral Science* (2004), Volume 40, Number 4 (December) which is devoted to this discussion.
2. Golembiewski, 1998:5.
3. Hornstein, 2001:225.
4. Bazigos and Warner, 1997.
5. Beckhard, 1969:9–19.
6. Nicoll, 1998a.
7. Nicoll, 1998c.
8. Burke, 1997:7.
9. Nicholl, 1998b.
10. Nicholl, 1998a.
11. French and Bell, 1995:4.
12. Cummings and Worley, 1997:28–30.
13. Cummings and Worley, 1997:49–51.
14. Cummings and Worley, 1997:51.
15. Lewin, 1947.
16. French and Bell, 1995:326–35.
17. French and Bell, 1995:334.
18. Oswick and Grant, 1996:2.
19. Cummings and Worley, 1997:17–19.
20. Burke, 1997:7.
21. Burke, 1997:7.
22. Nicholl, 1998c.
23. Nicholl, 1999.
24. Gelinas and James, 1999.
25. Blake et al., 2000:60.
26. Blake et al., 2000:54.
27. Blake et al., 2000:55–56.
28. Blake et al., 2000:59.
29. Blake et al., 2000:59–60.
30. Blake et al., 2000:60.
31. Marshak, 1993.
32. Fagenson-Eland, Ensher and Burke, 2004: 461
33. Manning and Binzagr, 1996:269.
34. See Worley et al. 1996.
35. See Manning and Binzagr, 1996; Fuller, Griffin, and Ludema, 2000; Bunker and Alban, 1992, 1997; Axelrod, 1992; Levine and Mohr, 1998; Klein, 1992; Emery, 1992; Dannemiller and Jacobs, 1992; Holman and Devane, 1999.
36. Manning and Binzagr, 1996:269.
37. Manning and Binzagr, 1996:271–72.
38. Manning and Binzagr, 1996:282.

39. Axelrod, 2001:22.
40. Bunker and Alban, 1992:477.
41. Axelrod, 1992:507.
42. Axelrod, 2001:22.
43. Axelrod, 2001:25.
44. Bunker and Alban, 1992:473.
45. Dannemiller and Jacobs, 1992:497.
46. Weisbord, 1992b:5.
47. For example, see Weisbord, 1992a:xii.
48. Fuller, Griffin, and Ludema, 2000:30–31.
49. Weisbord, 1992b:9.
50. Weisbord, 1992b:10.
51. Fuller, Griffin, and Ludema, 2000:31.
52. For example, see Weisbord, 1992b:9.
53. Golembiewski, 1999a:6; see also Blake et al., 2000:54.
54. Golembiewski, 1999b:5.
55. Herman, 2000:109.
56. Herman, 2000:110.
57. Cited in Herman, 2000:109.
58. Weick, 2000.
59. Weick, 2000.
60. Weick, 2000:228–29.
61. Weick, 2000:229–32.
62. Weick, 2000:235–36.
63. Weick, 2000:232.
64. Weick, 2000:234–35.
65. Weick, 2000:235.
66. Weick, 2000:235–36.
67. Weick, 2000:236–37.
68. Weick, 2000:238.
69. Helms Mills, 2003.
70. Helms Mills, 2003:4.
71. Helms Mills, 2003:124–80.
72. Bolman and Deal, 2003:19.
73. Bolman and Deal, 2003:13.
74. Balogun and Johnson, 2004:545.

Implementing Change: Change Management, Contingency, and Processual Approaches

Learning objectives

On completion of this chapter you should be able to:

- Appreciate more clearly the organizational change approaches underpinning the *director* and *navigator* images of managing change.
- Understand the change management approach to change.
- Outline contingency approaches to change.
- Appreciate current debates between OD and change management approaches to change.
- Be familiar with the processual approach to managing change.
- Reflect upon your own approach to managing change.

This chapter continues from the previous chapter by considering the other two images of managing change, the *director* and *navigator* images, which also have strong foundations in the organizational change field (as distinct from the organization theory field) and also assume, in various ways, that the change manager has an important influence on the initiation, support, and outcomes of organizational change.

We commence this chapter by considering the *director* image. This image underpins the change management approaches that are often associated with the work of many large consulting companies. Adherents to these approaches take a strategic view of organizational change and make no apology for taking a pragmatic, managerialist view of how to go about achieving lasting organizational change. Within the change management field are a variety of models to choose from, each with a series of steps that need to be followed.

One consequence of this variety is that it is not clear which change management model should be followed or what criteria should be used to choose among the models offered.

Addressing this problem are contingency approaches. These are still underpinned by the *director* image, but rather than claiming to have the "one best approach" for all types of organizational change, contingency change theorists and practitioners take an "it depends" approach in which the style of change, especially the style of change leadership, is dependent on the scale of the proposed change and the readiness of staff to receive it.

However, this notion of getting the right "fit" between the type of change and the manner for achieving it runs counter to processual approaches to viewing change. Drawing on the *navigator* image, these approaches see change as a political and disputed process that emerges over time and varies according to the context in which it is attempted.[1] These approaches are outlined in the discussion that follows.

DIRECTOR IMAGE OF MANAGING CHANGE: CHANGE MANAGEMENT AND CONTINGENCY APPROACHES

In this section we consider first a variety of change management approaches to organizational change and debates associated with whether they have supplanted the OD approaches discussed in the previous chapter. We then discuss the contingency approaches and consider why their impact has been less prevalent than the change management approaches.

Change Management Approaches

Common to the various *change management* approaches is that they provide multistep models of how to achieve large-scale, transformational change. Table 8.1 provides examples of these models that entail anywhere from a 5-step to a 12-step version of how change should proceed. These (and other) models differ not just in terms of the number of steps but whether all steps need to be followed, whether they need to be followed in sequence, and whether they need to be adapted to specific settings.[2]

Pendlebury et al.[3] argue that although their "Ten Keys" model may be adapted to suit particular change circumstances, omission of the various keys will likely lead to transformational failure. Most keys need to be implemented simultaneously and continuously during a change process, although some play a greater role in differing change phases compared to others. For example, they point out that:

- *Discontinuous change* is more likely to be associated with static environments and in this situation all keys "need to be applied scrupulously," whereas
- *In dynamic environments*, where change is continuous, keys two (mobilize), three (catalyze), seven (handle emotion), and eight (handle power) "will be less vital"[4] since staff will be more accustomed to change.

In this model, adapting the method appears to mean weighing the *degree* to which various keys are applied, not *whether* they are applied.

Nadler[5] maintains, in relation to his "12 Action Steps" change management framework, that it "can be adapted and applied by executives and managers at every level of

TABLE 8.1 Planned Change Management Models

Source: The models are paraphrased from the authors as listed in each column.

Pendlebury, Grouard, and Meston (1998) *Ten Keys*	Nadler (1998) *12 Action Steps*	Kanter, Stein, and Jick (1992) *Ten Commandments*	Taffinder (1998) *Transformation Trajectory*
1. Define the vision	1. Get support of key power groups	1. Analyze the need for change	1. Awaken
2. Mobilize	2. Get leaders to model change behavior	2. Create a shared vision	2. Conceive the future
3. Catalyze	3. Use symbols and language	3. Separate from the past	3. Build the agenda of change
4. Steer	4. Define areas of stability	4. Create a sense of urgency	4. Deliver big change
5. Deliver	5. Surface dissatisfaction with the present conditions	5. Support a strong leader role	5. Master the change
6. Obtain participation	6. Promote participation in change	6. Line up political sponsorship	
7. Handle emotions	7. Reward behavior that supports change	7. Craft an implementation plan	
8. Handle power	8. Disengage from the old	8. Develop enabling structures	
9. Train and coach	9. Develop and clearly communicate image of the future	9. Communicate and involve people	
10. Actively communicate	10. Use multiple leverage points	10. Reinforce and institutionalize change	
	11. Develop transition management arrangements		
	12. Create feedback		

the organization, providing immensely useful tools for initiating, leading, and managing change in every corner of the organization."[6] He depicts discontinuous change as being a continuous cycle rather than a linear process and identifies three core elements that need to be managed during the transformational process:[7]

- The need to manage organizational *power*, as depicted in steps 1 to 4 (see Table 8.1).
- The need to *motivate* people to participate in the change, in particular dealing with the anxieties associated with change, as depicted in steps 5 to 8.
- The need to manage the *transition* itself, as depicted in steps 9 to 12.

While pointing to the importance of all steps, Nadler accepts that some steps will need to be emphasized more in some change situations compared to others and that the order of the steps may vary according to the change situation.[8] Taffinder[9] makes similar points in relation to his five "transformation trajectories" (see Table 8.1). These trajectories are not linear but multidimensional; their starting points are staggered; some actions are dependent upon others' actions; however, their sequence is context specific, as is the emphasis that needs to be placed on each transition line.

Similar to the models presented in Table 8.1 is the work of Ghoshal and Bartlett,[10] who argue for the importance "of sequencing and implementation of activities in a change process."[11] They identify three distinct but interrelated transformational change phases:

- *Rationalization* (streamlining company operations).
- *Revitalization* (leveraging resources and linking opportunities across the whole organization).
- *Regeneration* (managing business unit operations and tensions, while at the same time collaborating elsewhere in the organization to achieve performance).[12]

They claim that while change is often presented as difficult and messy, there is nothing mystical about the process of achieving change with effective changes following the rationalization, revitalization, and regeneration sequential process.[13] Going through these change phases is not necessarily easy, with the process being akin to the transformation of a caterpillar into a butterfly: "It goes blind, its legs fall off, and its body is torn apart as the beautiful wings emerge. Similarly, transforming a hierarchical bureaucracy into a flexible, self-generating company can be painful, and it requires enormous courage from those who must lead the process of change."[14]

Of the change management models presented in Table 8.1, Kanter et al.[15] adopt the most reflective position in commenting upon the utility of their "Ten Commandments":

- First, they point out that how they are practiced and interpreted will vary according to the particular change maker group in question (strategists, implementers, and recipients). For example, while change strategists may view a change as urgent, a change recipient might view it quite differently if, in their eyes, it may lead to them being laid off.
- Second, multiple changes may be in progress so that what constitutes the notion of the past may be difficult to determine.
- Third, the change commandments need to be tailored to the needs of each organization; the commandments themselves may even form the source of debate within an organization in terms of how best to proceed.
- Fourth, they highlight the need for communication about change to be not just about passing on information but about allowing differing voices to be heard in the change process and engaging in dialogue with differing groups affected by the change.
- Fifth, they note that underpinning the 10 commandments is an assumption of action: "But this focus on action assumes a level of control that simply doesn't exist when large-scale change is being implemented. Those who want to embrace change must be as adept at *reacting* as they are at acting."[16]
- Sixth, they point to a paradox underlying the 10 commandments—that they help provide change strategists and implementers with the means of controlling change

at precisely the time that the opposite is required: "while the commandments may serve to minimize failure, maximize control and predictability, and define the end state, a transformation may actually require maximizing experimentation and risk taking, tolerating unknowable consequences, and evolving toward—rather than targeting—an end state."[17]

- Seventh, they point out that although the change model calls for a strong leader, the reality may be one of multiple leaders in an organization "wrestling with how change is to be managed, and by whom."[18]

Given these ambiguities, they maintain that "muddling along" and taking one stage at a time may be the most appropriate means of handling complex changes.[19] They conclude that "(a)lthough managing change will never be easy, with the right attitude and approach, it can be a most gratifying adventure."[20]

Possibly one of the best-known change management models is John Kotter's eight-step model.[22] First published in 1995 as an article in the *Harvard Business Review* (*HBR*), it became *HBR*'s most requested article for reprints in that year.[23] Subsequently, the article was expanded in 1996 into a book titled *Leading Change*, which was expanded further in 2002 with another book titled *The Heart of Change*. Table 8.2 provides a summary of his model.

TABLE 8.2 Kotter's Eight-Step Change Management Model

Source: Adapted from Kotter, 1995:61; 1996:21.

Step	Actions
1. Establish the need for urgency	• Perform market analyses • Determine problems and opportunities • Use techniques to focus people's attention on the importance of change to meet these challenges
2. Ensure there is a powerful change group to guide the change	• Create team structures to help drive the change • Ensure teams have sufficient power to achieve the desired change
3. Develop a vision	• Develop a vision that provides a focus for the change
4. Communicate the vision	• Role model the behavior implied by the vision • Use multiple channels to constantly communicate the vision
5. Empower staff	• Remove organizational policies and structures that inhibit achievement of the vision • Encourage risk taking
6. Ensure there are short-term wins	• Wins help support need for change • Rewarding "wins" helps to provide motivation
7. Consolidate gains	• Continue to remove organizational policies and processes that inhibit change • Reward those who engage positively with the change • Establish new, related change projects
8. Embed the change in the culture	• Link change to organizational performance and leadership

EXERCISE 8.1

Experiencing Change

This exercise is designed for people who have had some experience of organizational change. For those who lack this experience, you may wish to get someone else's perspective on what follows and use this information to frame your responses.

In any change process there are usually three change groups:[21]

- *Change strategists* are those individuals or groups who legitimate or sanction organizational changes. Most often these people occupy senior management positions.
- Those who are responsible for implementing change, often middle management, are known as *change implementers.*
- Those people who are the recipients of change (knowledge, skills, attitudes, etc) are known as *change recipients.*

Divide into two groups: those who have been change strategists/implementers and those who have been change recipients.

Change Strategists/Implementers Group

1. What type of change did you attempt? (List these in your group.)
2. How was the change received by the change targets?
3. What was the most frustrating part? Why? (List these in your group.)
4. How would you rate your success in achieving the desired change? What would you do differently next time? Why?

Change Recipients Group

1. What types of changes were attempted? (List these in your group.)
2. What was your response to the attempted change?
3. What was the most frustrating part? Why? (List these in your group.)
4. How would you rate management's implementation of the change? What should they do differently next time? Why?

Process

Each group will have 25 minutes to respond to the above questions. Appoint a spokesperson to give a 5-minute presentation to the rest of the class. What similarities and differences emerge looking at change from these different perspectives?

While Kotter acknowledges that his framework simplifies the change process and that "even successful change efforts are messy and full of surprises,"[24] he maintains that following the eight phases he outlines are important for achieving successful change and that "[s]kipping steps creates only the illusion of speed and never produces a satisfying result."[25] He argues that successful change follows a "see–feel–change" pattern in which problems need to be presented in a compelling way that captures the attention of others; this awakens in them feelings about the need for change; and the change itself reinforces new behaviors. Without dismissing an alternative "analysis–think–change" pattern, he argues that the "see–feel–change" pattern is more motivating for people to engage in change.[26]

EXERCISE 8.2

Developing Your Own Change Management Model

Table 8.1 sets out five change management models:

- Compare and contrast the various steps in these models. What is left out of different models?
- Create your own composite model—do this part of the activity in a group if possible.
- Is there a preferred sequence of steps? Why?
- Identify two or three key management skills associated with each step. Which ones are you strongest on? Weakest on?
- Where you have experience of organizational change, which steps have been best handled? Worst handled? Why?

Is Change Management Supplanting OD?

Some writers argue that as the relevance of OD came into question, so did this lead to a rise in interest in change management models. This raises the question of whether change management models are supplanting OD. There is no simple way of answering this question. However, what is interesting is to analyze the key social science electronic database, ABInform. We conducted a count of articles with the words "organization development" and "change management" in their titles over the period 1985 to 2001. Figure 8.1 reveals some interesting patterns, with the vertical axis representing the number of publication titles and the horizontal axis the time period. In total there were 148 references to OD articles and 134 references to change management articles. However, a study of the pattern shows an interesting shift. OD dominated discussion from 1985 to 1995 (except for two years, 1988 and 1991), but since 1996 references to change management have dominated. Indeed, 57 percent (76/134 total) of all change management references appeared from 1996 to 2001, compared to only 28 percent (41/148) of all OD references. This implies that since the mid-1990s, there appears to be a general increase in the use of the term "change management" and a comparative decline in the use of the term "organization development."

Very clearly, this is a limited test of the level of continuing interest in these two change traditions. For example, neither term captures all that encompasses each field; other articles are undoubtedly in the database that are relevant to each field but that do not mention either one or the other of the terms in their titles; and the database represents what is being written about—the discourse of change—which is not necessarily a reflection of what is actually being practiced in organizations. Nevertheless, and acknowledging these limitations, the table does provide an indication of what appears to be an increase in attention being paid to the term "change management" and a decrease in the use of the term "organization development" as an organizational change title. However, OD has been around for a long time and remains a staple part of many change agents' repertoires. As argued in the previous chapter, it may be under threat and going through a period of deep introspection, but its lasting influences are straightforward and undeniable.

FIGURE 8.1 ABInform—Change Management versus Organization Development

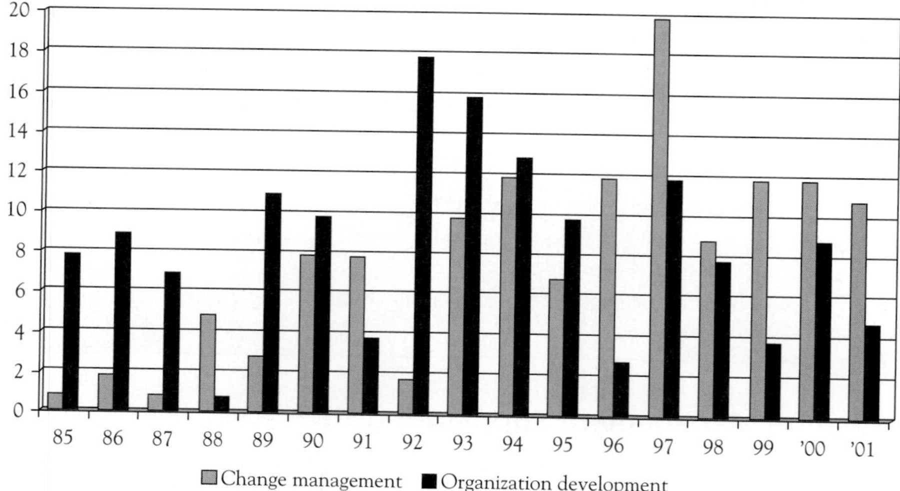

OD–Change Management Debates

Change management as a field is depicted by OD writers as the brash child of the large consulting companies. Lacking the underlying tenets of the OD value system, it is seen as a set of value-neutral change practices harnessed-up to assist management in achieving greater financial performance in their organizations.[27] Consultants are not facilitators or coaches (as in an OD model) so much as directors and advisers on best practices and strategies. Integration is at the heart of change management, aligning new changes to desired outcomes.

This has led to a debate about the relationship between OD and change management, a term often associated with fundamental, strategic change. Church sees, under the influence of non-OD change consultants, a shift in mentality of some OD practitioners toward a vendor mindset. This, he argues, is one of three forces "converging on the ultimate demise of O.D. as a field."[28] (The other two forces are a shift in OD values away from humanism toward a bottom-line focus and a lack of clarity regarding what it is that unifies the OD field.[29]) While some OD advocates seek greater clarification of what constitutes the OD field,[30] or of trying to figure out how the field should be "rewired,"[31] for other writers OD is now largely irrelevant: OD practitioners lack an understanding of business practices, OD departments in organizations are not growing, and there is a lack of interest in OD by both executives and MBA students.[32]

While drawing on a number of OD's techniques, change management is said to have supplanted rather than extended OD as a new field. This has occurred in three ways:

- First, theoretically, this new field has a broader scope than OD, considering human performance and development as one feature of organizational change efforts but related to other issues such as technology, operations, and strategy.

EXERCISE 8.3

OD versus Change Management: The Great Debate

Think about the arguments about OD and change management approaches to organizational change in this chapter and in the previous chapter. As an in-class exercise, divide into two groups, with one the "OD group" and the other the "change management" group. Debate one or both of the following propositions:

"That the demise of OD is long overdue."

or

"Change management approaches lack a concern for humanity."

- What conclusions do you reach?
- What key issues emerged?

- Second, the role of the classic OD practitioner is as a third-party facilitator or coach. Contrary to this, the change management consultant operates with technical knowledge and as part of a team consisting of skill sets that cover a range of strategy and organizational areas.
- Third, OD is presented as changing individual attitudes and ideas as a prelude to wider structural changes in an organization. Change management is contrasted with this on the grounds that it is through structural changes that new behaviors are assumed to emerge.[33]

Defenders of OD accept a number of limitations of the field. However, they point to an alignment of change management with management consulting and criticize it for adopting faddist, holy-grail-type solutions to client problems in which the consultant is an "omniscient expert."[34] They claim that proponents of change management have misrepresented the OD field. They point to how its scope has grown to include strategic issues with its practitioners now approaching organizational problems from "a holistic and integrated perspective."[35] They argue the need for a people-focused perspective on organizations and maintain "that creating a new discipline based on the models of consulting firms is misguided."[36]

In reply, supporters of change management models acknowledge evidence of a more strategic focus in OD but criticize the profession for still being dominated by traditional practitioner perspectives. Some of the language may have changed but not the underlying practices. They indicate that it is through embracing the change management field with its strategic focus and working with planners and information technology specialists that OD practitioners can collaborate to achieve organizational change.[37]

For their part, OD practitioners are concerned about integrating OD with change management, one writer "wondering whether or not this is simply a specious attempt on our part on having our cake and eating it too, an effort at keeping our values while becoming relevant to business executives. Right now I think this is probably the case."[38]

Clearly this debate has yet to be fully played out, although Heracleous[39] concludes that greater interaction is needed between the OD field and the strategic change management field, neither side being sufficiently aware of how the potential of the other can enhance radical organizational change.

Contingency Approaches

While change management models contain variation and flexibility, an underlying assumption is that there is "one best way" of producing organizational change—although it is not clear which of the various models offered is the best one for the manager of change to follow. Contingency theorists challenge this assumption and argue that the style of change will depend upon the scale of the change and the receptivity of organizational members for engaging in the change.

The best-developed change contingency approach is associated with the work of Dexter Dunphy and Doug Stace. In their book, published in 1990, titled *Under New Management*, they set out a comprehensive "it depends" approach to understanding the style of change that should be adopted. This was subsequently developed in their 1994 (first edition) and their 2001 (second edition) book *Beyond the Boundaries* as well as in other articles.[40] The initial research for their approach was based on a sample of 20 Australian organizations. They argue that the style of change (collaborative, consultative, directive, or coercive), as well as the scale of the change (fine-tuning, incremental adjustment, modular transformation, or corporate transformation) has to be matched to the needs of the organization.[41] Their model is set out in Figure 8.2.

They identify five main change approaches:

- By *developmental transitions*, they refer to situations in which there is constant change as a result of the organization adapting itself to external, environmental changes. The primary style of leadership is consultative, where the leader acts in the capacity of a coach aiming to gain voluntary, shared commitment from organizational members to the need for continual improvement.
- In *task focused transitions*, the change management style is directive with the change leader acting as a captain seeking the compliance of organizational members to redefine how the organization operates in specific areas. While directive leadership means that the overall change is driven from the top, this may translate into a

FIGURE 8.2 Dunphy/Stace Contingency Model of Change

Source: Stace and Dunphy, 2001:109. Reproduced with permission of McGraw-Hill Australia Pty. Limited.

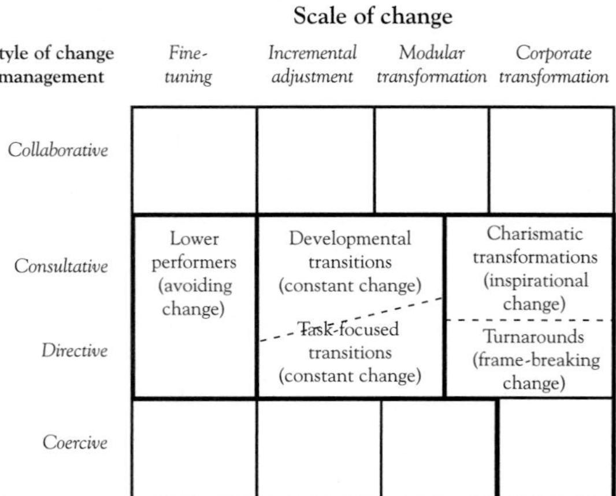

more consultative approach by managers operating lower down in the organization who are required to implement the changes.

- With *charismatic transformation*, people accept that the organization is out of step with its environment and that there is a need for radical, revolutionary change. Helping to create a new identity and a paradigm shift in the way in which the organization conducts its operations, the charismatic leader is able to operate symbolically to gain emotional commitment of staff to new directions.
- Whereas charismatic transformation is aimed at inspirational change, *turnarounds* are aimed at frame-breaking changes. Turnaround change leaders operate as commanders utilizing their positions of power to force required changes through the organization. This coercive/directive change style is argued to be needed where there is little staff support for change and little time available to the organization to seek their engagement and participation in how the organization should be reshaped.
- A fifth category in their model, *Taylorism*, is associated with fine-tuning, paternalistic approaches to managing change.[42]

In their view, one way of thinking of these approaches is to view them as differing "paths of change"[43] that organizations might adopt at different periods of time. For example, they propose that:

- Where organizations predominantly use fine-tuning, they will probably need to use charismatic transformation or turnaround at some stage to reinvigorate themselves.
- In order for turnarounds to be successful over time, a variety of task-focused transitions in different business units are likely to be needed.
- Because of the difficulty of keeping charismatic transformations going over the longer term, developmental transitions are likely to be needed to embed the changes into the organization.
- Where developmental or task-focused transitions are not seen to be delivering the desired changes, then charismatic transformations or turnaround change strategies are likely to be called for.[44]

They suggest that, overall, their research indicates that medium- to high-performance organizations are likely to be using consultative and directive change management styles while those using fine-tuning or Taylorism are likely to be least successful, especially given the hypercompetitive business environment.[45] Notwithstanding this, they argue that rather than having a dominant ideology of how change should occur in an organization, more effective managers and organizations are more comfortable adopting differing change styles depending upon the prevailing circumstances.[46]

Another contingency approach has recently appeared in the work of Huy,[47] who categorizes change into four ideal types:

- The *commanding* change intervention is one where the time period is short term, abrupt, and rapid. Change is usually implemented by senior executives who demand compliance from organizational members. Changes may well include downsizing, outsourcing, and divestments.
- The *engineering* intervention is oriented toward a medium-term, relatively fast-change perspective and often assisted by work design analysts who assist in changing work and operational systems. The change agent acts as an analyst in this process.

EXERCISE 8.4

Does This Go with That? What's Your Experience?

The contingency approach to change identifies five change styles:

- Developmental transitions
- Task-focused transitions
- Charismatic transformations
- Turnarounds
- Taylorist

In groups, see if you can conduct research to identify examples of organizational changes that fall into one or more of the above categories.

- To what extent were these successful? Using what criteria?
- Can you identify change "paths," that is, where an organization used more than one change process at different points in time? Can you find out whether the leader adopted a different style, for example, directive in one change; participative in another?
- Are you able to determine if there was a credibility issue that needed to be addressed where this occurred? Do you know how successful this was? What new skills might have been required?
- Were these mainly top-down or bottom-up changes? Or were they a combination of these two? What implications emerge from this?

- The *teaching* intervention takes a more gradual, longer-term OD change perspective. Assisted by outside process consultants, staff are taught how to probe their work practices and behaviors to reveal new ways of working.
- The *socializing* intervention is also gradual and long term. It sees change as developing through participative experiential learning based on self-monitoring, democratic organizational processes.[48]

Each ideal type has its limitations. The commanding approach may lead to resentment and rarely produces lasting behavioral change; the teaching approach is very individualistic and may not be aligned to corporate strategic objectives; the engineering approach may not encourage collaboration and spread of change across business units; and the socializing approach may lead to overfocusing on individual work groups rather than on how they may operate as part of a larger, corporate collective.[49]

Why Contingency Approaches Are Not Dominant

It is interesting to consider why the contingency approaches are less prevalent than change management approaches. In making this statement, we note that contingency approaches are framed around questions concerning the applicability of change management programs to differing times and situations. In a recent edition of the *Academy of Management Journal* these questions of time and situation were referred to by Pettigrew et al.[50] as the "more difficult questions" but ones that are "largely unstudied and inadequately understood" in the change field. We identify the following contributing reasons for the relative lack of "voice" given to contingency approaches:

- First, the notion of "fitting" an organizational change program to the type of change required may be easier to articulate in theory than to deliver in practice. Differing perceptions may exist about what is the required fit and what is the best strategic set of actions to employ.
- Second, compared to the "off-the-shelf" neatness and simplicity offered by the change management models outlined above, contingency approaches are more ambiguous and require greater choice and decisions by managers about what type of change situation they are facing and therefore which avenue to pursue.
- Third, the main focus of contingency approaches is on the specific style of leadership, matched to the scale of required change, rather than on a specific set of change action steps. Hence, contingency approaches may be less attractive in practice to senior managers who lack the skills to adopt differing modes of leading, depending upon the particular change circumstances.
- Fourth, if an organization is to adopt differing "paths of change" and employ differing styles of change leadership at differing times and in association with differing changes, this raises the question about the credibility or sincerity with which staff view senior management actions—adopting differing behaviors at differing times, sometimes participative and sometimes directive.
- Fifth, there is a question about "what" is contingent to managing change. Are there some things that are not contingent but are universal to all changes (and if so, what? why? and how do we know this with any certainty?) and are there other things that vary (and if so, what? why? and how do we know this with any certainty?).

NAVIGATOR IMAGES OF MANAGING CHANGE: PROCESSUAL APPROACHES

Processual approaches share an assumption with contingency theory that change unfolds differently over time and according to the context in which the organization finds itself; however, they part company from contingency theory in assuming "that change should not be and cannot be solidified, or seen as a series of linear events within a given period of time; instead, it is viewed as a continuous process,"[51] one that has "no clear beginning or end."[52]

Pettigrew's extensive and detailed study of change and stability from the 1960s to the 1980s in *Imperial Chemical Industries* (ICI), a major UK chemical company, provides the backdrop to the development of this approach. Pettigrew starts off from a position of being critical of linear, rational, and planned theories of change. For him, the key to understanding organizational change "is to identify the variety and mixture of causes of change, to examine the juxtaposition of the rational and the political, the quest for efficiency and power, the role of exceptional men (sic) and of extreme circumstances, the untidiness of change, forces in the environment, and to explore some of the conditions in which mixtures of these occur."[53] He argues for a political and contextual view of change: Change is best understood as a complex interplay between content, process, and context.[54] This recognizes that there are different interest groups in organizations that have differing rationalities around goals, time, language, and behavior, all of which influence how organizational change occurs.[55]

He points out that change at ICI went through periods of revolution followed by relatively long periods of stability or incremental adjustments.[56] New rationalities and changes from the existing order emerged through:

> insubordinate minorities, often in very senior line positions sensing environmental change and organizational inertia, developing a widening caucus of concern around new problem areas for the firm, using cognitive and analytical skill to fashion new rationalities and ideas to compete in the strategy formulation process, and seizing on the opportunities provided by environmental change to put together new marriages of strategic content and context.[57]

Adopting a political and cultural view of change for Pettigrew means recognizing "that intervening in an organization to create strategic change is likely to be a challenge to the dominating ideology, culture, and systems of meaning and interpretation, as well as the structures, priorities, and power relations of the organization."[58] This situation "makes it clearer why and how the processes of sensing, justifying, creating, and stabilizing strategic change can be so tortuous and long."[59]

What Does Managing Change Mean from a Processual Approach?

Pettigrew argues that "creating strategic change is in essence a long-term conditioning, educating, and influence process designed to establish the dominating legitimacy of a different pattern of relation between strategic context and content."[60] This means that managers of change need to examine the context of change in order to identify sources of continuity as well as performance gaps and misfits: "Context and continuity shape the starting point in which change processes emerge, falter, and proceed."[61] By context he refers to *external context* (economic, political, and competitive environment) as well as *internal context* (strategy, structure, culture, and power relations). In this sense, context provides both constraints *and* opportunities for managers of change.[62] For him the challenging question is: "Is it possible to describe and codify the tasks and skills appropriate for such a contextually sensitive activity as managing strategic change without reducing the change process to a mechanical and over-determined set of phases or stages and the activities of changing to a set of platitudinous generalities?"[63]

In seeking to answer this question, he draws on and extends the work of Johnston[64] and highlights a number of stages to engaging in the management of change:[65]

- One is a *problem-sensing* stage, which is important in a highly political environment. This entails signaling and spreading throughout the organization, through discussion and decision making, the legitimacy of certain problems as requiring attention.
- Next is the *development of concern* about the problem, a process that involves establishing broad buy-in at a variety of levels throughout the organization. This is an educational process entailing meetings and data integration and providing space and opportunity for people to challenge conventional wisdom.
- The third stage involves gaining *acknowledgment and understanding of the importance of the problem*. This period entails a persistent championing role and is important to enable new rationalities to emerge alongside new diagnoses of problems and solutions.

- A *planning and acting stage* involves clarifying future directions and objectives and putting in place transition managers to enable the transition to occur. This involves senior management establishing a tension within the organization between the current state of things and what is needed for the future: middle managers need to use this tension to create momentum for change through establishing targets and the like.
- Finally, *stabilizing change*, or "making things which happen stick,"[66] includes changing the organization's systems (HR, IT, etc.) in order to reinforce and support the changes.

These stages are reminiscent of the "*n*-step" prescriptions of change management models. Yet, in a later book, Pettigrew and Whipp[67] wrestle with the question of how change should be managed. Drawing on seven case studies of companies involved in strategic change, they reaffirm the relevance of the above stages in managing change.[68] However, they conclude that their studies question "any easy unitary notions of managing change and competition."[69] Returning to the ICI study, what is interesting is that Pettigrew's book is over 500 pages in length, but the discussion of the process of how managers can achieve strategic change occupies only six pages (pages 471–76). This imbalance points to the difficulty of processual approaches in providing a menu-driven way of achieving organizational change. This is not surprising given the messiness of change processes to which they point and the difficulties of controlling all of these in any change process. In this regard, it is probably fair to say that the processual approach is probably better at providing a detailed analysis and understanding of change retrospectively rather than prescriptively providing steps for the change manager to follow in any detailed manner.

Indeed, when another writer in this tradition, Patrick Dawson, did provide a prescriptive set of steps for achieving organization change, he was later criticized for this for falling back on the logic of change management approaches and failing to convey the subtleties and complexities of change that processual approaches uncover.[70] In his latest book, Dawson makes clear that he does not seek to offer managers prescriptions for achieving successful change.[71] Instead, he tries to establish the "practical value" of the processual approach in a reflective way, urging managers of change to gain an awareness of the critical change issues facing them rather than providing them with prescriptive change management recipes.[72] He lists 10 "lessons":[73]

1. Simple, linear change recipes should be challenged.
2. Change strategies will need to be adapted in light of the reactions and politics they create.
3. Change takes time and is unlikely to entail continual improvement.
4. Taken-for-granted assumptions need to be questioned along the way.
5. Change managers need to learn from stories of experiences of change, including those of individuals at all levels.
6. Training programs need to be aligned with desired changes.
7. Communication needs to occur in context, sensitive to competing narratives and political processes.
8. The substance of change is itself likely to alter as it unfolds in line with other internal and external contexts.

9. Political processes will be central to how quickly change outcomes occur.
10. Change involves interwoven, often contradictory processes as well as rewriting of accounts of the past and expectations of the future.

While these lessons have interesting and intuitive value, they may be less appealing to change managers seeking solutions and specific guidelines for producing change. Change managers are likely to find the processual approach both illuminating—identifying the undercurrents of change, the shifting terrain that can only be partially controlled in any change process—and frustrating—that how they should move from reflection and "lessons" to action is not well specified. This remains, perhaps, the greatest challenge of the processual approach. While its strength is clearly of an analytical, academic understanding of the political, cultural, and contextual messiness of change, how this gets translated into practice for managers of change is likely to be fertile ground for future work in this tradition.

Conclusion

The change management and contingency approaches were associated in Chapter 2 with a *director* image of managing organizational change. While recognizing that all images represent a simplification of any position, the *director* image points to the underlying assumption of these two approaches that by following a predetermined set of steps, intended change outcomes can be achieved. What is clear is that there are a variety of change management models upon which the manager of change may draw; what is less clear is the criteria that they should use in making this selection.

This points to a deeper issue that has been leveled at these models, which is that their claims are often made on the basis of thin empirical evidence. For example, in Pettigrew's[74] critique of Ghoshal and Bartlett's "three Rs" change model, he points to the lack of systematic evidence presented in support of it. He argues that their model is based on conjecture so that "it is difficult for the reader to disentangle what the authors have found empirically from what they would like to see."[75] One key challenge is for change management models to therefore provide a firmer footing in the form of systematic rather than anecdotal empirical evidence to support the advice they offer. This assessment of the extent to which change management models draw upon systematic empirical data may be one way in which managers of organizational change can differentiate among the competing models offered.

In Chapter 2 we identified the processual approach with the *navigator* image of managing organizational change. The *navigator* image accepts that management of change will always be in part unpredictable, with events impinging upon change processes over which they have only limited control. For example, Kanter et al.[76] point to the case of Northwest Airlines and the way, in the mid-1980s, the plan for cultural change was disrupted by its acquisition of Republic Airlines, which was followed by union-led strikes over the mismanagement of the merger. Later, the crash of Northwest flight 255—in which 156 people were killed after taking off from Detroit—compounded their problems. Then, toward the end of the 1990s, Northwest was itself subject to a hostile takeover, and then a more friendly takeover—which nevertheless saw most of Northwest senior management resign. As Kanter et al.,[77] comment, "So much for planned changes."

It is therefore up to the *navigator* to steer a path between that which is intended and controllable and that which is unanticipated and emerges along the way. Of interest to this position is the argument by Pettigrew[78] that we should abandon dichotomization of change outcomes into either planned or emergent. Rather, we should identify "the mutualities and complementarities of planned and emergent change."[79] Ironically, this may be best achieved at the level of the practicing change manager; as Weick notes, for middle managers, exactly what constitutes "emergent and planned change begin to become indistinguishable" as they deal with "fragments of frontline detail and fragments of a bigger picture."[80]

In this chapter and the previous one, we have identified differing approaches to managing organizational change. For the reflective manager of change, we suggest that they remain open to the insights offered from each of these approaches. This does not mean that "anything goes" but rather that they remain open to seeing "what goes best" in any change situation. Alternatively, it remains open to them to develop their own approach to managing change that draws upon the ones offered in these chapters. As Jean Bartunek says: "The ability to discern between competing approaches to change and their likely value may be one of the most important skills for managers to learn."[81]

TABLE 8.3 Chapter Reflections for the Practicing Change Manager

- Do you work with a one-size-fits-all approach to managing change? To what extent do you match your change approach to the scale, timing, and readiness of your staff to the change?
- How skilled are you in adopting more than one change style? On what skills do you need to work more in order to achieve this flexibility? Are you more comfortable managing top-down, bottom-up, or somewhere between these two?
- Is there a dominant change mode in your organization? If so, how appropriate is it? What would you need to do to replace it or modify it with another approach?
- How do you deal with multiple changes that are simultaneously present in your business unit but are at different stages and phases?

Supplemental Reading

Beer, M., and Nohria, N. 2000a. Resolving the tension between theories E and O of change. In *Breaking the code of change*, ed. M. Beer and N. Nohria, 1–33. Boston: Harvard Business School Press.

Dawson, P. 2003. *Understanding organizational change: The contemporary experience of people at work*. London: Sage.

Farias, G., and Johnson, H. 2000. Organizational development and change management: Setting the record straight. *Journal of Applied Behavioral Science* 36(3):376–79.

Ghoshal, S., and Bartlett, C. A. 2000. Rebuilding behavioral context: A blueprint for corporate renewal. In *Breaking the code of change*, ed. M. Beer and N. Nohria, 195–222. Boston: Harvard Business School Press.

Huy, Q. N. 2001. Time, temporal capability, and planned change. *Academy of Management Review* 26(4):601–23.

Kotter, J. P. 1996. *Leading change*. Boston, MA: Harvard Business School Press.

Nader, D. A. 1998. *Champions of change: How CEOs and their companies are mastering the skills of radical change*. San Francisco: Jossey-Bass.

Pettigrew, A. M., Woodman, R. W., and Cameron, K. S. 2001. Studying organizational change and development: Challenges for future research. *Academy of Management Journal* 44(4):697–713.

Quinn, R. E. 1996. *Deep change: Discovering the leader within*. San Francisco: Jossey-Bass.

Stace, D., and Dunphy, D. 2001. *Beyond the boundaries: Leading and recreating the successful enterprise*. 2nd ed. Sydney: McGraw-Hill.

THE STRIKE

On Friday, July 18, 2003, British Airways (BA) staff in Terminals 1 and 4 at London's busy Heathrow Airport held a 24-hour wildcat strike. The strike was not officially sanctioned by the trade unions but was a spontaneous action by over 250 check-in staff who walked out at 4 p.m. The wildcat strike occurred at the start of a peak holiday season weekend, which led to chaotic scenes at Heathrow. Some 60 departure flights were grounded and over 10,000 passengers left stranded.[82] The situation was heralded as the worst industrial situation BA had faced since 1997 when a strike was called by its cabin crew.[83] BA's response was to cancel its services from both terminals, apologize for the disruption, and ask those who were due to fly not to go to the airport as they would be unable to service them.[84] BA also set up a tent outside Heathrow to provide refreshments and police were called in to manage the crowd.[85] BA was criticized by many American visitors who were trying to fly back to the United States for not providing them with sufficient information about what was going on.[86] Staff returned to work on Saturday evening, but the effects of the strike flowed on through the weekend. By Monday morning, July 21, BA reported that Heathrow was still extremely busy: "There is still a large backlog of more than 1,000 passengers from services cancelled over the weekend. We are doing everything we can to get these passengers away in the next couple of days."[87]

As a result of the strike, BA lost around £40 million and its reputation was severely dented. The strike also came at a time when BA was still recovering from other environmental jolts, such as 9/11, the Iraqi war, SARS, and inroads on its markets from budget airlines.[88] Afterwards, BA revealed that it lost over 100,000 customers as a result of the dispute.[89]

THE CHANGE ISSUE: SWIPE CARDS

BA staff were protesting the introduction of a system for electronic clocking-in that would record when they started and finished work for the day. Staff were concerned that the system would enable managers to manipulate their working patterns and shift hours. The clocking-in system was one small part of a broader restructuring program in BA, titled the *Future Size and Shape* recovery program.[90] Over the previous two years, this had led to approximately 13,000, or almost one in four jobs, being cut within the airline. As *The Economist* noted, the side effects of these cuts were emerging, with delayed departures resulting from a shortage of ground staff at Gatwick and "a high rate of sickness causing the airline to hire in aircraft and crew to fill gaps. Rising absenteeism is a sure sign of stress in an organization that is contracting."[91]

For BA management, introduction of the swipe card system was a way of modernizing BA and "improving the efficient use of staff and resources."[92] As one BA official was quoted as saying: "We needed to simplify things and bring in the best system to manage people."[93]

For staff it was seen as a "prelude to a radical shake-up in working hours, which would lead to loss of pay and demands to work split shifts."[94] As one check-in worker was quoted as saying: "This used to be a job which we loved but we are now at the end of our tether. What comes next? They will probably force us to swap shifts without agreement and all this for less money than working at Tesco [a supermarket]."[95]

One writer argued that "the heart of the issue is that the workforce wants respect"; it was not until the wildcat strike that CEO Rod Eddington was even aware that "there was a respect deficit to be plugged." Specifically, staff were concerned that "BA will try to turn them into automata, leaving Heathrow at quiet times of the day only to be brought back at busiest moments, while not paying any extra for the disturbance. Women, in particular, want to preserve their carefully constructed capacity to balance the demands of work and home."[96] Although BA denied that the system would be used to make staff alter their working hours at little notice, staff did not accept this promise—wondering why it was being introduced in the first place if that was not the intended use. As one union official was quoted: "We know that BA breaks its agreements."[97] Another worker said that the strike was meant to be a "short, sharp, shock" for BA: "They would then be able to bring us in any time they wanted, which is just not on, especially for those of us with families."[98]

THE CHANGE PROCESS FOR INTRODUCING THE SWIPE CARD

Unions argued that the walkout was triggered by senior management at BA "abandoning talks over the introduction of smart cards and announcing their forced imposition at just five days' notice."[99] It was this unilateral decision by BA to introduce the swipe card, and a lack of adequate consultation with affected staff, that was cited as a key reason for the strike.[100] Even BA's pilots, who did not oppose a check-in system, were said to be sympathetic "with the . . . check-in staff over the way that the airline had mishandled the introduction of the swipe cards."[101] One commentator labeled the change process as a "commercial disaster" serving as "an important warning—about the dangers of management by diktat, certainly, but, more profoundly, about an incipient revolt against the close control and monitoring of our lives and movements that modern information technology enables."[102]

The Economist argued that management's "big mistake was to introduce a new working practice at the start of the summer quarter when the airline makes all its money."[103] Similarly, *The Times* wrote that this was a major management blunder: "To pick July, the start of the peak holiday season, to launch an unpopular new clock-in system, is asking for trouble. To push through a scheme without realizing the extent of the resistance by those involved suggests a management aloof from the mood of its employees. And to allow managers to give contradictory statements on the use of the new cards seems guaranteed to foment mistrust."[104]

As Hutton argued, with 20,000 other BA workers using the swipe card system, "Imposing them after months of inconclusive talks must have seemed—especially given the pressure to contain costs, with the airline set to report its worst ever quarterly loss of £60 million this week—a risk worth taking. It was a massive miscalculation of the workforce's mood."[105] This miscalculation was related to staff cynicism and bitterness about the redundancy program that had been conducted, staff fears of a lack of consultation, poor pay rates, and dissatisfaction with management having enormous knowledge on which to act in the future.

The Guardian echoed this viewpoint, noting that the "trigger was undoubtedly the cack-handed way BA management at Heathrow tried to force the introduction of swipe cards at exactly the wrong time, when the peak of the summer boom was approaching. They should have known how important it was to approach any potential changes in the working patterns of women juggling with childcare schedules in a very sensitive way."[106]

Rod Eddington, chief executive of BA, acknowledged that it was wrong of his senior management to introduce the new clock-in system in the way they did; he was quoted as saying on BBC Radio, in response to a statement put to him that BA had been guilty of "bad management" and "crass stupidity" for not predicting the level of anger to the swipe card: "With the gift of hindsight, it's difficult to disagree with you."[107]

THE RESOLUTION

As a result of the walkout, BA announced on Tuesday, July 22, that it would hold talks with representatives from three unions—Amicus MSF, Transport and General Workers Union, and GMB—and put back introduction of the swipe cards until noon on Wednesday, July 23.[108] Following further talks, it was finally announced on July 30 by BA that they had reached agreement with the unions to delay making the swipe card system operational until September 1. They also agreed to a 3 percent pay rise to administrative staff for 2003, not on the basis of introducing the swipe card system but based on being "confident that the remaining Future Size and Shape cost efficiencies will be delivered."[109]

As one person observed: "You have to ask, how important was this scheme to the future operation of BA in the first place? How much money was it going to save and wouldn't it be better to wait a few months for discussion to reassure the staff they are not going to get turned over?"[110]

Questions

Review the swipe card story, drawing on each of the following change perspectives discussed in Chapters 7 and 8:

- Organization development
- Sense-making
- Change management
- Contingency
- Processual

1. From each change perspective, what are the key issues to understanding the wildcat strike?
2. Assume that you have been retained as a change consultant by BA management to advise them on how to avoid such a situation in the future. What lessons emerge from each perspective and what recommendations would you draw from each in constructing your advice to BA management? If appropriate, role-play the presentation of this advice to senior management of BA.
3. Is there one change perspective, or a combination of change perspectives, that provides the best way of understanding the swipe card issue? Why?
4. What broad conclusions emerge from this analysis?

TABLE 8.4 Additional Case Studies

Canadian Fishing Company (A)
Wood, A. R., & Stuart, I. (1998) *Richard Ivey School of Business*
PLAY! Multimedia Case
Harder, J. W. (2001) *Darden Business Publishing*
State Farm Insurance—Michigan Region Multimedia Case
Isabella, L. A., & Forbes, T. (2003) *Darden Business Publishing*

Bibliography

Anonymous. 2003a. Strike action grounds BA flights. *BBC News*, July 18. http://www.bbc.co.uk.

Anonymous. 2003b. Strike a blow for BA's reputation. *CNN.com*, July 22.

Anonymous. 2003c. Britain: Terminal; British Airways. *Economist*, no. 8334 (July 26):31.

Anonymous. 2003d. Air pocket—British Airways has run into rough weather. *Times* (London), July 29:17.

Anonymous. 2003e. Back from the brink—Both sides can learn from the BA dispute. *Guardian* (Manchester), August 1:25.

Bartunek, J. M. 2003. Foreword. In *Making sense of organizational change*, ed. J. Helms Mills, ix–xi. London: Routledge.

Behar, D. 2003. BA "to back down in Heathrow strike." *Daily Mail* (London), July 30:32.

British Airways News Release. 2003. Operational update July 19 at 7 pm. *British Airways Online Press Office*, July 19. http://www.ba.com.

British Airways News Release. 2003. Latest news on operational disruption—Monday 21 July at 8am. *British Airways Online Press Office*, July 21. http://www.ba.com.

British Airways News Release. 2003. Talks with unions to be reconvened on Tuesday July 22. *British Airways Online Press Office*, July 21a. http://www.ba.com.

British Airways News Release. 2003. British Airways signs agreement with trades union. *British Airways Online Press Office*, July 30. http://www.ba.com.

British Airways News Release. 2003. First quarter loss. *British Airways Online Press Office*, July 31. http://www.ba.com.

Church, A. H. 1999. From the editor—The future of O.D. *Organization Development Journal* 17(1):2–3.

Clark, A. 2003a. BA bosses share the blame. *Guardian* (Manchester), August 1.

Clark, A. 2003b. BA strike robbed Heathrow of record. *Guardian* (Manchester), August 12.

Dawson, P. 1994. *Organizational change: A processual approach*. London: Chapman.

Dawson, P. 2003. *Understanding organizational change: The contemporary experience of people at work*. London: Sage.

Deaner, C. M. D., and Miller, K. J. 1998. Organization development: An evolving practice. *Organization Development Journal* 16(3):11–18.

Dunphy, D., and Stace, D. 1990. *Under new management: Australian organizations in transition*. Sydney: McGraw-Hill.

Farias, G., and Johnson, H. 2000. Organizational development and change management: Setting the record straight *Journal of Applied Behavioral Science* 36(3):376–79.

Ghoshal, S., and Bartlett, C. A. 1996. Rebuilding behavioral context: A blueprint for corporate renewal. *Sloan Management Review* 37(2):23–36.

Ghoshal, S., and Bartlett, C. A. 2000. Rebuilding behavioral context: A blueprint for corporate renewal. In *Breaking the code of change*, ed. M. Beer and N. Nohria, 195–222. Boston: Harvard Business School Press.

Heracleous, L. 2000. The role of strategy implementation in organization development. *Organization Development Journal* 18(3):75–86.

Hornstein, H. 2001. Organizational development and change management: Don't throw the baby out with the bath water. *Journal of Applied Behavioral Science* 37(2):223–26.

Hutton, W. 2003. How BA clipped its own wings. *Observer*, July 27.

Huy, Q. N. 2001. Time, temporal capability, and planned change. *Academy of Management Review* 26(4):601–23.

Johnston, A. V. B. 1975. Revolution by involvement. *Accountancy Age* 7(36) (September 17):11.

Jones, A. 2003. BA "swipe card" dispute talks continue. *PA News*, July 24.

Kanter, R. M., Stein, B. A., and Jick, T. D. 1992. *The challenge of organizational change: How companies experience it and leaders guide it*. New York: Free Press.

Kotter, J. P. 1995. Leading change: Why transformation efforts fail. *Harvard Business Review* 73(2):59–67.

Kotter, J. P. 1996. *Leading change*. Boston, MA: Harvard Business School Press.

Kotter, J. P., and Cohen, D. S. 2002. *The heart of change: Real-life stories of how people change their organizations*. Boston, MA: Harvard Business School Press.

McGreevy, R., and Johnston, C. 2003. Thousands stranded by Heathrow walkout. *Times* (London), July 19:2.

Nadler, D. A. 1998. *Champions of change: How CEOs and their companies are mastering the skills of radical change*. San Francisco: Jossey-Bass.

Palmer, I., and Hardy, C. 2000. *Thinking about management: Implications of organizational debates for practice*. London: Sage.

Pendlebury, J., Grouard, B., and Meston, F. 1998. *The ten keys to successful change management*. England: John Wiley & Sons Ltd.

Pettigrew, A. M. 1985. *The awakening giant: Continuity and change in Imperial Chemical Industries*. Oxford: Basil Blackwell.

Pettigrew, A. M. 2000. Linking change processes to outcomes: A commentary on Ghoshal, Bartlett, and Weick. In *Breaking the code of change*, ed. M. Beer and N. Nohria, 243–65. Boston: Harvard Business School Press.

Pettigrew, A., and Whipp, R. 1991. *Managing change for competitive success*. Oxford: Blackwell.

Pettigrew, A., and Whipp, R. 1993. Understanding the environment. In *Managing change*, ed. C. Mabey and B. Mayon-White. London: Open University/Chapman.

Pettigrew, A. M., Woodman, R. W., and Cameron, K. S. 2001. Studying organizational change and development: Challenges for future research. *Academy of Management Journal* 44(4):697–713.

Quinn, R. E. 1993. The legitimate change agent: A vision for a new profession. ODC Distinguished Speaker Address, Academy of Management Meeting, Atlanta, Georgia.

Quinn, R. E. 1996. *Deep change: Discovering the leader within*. San Francisco: Jossey-Bass.

Stace, D. A. 1996. Dominant ideologies, strategic change, and sustained performance. *Human Relations* 49(5):553–70.

Stace, D., and Dunphy, D. 2001. *Beyond the boundaries: Leading and recreating the successful enterprise*. 2nd ed. Sydney: McGraw-Hill.

Sull, D. N. 1999. Why good companies go bad. *Harvard Business Review* 77(4):2–10.

Taffinder, P. 1998. *Big change: A route-map for corporate transformation*. Chichester: John Wiley & Sons Ltd.

Tran, M. 2003a. BA staff take a swipe at new security system. *Guardian* (Manchester), July 22.

Webster, B. 2003a. Staff sign in, but do not sign out. *Times* (London), July 28:2.

Webster, B. 2003b. Jets half-empty as passengers desert airline, BA pilots warn. *Times* (London), July 29:2.

Weick, K. E. 2000. Emergent change as a universal in organizations. In *Breaking the code of change*, ed. M. Beer and N. Nohria, 223–41. Boston: Harvard Business School Press.

Worren, N., Ruddle, K., and Moore, K. 1999. From organizational development to change management: The emergence of a new profession. *Journal of Applied Behavioral Science* 35(3):273–86.

Worren, N., Ruddle, K., and Moore, K. 2000. Response to Farias and Johnson's commentary. *Journal of Applied Behavioral Science* 36(3):380–81.

Notes

1. Pettigrew et al., 2001.
2. Palmer and Hardy, 2000:171–73.
3. Pendlebury et al., 1998:40–41.
4. Pendlebury et al., 1998:49.
5. Nadler, 1998.
6. Nadler, 1998:8.
7. Nadler, 1998:82–108.
8. Nadler, 1998:92.
9. Taffinder, 1998:40–42.
10. Ghoshal and Bartlett, 2000.
11. Ghoshal and Bartlett, 2000:196.
12. Ghoshal and Bartlett, 2000:199–200.
13. Ghoshal and Bartlett, 2000:220.
14. Ghoshal and Bartlett, 2000:221.
15. Kanter et al., 1992:385–91.
16. Kanter et al., 1992:389.
17. Kanter et al., 1992:390.
18. Kanter et al., 1992:390.
19. Kanter et al., 1992:390.
20. Kanter et al., 1992:392.
21. See Kanter et al 1992: 375–82
22. Kotter, 1995, 1996.

23. Kotter, 1996:ix.
24. Kotter, 1995:67.
25. Kotter, 1995:59.
26. Kotter, 2002:10–13.
27. Nicholl, 1998a.
28. Church, 1999:2.
29. Church, 1999:2–3.
30. Deaner and Miller, 1998.
31. Herman, 2001:115.
32. Quinn, 1993, cited in Worren et al. 1999:273–74.
33. Worren et al., 1999:274–80.
34. Hornstein, 2001:224.
35. Farias and Johnson, 2000:377.
36. Farias and Johnson, 2000:378.
37. Worren et al., 2000:381.
38. Nicoll, 1998.
39. Heracleous, 2000:77.
40. For example, see Stace, 1996.
41. Stace, 1996:557.
42. See Stace and Dunphy, 2001:108–93
43. Stace, 1996:561.
44. Stace, 1996:562.
45. Stace and Dunphy, 2001:108.
46. Stace, 1996:566
47. Huy, 2001.
48. See Huy, 2001:610–11.
49. See Huy, 2001:612.
50. Pettigrew et al., 2001:704.
51. Burnes, 1996:187.
52. Pettigrew, 1985:453.
53. Pettigrew, 1985:24.
54. Pettigrew, 1985:439.
55. Pettigrew, 1985:42–43.
56. Pettigrew, 1985:452–53.
57. Pettigrew, 1985:440.
58. Pettigrew, 1985:443.
59. Pettigrew, 1985:443.
60. Pettigrew, 1985:454.
61. Pettigrew, 1985:455.
62. Pettigrew, 1985:455.
63. Pettigrew, 1985:471.
64. Johnston, 1975.
65. Pettigrew, 1985:473–76.
66. Pettigrew, 1985:476.

67. Pettigrew and Whipp, 1991.
68. For example, see Pettigrew and Whipp, 1991:165–66, 280–81.
69. Pettigrew and Whipp, 1991:292.
70. Dawson, 2003:173.
71. Dawson, 2003:11.
72. Dawson, 2003:173.
73. Paraphrased from Dawson, 2003:173–76.
74. Pettigrew, 2000:247–49.
75. Pettigrew, 2000:249.
76. Kanter et al., 1992:374.
77. Kanter et al., 1992:374.
78. Pettigrew, 2000.
79. Pettigrew, 2000:246.
80. Weick, 2000:232.
81. Bartunek, 2003:xi.
82. Anonymous, 2003a.
83. Anonymous, 2003b.
84. BA News Release, July 19, 2003.
85. Anonymous, 2003c.
86. Anonymous, 2003b.
87. BA News Release, July 21, 2003.
88. Anonymous, 2003c.
89. Clark, 2003b.
90. BA News Release, July 31, 2003.
91. Anonymous, 2003c.
92. BA Press Release, July 30, 2003.
93. Tran, 2003.
94. Behar, 2003. Reproduced with permission of Solo Syndication, Ltd.
95. Jones, 2003.
96. Hutton, 2003. Copyright Guardian Newspapers Limited, 2003.
97. Webster, 2003a.
98. McGreevy and Johnston, 2003.
99. Clark, 2003a.
100. Tran, 2003.
101. Webster, 2003b.
102. Hutton, 2003. Copyright Guardian Newspapers Limited, 2003.
103. Anonymous, 2003c.
104. Anonymous, 2003d. Copyright © 2003 NI Syndication, London. Reproduced with permission.
105. Hutton, 2003. Copyright Guardian Newspapers Limited, 2003.
106. Anonymous, 2003e. Copyright Guardian Newspapers Limited, 2003.
107. Clark, 2003a.
108. BA News Release, July 21a, 2003.
109. BA News Release, July 30, 2003.
110. Behar, 2003. Reproduced with permission of Solo Syndication, Ltd.

Chapter Nine

Linking Vision and Change

Learning objectives

On completion of this chapter you should be able to:

- Appreciate how approaches to vision and change differ, depending on the image held of managing organizational change.
- Identify the attributes of what makes a meaningful vision.
- Have a good understanding of how the context in which a vision is developed relates to the meaningfulness of the vision.
- Understand different techniques and processes for developing vision.
- Articulate why some visions are less effective than others.
- Appreciate why some visions may fade over time.
- Outline current arguments concerning the relationship of vision to organizational change.

The various change management models outlined in Chapter 8 (see Table 8.1) provide a straightforward message to managers: You need to get the vision right if you want to have any chance of achieving successful organizational change. For Victor and Franckeiss,[1] "It is imperative that change is aligned with a clear vision and business strategy and that subsequent activities and interventions are coordinated and consistent." Hinterhuber and Popp[2] maintain having a vision is behind any new, entrepreneurial activity or major corporate change program. Having a strategic vision is linked to competitive advantage, enhancing organizational performance, and achieving sustained organizational growth.[3] Clear visions enable boards to determine how well organizational leaders are performing and identify gaps between the vision and current practices.[4] Organizations preparing for transformational change regularly undertake "revisioning"[5] exercises to help guide them into the future. The visioning process itself can enhance the self-esteem of the people who participate in it because they can see the potential fruits of their labors.[6]

Conversely, a "lack of vision" is associated with organizational decline and failure.[7] As Beaver[8] argues, "Unless companies have clear vision about how they are going to be distinctly different and unique in adding and satisfying their customers, then they are likely to be the corporate failure statistics of tomorrow." Lacking vision is used to explain why companies fail to build their core competencies despite having access to adequate technical resources to do so.[9] Business strategies that lack visionary content may fail to identify when change is needed.[10] Lack of an adequate process for translating shared vision into collective action is associated with the failure to produce transformational organizational change.[11]

Vision appears to have come of age. Some writers see it as a "sacred concept" with visionary managers treated in the popular media as "gods."[12] Given this situation, it is surprising that it is still a concept on which there are relatively few empirical studies and about which there is a lack of agreement concerning its definition,[13] or how to measure it.[14] Many prescriptive books and articles outline the "one best way" of getting a vision but, as Raynor[15] writes, "no two read alike." Other writers suggest that a preoccupation with vision has led to it being overworked and trivialized,[16] with many vision statements being "either generic nonsense or bland gibberish."[17] Reflecting such arguments, Levin[18] points out that discussion on vision "has alternated between being construed as a faddish and trendy concept and being viewed as a fundamental attribute of effective leadership." This means that for some commentators, "vision as a term is in danger of losing its value";[19] others take a different position and suggest that confusion over the use of the term and its meaning does not invalidate the need for a vision to keep a company moving in the right direction.[20]

These different positions reflect a deeper issue, which is that the way vision is linked to change depends on the image of managing change that is utilized. Table 9.1 sets out how each image entails different understandings of this linkage. We invite the reader to use this table as a guide to what is discussed in this chapter, referring back to it to identify how different images direct attention to some issues and approaches rather than others. We commence the chapter by showing that whether visions are meaningful will depend on three features. The first relates to the *content* or the attributes of the vision (what it is and says). The second relates to the *context* in which the vision is utilized (where it is used and by whom). The third relates to the *process* by which the vision is developed (how it emerges and who has input into it). Following this we identify why visions may fail to produce their intended effects. Finally, we focus on three contentious issues relating to the role of vision in organizational change: whether vision initiates and drives change or rather emerges as change unfolds; whether vision helps or hinders change; and whether vision is best understood as an attribute of heroic leaders or of heroic organizations.

CONTENT OF MEANINGFUL VISIONS

What it is about vision statements that makes them visionary has provoked much discussion. Some seek answers to this question by focusing on the content of the vision. Others seek answers by focusing on the context in which it is utilized. Still others direct attention to the role of leaders in articulating the vision and the process by which it is

TABLE 9.1 Images of Managing Change and How They Relate to Vision

Image of Managing Change	Link between Vision and Change	Issues to Which Image Directs Attention and That Are Found in This Chapter
Director	Vision is something that is essential to producing successful organizational change. It should be articulated early on and it is up to leaders to do this.	• Vision drives change. • Need for clear vision aligned with business strategy, mission, and goals. • Analytical and/or benchmarking approaches utilized. • Organizational context will affect impact of vision in producing change (e.g., **rigid, overmanaged, liberated** organizations).[21] • Vision telling or selling approach to inform people of what will be the vision and why. Top-down responsibility.
Navigator	Vision is important but not necessarily able to be achieved because of competing visions that exist among various organizational parties and stakeholders.	• Vision produced through debates among different groupings within and across the organization. • Assumption that "vision collision" can occur—where differing organizational groups have competing visions. Need for change managers to navigate the change through these competing visions.
Caretaker	Vision is in many ways immaterial to the way change will proceed. Inexorable forces, often external to the organization, will have the most influence on change—change is rarely the outcome of visionary actions.	• Visionary or charismatic change leaders will only have limited impact where the vision is not directly related to the inexorable events unfolding in the organization.
Coach	Vision is something that is important and is more likely to emerge through the facilitation skills of the change leader interacting with his or her followers, shaping their agendas and desired futures.	• Vision produced through consultation and co-creation techniques. • Assumption that vision will fail where there is little participation in its development.

TABLE 9.1 Images of Managing Change and How They Relate to Vision—*(concluded)*

Image of Managing Change	Link between Vision and Change	Issues to Which Image Directs Attention and That Are Found in This Chapter
Interpreter	Vision is the ability to articulate the inner voice of the organization, that which is lived, be it core ideology or values, and that underpins the identity of the organization.	• Intuitive approach to vision development, relying on imagination and imagery. • Vision seeks out the "inner-voice" of the organization to touch the "core of the system"[22] • Vision may emerge or is revealed during change—not as a driver of change. • May entail use of framing, scripting, and staging techniques.[23]
Nurturer	Vision is emergent from the clash of chaotic and unpredictable change forces. It may be possible to enact vision for particular periods, but because of the shifting, competitive and fragmented contexts in which organizations operate visions are likely to be temporary and always in the process of being rewritten.	• Visionary change leaders will be of transitory importance to any change as they are unlikely to be able to predict with accuracy the outcome of chaotic, systemwide forces that produce change. • Vision may be an attribute more of organizations rather than individuals—it is what endures through chaotic circumstances.

developed. In this section we address arguments about what a good vision is by focusing on the *content* of the vision, including its attributes, its style, and how it is differentiated from mission and organizational values.

Vision Attributes

Table 9.2 sets out a range of definitions of organizational vision. Most include reference to a future or ideal to which organizational change should be directed. The vision itself is presented as a picture or image that serves as a guide or goal. Depending on the definition, it is referred to as inspiring, motivating, emotional, and analytical. For Boal and Hooijberg,[24] effective visions have:

- A *cognitive* component (which focuses on outcomes and how to achieve them).
- An *affective* component (which helps to motivate people and gain their commitment to it).

However, they also point out that "Unfortunately, little is known about what the essential properties of a vision are, or how to craft a vision that has either charismatic

TABLE 9.2 Definitions of Organizational Vision

- "A clear mental picture of a future goal created jointly by a group for the benefit of other people which is capable of inspiring and motivating those whose support is necessary for its achievement." (Johnson, 1999:337)
- "[A]n ideal that . . . represents or reflects the shared values to which the organization should aspire." (Kirkpatrick et al., 2002:139)
- "[A] hypothetical cognitive image that pulls together beliefs about ideal ways of doing things and what the future can be." (Thoms and Greenberger, 1995, cited in Thoms and Greenberger, 1998:4)
- "[A] set of idealized goals established by the leader that represent a perspective shared by followers." (Conger and Kanungo, 1998:156, cited in Berson et al., 2001:55)
- "[A] picture or view of the future. Something not yet real, but imagined. What the organization could and should look like. Part analytical and part emotional." (Thornberry, 1997:28)
- "[A]n orientation point that guides a company's movement in a specific direction. If the vision is realistic and appeals both to the emotions and the intelligence of employees, it can integrate and direct a company." (Hinterhuber and Popp, 1992:4)
- "[T]he shared understanding of what the firm should be and how it must change." (Shoemaker, 1992:67)
- "[A] picture of a destination aspired to, an end state to be achieved via the change. It reflects the larger goal people need to keep in mind while concentrating on concrete daily activities." (Kanter et al., 1992:509)
- "[S]hows the direction change will take and the goal it is to achieve. It is the one stable element in the process and acts as its guiding light from beginning to end amidst the chaos of change." (Pendlebury et al., 1998:53)
- "[A]n ambition about the future, articulated today; it is a process of managing the present from a stretching view of the future." (Stace and Dunphy, 2001:78)

or transformational effects." Nevertheless, as set out in Table 9.3, many writers have presented their views on the key elements that constitute a good vision.

As can be seen, many of the characteristics are held in common by these authors, such as it being clear, desirable, challenging, feasible, and easy to communicate. Nutt and Backoff[25] identify four generic features of visions that are likely to enhance organizational performance:

- *Possibility*, by which they mean that visions should entail innovative possibilities for dramatic organizational improvements.
- *Desirability* of the vision, by which they mean the extent to which it draws upon shared organizational norms and values about the way things should be done.
- *Actionability*, by which they mean the ability of people to see in the vision actions that they can take that are relevant to them.
- *Articulation*, by which they mean that the vision has imagery that is powerful enough to communicate clearly a picture of where the organization is headed.

For Pendlebury et al.,[26] vision has three components:

- *Why the change is needed* (the problem). It helps to validate the need for the change.
- *The aim of the change* (the solution). It helps to gain appreciation of the gap between the current state of the organization and the envisioned future. However, the solution must be:
    - Seen to be credible and directly address the problem.

TABLE 9.3 Characteristics of Good Visions

Jick[a]	Kotter[b]	Metais[c]	Johnson[d]	El-Namaki[e]
• Clear and concise • Memorable • Exciting and inspiring • Challenging • Centered on excellence • Both stable and flexible • Achievable and tangible	• *Imaginable*—It conveys picture of what future will look like • *Desirable*—It appeals to long-term interests of stakeholders, for example, employees, customers, stockholders • *Feasible*—It embodies realistic, attainable goals • *Focused*—It provides guidance in decision making • *Flexible*—It is general enough to enable individual initiative and alternative responses to changing environments • *Communicable*—It can be explained in five minutes	• It is a *dream*—it provides emotional involvement • It is *excessive*—and not attainable within current actions or resources • It is *deviant*—it breaks conventional thinking and frames of reference	• It visualizes a future aim • It is contributed to from a variety of sources • It implicates the need for people with specialist skills • It can be communicated easily • It has a powerful motivational effect • It serves an important need • It is aligned with the values of prospective supporters	• *Coherence*—It integrates the company strategy and the future image of the company • *Translatable*—It is translatable into meaningful company goals and strategies • *Powerful*—It generates enthusiasm • *Challenging*—It is challenging for all organizational participants • *Unique*—It distinguishes the company from others • *Feasible*—It is realistic and achievable • *Idealistic*—It communicates desired outcome

[a]Adapted from Jick, 1989:2.
[b]Adapted from Kotter, 1996.
[c]Adapted from Metais, 2000:39.
[d]Adapted from Johnson, 1999.
[e]Adapted from El-Namaki, 1992, cited in Harris and Ogbonna, 1999:334.

  - Meaningful to all affected staff.
  - Capable of being realized given the skills of staff.[27]
- *The change actions that will be taken* (the means). It is how change actions will be mobilized and delivered.[28]

What is of interest in lists such as those produced by Nutt and Backoff[29] and Pendlebury et al.[30] is that they specify the desirable elements of a vision that help to ensure its success. What they leave out are the criteria against which each of these elements can be assessed. This suggests that the affective or "feel good" content of a vision is something that you know when you experience it but that is hard to specify in terms of measurable characteristics. Table 9.4 provides some examples of company vision statements.

TABLE 9.4 Examples of Vision Statements

Source: Taken from Katzenbach and the RCL Team, 1996:64–85.

"A Coke within arm's reach of everyone on the planet" (Coca Cola)
"Encircle Caterpillar" (Komatsu)
"Become the Premier Company in the World" (Motorola)
"Put a man on the moon by the end of the decade" (John F. Kennedy, April 1961)
"Eliminate what annoys our bankers and our customers" (Texas Commerce Bank)
"The one others copy" (Mobil)

EXERCISE 9.1
Finding the Vision "Wow" Factor

1. Find the vision statements of 10 different companies that you are interested in. You can get these either from annual reports or from online searches. If you prefer, take the vision statements outlined in Table 9.4.
2. Choose two different frameworks from Table 9.3.
3. Assess the vision statements in relation to the two frameworks.
4. What are your conclusions about each of the visions? Do they have the "wow" factor? Why?

Beyond Bumper Sticker Visions? Visions as Stories

Levin argues that many vision statements are like "bumper stickers" composed of empty words, encompassing in-vogue language and management speak. Further, they appear to be so similar that they could easily be interchanged across a variety of companies and lack inspiration for the staff for whom they are intended.[31] For him, one way of avoiding this situation is to provide stories of the future rather than just vision statements. Vision stories provide "a vividly detailed description of a future that people can readily picture and imagine."[32] He maintains that stories are more effective than simple vision statements because people can imagine themselves and their actions in the future. Table 9.5 outlines his process for producing vision stories. He cites Arthur Martinez, when CEO of Sears, as an example of someone adept at using visionary stories in his organization: Martinez required his senior management to write up stories about the nature of the businesses that they manage and how the customer relates to these businesses.[33]

Relationship of Vision to Mission and Goals

Vision is often confused with other terms such as mission statements, goals, and organizational values.[34] This has reached the point where "One person's vision is another person's mission."[35] Table 9.6 identifies one way of separating such concepts. For Levin, effective visions should "describe a future world where the mission is advanced and where goals and strategy are being successfully achieved in lockstep with

TABLE 9.5 Vision as Story-Telling

Source: Developed from Levin, 2000.

Step	Actions
Step 1. Becoming informed	Help CEO and leadership team articulate personal vision for future of organization • External impacts • Trends • Core beliefs
Step 2. Visiting the future	Project team five years forward • Reputation • What competitors and customers think of you • Contribution to community • What people say about your company
Step 3. Creating the story	Subgroups write in narrative form (1,500 words) • What's occurring in the marketplace • How are staff providing services and interacting with customers • What's the mood and what are people experiencing and feeling
Step 4. Deploying the vision	Story taken forward for discussion, examination, and refinement—sampling through parts of the organization • Explain purpose and desired outcomes • Present and discuss rationale • Summarize story and what is not negotiable • Obtain people's responses to it and possible changes

the organization's guiding philosophy and values."[36] As we shall see below, this integrated approach is similar to the position adopted by Collins and Porras.

Nutt and Backoff[37] regard vision as being similar to mission and goals in providing direction and identifying change actions that are needed. However, although goals and objectives may identify a result that is desired, such as better morale, they do not necessarily articulate the actions that are needed to produce this result. Nor do they usually address the role of organizational values in achieving the result. Whereas vision usually paints a picture of the future and is inspirational, mission statements are more purposive and instrumental in outlining what needs to be done.

Relationship of Vision to Market Strategy

Some writers argue that if they are to create competitive advantage, vision and strategy must be unconventional, often counterintuitive, and differentiated from those of other companies.[38] This can be seen in the arguments of Hay and Williamson,[39] who maintain that vision has an external and an internal dimension. The *external dimension* is a

TABLE 9.6 What's the Big Difference?

Source: Developed from Levin, 2000:93–98.

How Does Vision Compare to . . . ?	The Difference Is . . .
Mission	Mission depicts what the organization is and does . . . not where it is headed in the future.
Philosophy	Philosophy articulates values and beliefs about how work should be carried out . . . without prescribing what the future will look like.
Goals and strategy	Goals and strategy statements define specific outcomes. They articulate how the organization will progress toward the future . . . not what the actual future will be.

shared view within the organization of what are the market, customers, competitors, industry dynamics, and likely macroeconomic impacts on the market. They point to U.S. tire manufacturers such as Goodyear, Michelin, and Bridgestone/Firestone, the majority of which have a vision that sees the large car manufacturers as their main market and that work on high volume and market share to reduce costs. They contrast this to a relatively unknown company, Cooper Tire, which is ninth ranked in the United States for market share but ranks 28th in Fortune 500 industrial companies for delivering best total returns. This company's vision of the tire market is different, having a view that Americans are holding on to their cars longer and that the main market is therefore not car manufacturers but replacement tire outlets, particularly independent tire outlets. They argue that having a well-specified market vision such as this helps to identify how the company will grow and compete. At the same time, the vision needs to be aligned with the *internal dimension*, of organizational beliefs and values. It is through this that meaning is created throughout the organization about what it is that the organization does—and from here other strategic actions are taken such as the development of the mission, plans, objectives, and budgets.[40]

HOW CONTEXT AFFECTS VISION

In this section we address the relationship between vision and the *context* in which it is articulated, including organizational and cultural factors.

Nutt and Backoff[41] evaluate four organizational contexts in terms of their ability to produce visionary change. These abilities are assessed in relation to the degree to which there is acceptance of the need to change (change susceptibility) and the extent to which resources are on hand to engage in strategic change (resource availability).[42]

- *Rigid organizations* are classified as those that have little in the way of available resources and lack acceptance of the need for change. Associated with organizations such as Eastern and Pan Am before their collapse, they are likely to be both hierarchical and inflexible.
- *Bold organizations* have low resources but high acceptance of the need for change. They are characterized by more organic structures and being less rule-bound. These

are contexts in which visionary leadership is more likely to emerge, although this entails freeing up resources and ensuring that key stakeholders are carefully cultivated in the process of developing the vision.

- *Overmanaged organizations* have high resource availability but little acceptance of the need for change. Associated with a more stable environment and dominated by past practices that are seen to have worked well and to remain relevant, they are limited in their ability to accept the need for a new vision.
- *Liberated organizations* are those where visionary processes are likely to be most successful. Organizations such as Hewlett-Packard and Intel are characterized as having a high acceptance of the need for change and high availability of resources that can be utilized in the strategic change process.[43]

What this position highlights is that whether a vision will "take" in an organization relates to whether there is a contextual "trigger" that alerts people to the need for a new vision, something that "provides both meaning to the current situation and promise of salvation from the currently acute distress."[44] A range of triggers is possible including environmental turbulence and crises that require new strategies or ways of operating.[45] Other triggers may include when organizational performance is poor or when an organization passes through different phases of its life cycle such as moving from an entrepreneurial or start-up stage to a growth stage.[46] Having said this, in an alternative scenario, leaders may use their visionary attributes and frame interpretations of current situations so as to "create dissatisfaction with the status quo, a sense of distress, and a desire for change among followers."[47] In this sense, they *produce* a crisis situation through their visionary and rhetorical skills rather than wait for one to appear.

Finally, there is another way in which context is important to understanding why visions may "take" in one situation but not another. This relates to the national and cultural context in which the organization is embedded. For example, Wind and Main[48] point out that Donald Burr's People Express vision for the airline to "become the leading institution for constructive change in the world" was too vague and preposterous. However, they point out that in Japan the chairman of Canon, Ryuzaburo Kakur, refers to himself as an evangelist and that the organization is guided by "living and working together for the common good."[49] While it is similar in intent to Donald Burr's vision, they suggest that this statement resonates in Japan in a way that it would not in the United States as Japanese organizations are more aligned with the national and social interests of that society than are those in the United States.[50]

PROCESSES BY WHICH VISIONS EMERGE

In this section we identify different approaches to developing change visions.

Crafting the Vision

Holpp and Kelly[51] claim that getting a vision is "a little like dancing with a 500-pound gorilla. It takes a little while to get the steps down, but once the dance is over, you know you've really accomplished something." As outlined in Table 9.7, there are different approaches (or dances) that might be taken to develop a vision.

For some, "the vision must come from the top"[52] and is the responsibility of management, who usually task a small team with analyzing needs, identifying choices, and making recommendations on the nature of the change vision.[53] For others, its production is a collaborative effort involving the CEO and those who will be affected by it.[54] For example, Gratton[55] outlines how seven European companies engaged in a visioning process that was democratic and drew on a wide range of cross-functional groups rather than being top-down and imposed. She argues that letting the vision emerge from debates among multifunctional groups in an organization has the potential to lead to more creative visions and actions. It also ensures that the urgency and need for change are transmitted across the organization and provide executives with a better understanding of the risks and trade-offs involved in implementing the vision.[56]

Nutt and Backoff[57] identify three different processes for crafting a vision:

- *Leader-dominated approach*. The CEO provides the strategic vision for the organization. This is similar to the "telling" and "selling" strategies in Table 9.7. They point out that this approach is at odds with the philosophy of empowerment, which maintains that people across an organization should be involved in processes and decisions that affect them.
- *Pump-priming approach*. The CEO provides visionary ideas and gets selected people and groups within the organization to further develop these ideas within the broad parameters set out by the CEO. This adapting and shaping process is similar to the "testing" and "consulting" strategies in Table 9.7.

TABLE 9.7 Different Philosophies for Creating Vision

Source: Created from Bryan Smith, Chairman of Innovation Associates of Canada, as cited in Haapaniemi, 1996.

Vision Technique	What It Means	When It Is Used
Telling	CEO creates the vision and gives it to staff.	When involvement is not seen as important
Selling	CEO has a vision that he or she wishes to sell to staff.	When CEO is attracted to the vision and wants others in the organization to adopt it
Testing	CEO seeks organizational feedback on ideas he or she has about a vision.	When CEO wants to see which parts of the vision should be supported
Consulting	CEO seeks development of vision through creative input of staff. Ground rules and parameters set, but discussion is cascaded through the organization.	When CEO needs help in developing the vision
Co-creating	Creation of shared vision by CEO and organization. Process may involve alignment of visions at levels including personal, team, and group/departmental.	When CEO wants to identify shared, compatible, hierarchical visions throughout the organization

- *Facilitation approach*. Similar to the "co-creating" strategy in Table 9.7, it is one that draws more directly on participative management philosophies by engaging a wide range of people in a process of developing and articulating a vision. It is the CEO who acts as a facilitator, orchestrating the crafting process. For Nutt and Backoff,[58] it is this approach that is likely to produce better visions and more successful organizational change and performance as more people will have contributed to its development and therefore be more willing to act in accordance with it.

EXERCISE 9.2

What's the Business Press View on Vision?

1. Locate up to half a dozen recent articles from the business press that discuss vision in relation to specific companies going through organizational change. The change could be growth, decline, or some form of restructuring. (*Hint*: Use an electronic database search to assist you in locating relevant articles.)
2. How does each commentator link vision to the change?
3. Is vision an explanatory variable for understanding why a change succeeded or failed?
4. How would you rate the tone of the article in relation to vision: positive, neutral, or negative?
5. What overall message would a reader receive about vision after reading the article?
6. To what extent are the articles similar in perspective? Are there any points of difference? How would you explain these?
7. How influential do you think such articles are on the managers who read them?

Questions That Help to Develop a Vision

While the above frameworks identify the extent to which there is involvement throughout the organization in the development of the vision, they do not address directly the specifics on how to develop the actual vision itself. Some routines for producing vision are outlined in Table 9.8.

Holpp & Kelly[59] identify three differing approaches or sets of questions through which vision may be acquired: an *intuitive* approach, an *analytical* approach, and a *benchmarking* approach.[60]

The *intuitive* approach relies on the use of imagination and imagery to encourage staff to participate in vision development. Managers are asked to imagine doing their jobs in such a way that they achieve what they want from themselves and other people with whom they work.

- In the first step, they are asked to list up to 10 things that they want to achieve personally and professionally, and then prioritize these.
- In the second step, they focus on their current reality as a means of identifying the tension that exists between their lived experiences and their desired image.[61]
- In the third step, they are provided with support to help identify and achieve action plans to work toward achieving their vision.

TABLE 9.8 **The Vision Process**

Source: Developed from Gratton, 1996; Nanus, 1996; Shoemaker, 1992; Pendlebury et al., 1998.

Implementing Strategic Vision (Gratton, 1996)	Vision Retreat (Nanus, 1996)	Strategic Vision and Core Capabilities (Schoemaker, 1992:67)	Developing the Vision (Pendlebury et al., 1998:63–67)
1. Articulate the long-term vision 2. Identify strategic people and processes critical to achieving the vision 3. Assess alignment of the vision with current capabilities 4. Prioritize key actions to bridge from current reality to vision of the future	*Phase 1: Preparation.* Establish purpose and goals of the retreat *Phase 2: Initial meeting.* Two-day meeting with discussion on *vision audit* (character of organization), *vision scope* (who it includes and desired vision characteristics), and *vision context* (environmental issues) *Phase 3: Analysis and report cycle.* Facilitator prepares three scenarios of the future that are discussed among participants over a number of weeks *Phase 4: Final meeting.* One-day discussion and evaluation of vision alternatives and their strategic implications *Phase 5: Post-retreat activities.* Conclusions communicated throughout the organization including ways of implementing it	1. Generate scenarios of possible futures the organization may face 2. Do a competitive analysis of the industry 3. Analyze the core capabilities of the company and its competitors 4. Develop a strategic vision (best) aligned to the strategic options generated from steps 1–3	1. Formalize the need for change 2. Identify the issues that need to be addressed 3. Develop multiple visions 4. Choose an appropriate vision 5. Formalize the vision, ensuring it is clear and communicable

In the *analytical* approach, visions are not so much imagined as defined in relation to organizational or departmental missions and roles. Vision is closely related to organizational purpose with a focus on:

- Who is served by the organization.
- What it is that the organization does.
- Where it is that the organization places most of its efforts.
- Why it is that the organization focuses on particular work and goals.
- How the organization operationalizes these efforts.

Such questions "help guide organization or departments from where they are to where they want to be."[62]

In the *benchmarking* approach, a vision statement is developed by focusing on the actions and standards utilized by the organization's toughest competitors. This process involves:

- Asking what it is that their competitors do well.
- Asking how they can surpass this.
- Asking what would be the quantitative and qualitative measures that would indicate when this would be achieved.
- Identifying what it will be like and how it will feel when this standard has been achieved.[63]

Whereas the intuitive and analytical approaches are more internally focused, the benchmarking approach is more externally focused. Some potential downsides to each of these approaches can be appreciated:

- The *intuitive approach*, which broadly follows the tenets of an organization development approach, may produce personal visions that are disconnected from the core business of the organization and current or anticipated industry trends.
- The *analytical approach* serves more to align the organizational vision to the mission of the organization but pays less attention to the values and enduring guiding logics that may exist in the organization. It also may neglect the inspirational element often attached to vision by too closely aligning it with mission.
- The *benchmarking approach* assumes that the future of the organization continues to be aligned with current competitors. However, where transformational change is pursued, benchmarking against current competitors is not likely to be very helpful—compared to identifying who are likely to be the new competitors in an envisioned future. In Mintzberg's[64] view, this "requires not merely rearranging the established categories, but inventing new ones."

Connecting the Vision to the Organization's Inner Voice

Robert Quinn[65] has made an interesting contribution to the process of identifying change visions. He points out that, in many organizations, people want to know what the vision is and look to the CEO to provide it. Paradoxically, where vision statements are available, such as on corporate business cards, these are likely to be rejected as being in name only—they are not what people are "willing to die for."[66] He argues that developing a vision to guide organizational actions has to go beyond superficial statements and "confront the lack of integrity that exists in the system," an exercise for which few managers are well equipped.[67]

To illustrate his position, he tells the story of a speech Gandhi gave at a political convention in India. When he got up to speak, many in the audience left their seats and paid him little attention. However, as he spoke about what Indians really cared about, not politics but bread and salt, people gradually sat down again and listened to him. His message was unusual: "This small, unassuming man had journeyed through their heartland and captured the essence of India. He was vocalizing it in a way they could feel and understand. Such articulation is often at the heart of radical, deep change."[68] For Quinn, it is this ability to delve into the organization and find its bread and salt that makes a vision appealing, passionate, and beyond the superficial. This search for the "inner voice" of the organization is needed to find visions that resonate within the organization and narrow the gap between the talk and the walk.[69] Such "bread-and-salt" visions are achieved in a circular manner involving a bottom-up and top-down dialogue to touch "the core of the system."[70]

WHEN VISIONS FAIL

Change visions may fail when the objective is:

- *Too specific* (it fails to appreciate the inability to control change and how there is always a degree of uncertainty associated with its outcomes).
- *Too vague* (it fails to act as a landmark toward which various change actions are directed).
- *Inadequate* (it only partially addresses the problem to which it is directed.
- *Too unrealistic* (so that it is perceived as unachievable by staff).[71]

Jick adds that a vision is also likely to fail when leaders spend 90 percent of their time articulating it to their staff (but not necessarily in clearly understood terms) and only 10 percent of their time in implementing it.[72] Table 9.9 outlines a range of other reasons why visions may fail. In this section, we consider two further reasons for vision failure: the adaptability of the vision over time and the presence of competing visions.

Adaptability of the Vision over Time

Whereas some visions stand the test of time and remain applicable and adaptable to new situations and environments, others need to be overhauled in order to remain relevant. This situation is nicely demonstrated in Harris and Ogbonna's[73] investigation of two medium-sized U.K. retail companies and the impact on strategic change of the founders' vision. In both cases, the vision was established well over 100 years ago by the company founder and there was evidence of an escalation of commitment to the vision by ensuing management. In one, the vision was paternalistic (commitment towards staff) and focused on prudent growth. This led to a strong focus on sales and profitability in each new store location. These characteristics are still present in today's management of the company. The vision itself was seen as flexible and able to respond

TABLE 9.9 When Vision Fails

Source: Developed from Lipton, 1996:89–91.

Vision Fails When . . .	This Is Because . . .
The walk is different from the talk	When management does not walk the talk, or practice what they preach, the vision is treated by staff as empty and little more than a slogan
It is irrelevant	If it is developed in a vacuum, without managers listening to their staff, it will not be anchored in the reality of their lived experiences and will alienate the people to whom it is directed
It is treated as the holy grail	When unrealistic expectations are placed on the vision, or it is treated as a magic solution to all organizational problems, it is likely to fail
It is developed through a rearview mirror	Where visions are developed through analysis rather than imagination, they are more likely to be read than an uninspiring plan
It is too disconnected from the present	Visions need to recognize current obstacles so that they are seen as achievable and believable
Too abstract or too concrete	Visions must be idealistic, realistic, and tangible
Developed without using a creative process	Often it is the process as well as the final vision that is instrumental to achieving the organization's future
Little participation	Consensus building around the vision is needed, including activities to both develop and sufficiently diffuse the vision throughout the organization
Complacency	If the vision is seen to be a projection too far into the future, it will not be seen as urgent

to the prevailing environmental conditions facing the company. The researchers label the founder's vision as providing a "strategic dividend" for subsequent management.

By contrast, in the second company, the founder's vision was to have a store in every town in a particular geographic region. The other aspect of the vision related to the importance of family control of the company. The researchers argue that this vision still drives senior management within the company. However, in contrast to the first company, this vision serves as what they term a "strategic hangover." The closed nature of the vision has led successive management to make decisions out of step with change in environmental conditions facing the industry such as the movement of mega retail stores into the geographic region and a shift in focus of such stores from price to quality and service. The result was that the company almost faced financial ruin on two separate occasions. In relation to subsequent strategic change actions taken by management in these two companies, the authors present the view that "whether the original vision of the founder results in a legacy or a hangover is clearly dependent on the original flexibility of the strategy and the later environmental appropriateness."[74]

Presence of Competing Visions

Another reason why vision may fail is due to what Kanter et al.[75] refer to as vision "collisions," that is, the presence of multiple and conflicting visions. This can occur where the vision is crafted by organizational strategists who are convinced about the need for change—but this need is not shared by change implementers or change recipients, who may still be completing earlier changes already introduced into the organization. It also can occur where there is a gap between management's strategic vision and stakeholders' images and vision of the company, such as was the case with Nike. In the mid-1980s, Nike's vision of itself was one of meeting the needs of athletic footwear. However, the company found that a different market segment was buying their shoes: not athletes but people who were substituting casual shoes for sneakers. Nike responded by producing casual Nike shoes, which were unsuccessful as they failed to appreciate that the reason customers were purchasing the highly overengineered sneakers was because they appealed to their image.[76] In this case, the vision of the company was out of step with that which was being applied to it by consumers. Multiple, conflicting visions also can occur during the merger of companies. For example, Mitchell[77] cites the failure in 2000 of the merger between Deutsche Bank and Dresdner Bank as a case in point. In this merger, there was a "failure of management to persuade Deutsche's investment bankers of the vision for how the newly merged company would compete. Many key employees left, and the threat of mass walkout forced Deutsche to abandon the deal after considerable damage to the share price of both companies."[78]

LINKING VISION TO CHANGE: THREE DEBATES

In this section we identify three key debates on how vision is linked to organizational change. The first is whether vision is a proactive driver of change as opposed to emerging during the process of change. The second is whether vision helps or hinders change. The third is whether vision is best ascribed to heroic, charismatic leaders (and, if so, how) or whether it is best understood as an attribute of organizations.

Does Vision Drive Change or Emerge during Change?

Vision Drives Change

As noted above, the various change management models outlined in Chapter 8 give a prominent role to vision as a prerequisite for entering into organizational change. For example:

- For Kanter et al.,[79] vision is one of the first steps that is needed in organizational change. Without a vision, changes introduced by managers may seem arbitrary and unneeded. Vision provides clarity about the goals in introducing a change, particularly so that it is not written off by staff as yet another cost-cutting exercise. The vision helps to motivate staff in working toward the change and engaging them in what may appear to be daunting or risky actions.[80]
- For Pendlebury et al.,[81] the vision outlines "the extent of change, i.e. how profound it will be, how long it will take and in which domains it will operate." Having a vision at the start of change is needed for both transformational change (where it

outlines the broader strategic intent of the change and to which all actions are directed) as well as incremental or adaptive change (where the vision can be more specific in terms of specifying objectives or procedures for producing the change).[82]

The need for vision at the commencement of change is also embedded in the strategy literature, in particular in the use of the term *strategic intent* to represent vision. Most usually associated with the work of Hamel and Prahalad,[83] it is argued that "strategic intent envisions a desired leadership position and establishes the criterion the organization will use to chart its progress."[84] They point to Komatsu's "Encircle Caterpillar" and Canon's "Beat Xerox" as visionary statements that capture strategic intent. The strategic intent behind such statements was long term and encompassed a number of different change programs and actions over the short and medium term that were designed to work toward the long-term vision.[85] The strategic intent expressed the end that was desired without specifying or prescribing the necessary steps for achieving it along the way.

Vision Emerges during Change

An alternative argument is that while vision is important, it may be something that is not possible to articulate early on during transformational or discontinuous change. Shaw[86] takes such a position in arguing that organizational structures and management processes may need fundamental change and it is only after this process has begun that vision may be developed. This is because the current way these features are organized may inhibit the availability of information needed in order to develop the vision (such as customer expectations, market competition, etc.). The implication is that it is only after discontinuous change has commenced that such information will be available to assist in vision development. This means that "Those leading discontinuous change often 'soak' in the problems facing them, observe the results of their ongoing efforts, and then make changes as needed on a real-time basis."[87] To borrow a phrase from Robert Quinn,[88] this entails "building the bridge as you walk it."

Other writers take an even stronger stand in arguing that "the vision thing" is overrated in terms of driving change. This is the position adopted by Hilmer and Donaldson.[89] For them, it is business planning that produces successful change, not vision or visionary leaders. These authors maintain that by reanalyzing GE's corporate changes, it can be seen that "[t]here was no clear vision to guide the transformation"[90] and that Jack Welch's actions were pragmatic and "based on the application of conventional business ideas about the need for productivity improvement and high market share."[91] Multiple visions were produced over the period of his tenure and no clear vision emerged until "*after* much of the transformation had been accomplished."[92] For them, it was only vision rhetoric that was used along the way "to make the hierarchy's normal business decisions and operations function in a more acceptable way."[93]

Does Vision Help or Hinder Change?

Vision Helps Change

Tangible benefits are said to be associated with organizations that have skillful visions. Lipton[94] identifies five key ways in which skillful visions can enhance organizations:

- *Enhancing performance.* The Collins and Porras studies concluded that companies labeled as visionary were likely, over time, to deliver a greater dividend to shareholders compared to others.
- *Facilitating organizational change.* They accomplish this by providing a road map to facilitate the transition process.
- *Enabling sound strategic planning.* Plans that have embedded within them imagery of the future are more likely to inspire people to action.
- *Recruiting needed talent.* This applies particularly to the Generation Xers who want to maximize their incomes at the same time as feeling that they are engaging in challenges greater than simply making a profit.
- *Focusing on decision making.* This helps to develop the distinctive competencies that characterize the organization.[95]

Metais[96] supports this position in arguing that "strategic vision" helps to produce *stretch* in an organization; that is, it creates a feeling of incompetence resulting from the gap between the future and the current reality. This incompetence will facilitate creativity and the search for new ways of utilizing and acquiring needed resources. At the same time, it helps to *leverage* these resources, that is, identify new, innovative ways of utilizing them.[97] Together, stretch and leverage can be used to identify new strategic ways of achieving the vision, including change actions such as:

- *Flanking* (exploiting a weakness in a dominant competitor).
- *Encircling* competitors (by gaining greater control of the market).
- *Destabilizing* a market (by changing the competitive rules that operate).[98]

Along similar lines, Schoemaker[99] links strategic vision with helping to decide which products and markets an organization should pursue. Strategic management should then be used to align performance appraisals and incentive systems with the vision.

Vision Hinders Change

In going against the tide of praise for vision, others argue that it can hinder organizational change. This can occur when visionary or charismatic leaders (more on these people below) use an emotional appeal as the basis for engaging in change actions and neglect the necessary attention to operational detail that is needed to make the change work.[100] Associated with this is the problem that vision directs attention more to the future rather than to dealing with where the company is at the present. The failure of Boo.com is used to illustrate this argument.[101] This company raised $135 million to deliver on its vision of having a global presence in Internet-based clothing shopping. It launched operations in 17 different countries but had problems with slow software, which frustrated potential buyers:

> Boo's vision called for a broadband world of cool kids with large budgets. Boo's reality consisted of 56k modems, fussy buyers, and tight budgets. Boo was consistent with its vision but out of sync with its present landscape.[102]

Vision can hinder change where the wrong vision drives the change, where leaders overstimulate perceptions of crisis, or where the vision fails to produce what was promised and followers become disillusioned and lose confidence in the leader and the organization. The latter situation is thought to emerge where the gap between the vision and the available organizational skills to achieve it is too large.[103]

Vision development approaches that do not involve the people who will be affected are thought to have negative consequences for producing successful organizational change. For example, Robbins and Finley[104] point out that

> Where organizations go wrong is in assuming that the vision is some precious grail-like object that only the organizational priests are privy to—that it appears in a dream to the executive team, who then hold it up high for the rank and file to ooh and ahh over. . . The problem with the priestly approach to vision-and-mission is that the resulting vision is often a lot of garbage. The outcome, instead of being a useful reminder to keep to the change track, is a paragraph held to be so sacred that no one dares change it.

Vision can hinder change where, once it is developed, senior management become committed to it such that they are unwilling to reevaluate it and test its ongoing utility and relevance.[105] This is because to do so may challenge "the assumption that top management really is in control, really does have more accurate foresight than anyone else in the corporation, and already has a clear and compelling view of the company's future. Senior managers are often unwilling to confront these illusions."[106]

Visions can hinder companies when they are developed based upon sense-making processes that are linked to current or past sense-making practices. In the view of Lissack and Roos,[107] this is flawed since predicting the future on this basis reifies the desired outcome without enabling future changes to be built into it. Vision is based on the world in the future being stable and predictable. Outcomes are locked in and goals are set. The problem with this is that the vision acts against the organization pursuing new, unanticipated opportunities that may emerge in the future.[108]

For these authors, vision—and the strategic processes into which it is incorporated—is limited by other assumptions: One assumption is that organizational boundaries are well defined—such as staff, customers, and suppliers. In a world of fuzzy organizational networks, such assumptions are questionable.[109] A second assumption is that the identity of the organization is fixed and that the vision is built around this identity, for example, that Lego is a toy company. However, the identity of a company—what it does—is continuously changing through the actions of people at a variety of levels within it: "*Identity will always be somewhat unclear, and people will always want to talk about it.*"[110]

Rather than use vision, these authors argue in favor of what they term "coherence." By this they refer to "acting in a manner consistent with who you are given your present spot in the business landscape."[111] We suggest that it is unlikely that the term *coherence*, emphasizing ongoing discussions around boundaries and organizational identity, is likely to replace the term *vision*. However, the arguments of these authors are instructive in reminding us that organizational identities are not fixed but negotiated and changed over time and vision therefore needs to enable rather than disable such processes.

Is Vision an Attribute of Heroic Leaders or of Heroic Organizations?

Vision Is an Attribute of Heroic Leaders

Some writers claim that successful strategic organizational change will only occur when it is led effectively.[112] For Nadler such "heroic leaders" not only energize their

TABLE 9.10 Louis Gerstner on Vision

Louis V. Gerstner Jr, CEO of IBM, argued in a press conference in the mid-1990s that "the last thing IBM needs right now is a vision."[a] He later wrote that this was the "the most quotable statement I ever made."[b] This statement has often been cited as evidence that he downplayed or even dismissed the role of vision in organizational change. For example, Raynor[c] argues that "For a good many critics Gerstner's comment was greeted with a heartfelt 'it's about time'—that is, it is about time that a senior executive had the courage to speak up and put all that rhetoric about visions and missions in its place."

However, Gerstner argues that those who have portrayed this view of him have misinterpreted (or even misquoted) him, often failing to pay attention to the "right now" part of the statement. He maintains that IBM had a number of vision statements: it was now time to implement these, rather than engage in further visioning exercises because by that time "Fixing IBM was all about execution."[d]

[a]Gerstner, 2003:68.
[b]Gerstner, 2003:68.
[c]Raynor, 1998:368.
[d]Gerstner, 2003:71.

followers to engage in change, and provide enabling behavior and support to them to assist them, but provide them with a vision. This "envisioning" aspect of their role as change leaders "provides a vehicle for people to develop commitment, a common goal around which people can rally, and a way for people to feel successful."[113] The vision has to be clear, compelling, challenging, and credible—it also has to be reflected in the expressions and actions of the leader who is articulating it.[114] Nadler points to visionary leaders such as Jamie Houghton at Corning, who painted "an engrossing picture of a culture in which Corning would be one of the most competent, profitable, and respected corporations in the entire world." He cites Sun Microsystems' Scott McNealy as envisioning "an information world where people would be free to choose from a range of vendors rather than held captive by a single, all-powerful mega-corporation."[115]

Ironically, some of those who are cited as visionary leaders do not see themselves as visionary, "heroic," or as even subscribing to the importance of vision:

- Robert Eaton, who managed Chrysler after Lee Iacocca, downplayed "vision" in favor of "quantifiable short-term results."
- Bill Gates of Microsoft fame once declared that "Being visionary is trivial."[116]

Nevertheless, such people are depicted as expressing "a clear, appealing, challenging, and future-oriented picture of their organizations"[117]—all features of what are presented as the characteristics of effective visions.

Effective charismatic or visionary leaders, Gardner and Avolio[118] maintain, create "desired identity images" including trustworthiness, credibility, morality, innovativeness, esteem, and power. Drawing on a dramaturgical perspective, they argue that charismatic leaders secure such images in their followers and enact their visions through four processes:

- *Framing* is the art of managing the meaning of followers, getting them to accept the vision's interpretation and meaning by stressing its importance and aligning it with followers' values.
- *Scripting* extends framing, building upon it by coordinating and integrating more specific sets of ideas and actions. This entails:

- Casting (of appropriate roles).
- Dialogue (using various rhetorical devices to gain message appeal).
- Direction (of verbal and nonverbal behaviors).

- *Staging* is the selection of symbols, artifacts, props, and settings for reinforcing the vision.
- *Performing* refers to enacting the vision. This occurs through exemplification of required behaviors and promotion of themselves and their vision.

EXERCISE 9.3

Interviewing Followers

Your task is to interview three different employees—they can be in the same or different organizations. Get them to think back to an organizational change that they experienced and ask the following questions:

1. Were they presented with an organizational vision about the change? If so:
   - What was it?
   - What effect did it have on them?
   - Did they participate in developing the vision?
   - To what extent did the vision motivate them toward engaging in the change?
   - How central do they think vision is to achieving organizational change?
2. If your interviewees were not presented with an organizational vision, ask them the following questions:
   - Would a vision have helped them participate more in the change?
   - How central do they think vision is to achieving organizational change?

When you have completed your interviews, compare and contrast your responses. What general conclusions emerge regarding the relationship between vision and organizational change from the point of view of your respondents? What do you learn from this exercise?

It is important to note that while having a vision is deemed by many writers to be a prerequisite for being a successful change leader, others take a different view: to be an inspirational leader, vision is necessary but not enough by itself. In addition to vision and energy, the following are also needed:

- The ability to reveal personal weaknesses to followers (as a way of getting their trust).
- The ability to sense how things are in both the organization and the wider environment.
- The ability to display "tough empathy" with followers (satisfying what they need rather than what they really desire).
- Daring to be different (enabling them to signal and retain their separateness from their followers).[119]

The implication of this argument is that visionary leadership is important but enhanced by the addition of other qualities.

Vision Is an Attribute of Heroic Organizations

Collins and Porras[120] present the case that to produce visionary companies, charismatic, visionary leaders are not needed. As they put it, "Charisma's role in setting vision is vastly overrated."[121] Indeed, a charismatic leader may be an impediment to producing an enduring visionary company. This is because it is more important for companies to concentrate on being "clock builders, not time tellers." [122] The implication is that companies that are "built to last" require embedded visions, ideologies, and values rather than pronouncements from a single leader. It is up to a leader to catalyze a vision and create an organizational commitment to it, a process that can be achieved by a variety of management and leadership styles: "The key is to build an organization with vision, not simply to have a single charismatic individual with vision as the CEO."[123]

In their schema, vision consists of core ideology—which is unchanging and defines what the organization stands for and why it exists—and envisioned future is what the organization aspires to and changes toward over time.[124] Core ideology is the yin and is composed of core values and core purpose. *Core values* are the "timeless guiding principles" such as the HP Way, Walt Disney Company's imagination and wholesomeness, Procter & Gamble's product excellence, and Nordstrom's customer service. They found that most companies have only three to five shared, core values.[125] *Core purpose* defines the reason for existence of the company such as:

- 3M's "solve unsolved problems innovatively."
- Mary Kay Cosmetics' "give unlimited opportunity to women."
- McKinsey & Company's "help leading corporations and governments be more successful."
- Wal-Mart's "give ordinary folk the chance to buy the same things as rich people."[126]

Core purpose is something that "should last at least 100 years" and differs from goals and business strategies, which change constantly over time: "although purpose itself does not change, it does inspire change. The very fact that purpose can never be fully realized means that an organization can never stop stimulating change and progress."[127]

The yang is the *envisioned future*. It consists of BHAGs, or big hairy audacious goals, and vivid descriptions of what such goals will deliver. BHAGs are not just goals but daunting challenges with well-specified finishing lines toward which people can work. They may involve a:

- "Common enemy" logic such as Philip Morris's 1950s "knock off RJR as the number one tobacco company in the world" and Nike's 1960s "Crush Adidas."
- "Role model" logic such as Stanford University's 1940s goal of becoming "the Harvard of the West" and Watkins-Johnson's 1996 goal to "become as respected in 20 years as Hewlett-Packard."
- "Internal-transformational" logic such as GE's 1980s goal to "become number one or number two in every market we serve and revolutionize this company to have

> the strengths of a big company combined with the leanness and agility of a small company" and Rockwell's 1995 goal to "transform this company from a defense contractor into the best diversified high-technology company in the world."[128]

The second component of envisioned future, *vivid descriptions*, consists of vibrant, passionate, and engaging descriptions of what it will be like in the future when goals are achieved. Unlike core ideology, which can be discovered, "the envisioned future is a creative process"[129] engaging executives and others in the organization. An example of organizational vision is depicted in Table 9.11.

In their later work, they propose "industry foresight" as a more useful term to utilize rather than vision. Instead of the "dream" or "apparition" quality of a vision, foresight

EXERCISE 9.4

Delving into Your Organization's Vision

1. Choose an organization at which you are currently working or with which you are familiar (alternatively, choose the university at which you are currently studying).
2. As set out in Table 9.10, Collins and Porras[130] depict vision as composed of *core ideology* (core values, purpose) and *envisioned future* (big hairy audacious goals [BHAGs] and vivid descriptions).
3. Identify your organization's vision in these terms. You may wish to do this by examining company documents, talking to others, and reflecting on your own experiences.
4. To what extent does this vision help to drive change in your organization? How?
5. To what extent is this vision espoused *and* in use? How can you tell?

TABLE 9.11 Vision at Merck

Collins & Porras[a] argue that "complete visions" consist of a *core ideology* (core values and purpose) and *envisioned future* (big hairy audacious goals [BHAGs] and vivid descriptions). They give the following example of Merck, 1930s:

Core Ideology	**Envisioned Future**
Core Values	**BHAG**
• Social responsibility • Excellence • Science-based innovation	Transform from a chemical manufacturer to a world drug company with research capacity rivaling major universities
Purpose	**Vivid Description**
To preserve and improve human life	With the tools we have supplied, science will be advanced, knowledge increased, and human life win ever a greater freedom from suffering and disease. . .

[a]Collins and Porras, 1997:236–37.

represents deeper thought and insight into an industry and its trends. It goes beyond a focus on specific individuals and their heroic contributions to organizational success to a position where industry foresight is associated with, or the synthesis of, "many people's visions."[131]

In many ways, the work of Collins and Porras represents a sensitive treatment of the relationship between vision and change. In their work, vision (or industry foresight) is broken down into component parts, some of which remain stable and some of which change over time. Many change models that refer to the need for vision to guide an organizational change lack this degree of sophistication. Vision is often presented as something that guides change—and more often than not is handed down to the rest of the organization by the CEO or top-management team. However, in Collins and Porras' work, vision (as core ideology) serves as a background, enduring part of the organization. In itself, it does not so much guide change as reflect how it might be achieved (such as by following core values). It is the envisioned future of vision that may offer more concrete change direction, that is, what should be changed, and help to identify needed change actions.

EXERCISE 9.5

The Great Debates

Debate one or more of the following statements:

- "That vision is crucial in achieving successful organizational change."
- "That vision is an overrated concept."
- "That visionary leaders hinder organizational change."
- "That the success of a vision depends on the cultural context in which it is used."

Conclusion

Some writers claim that vision "has become one of the most overused and least understood words in the language."[132] Hence, rather than accepting at face value a central role for vision in producing successful organizational change, this chapter has gone backstage to examine the assumptions underpinning the concept. We have found wide variation in what vision means, what it should look like, how it should be produced, and what its relationship is to organizational change. We also have found debates about whether vision drives change or emerges during the process of change, whether vision helps or hinders change, and whether vision is best understood as an attribute of individuals or of organizations.

While the concept of vision seems to be in widespread use, its effectiveness is not always evident—some visions "take"[133] while others do not. Differing explanations for why this situation exists can be related back to the content of the vision, the process through which it is formed, the organizational and cultural context in which it is embedded, and the extent to which a leader is associated with its articulation. There is an additional problem to which Kim and Zeniuk[134] point, which is that the change vision "in use" may differ from the "espoused" vision. For some, vision is something that should last for 100 years or more;[135] for others, such as in the case study of Mentor Graphics Corporation (see below), it is open to constant change and renegotiation as business cycles change. In the latter case, vision statements were developed relatively quickly; this compares to the crafting of vision statements at AT&T, which took some two years, and at Steelcase, an office furniture manufacturer, where it took 18 months.[136]

The weight of commentator opinion seems to be that vision is important in assisting change and therefore worth having. While this may be true, care should be taken by the thoughtful change practitioner to ensure that it does not occupy a holy grail status in their organization—or in their own thinking. We are mindful of the way some concepts can acquire a taken-for-granted, "natural" status, both in language and in practice. Rather than change practitioners uncritically accepting the need for vision as a precursor to change, on the basis of arguments and debates outlined in this chapter, we maintain that the role of, and the need for, vision needs to be assessed specific to each change situation. We acknowledge that the nature of this assessment may itself be difficult and at the end of the day come down to a personal rather than a formally planned way of arriving at an answer to the question of whether vision (as opposed, for example, to planning) is needed. At the same time, and as outlined at the commencement of this chapter in Table 9.1, we suggest that, in part, the image of managing change will also influence the importance ascribed to vision. Rethinking or widening the images of managing change that are utilized will, by necessity, entail exploring new ways of understanding the centrality and role of vision in producing organizational change.

TABLE 9.12 Chapter Reflections for the Practicing Change Manager

- What criteria do you use in terms of figuring out whether a particular vision or vision statement is likely to be useful within your organization? What other things might you wish to take into account?
- What's your preference: a short vision statement or a longer vision story? Why? How do you use vision statements or stories?
- How do *you* separate vision from mission, planning, and goals? Is this an important distinction to make? How aligned is vision with these other concepts in your organization? Are there competing visions within your organization? How do these get resolved?
- What's your experience: Are visions more likely to "take" in some organizations or cultural contexts that you've been in compared to others? Why is this the case? What criteria can you develop to help assess when you should use vision to assist in organizational change?
- What process have you used, or seen used, to best craft a vision? Do you have a personal preference toward an intuitive as opposed to an analytical approach to vision development? Why?
- Is there an "inner voice" in your organization? What are the "bread-and-salt" issues? Are there "undiscussable" issues in your organization?
- What's your experience: When do visions fail or when does their effectiveness fade? Can visions be revitalized? How?
- What's your position: Does vision drive change? Does vision help change? Does vision need visionary leaders?

Supplemental Reading

Collins, J. C., and Porras, J. I. 1997. *Built to last: Successful habits of visionary companies*. New York: HarperCollins.

Gardner, W. L., and Avolio, B. J. 1998. The charismatic relationship: A dramaturgical perspective. *Academy of Management Review* 23(1):32–58.

Hinterhuber, H. H., and Popp, W. 1992. Are you a strategist or just a manager? *Harvard Business Review* 70(1):3–11.

Larwood, L., Falbe, C. M., Kriger, M. P., and Meising, P. 1995. Structure and meaning of organizational vision. *Academy of Management Journal* 38(3):740–69.

Levin, I. M. 2000. Vision revisited: Telling the story of the future. *Journal of Applied Behavioral Science* 36(1):91–107.

Lipton, M. 1996. Demystifying the development of an organizational vision. *Sloan Management Review* 37(4) (Summer):83–92.

Lissack, M., and Roos, J. 2001. Be coherent, not visionary. *Long Range Planning* 54:53–70.

Nutt, P. C., and Backoff, R. W. 1997. Crafting vision. *Journal of Management Inquiry* 6(4):308–28.

Raynor, M. E. 1998. That vision thing: Do we need it? *Long Range Planning* 31(3):368–76.

Schoemaker, P. J. H. 1992. How to link strategic vision to core capabilities. *Sloan Management Review* 34(1) (Fall):67–81.

Gerard Langeler, writing as president of Mentor Graphics Corporation, discusses the role of vision in his company over a 10-year period.[138] Formed in the early 1980s, Mentor Graphics started with an unarticulated vision to "Build Something That People Will Buy." On this basis, they spent a number of months interviewing potential customers and designing a computer-aided engineering workstation product.

At the same time, a competitor, Daisy Systems, was engaged in the same task and, in the early years, outcompeted Mentor Graphics. Eventually, "Beat Daisy" became the new vision, a vision driven by the need to survive as a business.

By 1985 their revenues were greater than Daisy's—their vision had been realized. The company continued to grow despite the recession but suffered from typical growth problems, including decline in product quality and problems of internal company coordination. Stock value also suffered and a number of staff approached Langeler seeking a new vision for the company.

The new vision was developed based on "Six Boxes," which represented the six different businesses in which they sought market leadership. The "Six Boxes" became a company mantra, but in the late 1980s, one of the businesses, computer-aided publishing, was not paying dividends. However, the fact that it constituted one of the "Six Boxes" meant that they could not shut it down—and be left with a "Five Boxes" vision! In this case, the existence of the vision disrupted the ability to make sound financial judgments. It also stopped them from moving more quickly to using Sun platforms, something they thought was too conventional for them.

A new vision was developed—the "10X Imperative"—that mirrored the push other companies were making toward quality through six-sigma programs and the like. However, customers didn't really understand the new vision: It was too abstract and elusive.

In 1989 yet another vision emerged: "Changing the Way the World Designs Together." In retrospect, Langeler depicts this vision as "the final extension of vision creep that began with Six Boxes."[139] It was very grand and had little to do with the actual businesses in which Mentor Graphics operated—including the development of its new 8.0 generation of software.

The realization, by the early 1990s, that the company's vision detracted from what the company was actually about led to the dumping of the vision and the replacement with one that echoed the early beginning of the company: "Our current short-, medium-, and long-term vision is to build things people will buy"[140] was seen as a more pragmatic vision for a company that had lost its way, caught up in a cycle of visions that were increasingly irrelevant to the company's core business and that inhibited their ability to make sound business decisions.

Questions

1. How would you describe the way vision was used at Mentor Graphics?
2. Did it strengthen or weaken the company? How? Why?
3. Of the reasons covered in this chapter relating to why visions may fail, which ones are applicable to Mentor Graphics?
4. Discuss issues of vision content, context, and process in how vision was introduced and changed at the company. What emerges from this?
5. Based on what happened in this company, what are the implications in terms of the three debates about vision discussed in this chapter (whether vision drives change or emerges during change, whether vision helps or hinders change, and whether vision is an attribute of heroic leaders or heroic organizations?
6. Of the six change images outlined in Table 9.1, which images of vision can be applied to this case study? What lessons emerge from this?

TABLE 9.13 **Additional Case Studies**

Carly Fiorina: The Change Leader
Gupta, V. (2004) *ICFAI Knowledge Centre, India*
FNB Metro: Waking up to Change
Ortlepp, K., & Gordon-Brown, C. (2004) *Wits Business School, University of the Witwatersrand, South Africa*
Nokia and MIT's Project Oxygen
Henderson, R. (2004) *Harvard Business School*
Bob Galvin and Motorola, Inc. (A)
Gentile, M., under direction of Jick, T. (1987) *Harvard Business School*
Charlotte Beers at Ogilvy & Mather Worldwide (A)
Steckler, N., under supervision of Ibarra, H. (1995) *Harvard Business School*

Bibliography

Beaver, G. 2000. The significance of strategic vision, mission and values. *Strategic Change* 9(4):205–207.

Berson, Y., Shamir, B., Avolio, B. J., and Popper, M. 2001. The relationship between vision strength, leadership style, and context. *Leadership Quarterly* 12(1):53–73.

Beyer, J. M. 1999. Taming and promoting charisma to change organizations. *Leadership Quarterly* 10(2):307–30.

Boal, K. B., and Hooijberg, R. 2001. Strategic leadership research: Moving on. *Leadership Quarterly* 11(4):515–49.

Collins, J. C., and Porras, J. I. 1991. Organizational vision and visionary organizations. *California Management Review* 34(1) (Fall):30–52.

Collins, J. C., and Porras, J. I. 1996. Building your company's vision. *Harvard Business Review* 74(5):65–77.

Collins, J. C., and Porras, J. I. 1997. *Built to last: Successful habits of visionary companies*. New York: HarperCollins.

Conger, J. A., and Kanungo, R. A. 1998. *Charismatic leadership in organizations*. Thousand Oaks, CA: Sage.

DeLisi, P. 1998. A modern-day tragedy: The Digital Equipment story. *Journal of Management Inquiry* 7(2):118–30.

Domm, D. R. 2001. Strategic vision: Sustaining employee commitment. *Business Strategy Review* 12(4):39–48.

El-Namaki, M. S. S. 1992. Creating a corporate vision. *Long Range Planning* 25(6):25–29.

Flower, J. 1992. 21st century innovators. *Healthcare Forum Journal*, March–April:70–75.

Folz, D. 1993. A culture of high performance. *Executive Excellence* 10(2) (February):17.

Gardner, W. L., and Avolio, B. J. 1998. The charismatic relationship: A dramaturgical perspective. *Academy of Management Review* 23(1):32–58.

Gerstner, L. V., Jr. 2003. *Who says elephants can't dance? Inside IBM's historic turnover*. New York: HarperBusiness.

Gratton, L. 1996. Implementing a strategic vision—key factors for success. *Long Range Planning* 29(3):290–303.

Haapaniemi, P. 1996. Shared vision. *Chief Executive*, July–August:16.

Hamburger, Y. A. 2000. Mathematical leadership vision. *Journal of Psychology* 134(6):601–11.

Hamel, G. 1996. Strategy as revolution. *Harvard Business Review* 74(4):69–82.

Hamel, G., and Prahalad, C. K. 1989. Strategic intent. *Harvard Business Review* 67(3):2–14.

Hamel, G., and Prahalad, C. K. 1994. Competing for the future. *Harvard Business Review* 72(4):122–28.

Harris, L. C., and Ogbonna, E. 1999. The strategic legacy of company founders. *Long Range Planning* 32(3):333–43.

Hatch, M. J., and Schultz, M. 2001. Are the strategic stars aligned for your corporate brand? *Harvard Business Review* 78(2):3–8.

Hay, M., and Williamson, P. 1997. Good strategy: The view from below. *Long Range Planning* 30(5):651–64.

Hilmer, F. G., and Donaldson, L. 1996. *Management redeemed: Debunking the fads that undermine our corporations*. New York: Free Press.

Hinterhuber, H. H., and Popp, W. 1992. Are you a strategist or just a manager? *Harvard Business Review* 70(1):3–11.

Holpp, L., and Kelly, M. 1988. Realizing the possibilities. *Training and Development Journal* 42(9) (September):48–55.

Hunt, J. W., and Laing, B. 1997. Leadership: The role of the exemplar. *Business Strategy Review* 8(1):31–42.

Jick, T. D. 1989. The vision thing. *Harvard Business School*, Note # 9-490-019.

Jick, T. D. 2001. Vision is 10%, implementation the rest. *Business Strategy Review* 12(4):36–38.

Johnson, M. 1999. A feasibility test for corporate vision. *Strategic Change* 8(6):335–48.

Kanter, R. M., Stein, B. A., and Jick, T. D. 1992. *The challenge of organizational change: How companies experience it and leaders guide it*. New York: Free Press.

Katzenbach, J. R., and the RCL Team. 1996. *Real change leaders: How you can create growth and high performance at your company*. London: Nicholas Brealey.

Kim, D., and Zeniuk, N. 1999. After fixing the crisis. In *The dance of change: The challenges to sustaining momentum in learning organizations*, ed. P. Senge, A. Kleiner, C. Roberts, R. Moss, G. Roth, and B. Smith, 183–86. New York: Currency Doubleday.

Kirkpatrick, S. A., Wofford, J. C., and Baum, J. R. 2002. Measuring motive imagery contained in the vision statement. *Leadership Quarterly* 13(2):139–50.

Kotter, J. P. 1996. *Leading change*. Boston, MA: Harvard Business School Press.

Kuratko, D. F., Ireland, R. D., and Hornsby, J. S. 2001. Improving firm performance through entrepreneurial actions: Acordia's corporate entrepreneurship strategy. *Academy of Management Executive* 15(4):60–71.

Langeler, G. H. 1992. The vision trap. *Harvard Business Review* 70(2):5–12.

Larwood, L., Falbe, C. M., Kriger, M. P., and Meising, P. 1995. Structure and meaning of organizational vision. *Academy of Management Journal* 38(3):740–69.

Levin, I. M. 2000. Vision revisited: Telling the story of the future. *Journal of Applied Behavioral Science* 36(1):91–107.

Lipton, M. 1996. Demystifying the development of an organizational vision. *Sloan Management Review* 37(4) (Summer):83–92.

Lissack, M., and Roos, J. 2001. Be coherent, not visionary. *Long Range Planning* 54:53–70.

Martin, P. E. 1992. Visioning and strategic planning—the measure of departmental self-esteem. *Cost Engineering* 34(11):21–23.

Metais, E. 2000. SEB group: Building a subversive strategy. *Business Strategy Review* 11(4):39–47.

Mintzberg, H. 1994. The fall and rise of strategic planning. *Harvard Business Review* 72(1):107–14.

Mitchell, C. 2002. Selling the brand inside. *Harvard Business Review* 80(1):5–11.

Nader, D. A. 1998. *Champions of change: How CEOs and their companies are mastering the skills of radical change*. San Francisco: Jossey-Bass.

Nadler, D. A., and Shaw, R. B. 1995. Beyond the heroic leader. In *Discontinuous change: Leading organizational transformation*, ed. D. A. Nadler, R. B. Shaw, A. E. Walton, & Associates, 217–31. San Francisco: Jossey-Bass.

Nanus, B. 1996. Leading the vision team. *The Futurist* 30(3) (May–June):21–23.

Nutt, P. C., and Backoff, R. W. 1997. Crafting vision. *Journal of Management Inquiry* 6(4):308–28.

Pendlebury, J., Grouard, B., and Meston, F. 1998. *The ten keys to successful change management*. England: John Wiley & Sons Ltd.

Prahalad, C. K., and Hamel, G. 1990. The core competence of the corporation. *Harvard Business Review* 68(3):79–90.

Quinn, R. E. 1996. *Deep change: Discovering the leader within*. San Francisco: Jossey-Bass.

Raynor, M. E. 1998. That vision thing: Do we need it? *Long Range Planning* 31(3):368–76.

Robbins, H., and Finley, M. 1997. *Why change doesn't work: Why initiatives go wrong and how to try again—and succeed*. London: Orion.

Schoemaker, P. J. H. 1992. How to link strategic vision to core capabilities. *Sloan Management Review* 34(1) (Fall):67–81.

Seurat, R. 1999. Sustained and profitable growth. *Business Strategy Review* 10(1) (Spring):53–56.

Shamir, B., and Howell, J. M. 1999. Organizational and contextual influences on the emergence and effectiveness of charismatic leadership. *Leadership Quarterly* 10(2):257–83.

Shaw, R. B. 1995. The essence of discontinuous change: Leadership, identity and architecture. In *Discontinuous change: Leading organizational transformation*, ed. D. A. Nadler, R. B. Shaw, A. E. Walton, and Associates, 66–81. San Francisco: Jossey-Bass.

Stace, D., and Dunphy, D. 2001. *Beyond the boundaries: Leading and recreating the successful enterprise*. 2nd ed. Sydney: McGraw-Hill.

Teal, T. 1996. The human side of management. *Harvard Business Review* 74(6):3–10.

Thoms, P., and Greenberger, D. B. 1995. The relationship between leadership and time orientation. *Journal of Management Inquiry* 4(3):272–92.

Thoms, P., and Greenberger, D. B. 1998. A test of vision training and potential antecedents to leaders' visioning ability. *Human Resource Development Quarterly* 9(1):3–19.

Thornberry, N. 1997. A view about "vision." *European Management Journal* 15(1):28–34.

Victor, P., and Franckeiss, A. 2002. The five dimensions of change: An integrated approach to strategic organizational change management. *Strategic Change* 11(1):35–42.

Wind, J. W., and Main, J. 1999. *Driving change: How the best companies are preparing for the 21st century*. London: Kogan Page Ltd.

Yearout, S., Miles, G., and Koonce, R. H. 2001. Multi-level visioning. *Training & Development* 55(3):31–39.

Notes

1. For example, see Victor and Franckeiss, 2002:41.
2. Hinterhuber and Popp, 1992:4.
3. Beaver, 2000:205; Kirkpatrick et al., 2002:140; Seurat, 1999:553–54.
4. Eadie and Edwards, 1993:12.
5. Flower, 1992:71.
6. Martin, 1992.
7. DeLisi, 1998:118.
8. Beaver, 2000:205.
9. Prahalad and Hamel, 1990:86.
10. Hamel, 1996:80.
11. Folz, 1993:17.
12. Lissack and Roos, 2001:55. This and subsequent quotes copyright © 2001 by and reproduced with permission of the Strategic Planning Society, www.sps.org/uk.
13. Larwood et al., 1995:740–41, 746.
14. Kirkpatrick et al., 2002:140.
15. Raynor, 1998:368.
16. Jick, 1989:1.
17. Beaver, 2000:205.
18. Levin, 2000:91.
19. Hunt and Laing, 1997:32.
20. Wind and Main, 1999:101.
21. Nutt and Backoff, 1997:316–17.
22. Quinn, 1996:198–210.
23. Gardner and Avolio, 1998:39–46.
24. Boal and Hooijberg, 2001:527.
25. Nutt and Backoff, 1997:312–14.
26. Pendlebury et al., 1998:56–57.
27. Pendlebury et al., 1998:58.
28. Pendlebury et al., 1998:60.
29. Nutt and Backoff, 1997:312–14.
30. Pendlebury et al., 1998:56–57.
31. Levin, 2000:92–93.
32. Levin, 2000:93.
33. Cited in Domm, 2001:47.
34. Raynor, 1998; Thornberry, 1997:29; Levin, 2000:92.
35. Yearout et al., 2001:31.
36. Levin, 2000:95.
37. Nutt and Backoff, 1997:309–10.
38. Teal, 1996:5.
39. Hay and Willliamson, 1997:655–56.
40. Hay and Willliamson, 1997:656–58.

41. Nutt and Backoff, 1997:316–17.
42. Nutt and Backoff, 1997:316.
43. Nutt and Backoff, 1997:317.
44. Shamir and Howell, 1999:260.
45. Nutt and Backoff, 1997:315.
46. Shamir and Howell, 1999:262–72.
47. Shamir and Howell, 1999:261.
48. Wind and Main, 1999:102.
49. Wind and Main, 1999:102.
50. Wind and Main, 1999:102–103.
51. Holpp and Kelly, 1988:48.
52. DeLisi, 1998:118.
53. Pendlebury et al., 1998:63.
54. Kuratko et al., 2001:68.
55. Gratton, 1996:291.
56. Gratton, 1996:302.
57. Nutt and Backoff, 1997:312–14.
58. Nutt and Backoff, 1997:318.
59. Holpp and Kelly, 1998.
60. Holpp and Kelly, 1998.
61. Holpp and Kelly, 1998:50.
62. Holpp and Kelly, 1998: 52.
63. Holpp and Kelly, 1998:52.
64. Mintzberg, 1994:109.
65. Quinn, 1996.
66. Quinn, 1996:195–97.
67. Quinn, 1996:197.
68. Quinn, 1996:199.
69. Quinn, 1996:198–205.
70. Quinn, 1996:210.
71. Pendlebury et al., 1998:61–63.
72. Jick, 2001:36.
73. Harris and Ogbonna, 1999:336–39.
74. Harris and Ogbonna, 1999:340.
75. Kanter et al., 1992:385.
76. See Hatch and Schultz, 2001:6.
77. Mitchell, 2002.
78. Mitchell, 2002:10.
79. Kanter et al., 1992:383.
80. Kanter et al., 1992:509.
81. Pendlebury et al., 1998:54.

82. Pendlebury et al., 1998:55.
83. Hamel and Prahalad, 1989.
84. Hamel and Prahalad, 1989:4.
85. Hamel and Prahalad, 1989:4.
86. Shaw, 1995:67.
87. Shaw, 1995:67.
88. Quinn, 1996:83–88.
89. Hilmer and Donaldson, 1996:125–27.
90. Hilmer and Donaldson, 1996:126.
91. Hilmer and Donaldson, 1996:127.
92. Hilmer and Donaldson, 1996:126.
93. Hilmer and Donaldson, 1996:127.
94. Lipton, 1996.
95. Lipton, 1996:84–85.
96. Metais, 2000.
97. Metais, 2000:39–40.
98. Metais, 2000:40–46.
99. Schoemaker, 1992:79.
100. Beyer, 1999:321–22.
101. Lissack and Roos, 2002:61.
102. Lissack and Roos, 2002:61.
103. Beyer, 1999:321–22.
104. Robbins and Finley, 1997:175.
105. See Hamel and Prahalad, 1994:123.
106. Hamel and Prahalad, 1994:123.
107. Lissack and Roos, 2002.
108. Lissack and Roos, 2002:54.
109. Lissack and Roos, 2002:57.
110. Lissack and Roos, 2002:58 (italics in original).
111. Lissack and Roos, 2002:61.
112. Nadler, 1995:217–18.
113. Nadler, 1995:219.
114. Nadler, 1995:219.
115. Nadler, 1998:276.
116. Cited in Lipton, 1996:86.
117. Lipton, 1996:86.
118. Gardner and Avolio, 1998:39–46.
119. Goffee and Jones, 2000:63–70.
120. Collins and Porras, 1997:7–8. Copyright © 1996 by Harvard Business Review. Reproduced with permission of Harvard Business School Publishing.
121. Collins and Porras, 1991:51.

122. Collins and Porras, 1997:8.
123. Collins and Porras, 1991:51.
124. Collins and Porras, 1996:66.
125. Collins and Porras, 1996:66–67.
126. Collins and Porras, 1996:69.
127. Collins and Porras, 1996:69.
128. Collins and Porras, 1996:72.
129. Collins and Porras, 1996:75.
130. Collins and Porras, 1997.
131. Hamel and Prahalad, 1994:128.
132. Collins and Porras, 1996:66.
133. Jick, 1989:6.
134. Kim and Zeniuk, 1999:184–85.
135. Collins and Porras, 1991:30.
136. Examples cited in Raynor, 1998:369.
137. This case was developed from Langeler, 1992.
138. Langeler, 1992.
139. Langeler, 1992:11.
140. Langeler, 1992:12.

Strategies for Communicating Change

Learning objectives

On completion of this chapter you should be able to

- Identify communication strategies appropriate to different images of managing change.
- Appreciate a variety of strategies involved in communicating change.
- Identify key elements involved in the communication process.
- Describe appropriate communication strategies for announcing organizational change.
- Understand how successful communication processes will vary depending on the stage and type of organizational change.

How change gets communicated and talked about is crucial to its success. The importance of communication during change has been linked to facilitating vision, enhancing feedback, providing social support, and helping to modify change as it unfolds.[1] Communication has been linked to the success of research and development project groups,[2] to establishing the trustworthiness of managers,[3] and to persuading individuals to be involved in change innovations.[4] A KPMG survey of managers in 131 of Canada's top corporations found that managers viewed communication as the most important factor in achieving successful changes such as mergers, downsizing, and reengineering.[5] A survey of 410 top managers in Fortune 1000 firms found that "clear and consistent communication" was deemed by them to be integral to achieving successful organizational change.[6]

Failure to tackle appropriate change communication strategies can have deleterious consequences. A study of 43 U.S. organizations in the midst of major change found that most companies had not developed a strategy for announcing the change, which led to the emergence of counterproductive rumors.[7] A Wyatt Company study of CEOs in 531 U.S. organizations found that if they had had their time over again in going through a major restructuring, they would have focused more on communication with their employees.[8] In Beer and Eisenstat's[9] in-depth study of 12 companies engaged in strategic change, they categorized 10 of them as having poor vertical communication leading to cynicism in staff and a perception by them that there was a lack of openness by senior management about the change. In her survey of change implementers, Lewis[10] concluded that communication was ranked as among the most problematic issues that they had to deal with.

We divide up our discussion of communication into two chapters, this one dealing with communication *strategies* and the next dealing with the *skills* needed for putting those strategies in place. This division is based on the view that there is no point being able to identify the communication strategies that are needed to produce successful organizational change without an understanding of the skills that are involved in implementing those strategies. Conversely, there is no point in utilizing a set of communication skills if these are not part of a well-thought-out and targeted change communication strategy.

In arriving at this position, we suggest that the image of managing change will influence both the communication strategies and skills that change managers will focus on. For example, Gayeski and Majka[11] point out one of the problems facing communicators is their expectation of what they can achieve. They argue that a mechanical (*director*) image of organizations has dominated our understandings so that an image of control and manageability has been associated with organizational communication. They claim that this image is outmoded and better understood in terms of chaos and complexity theories (*nurturer* image). Accepting an image such as this may decrease the frustration of not being able to control events in the way that is often assumed in the mechanical image. Change managers may be able to shape but not always control the communication of change. More generally, each of the six images of change outlined in Chapter 2 has associated with it a different underlying strategy for communicating change. Table 10.1 provides a summary of these (this table is extended in the next chapter to indicate the specific skills associated with these communication strategies).

In this chapter on communication strategy, we first outline a classic model of the communication process and point to how issues of language, power, gender, and emotions are important to understanding how it operates. Where readers already have an understanding of the basic communication process, we suggest that they move on to the second part of the chapter, where we focus on the dilemmas concerning the change manager's communication strategy: whether you can communicate too much, how the strategy is linked to the type of change and the phases of a change, and whether the strategy acts to "get the word out" or to get "buy-in." Third, we enter the terrain of assessing the appropriateness of using differing media in communicating change. Here we address the richness of the media and discuss where responsibility lies for communicating change. As we go through these various areas, we invite the reader to refer back to Table 10.1 as a guide for understanding the emphasis that different images of managing change place on the topics discussed.

THE COMMUNICATION PROCESS

In this section we outline a basic communication process model and then deepen the discussion by considering the way language, gender, power, and emotions affect how it operates.

TABLE 10.1 Relationship of Change Images to Purpose of Communication

Image of Managing Change	Purpose of Communication
Director	Ensure people understand what is going to happen and what is required of them. Provide them with answers to the why, what, who, how, and when questions—including the "value-proposition" involved in the change. Where a contingency perspective is involved, this may mean modifying the type of information provided and leadership style to make these "fit" the type of change involved and the level in the organization at which the change message is pitched. Communication strategies need to ensure that there is no message overload (communicating too much through "spray and pray" techniques) or message distortion (incorrect message sent out).
Navigator	Similar to *director* image in terms of outlining the nature of the change to staff, but pay attention to identifying alternative interests (including gender differences), power relationships, and actions that may disrupt the proposed change. This enables these to be either dealt with or the change itself replotted in order to produce the best change outcomes possible in the current situation. "Tell and sell" communication techniques are used to try to win people over to the change.
Caretaker	Focus is on letting people know about the "why" of change, that is, the inevitability of the changes and how best to cope or survive them. "Identify and reply" (reactive) communication strategy is used.
Coaching	Focus is on ensuring people share similar values and are aware of what actions are appropriate to these values. Coaches model consistency in actions and words. Whereas the focus of the *director* is more on "getting the word out" about the change, the focus of the *coach* is "getting buy-in" to the change through shared values and the use of "positive emotions." Team-based rather than top-down, CEO-led communication styles are most favored. "Underscore and explore" interactions are used to engage in dialogue about the change.
Interpreter	*Interpreters* provide staff with a sense of "what is going on" through story telling, metaphors, and so on. *Interpreters* are aware of the multiple *sense-making* that goes on in organizations from different groups about any proposed change. Their focus is on *sense-giving* to different groupings across the organization (and outside); that is, presenting the most persuasive account of the change to ensure that as many people as possible share common understandings of the change. They recognize that not all will buy in to the story of change, but the aim is to provide the most dominant account. "Rich" communication media are most favored.
Nurturer	The *nurturer* image leads change managers to reinforce the view that processes cannot always be predicted and that often outcomes will occur that are innovative and creative for an organization even though few people could have anticipated what these might be prior to their occurrence.

FIGURE 10.1 A Model of Communication

Source: Nelson and Coxhead, 1997:40. Copyright © 1997 John Wiley & Sons, Limited. Reproduced with permission of the publisher.

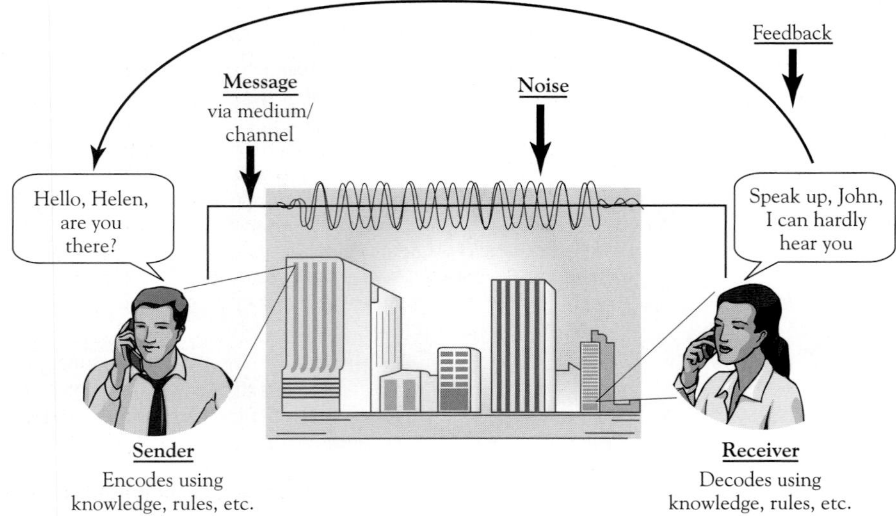

Modeling the Communication Process

The communication "mix" covers a variety of areas including content, voice, tone, message, audience, medium, frequency, and consistency.[12] Figure 10.1 outlines a simple communication model and what Nelson and Coxhead[13] term its "principal components" are set out in Table 10.2. These authors highlight three potential problems during the communication process:[14]

- *Message overload* occurs when information acquisition is overbalanced compared to an individual's response capabilities.
- *Message distortion* occurs when meanings are misinterpreted through intentional or unintentional problems relating to the sending or receiving of the message.
- *Message ambiguity* occurs when an organization has a vision but is not prescriptively clear on how to achieve it.

Avoiding such problems, these authors argue, will occur when a common language about the change is adopted and when top management consistently models the desired behaviors. For them, enhancing the involvement and self-esteem of employees and utilizing specialist personnel to monitor the change process will be of assistance.[15]

Influence of Language, Power, Gender, and Emotion

Simple change communication models are useful for identifying why some communication breakdowns occur, but greater knowledge is needed of the impact on the change communication process of other influences such as the following.

Gender, Language, and Power

Tannen[16] points out that language doesn't just communicate ideas but reflects and reinforces underlying social relationships. She provides the example of the following

TABLE 10.2 Principal Components of a Simple Model of Communication

Source: Adapted from Nelson and Coxhead, 1997:39–40.

1. *Message*	Verbal and nonverbal attempts to trigger meaning
2. *Feedback*	Providing a response to the sender in order to see if the intended meaning was conveyed
3. *Channel*	The medium through which the message was sent (e.g., face-to-face, e-mail, letter, video, etc.)
4. *Sender/receiver*	Individuals who, respectively, send or receive messages
5. *Encoding/decoding*	The creation, transformation, and deciphering of messages. This may be affected by a range of individual states including emotions, values and beliefs, and prior knowledge
6. *Noise*	Other distractions that exist in the communication environment and may act to interfere with the transmission of meaning

statements, each of which requires the same action from a person but signals differing information about the relationship of that person to the one doing the talking:[17]

- "Sit down!" This signals higher status of the person uttering the statement; perhaps it indicates anger and no need to engage in pleasantries.
- "I would be honored if you would sit down." This signals respect, or possibly sarcasm, depending on the tone of voice and the situation.
- "You must be so tired. Why don't you sit down?" This signals either a concern and closeness for the person, or condescension.

Gender differences also affect the communication process. Here are three examples:

- *Getting credit*. In her research, Tannen found that men tend to claim credit through the use of the word "I"; women are more likely to use the word "we," even in situations where they had specifically taken actions by themselves.
- *Confidence and boasting*. "[W]omen are more likely to downplay their certainty and men are more likely to minimize their doubts."[18]
- *Asking questions*. Women are more likely to ask questions than men; the downside to this is that male managers may interpret women as knowing less than their male peers.[19]

Other gender differences relate to how feedback is given and received, how compliments are exchanged, and whether the communication is direct or indirect.[20]

The use of language and how it reflects underlying power and gender relationships points to deeper dimensions relating to why communication processes can break down during organizational change (as well as during periods of stability). For example, where change managers seek staff input into a specific change, how this is asked for—and the language used—may reinforce underlying power differences. Telling staff to provide input may have different results than using language that conveys respect for their opinions (as in the "sit down!" example above). An understanding of potential gender differences in the communication process will remind change managers to reflect on the accuracy of their assumptions and conclusions about particular individuals.

For example, an assessment by a male manager of how well a woman is coping with change, compared to other men in the same organizational unit, may be: "She seems very uncertain since she is always asking questions about it." However, this conclusion may have more to do with gender differences related to a willingness to ask questions (about the change) than to real differences in attitude toward the change itself.

EXERCISE 10.1

Listen to Who's Talking!

Tannen[21] points out that the way we communicate reinforces differences in power and gender relationships. This can affect our interpretations of what we think is going on in a particular situation.

1. Observe a work meeting—preferably with up to 10 people.
2. Listen to the language being used: What different types of languages in use can you observe (e.g., commanding language, respectful language, concern language, condescension language)?
3. Do individuals tend to use one type of language in their interactions?
4. Who does most of the talking? Who asks most of the question?
5. To what extent does the talk convey information about power and gender differences? (Who takes credit? exudes confidence? asks questions?)
6. What general conclusions do you draw from this analysis about the way language constructs and reinforces differences within the organization?
7. As a change manager, how will your awareness of these differences influence your future interactions with staff?

Emotion and Communication

Some writers are critical of communication of change models for being too rational and cognitive and largely ignoring the role of emotions in organizational change. Although it is mentioned in models such as in Figure 10.1, the focus on emotions is often yet another burden for the change manager to address—another dimension contributing to change communication breakdown. An alternative view is that the emotional side of change can, itself, be "a potential tool for securing the willingness, commitment, and efforts of subordinates in the process of the change."[22] Fox and Amichai-Hamburger point to a need to seek congruence between our cognitive perception of a change and our emotional understanding of it. It is through emotional appeals that urgency can be communicated, vision instilled, and powerful change coalitions established.[23] Bringing about "positive emotions" that produce "excitement and anticipation" around a change program entails paying attention to four areas (see Table 10.3).

Understanding the emotional side of change is important. However, whether change managers can always produce positive emotional responses to a change by following the advice of these authors is open to question on four grounds: First, there is an underlying assumption that emotions are produced and contained within the surrounds of the organization. The impact of external stimuli (the way friends and family talk about a change with the staff member; how the press presents the change, etc.) seems to be ignored. Second, an underlying assumption is that all people respond in the same way to the same emotional appeals. This ignores the differing motivations people take to their work and

TABLE 10.3 **Getting Emotional Commitment**

Source: Developed from Fox and Amichai-Hamburger, 2001:87–92.

Getting Emotional Commitment Means Addressing the Following Issues	How This Is Done
Core Message Regarding the Change	
• Emotional arguments	Use of negative words helps convey what will occur if the change fails; positive words help depict success of change program in the future
• Metaphors	Drawing on metaphors that already have meaning to staff helps produce an image of the future and makes the "strangeness" of the future more familiar
Packaging the Message	
• Emotional mode of communication	Create attention through use of multiple forms including music, colors, slogans, and pictures; avoid overexposure to any one form
• Humor	Humor helps create a sense of ease and lessens the gap between manager and staff
• Display emotions	During presentations, use of appropriate feelings, speech tones, body language, and facial expressions helps create warmth and confidence
• Characteristics of change leaders	Credibility and attractiveness of the message is more likely when there is a perception that the message conveyed is congruent with the actions and behaviors of the manager concerned
Behavior of Change Managers to Staff	
• Fairness and justice	Decisions should be seen to be fair and follow legitimate, recognized procedures; staff should have the opportunity to voice issues and emotions in relation to the change
Setting	
• Group dynamics	Groups and teams should be used to gain commitment to the change
• Ceremonies	Celebrations help to stimulate emotions and reinforce the positive aspects of the change and what it is achieving; they also can signal departure from the past
• Pleasant atmosphere	Work at producing positive feelings toward the change by talking about it in tones that are not formal and cold

how this affects their perceptions of a change; it also ignores that different cultures express emotions in differing ways—and how this impacts upon diverse workforces. Third, the skills of a change manager in "managing emotions" will be mixed; not all will have the skills—or credibility, especially based on their past actions—to deal with the emotional responses of staff to change. What this highlights is that, while the emotional side of change needs to be acknowledged, not all change managers will be equally adept in achieving positive emotional responses to particular changes. Fourth, it may be easier to achieve positive emotional responses to some changes and not others.

STRATEGIES FOR COMMUNICATING CHANGE

In this section we focus on a range of communication strategy dilemmas confronting the change manager—including whether you can communicate too much, how to get staff "buy-in," and how to go beyond a "spray and pray" information strategy. We conclude this section by looking at two contingency approaches to thinking about communication strategy: one that links it to the type of change and a second that links it to differing phases of a change.

Can You Communicate Too Much?

One of the often-heard expressions is "we need more communication around here." Many writers and practitioners take the position that you cannot overcommunicate, a message that appears to have been part of the communication of the Ford 2000 change strategy (see Table 10.4).

This view that "you cannot overcommunicate" is not necessarily shared by all change agents and researchers. Geigle and Bailey[24] report on a business process reengineering that occurred in a federal agency and affected around 400 people. The reengineering change team was committed to a strategy of organizationwide communication and openness regarding the change project to a degree that was thought to be unprecedented in the organization's change history. The outcome of this strategy was change recipient anxiety and cynicism about the change. Two factors were behind this.

First, participants suffered information overload: "It's almost like they know with all this information, we won't read it." Information overload is even more problematic in companies where participants are already in receipt of a high volume of other information. For example, at Intel, an average of 3 million e-mail messages are received each day with some people getting up to 300 messages daily. As one Intel computing productivity manager, Nathan Zeldes, is quoted as saying: "We're so wrapped up in sending e-mail to each other, we don't have time to be dealing with the outside."[25]

Second, and in relation to the federal agency example, the communication strategy did not involve real participation as had been anticipated. When the reengineering team gained feedback, it did not have a strategy for incorporating this into the change program: "Even with all the information out there, I still feel like—they may be informing me of everything that's going on, but I have absolutely zero say in what goes on."

The authors conclude that there may well be symbolic importance in announcing and pursuing an open communication strategy during a change project but this by itself is not sufficient to achieving successful change. In their view, a change team is at its best when its members act not as reporters of information about the change but as sense-makers facilitating understanding for change recipients and helping them to identify (filter and distill) what is important in the information that is provided.[26] This distinction is instructive since it appears that change managers act more often as reporters than sense-makers. For example, based on the results of her survey of organizational change, Lewis[27] argues that implementers most often disseminate rather than solicit information during planned changes.

Getting the Word out or Getting Buy-in?

The federal agency example depicts the difference between what is referred to as "getting the word out" about a change (providing information) as opposed to "getting

TABLE 10.4 Communicating at Ford—Past and Present

Ford 2000 Communication Strategy[a]

In the mid-1990s, the Ford 2000 change program was launched, aimed at transforming a 90-year-old company facing decline through competition and needing to streamline operations and lower costs of production.

It used a variety of multimedia communication techniques to create in people a sense of urgency and to help instill the need to engage in the change. A cascade strategy of face-to-face meetings with top executives, then managers, then supervisors and employees was designed to bring the message to the front line. A weekly publication, *Grapevine*, was faxed throughout the organization to the top 3,000 global managers, who were expected to convey information to their staff. This was later replaced by an electronic publication called *Insight* that enabled more tailoring of information to specific areas of the organization. Videotapes of planned changes also were used frequently throughout Ford, including being fed worldwide to its 350 locations. Quarterly surveys of employees were conducted to gauge whether the Ford 2000 message was being received.

At the same time, two-way information sharing sessions were encouraged through "town-hall" face-to-face meetings and twice a year there was a global broadcast from Ford's headquarters in Dearborn, Michigan, during which employees had access to open phone lines to ask questions. Ford's in-house television network, FCN-TV, was used weekly, during which executives were available to respond to company interviewers about changes.

"We tried to mix news with what people wanted to know and what they needed to know," says Sara Tatchio, who was executive producer of FCN-TV. "Our job was to overcommunicate, share everything, and make employees part of the team."[b]

One challenge faced by Ford was how to communicate the change message to its culturally diverse workforce, including plants in Latin America and Asia where there was little available in terms of established communication media. A mixture of newspapers and teletext media was used with a focus on delivering the key themes of the change program.

"The idea was and continues to be communicate, communicate, and communicate, until you get sick and tired of communicating," says David Scott, Ford's recently retired vice president of public affairs. "That's when people are only beginning to get the message."[c]

A New CEO and a New Way of Communicating

In the aftermath of serious financial and quality issues that arose toward the end of CEO Jacques Nassar's reign at Ford, the company looked to its new leader, Bill Ford Jr., to reestablish the organization that his great-grandfather had started in 1903. Bill Ford's most outstanding quality as a leader is reportedly the way through which he communicates. Irvine Hockaday, a longtime Ford director, stated: "Bill is an excellent communicator and has a deep well of trust and affection from many of [the employees, dealers, union officials and suppliers]."[d]

Ford places his emphasis on communicating with investors worldwide to prove that Ford can progress as a company and continue to survive. Although he has been criticized for his lack of experience in executive positions, Bill Ford Jr. has reportedly won supporters over with his inspiring and dramatic speeches—one of his more developed skills.[e]

[a]Adapted from Harvard Management Communication Letter, 1999:9–11. Copyright © 1999 Harvard Business Review. Reproduced with permission of Harvard Business School Publishing.
[b]Harvard Management Communication Letter, 1999:10.
[c]Harvard Management Communication Letter, 1999:11.
[d]Taylor, 2003.
[e]Morris, 2002.

staff buy-in" (participation) to the change. Guaspari[28] takes up this issue and points out that many people rank communication as important to a change effort as it is the way "[t]o get the word out."[29] In his view it is arrogant to assume that management know what is right and what is needed to make a change successful; instead, what they need to do is to get people informed about what is going on. Newsletters, speeches, videos, and memos are harnessed to achieve this end.

Contrasted to this is a view of communication as obtaining "buy-in" from people in relation to the change—including getting information from them that will be useful in achieving the change, identifying what is important to them, and uncovering what they see as the costs and benefits of the change.[30] Allied with this is the process of identifying for people how they will benefit from it. Guaspari refers to this latter process as being able to provide a clear value proposition that will touch individual staff in a way that motivates them toward the change (see Table 10.5).

Getting people to "buy in" may depend upon what it is that they are buying into: whether they perceive it as favorable to them and whether the change has been adequately justified to them. Research indicates that justifying and "educating" people about the need for change relate positively to both whether they perceive the *outcome* of the change as fair (outcome fairness) and whether they perceive the *process* of achieving the change as fair (procedural fairness).[31] In Daly's study of 183 employees who worked for private-sector organizations that had relocated to Chicago, he found that managerial justification for the move was especially important when the move was not looked on favorably by staff (but justification was not as important where the move was viewed favorably).[32] He concludes that some managers might be tempted by his findings to avoid explaining change decisions to employees if they perceive that the change outcomes will be favorable to them. However, what Daly points out is that this situation clearly does not apply in relation to judgments about procedural fairness:

> employees are likely to expect an explanation for a change decision regardless of whether the outcomes are positive or negative. . . If those employees are not given an explanation for the event, they are likely to feel that the procedures used to make and implement the decision were unfair, leading in many cases to resentment against the decision process and the decision makers.[33]

TABLE 10.5 Change through Value Propositions

Guaspari[a] argues that it is important for companies to be able to identify the "value proposition" involved in a change; that is, how the change will achieve useful outcomes to the company, customers, and employees. He provides examples of this:

- "As a result of the new skills you'll learn in order to perform your job in the newly reengineered organization, you will have significantly increased your value internally and your marketability externally."
- "The work will be backbreaking. The pace will be relentless. You stand to make a ton of money."
- "We are making these changes to enable us to rewrite the rules in our industry, to improve by orders of magnitude the value we can create for our customers."[b]

[a]Guaspari, 1996.
[b]Guaspari, 1996:35.

TABLE 10.6 **Communicating Change**

"Communicating for Change"[a]	"A Dozen Tips"[b]	"Questions to Consider"[c]
1. Explain how change will unfold. • What is it? • How will it affect me? 2. Discuss the need for change. • The context. • Who decided on the need for change. • Why the status quo cannot continue. 3. Establish the business case for the change. • Describe the future. • Outline the benefits to the organization, work unit, specific individuals. 4. Determine the plan for change. • What are the new roles, expectations, responsibilities, relationships, skills, and performance measures? • How will the organization support individuals to help them adapt to and achieve these changes?	1. Specify the nature of the change. 2. Explain why. 3. Let staff know the scope of the change, including the good and the bad news. Continually repeat the purpose of the change and how it will occur. 4. Use graphics. 5. Make the communication two-way. 6. Target supervisors. 7. Support change with new learning. 8. Point to progress emanating from the change. 9. Don't limit communications to meetings and print. 10. Institutionalize information flow about the change. 11. Model the changes yourself.	1. Why . . . • The need for change? • This type of change? • Now? • It involves various parts of the organization? 2. What . . . • The change is? • Will be affected? • Needs to be prepared? • Will success look like? 3. Who . . . • Will be affected? • Will have input? • Will tell people about the change? • Should receive which specific change messages? 4. How . . . • Will the change proceed? • Can the change be facilitated? • Will people know if the change is successful? 5. When . . . • Will the changes take place? In what time frame? • Will messages be communicated about the change?

[a]Adapted from O'Neill, 1999:24.
[b]Adapted from Saunders, 1999.
[c]Adapted from Axley, 2000.

Daly's findings are broadly in line with other research on trust, which identifies how managers are more likely to be trusted by staff when they:

- Provide accurate information and feedback.
- Adequately explain the basis for their decisions.
- Use open communication, enabling exchange of ideas between them and their staff.[34]

In this regard, Table 10.6 outlines the types of questions to which staff are often looking for answers in confronting a new change.

FIGURE 10.2 Communication Strategy Continuum

Source: Clampitt et al., 2000:47–49.

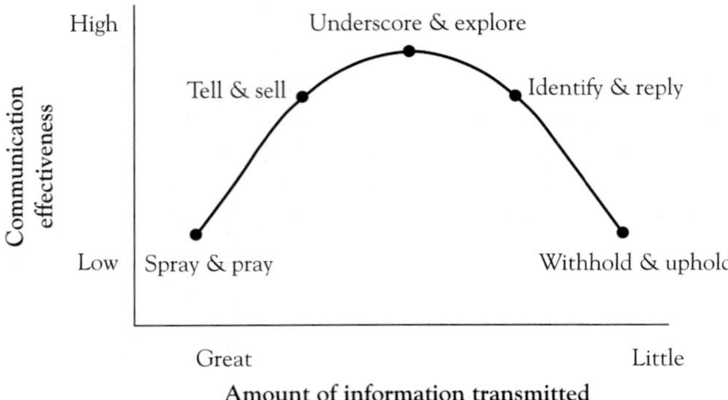

TABLE 10.7 Communication Strategies

Source: Adapted from Clampitt et al., 2000:47–49.

Strategy	Content of Strategy
Spray and pray	Employees are showered with a wide variety of information. More information is assumed to equal better communication. Managers pray that staff will pick up on what is needed to be done. The upside of this strategy is that staff are exposed to extensive company information. The downside is that staff are often unable to discern significant from insignificant information; understand what is happening but not why; and are overloaded with information.
Tell and sell	Information is provided to staff, but it is limited to core organizational issues. Management attempts to both inform staff about changes and sell them on why they are required. The downside of this approach is the potential for employee skepticism and cynicism since no meaningful dialogue is entered into with them; they become the passive recipients of the next wave of change proposals.
Underscore and explore	Fundamental issues remain the focus, but management engages employees in a dialogue about the change process and seeks to identify obstacles and misunderstandings that will need to be addressed.
Identify and reply	A defensive strategy, it is used to identify and respond to employee rumors and innuendos regarding changes and work practices. It is an attempt to help staff make sense out of issues that are confusing to them. The downside of this strategy is that it is reactive and assumes, usually inaccurately, that staff know the key strategic and organizational issues that need to be addressed.
Withhold and uphold	Information is withheld until it is absolutely necessary to release it, and management adopts a party line on issues that they uphold publicly. Information is not open and a bitter staff culture is likely to be the result.

Beyond Spray and Pray

As is evident in the above discussion, a variety of communication strategies exist, and Figure 10.2 and Table 10.7 document a number of these.

Clampitt et al.[35] argue that the *spray and pray* strategy (which characterizes the federal agency example) and the *withhold and uphold* strategy are least likely to be effective in achieving organizational performance, whereas the *underscore and explore* strategy "maximizes organizational potential by creatively synthesizing executives' initiatives and employee concerns."[36] They suggest that on occasion more than one strategy can be used concurrently. For example, in one organization, the spray and pray strategy, also known as the "communication clutter" strategy,[37] was used generally in "bombarding" staff with information on organizational performance; however, when it was faced with organizational changes such as downsizing and operational changes, a "withhold and uphold" strategy was adopted specifically on these issues. Executives adopted this latter strategy to reduce exposing employees to promises about the future that they were not able to deliver. The effect of this dual approach was not well received by staff: "Providing all the information employees could possibly want while avoiding the issues they cared about most bred discontent and mistrust."[38]

EXERCISE 10.2

Opening up Your Information Coffers?

Think back to a recent organizational change.

1. Did your organization have a strategy for announcing the change? (See Tables 10.6 and 10.9 for some examples.)
2. What information strategy did it use for conveying information during the change? Did it adopt one or more of the strategies outlined by Clampitt et al.[39] (see Figure 10.2)? Was the same strategy adopted consistently and for all members of the organization?
3. On a scale of 1 (= ineffective) to 5 (= very effective), how would you rate the overall communication strategy?
4. With 20/20 hindsight vision, what changes would you make?
5. How appropriate are your recommendations likely to be for future organizational changes? Will they depend upon the changes themselves?

Contingency Approaches to Communication Strategies

In Chapter 8 we came across the contingency perspective on organizational change. This perspective has been applied to understanding what type of change communication strategy should be used. There are two versions of this: one that adopts a view that the communication strategy is contingent on the *type* of change and another that maintains that it is contingent on the *stage* of a particular change. These views are outlined below.

Your Communicating Strategy Depends on the Type of Change

Stace and Dunphy[40] adopt a contingency view, pointing out that the communication strategy needs to be appropriate to the particular type of organizational change:

- *Developmental or incremental* transitions aim for widespread involvement and emphasize face-to-face communication as well as the use of change teams to identify initiatives and broaden commitment.
- *Task-focused* transitions endeavor to align behavior with top-management initiatives and are primarily top-down in nature with greater emphasis placed on formal communication processes such as e-mail broadcasts, memos, and so on.
- *Charismatic* transformations seek to gain emotional commitment to a new way of proceeding and entail more personalized forms of communication that enable top-down communication with at least some symbolic two-way communication media.
- *Turnarounds* occur at times of organizational crises and draw on formal, top-down modes of communication that endeavor to force people to comply with the new direction.[41]

They outline how each approach varies in terms of communicating the goals of the change process, who is to be involved in the change, the kinds of issues that will be addressed, the communication channels and directions (top-down, lateral, one-way/two-way) that will be used, and the balance of power that will need to be managed among relevant parties.[42]

Your Communication Strategy Depends on the Stage of the Change

Adopting a differing contingency focus, Reardon and Reardon[43] suggest that the communication strategy that is needed to produce successful organizational change differs depending on the *stage* of the change process. They identify four leadership styles, which entail different communication processes and strategies:

- In the *commanding* style, leaders are performance and results oriented and communication mainly entails directing people toward various tasks.
- In the *logical* style, leaders employ strategic actions as a result of discovering the range of alternatives available to them through analysis and reasoning. The communication style is one of explanation such as why a particular change is needed and what the long-term goals are.
- In the *inspirational* leadership style, the leader develops a vision of the future and seeks to encourage the cohesiveness of organizational members around the vision. Communication entails the creation of trust, getting people to mobilize around a particular change effort.
- In the *supportive* leadership style, the leader is concerned with creating consensus and an open working environment; involvement is the main communication process.

The authors argue that these four leadership styles, with their differing communication foci, need to be employed at different stages of a change process. They identify five main stages of change:

- In the *planning* stage, the focus is on identifying what needs to change and a combination of logical and inspirational leadership styles is most appropriate.
- In the *enabling* stage, in which people are selected and trained for the change process, a combination of logical, inspirational, and supportive styles is needed.

- In the *launching* stage, the change commences and entails a series of steps and goals that are best met by logical and commanding styles.
- In the *catalyzing* stage, inspirational and supportive leadership styles are needed to help motivate people to become engaged in, and assist with, the change effort.
- In the *maintaining* stage, people are encouraged to continue with a change effort even in the face of obstacles that confront them. Inspirational and supportive communication styles assist in this regard.

Reardon and Reardon[44] claim that their Leadership Style Inventory (LSI) questionnaire enables identification by individuals of their dominant communication and leadership styles. They acknowledge that one implication of their argument is that because different communication styles are required at different phases of a change, no one leader is likely to be appropriate to all of the change stages.

In our assessment, some words of caution are warranted in relation to this approach, given what we see as some inherent difficulties with it:

- The different stages of change are based on a linear logic rather than, for example, a circular or chaos view (see Chapter 2).
- Multiple changes may occur at one and the same time, which raises questions about the style change managers should invoke when they are involved in more than one concurrent change.
- Change phases themselves may be difficult to identify in practice—particularly knowing when one has been completed and the next one has commenced.
- The model is highly prescriptive in terms of what style of communication is needed and when. This prescription is presented as fact without specifying the evidence for this.
- A question remains about whether administering a one-off survey is an adequate means of establishing leadership and communication styles.

COMMUNICATION MEDIA

An important part of the communication process relates to the media that will be used. A number of differing media have already been referred to in passing and we now devote more attention to issues and arguments about their use. First, we discuss the "richness" of the various communication media. Second, we address who should do the communicating: senior managers or supervisors? Third, we look at various types of change management teams.

Media Richness

As already alluded to in the outline of Stace and Dunphy's contingency communication approaches, a range of standard organizational media can be used to communicate change. Lengel and Daft[45] refer to these in terms of their "richness"; that is, the extent to which the communication style entails interpersonal contact. Figure 10.3 presents what they term a "media richness hierarchy."

They argue that nonroutine, difficult management problems are best dealt with using media-rich communication sources such as face-to-face meetings; routine issues should

FIGURE 10.3 Media Richness Hierarchy

Source: Lengel and Daft, 1998:22.

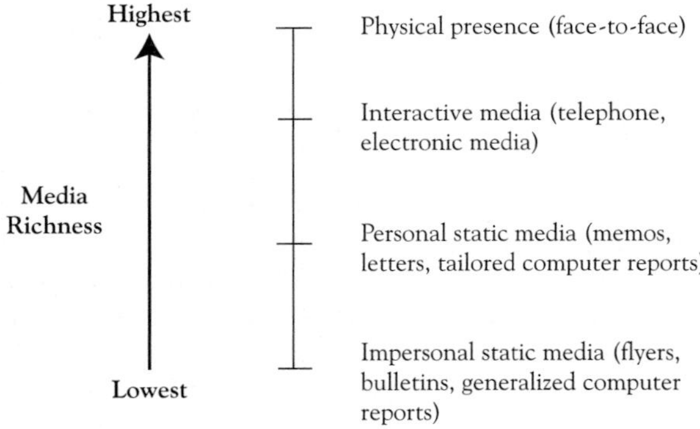

use "leaner" forms (more impersonal, static media such as e-mails, newsletters, etc.) so that they do not lead to a "data glut" and create "surplus meaning" beyond that really required to deal with the issue.[46] Using the same framework, Ashkenas et al.[47] maintain that whereas face-to-face communication is best suited to achieving the shaping of behaviors, at the other end of the spectrum impersonal static media are better suited to sharing information.

These strategies indicate that incremental changes, if they simply build upon current practices, may be relatively "routine" and require a differing communication medium to more radical, widespread changes that may challenge, change, or alter in nonroutine ways current organizational practices. Where the latter occurs in a large organization, the ability to deliver communication "richness" is more difficult because of the scale of the organization. In this case, in announcing an organizational change, the change manager will need to consider a variety of trade-offs (see Table 10.8).

Other change agents tend to adopt a particular communication medium for all situations. For example, Larkin and Larkin[48] state that face-to-face is best. They acknowledge that videos and publications may be useful for conveying technical information but maintain that both are limited in terms of their ability to communicate change itself. The problem with videos is that they will not be taken seriously by their intended audience; similarly, using satellite hookups for live speeches and questions and answers are likely to result in management platitudes and/or serve as an incendiary device for disaffected staff; company publications likewise come in for criticism in terms of often being incomprehensible and lacking in credibility. In practice, it is likely that a portfolio of communication strategies is likely to be needed, tailored to the particular change situation.

Who Is Responsible for Communicating the Change?

A common view is that CEOs should be personally involved in the communication of change in order to show their commitment to it. They should not delegate this activity to others in the organization. A differing position is that supervisors are the best conduit

TABLE 10.8 Issues in Announcing Major Organizational Changes

Source: Developed from Smeltzer, 1991:11–14.

Component	Issues
Verbal message	
• *Style*	• Different styles may be used; for example, a "telling," authoritarian style compared to a persuasive, "selling" style.
• *Coverage*	• A balance is needed between retaining confidential company information and knowledge that greater buy-in is likely when the rationale is understood
• *Source*	• The message source will influence how the message is perceived. The more power one has, the more autocratic one is able to be in announcing a change; however, generating trust is also important.
Channel	Trade-offs occur in terms of communication "richness"; that is, the extent to which announcements are made personally, one-on-one or face-to-face, compared to memo and other written forms. "Richer" forms lead to greater accuracy but take a great deal of time.
Timing	This entails two considerations. The first is the timing of the message: Is it "forced" onto employees only at a time desired by management? Is the timing such that it can lessen the emergence of rumors? The second is the amount of time it takes to announce the change: Elaborate announcements may be too time-consuming.

EXERCISE 10.3

Getting the (Change) News: What Media Work Best for You?

Imagine that you are an employee of a large organization about to go through a restructuring. Think about the following issues:

1. What information would you like?
2. From whom would you prefer to get this information? Why?
3. In what format would you prefer to get it: individually, in a group, other?
4. What would be the best source (media) for you to get this information—consider the range of media referred to in this chapter, from low to high media richness? What would be the worst way of getting this information? Why?
5. As a manager of change, in the future, how might you use these insights in terms of forming a media communications strategy?

since they are more likely to be trusted by staff.[49] Larkin and Larkin[50] adopt the latter position in their preference for face-to-face media. They maintain that such meetings should not occur in large groups but be more strategic, especially involving frontline supervisors. The latter will be in contact with frontline staff and be better able to communicate with them about the change.[51] To this end, they propose a two-stage strategy for briefing supervisors during a major change (see Table 10.9).

TABLE 10.9 Strategy for Briefing Supervisors about Major Change

Source: Adapted from Larkin and Larkin, 1996:102–103.

Round One: Seek Opinions and Recommendations of Supervisors		Round Two: Reporting Back to Supervisors	
What to Do	**Why**	**What to Do**	**Why**
A senior manager meets with 8 to 10 supervisors.	Meeting as a single manager rather than as a team of managers conveys to them that you are not afraid of their opinions.	The same manager meets with the same group of supervisors.	This ensures that they are dealing with a tangible representative of management.
Divide a single piece of paper into two columns, a not-willing-to-change column (you describe items in this column) and a willing-to-change column (they make recommendations here).	This makes it clear that you are not playing with them—by specifying what you are not going to change. This allows them to provide a forum for recommendations for you to take back to the senior change management team.	Hand out a single sheet of paper with the recommendations of the supervisors and senior management responses. Answer questions but avoid arguments and excessive defense.	You are conveying to them what has happened in regard to their recommendations—not trying to convince them about the relative merits of what has happened.
Ensure that they understand that final decisions rest with the senior change management team; make sure the meeting takes no longer than 90 minutes.	This helps to clarify that you are seeking their opinions and not obtaining their permission. Keeping the meeting relatively short is important for keeping it focused.	Distribute a booklet outlining the change and draw their attention to its major features.	This will assist them in identifying the face-to-face conversations they will need to have with their staff

John Barnett, when he became CEO of Molson Breweries, introduced widespread changes across its Canadian operations. He held this focus on the importance of the supervisor as a key link in the communication process. Initially he engaged in a variety of up-front meetings across the organization to explain the change. Subsequently, however, he concluded that it was more important that the change message be received by someone who was trusted by staff—such as their immediate supervisor.[52]

Tag Teams

For Duck,[53] rather than emphasizing the role of either the CEO or supervisors, an important part of managing change is "managing the conversation between the people leading the change effort and those who are expected to implement the strategies."

TABLE 10.10 Communicating Change with Tag Teams

Source: Olofson, 1999:42.

USAA is a financial services company that employs 18,500 people, has 3 million customers, and is based in San Antonio, Texas. In moving through an organizational change, it adopts a method of using "tag teams" to ensure that change occurs at the same time, minimizing disruption to existing operations. A core team works on a particular change but is joined by "tag teams" made up of volunteers from different parts of the organization who attend core team meetings and deliberations. They are charged with asking questions about how change initiatives will affect customer services and with conveying concerns and fears of their fellow colleagues in relation to the change. After the meetings, they return to their jobs and act as an informal conduit, conveying information back to their colleagues and work group.

She maintains that managers often fail to realize that they are sending out messages even when they are not formally communicating with change recipients. For example, a change task force may meet in isolation from change recipients to identify how to accomplish a change. They may feel that there is no need to communicate more widely in the organization during this period. She points out that this "virtually guarantees that the change effort will fail" since people will be aware that the change task force is meeting, rumors will circulate, and people will avoid buy-in to the final outcome.[54] She argues that one way of avoiding this situation is to use what she terms a transition management team to manage large-scale organizational change (see Table 10.10 for an example of this).

Among its responsibilities, the transition management team needs to stimulate conversation across functional, isolated parts of the organization as a way of shifting information across organizational boundaries. She maintains that "Early, open-ended conversations often result in the most productive outcomes";[55] the transition management team should avoid closing down conversations early on in the pursuit of quick results. The idea of change as managing conversations will be taken up in more detail in the following chapter.

Conclusion

In this chapter, we have seen that the concept of communications strategy is important to producing successful organizational change. The strategy needs to be oriented to issues such as what needs to be communicated, to whom, by whom, at what points in a change process, and what the intention is in communicating: whether to get buy-in or to get the word out. The various forms of media that can be drawn upon in communicating change also need to be considered. However, as outlined in Table 10.1, which issues outlined in this chapter receive focus in a communication strategy are most likely to depend on the images of managing change that are held. In the next chapter, we develop this idea by looking at the way these images also influence what communication skills are most likely to be utilized during an organizational change.

TABLE 10.11 Chapter Reflections for the Practicing Change Manager

- In what ways does your use of language reinforce power and gender differences within your organization? What effect do you think this has in terms of how your change message is received? What modifications would you make?
- Do you see yourself as being more of a reporter of information to staff rather than a sense-maker, helping them to understand change actions and distilling information and seeking input from them?
- To what extent do you focus on getting the word out, rather than seeking staff buy-in? Do you adopt different approaches depending upon the type of change? Do you "spray and pray" information or do you "underscore and explore"?
- Are you more comfortable adopting "rich" communication media (face-to-face meetings, etc.) or more "leaner" forms (e-mail, newsletters, etc.)? Do you adopt different forms depending upon the type of change? With which ones have you had the most success and why?
- What's your view: How central should CEOs and supervisors be in the change communication process? What are the key issues from your point of view?

Supplemental Reading

Beer, M., and Eisenstat, R. A. 2000. The silent killers of strategy implementation and learning. *Sloan Management Review* 41(4) (Summer):29–40.

Clampitt, P. G., DeKoch, R. J., and Cushman, T. 2000. A strategy for communicating about uncertainty. *Academy of Management Executive* 14(4):41–57.

Fox, S., and Amichai-Hamburger, Y. 2001. The power of emotional appeals in promoting organizational change programs. *Academy of Management Executive* 15(4):84–95.

Lengel, R. H., and Daft, R. L. 1998. The selection of communication media as an executive skill. *Academy of Management Executive* 11(3):225–32.

Lewis, L. K. 2000a. "Blindsided by that one" and "I saw that one coming": The relative anticipation and occurrence of communication problems and other problems in implementers' hindsight. *Journal of Applied Communication Research* 28(1):44–67.

Pettigrew, A. M., Woodman, R. W., and Cameron, K. S. 2001. Studying organizational change and development: Challenges for future research. *Academy of Management Journal* 44(4):697–713.

Reardon, K. K., and Reardon, K. J. 1999. "All that we can be": Leading the U.S. Army's gender integration effort. *Management Communication Quarterly* 12(4):600–17.

Saunders, R. M. 1999. Communicating change: A dozen tips from the experts. *Harvard Management Communication Letter* 20(8):2–3.

Smeltzer, L. R. 1991. An analysis of strategies for announcing organization-wide change. *Group & Organization Studies* 16(1):5–24.

Stace, D., and Dunphy, D. 2001. *Beyond the boundaries: Leading and recreating the successful enterprise*. 2nd ed. Sydney: McGraw-Hill.

Cheryl Ways, a 30-year-old IT professional, took a call at around 9 p.m. on October 15, 2001, from her husband, who rang complaining about her still being at work and asking her when she was coming home. Most of her co-workers had already left for the day, but she worked on for another half hour before shutting down her computer and heading out of Agilent Technology's empty building. What's remarkable about this story is that Cheryl had been told three weeks earlier that she was soon going to be laid off. So what was she doing, still working hard for the company putting in long hours just before being finally let go?[57]

Ways was one of 8,000 staff at Agilent Technology who were cut from the firm during 2001[58] and one of 2 million people throughout corporate America who lost their jobs that year.[59] A technology and electronics manufacturer and maker of measuring and testing equipment,[60] Agilent Technologies was spun off from Hewlett-Packard during 1999.[61] Hewlett-Packard was known for its "precept that workers will give their best if they're treated honestly and listened to"[62] and this philosophy was emulated by Agilent. Maintaining an open style of communication through e-mails, meetings, and other media, senior management openly acknowledged that downsizing went against the embedded HP way of caring for staff.[63]

Prior to commencing downsizing, Agilent tried other solutions to their business woes. Faced with a 23 percent decline in sales, a sharp fall in orders, and a falling share market, the company put in place a pay cut of 10 percent to save costs. This was seen as a temporary measure, with Agilent's CEO Ned Barnholt predicting a "slow and gradual recovery."[64] The company tried other cost-saving measures such as reducing external consultants and hirings and calling on staff to limit travel and other discretionary spending.[65] There weren't clear guidelines for how to do this or how much savings were needed. As Juan Yamuni, an international treasury analyst, said: "Top management was good about guiding you instead of getting a direct order."[66] It also tried to minimize layoffs by reducing variable pay such as stock options and bonuses.[67]

Despite laying off 8,000 workers (20 percent of the company) in 2001, the following year the company was listed at number 31 on *Fortune's 100 Best Companies to Work For*.[68] This suggests that, for the most part, it had retained the trust of its employees and displayed empathy toward their plight.[69] Staff knew what was going on through a "barrage of emails and face-to-face meetings with top management down; even the tired sound in the CEO's voice as he delivered news of mass layoffs."[70] Other forms of communication with staff included a newsletter call *InfoSparks* that came out twice a week, "coffee talks," brainstorming meetings, and public-address-system speeches. When staff were laid off, Barnholt decreed that there were to be no across-the-board cuts, that specific staff would be identified, and that they would be told directly by their managers. The 3,000 managers were given a daylong training session with an outplacement agency to assist them in delivering the bad news.[71]

According to Karen Scussel, vice president of HR Operations: "The main thing is to keep the communications open . . . That's how we're maintaining morale. The main employee morale issue is anxiety, and we've learned a lot about how to deal with it."[72] She also said, "We keep talking about what we believe in, what our core values are. We keep talking about hanging in there. Employees have come to believe in our purpose."[73] And it seems to have worked, at least for a while. Staff realized that management would prefer to continue with the HP values—but recognized the financial difficulties facing the company. As Cheryl Ways said about being let go, "I felt horrible that they had to do this"; working hard up to the end was her "gift" to her co-workers who remained, "to leave my job in the best possible way."[74]

For others, working hard right up to the end was for other reasons, such as trying to prove themselves in order to stop the decision to close down various parts of the company. For example, Dave Allen, the general manager of Agilent's semiconductor factory at Newark, California, announced in September 2002 that the division would be closed and shifted to Colorado and that most would lose their jobs within the year. Production at the plant initially dropped but then increased. Asked about this phenomenon, one of the workers at the factory, Mary Dominguez, said, "[M]aybe Fort Collins won't work. And maybe they'll let us stay."[75]

The early optimism of a gradual recovery seems to have faded, with the staff who remain feeling the pressure; as Steve Peterson, a global online manager, said, "We are just really working hard and are discouraged that things are not better."[76] In November 2002, it was announced that 2,500 more jobs would be eliminated and in February 2003 it was announced that a further 4,000 jobs would follow suit.[77] Whether Agilent's open communication style will be enough to retain people's motivation into the future is likely to be sorely tested under these conditions.

Questions

1. How would you describe Agilent Technology's communication process for dealing with downsizing?
2. Which approach—"getting the word out" or "getting buy-in"—best characterizes the communication process? Why?
3. Apply Stace and Dunphy's contingency approach to the case. What emerges from your analysis?
4. What assessments would you make of the media used by the company?
5. What are the limits to an open communication style when faced with ongoing rounds of downsizing? What else might be done by management to retain staff motivation?

TABLE 10.12 **Additional Case Studies**

Airbus: From Challenger to Leader
Subhadra, K., & Dutta, S. (2003) *ICFAI Knowledge Centre, India*
Louis V. Gerstner Jr.—The Man Who Turned IBM Around
Gupta, V., & Prashanth, K. (2003) *ICFAI Knowledge Centre, India*
Redesigning Nissan (A): Carlos Ghosn takes Charge
Manzoni, J-F; Hughes, K., & Barsoux, J-L. (2001) *INSEAD, Fountainbleau*

Bibliography

Anastasiou, S. 1998. Communicating change. *New Zealand Management* 45(9) (October):86.

Anonymous. 2000. Agilent will cut jobs and move operations amid restructuring. *The Wall Street Journal* 236(31) (15 August):A18.

Anonymous. 2001. Business brief—Agilent Technologies Inc.: Employees' pay is cut 10% in effort to avoid layoffs. *The Wall Street Journal* 237(68) (April 6):B5.

Anonymous. 2003. Technology brief—Agilent Technologies Inc.: Loss is posted for 1st quarter; more job cuts are announced. *The Wall Street Journal*, February 24:B4.

Ashkenas, R., Ulrich, D., Jick, T., and Kerr, S. 1995. *The boundaryless organization: Breaking the chains of organizational structure*. San Francisco: Jossey-Bass.

Axley, S. R. 2000. Communicating change: Questions to consider. *Industrial Management* 42(4):18–22.

Barrett, F. J., Thomas, G. F., and Hocevar, S. P. 1995. The central role of discourse in large-scale change: A social construction perspective. *Journal of Applied Behavioral Science* 31(3):352–72.

Beer, M., and Eisenstat, R. A. 2000. The silent killers of strategy implementation and learning. *Sloan Management Review* 41(4) (Summer):29–40.

Berner, R., and Coy, P. 2002. Keeping a lid on unemployment. *BusinessWeek*, no. 3774 (March 18):28.

Clampitt, P. G., DeKoch, R. J., and Cushman, T. 2000. A strategy for communicating about uncertainty. *Academy of Management Executive* 14(4):41–57.

Cullen, L. T., Berestein, L., Coady, E., Parker, C., Roston, E., and Sattley, M. 2002. Where did everyone go? *Time* 160(21) (November 18):64–66.

Daly, J. P. 1995. Explaining changes to employees: The influence of justifications and change outcomes on employees' fairness judgments. *Journal of Applied Behavioral Science* 31(4):415–28.

Duck, J. D. 1993. Managing change: The art of balancing. *Harvard Business Review* 71(6):109–18.

Fox, S., and Amichai-Hamburger, Y. 2001. The power of emotional appeals in promoting organizational change programs. *Academy of Management Executive* 15(4):84–95.

Gayeski, D. M., and Majka, J. 1996. Untangling communication chaos: A communicator's conundrum for coping with change in the coming century. *Communication World* (CW Special Supplement) 13(7):22–26.

Geigle, S. L., and Bailey, M. R. 2001. When communication fails: An analysis of the influence of communication practices during change. Paper presented at Western Academy of Management Conference, Sun Valley, Idaho, April 5–7.

Guaspari, J. 1996. If you want your people to buy-in to change, you have to sell them. Yes, sell them. *Across the Board* 33(5) (May):32–36.

Harvard Management Communication Letter. 1999. If it ain't broke, fix it anyway: Communicating to create change at Ford. *Harvard Management Communication Letter* 2(5):9–11.

Hutt, M. D., Walker, B. A., and Frankwick, G. L. 1995. Hurdle the cross-functional barriers to strategic change. *Sloan Management Review* 36(3) (Spring):22–30.

Johnson, J. D. 1990. Effects of communicative factors on participation in innovations. *Journal of Business Communication* 27(1) (Winter):7–22.

Larkin, T. J., and Larkin, S. 1996. Reaching and changing frontline employees. *Harvard Business Review* 74(3):95–104.

Lengel, R. H., and Daft, R. L. 1998. The selection of communication media as an executive skill. *Academy of Management Executive* 11(3):225–32.

Lewis, L. K. 1999. Disseminating information and soliciting input during planned organizational change: Implementers' targets, sources, and channels for communicating. *Management Communication Quarterly* 13(1):43–75.

Lewis, L. K. 2000a. "Blindsided by that one" and "I saw that one coming": The relative anticipation and occurrence of communication problems and other problems in implementers' hindsight. *Journal of Applied Communication Research* 28(1):44–67.

Lewis, L. K. 2000b. Communicating change: Four cases of quality programs. *Journal of Business Communication* 37(2):128–55.

McGarvey, R. 2002. Leading in lean times: Tips and tricks to keeping a workforce motivated. *Electronic Business* 28(12) (December):60–63.

Morris, B. 2002. Can Ford save Ford? *Fortune* 146(10) (November 18):38–47.

Nelson, T., and Coxhead, H. 1997. Increasing the probability of re-engineering/culture change success through effective internal communication. *Strategic Change* 6(1):29–48.

Olofson, C. 1999. Make change, minimize distractions: What's your problem? *Fast Company* 42(21) (January):42.

O'Neill, M. 1999. Communicating for change. *CMA Management* 73(5) (June):23–24.

Price Waterhouse Change Integration Team. 1996. *The paradox principles: How high-performance companies manage chaos, complexity, and contradiction to achieve superior results*. Burr Ridge, IL: Richard D. Irwin.

Reardon, K. K., and Reardon, K. J. 1999. "All that we can be": Leading the U.S. Army's gender integration effort. *Management Communication Quarterly* 12(4):600–17.

Roth, D. 2002. How to cut pay, lay off 8,000 people, and still have workers who love you. *Fortune* 145(3) (February 4):40–44.

Saunders, R. M. 1999. Communicating change: A dozen tips from the experts. *Harvard Management Communication Letter* 20(8):2–3.

Smeltzer, L. R. 1991. An analysis of strategies for announcing organization-wide change. *Group & Organization Studies* 16(1):5–24.

Smith, D. 1998. Invigorating change initiatives. *Management Review* 87(5) (May):43–48.

Stace, D., and Dunphy, D. 2001. *Beyond the boundaries: Leading and recreating the successful enterprise*. 2nd ed. Sydney: McGraw-Hill.

Taffinder, P. 1998. *Big change: A route-map for corporate transformation*. Chichester: John Wiley & Sons Ltd.

Tannen, D. 1995. The power of talk: Who gets heard and why. *Harvard Business Review* 73(5):138–48.

Taylor, A., III. 2003. Getting Ford in gear. *Fortune* 147(9) (May 12):103.

Whitener, E. M., Brodt, S., Korsgaard, M. A., and Wermer, J. M. 1998. Managers as initiators of trust: An exchange relationship framework for understanding managerial trustworthy behavior. *Academy of Management Review* 23(3):513–30.

Williams, M. 2001. Agilent reports a hefty loss, plans job cuts. *The Wall Street Journal* 238(36) (August 21):A3.

Notes

1. Lewis, 2000a:45–46.
2. Hutt, Walker, and Frankwick, 1995:23.
3. Whitener et al., 1998:517.
4. Johnson, 1990:20.
5. Barrett and Luedecke, 1996.
6. Smith, 1998:46.
7. Smeltzer, 1991:18.
8. Larkin and Larkin, 1996:95.
9. Beer and Eisenstat, 2002:29–32.
10. Lewis, 2000b:63.
11. Gayeski and Majka, 1996.
12. Price Waterhouse Change Integration Team, 1996:13.
13. Nelson and Coxhead, 1997:39.
14. Nelson and Coxhead, 1997:39–42.
15. Nelson and Coxhead, 1997:42–45.
16. Tannen, 1995:141–42.
17. Tannen, 1995:140.
18. Tannen, 1995:142.
19. Tannen, 1995:141–42.
20. Tannen, 1995:143–47.
21. Tannen, 1995.
22. Fox and Amichai-Hamburger, 2001:85.
23. Fox and Amichai-Hamburger, 2001:86.
24. Geigle and Bailey, 2001.
25. Overhold, 2001.
26. Geigle and Bailey, 2001.
27. Lewis, 1999:65.
28. Guaspari, 1996. Reproduced with permission of the publisher.
29. Guaspari, 1996:36.
30. Guaspari, 1996:36.
31. Daly, 1995:424. Copyright © 1995 Sage Publications. Reproduced with permission of the publisher.
32. Daly, 1995:422–23.
33. Daly, 1995:426.
34. Whitener et al., 1998:517.

35. Clampitt et al., 2000:47. This and subsequent quotes reproduced with permission of Academy of Management Executive through Copyright Clearance Center.
36. Clampitt et al., 2000:49.
37. Anastasiou, 1998:86.
38. Clampitt et al., 2000:52.
39. Clampitt et al., 2000.
40. Stace and Dunphy, 2001.
41. Stace and Dunphy, 2001:190–91.
42. Stace and Dunphy, 2001:157.
43. Reardon and Reardon, 1999.
44. Reardon and Reardon, 1999:602.
45. Lengel and Daft, 1998:226.
46. Lengel and Daft, 1998:227–29.
47. Ashkenas et al., 1995:76.
48. Larkin and Larkin, 1996:97–101.
49. Lewis, 1999:50.
50. Larkin and Larkin, 1996.
51. Larkin and Larkin, 1996:97–101.
52. Story as told by Taffinder, 1998:170.
53. Duck, 1993:110.
54. Duck, 1993:110–11.
55. Duck, 1993:117.
56. This case was adapted and developed from a number of sources.
57. Roth, 2002:41.
58. McGarvey, 2002:62.
59. Roth, 2002:41.
60. Anonymous, 2003.
61. Roth, 2002:43.
62. Roth, 2002:43.
63. McGarvey, 2002:62.
64. Williams, 2001.
65. Anonymous, 2001.
66. Roth, 2002:43.
67. Berner, 2002.
68. Cullen et al., 2003.
69. Roth, 2002:40.
70. Roth, 2002:42.
71. Roth, 2002:44.
72. McGarvey, 2002:62.
73. McGarvey, 2002:62.
74. Roth, 2002:42.
75. Roth, 2002:44.
76. Cullen et al., 2003.
77. Anonymous, 2003.

Skills for Communicating Change

Learning objectives

On completion of this chapter you should be able to:

- Identify communication skills appropriate to different images of managing change.
- Appreciate the breadth of skills needed as a change manager in communicating change.
- Understand the role of toxic handlers in the change process.
- Assess the different change conversations needed in a change process.
- Adapt your change language to ensure that it is coherent and aligned with desired changes.
- Make your change communication strategies relevant to both internal and external stakeholders.

Collins[1] argues that much of the change communication literature is unitarist in its assumptions; that is, it assumes that different interests of managers and staff can be resolved in a change process. This is an assumption best associated with both the *director* and *coach* images of managing change. From a unitarist perspective, breakdowns occur when communication processes are inadequate, when meanings have been misunderstood, or when inappropriate values are held. The assumption is that good skills in communicating change can resolve such problems.

Collins compares this position to a political, pluralist view of the change process in which outcomes are less the result of well-functioning communication skills and strategies and more the result of negotiation of differing individuals and groups pursuing often divergent paths and aims,[2] a position that draws on the *navigator* and *interpreter* images of managing change. This position assumes that some changes may cut across different interests within an organization in such a way that change managers need to recognize that no matter how well developed their change communication skills are, they will not necessarily be enough to resolve deep underlying differences within an organization or among external stakeholders who hold fundamentally different

TABLE 11.1 Relationship of Change Images to Communication Skills

Image of Managing Change	Purpose of Communication	Key Communication Skills
Director	The purpose is to ensure people understand what is going to happen and what is required of them, by providing them with answers to the why, what, who, how, and when questions—including the "value-proposition" involved in the change. Where a contingency perspective is involved, this may mean modifying the type of information provided and leadership style to make these "fit" the type of change involved and the level in the organization at which the change message is pitched. Communication strategies need to ensure that there is no message overload (communicating too much through "spray and pray" techniques) or message distortion (incorrect message sent out).	Sending of clear, unambiguous messages about the need for change Management of external stakeholders—where necessary, use of excuses, justifications, statements of regret, dissociation, disclaimers, and so on
Navigator	This is similar to *director* image in terms of outlining the nature of the change to staff but pay attention to identifying alternative interests (including gender differences) and power relationships and actions that may disrupt the proposed change. This enables either these to be dealt with or the change itself replotted in order to produce the best change outcomes possible in the current situation. "Tell and sell" communication techniques are used to try to win people over to the change.	Critical listening skills Persuasion accounts Negotiation Selling of change, upward and downward Appeal through deals
Caretaker	The focus is on letting people know about the "why" of change; that is, the inevitability of the changes and how best to cope or survive them. "Identify and reply" (reactive) communication strategy is used.	Discriminative and therapeutic listening skills
Coach	The focus is on ensuring people share similar values and are aware of what actions are appropriate to these values. *Coaches* model consistency in actions and words. Whereas the focus of the *director* is more on "getting the word out" about the change, the focus of the *coach* is "getting buy-in" to the change through shared values and the use of "positive emotions." Team-based rather than top-down, CEO-led communication styles are most favored. "Underscore and explore" interactions are used to engage in dialogue about the change.	Appreciative listening skills Toxic handling Dialogue Community building Appeals through ideals Attention to emotions

TABLE 11.1 Relationship of Change Images to Communication Skills—*(concluded)*

Interpreter	*Interpreters* provide staff with a sense of "what is going on" through story telling, metaphors, and so forth. *Interpreters* are aware of the multiple *sense-making* that goes on in organizations from different groups about any proposed change. Their focus is on *sense-giving* to different groupings across the organization (and outside); that is, presenting the most persuasive account of the change to ensure that as many people as possible share common understandings of the change. They recognize that not all will buy in to the story of change, but the aim is to provide the most dominant account. "Rich" communication media are most favored.	Storytelling, connecting the dots Engaging in change conversations, including initiative, understanding, performance, and closure conversations Aligning of discourse to type of change desired—ensuring imagery used is consistent with change type being presented
Nurturer	The *nurturer* image leads change managers to reinforce the view that processes cannot always be predicted and that often outcomes will occur that are innovative and creative for an organization even though few people could have anticipated what these might be prior to their occurring.	Discriminative and therapeutic listening skills

worldviews. They will, however, endeavor to be highly influential among these different world views.

Where changes are inevitable, as in the *caretaker* image, or the result of unpredictable chaotic influences such as with the *nurturer* image, then the change skills drawn upon are those that are likely to involve discriminative and therapeutic listening skills, in particular listening out for when it is necessary to explain why changes are occurring, rather than justifying the need for the change. Table 11.1 outlines in more detail the types of communication skills associated with these six images of managing change.

In what follows, we explore the range of communication skills associated with these images and the reader is invited to refer back to Table 11.1 as a guide for what follows in this chapter, providing an indication of which communication skills particular images are most likely to focus on. We commence by discussing listening and storytelling as communication skills, the skills involved in selling ideas upward in an organization, and the skills involved in being a "toxic handler" of change.

Second, we focus on the concept of change conversations, outlining the different types of change conversations needed in different phases of a change process. We alert change managers to how they may send out contradictory messages to staff when they fail to align their language to their desired change. More generally, we look at the need to create a common change language when the change involves different groups.

Finally, we raise an often-neglected issue in the change literature, which is the need to focus on skills related to communicating change with the outside world. Specifically, we discuss how to sell internal organizational changes to external stakeholders; we then conclude with crisis management as a specific type of change management and discuss skills associated with repairing corporate reputation with external stakeholders.

COMMUNICATION SKILLS FOR ENGAGING OTHERS IN THE CHANGE PROCESS

In this section, we address four skills involved in engaging others in a change process: listening, storytelling, upward selling, and toxic handling.

Listening as a Communication Skill

If communication about change entails a dialogue, then inevitably listening becomes a central communication skill. Wolvin and Coakley[3] outline five views on listening, which are set out in Table 11.2.

Gerard and Teurfs[4] argue that it is through listening, dialogue, and community building that change occurs. Transformation ensues when a collaborative culture emerges based on shared meaning and mutual understanding of thoughts and feelings. This involves skills such as:

- *Suspending judgment* (in order to produce an open atmosphere of trust).
- *Identifying assumptions* (to reveal misunderstandings).
- *Listening* (to enable learning).
- *Inquiring and reflecting* (in order for new collective understandings to emerge).[5]

They claim that creating community through dialogue leads to three types of cultural transformations: *behavioral transformation* (involving new norms and behaviors), *experiential transformation* (whereby groups learn how community might be achieved), and *attitudinal transformation* (in which individualism is replaced by collaboration).[6]

On a critical note, this approach is clearly optimistic in terms of organizational communities being able to overcome underlying power, conflict, and other differences. It is also silent in relation to how strategic change is produced through this version of communicating change: The aim seems to be the development of communities, but, at a corporate level, these communities may lack broader strategic focus and direction.

Telling Stories

One underrecognized change management communication skill is storytelling. People tell stories in conversations "to keep the organization from repeating historically bad choices and to invite the repetition of past successes."[7] In studying a U.S. firm called "Gold" consisting of 300 employees and operating in a number of states, David Boje wrote that the CEO told a series of stories in a strategic planning session with his vice presidents in order to enact with them a view of what changes were needed in the organization. In his analysis of a particular story, Boje says of the CEO:

> His ability to enact a performance that coaxes his executives to identify with his relevant experiences in analogous situations gives his scenario for change a good deal of credibility. The executives are beginning to buy into the future scenario. To implement

TABLE 11.2 Listening as a Change Management Skill

Source: Adapted from Wolvin and Coakley, 1996:151–54.

Wolvin and Coakley suggest that there are five different modes of listening that good communicators can become skilled in recognizing and using.

Type of Listening	Usage	Example
Discriminative listening	Determining significance of auditory/visual messages	In a meeting but selecting the messages that are listened to so that another activity, such as answering the phone, also can be done
Comprehensive listening	Striving to understand message for later recall/use	Recalling the names of new colleagues
Therapeutic listening	Helping others	Listening to problems that staff may have and offering counsel
Critical listening	Evaluating message	Listening to a business issue, interpreting it, and then analyzing/making a judgment
Appreciative listening	Involving discriminative and comprehensive listening	Making light of a message and gaining amusement or pleasure from it, for example, a joke

> this change, several divisions will be put on the block so Gold can focus on its main business. . . There are elements of reform, bloodletting (firings), and death (selling off divisions) as the need pattern becomes envisioned in this story.[8]

One implication of this argument is that effective change managers are likely to be effective storytellers. Curiously, while "storytelling can be a useful tool for managers trying to cope with rapid change,"[9] Boje points out that this is a change management skill that receives little attention or management training.[10]

Selling Change Upward

New ideas for change can be pushed *upward* through the organization from staff and various modes of argument (intangible media) can be used to gain managerial attention in support of change ideas. Dutton et al.[11] refer to these change skills as the linguistic and persuasive routines associated with "issue selling"; that is, the processes whereby individuals seek to present to senior managers specific changes that they would like to see occur. The concept of "issue selling" is based on a view of organizations as

> a cacophony of complementary and completing change efforts, with managers at all levels joining the fray and pushing for issues of particular importance to themselves. Indeed, it may be most accurate to portray an organization as a pluralistic marketplace of ideas in which issues are "sold" via the persuasive efforts of managers and "bought" by top managers to set the firm's strategic direction.[12]

Dutton et al.[13] studied idea "selling" in a large, northeastern rural hospital. One of their findings relates to how ideas were packaged. They divide packaging into two groups. The first relates to how the ideas are *presented*. Three key tactics are:

- Linking the idea to the logic of the business plan.
- Raising the proposal continuously.
- Packaging the issue incrementally so that the size of the change does not appear to be too large.

The second relates to what they termed *bundling*, that is, linking it to other ideas and issues. This is achieved by tying the issue to goals that are highly valued such as:

- Profitability
- Market share
- Organizational image
- Concerns of key stakeholders

Part of this involves identifying to whom issues are sold, who is targeted for involvement in the selling, and the selling process itself: formality, preparation, and timing.[14] While this is not yet central to the change communication literature, these authors have pinpointed a hitherto neglected, but important, skill for communicating organizational change.

EXERCISE 11.1

Sales Pitch!

Dutton et al.[15] outline a range of issues associated with "selling upwards" change ideas in organizations. Think about something that you would like to see changed in your organization. Your task is to figure out how to sell this issue upward to senior management.

1. What idea *presentation* techniques will you use:
   - Link it to the business plan?
   - Raise the proposal continuously?
   - Package the issue incrementally?
2. What *bundling* techniques will you use, for example:
   - Tie it to profitability?
   - Tie it to market share or organizational image?
   - Tie it to concerns of key stakeholders?
   - Tie it to other issues, such as . . . ?
3. What other *presentation and bundling* arguments have worked well for you in the past? Which new ones might you try?
4. What barriers do you face in using these techniques? How might these be overcome?
5. Now . . . go ahead and try it!

Toxic Handlers

Frost and Robinson[16] have coined the term "toxic handlers" to describe people whose skills extend to helping others deal with the organizational pain that can be associated with change. Change can be toxic to staff through either unrealistic expectations or targets, internal competition, or belligerent and angry bosses, all of which can result in "confusion, fear, and anguish among employees."[17] Toxic handlers "take the heat" and "voluntarily shoulder[] the sadness, frustration, and anger"[18] present within organizations. Table 11.3 outlines an example of a toxic handler and five ways in which toxic handlers work.

Toxic handlers act as sponges, soaking up the ill-effects of change processes and acting as intermediaries between staff and toxic organizational policies and bosses. The irony is, of course, that toxic handlers themselves can become burned out by their pain-relieving activities, which they engage in usually on top of their regular job. A second irony is that where toxic handlers emerge, this may stop organizations—and their managers—from addressing the roots of organizational change "pain"—and the need for toxic handlers in the first place.

EXERCISE 11.2

Handling Your Own Toxic Waste

1. Read Table 11.3 about toxic handlers.
2. Have you ever been or observed a toxic handler? If so:
   - How did this emerge?
   - How long did it last?
   - What were your/their greatest challenges?
   - How did you/they manage the burnout factor?
3. Have you ever been helped by a toxic handler? If so:
   - How did this emerge?
   - How long did it last?
   - How helpful were they?
   - What was the end result?
4. Compare and contrast your experiences with others. What common features emerge?

CHANGE CONVERSATION SKILLS

This section commences with the idea that change entails the use of different change conversations at different phases of a change. We then explore a second, related view that emphases the importance of linguistic coherence in different conversation phases. Third, we outline why there is a need for change managers to align their use of change language with the type of change that they are trying to produce. Fourth, we discuss the importance of creating a shared change language among different parties involved in the change.

TABLE 11.3 Toxic Handlers

Frost and Robinson[a] tell the following story:

Michael, a senior project manager in a public utility, worked with a group of 24 engineers. A new CEO was appointed whose style included making fun of people, openly criticizing them, and generally walking all over them. People became scared, felt betrayed, some were hospitalized with ulcers, and productivity declined rapidly as people contemplated leaving. Michael intervened in the situation for a period of three years until the CEO was finally fired by the board. He allowed his colleagues to express their frustrations to him in private, was often the one who spoke up in public when the CEO picked on someone, and helped the CEO by translating policies and actions and trying to present them as being not as bad as they appeared. After the CEO departed, Michael's colleagues informed him that a major reason why they had stayed on was the compassionate and smoothing role that he adopted on their behalf.

Frost and Robinson[b] outline five ways that *toxic handlers* operate:

- *Listening empathetically*, such as by cooling people down when they are angry and frustrated.
- *Suggesting solutions*, by helping to solve problems and providing advice about how to proceed.
- *Working behind the scenes*, easing pain, for example, by helping to get disaffected staff transferred to more congenial departments.
- *Carrying the confidences of others*, like priests, listening to and keeping secret individuals' fears and anguish.
- *Reframing difficult messages*, by presenting difficult messages in a language that makes them more manageable and palatable.

[a]Frost and Robinson, 1999:97–98.
[b]Frost and Robinson, 1999:99–100.

Talking in Stages

Ford and Ford[19] do not view communication as a tool for producing intentional organizational change; rather, and in line with the introduction to this chapter, it is within and through communication that change occurs. This means that "the management of change can be understood to be the management of conversations."[20] They draw upon *speech act theory* to argue that change can be thought of as occurring through four types of change conversations.[21] *Initiative conversations* bring attention to the need for change, whether reactive or proactive. This may take the form of:

- *An assertion* ("We have to bring the finances under control.").
- *A request* ("Can your business unit be restructured to achieve greater operating efficiencies?").
- *A declaration* ("We are going to increase our market share.").

Conversations for understanding provide an opportunity for people to gain a greater appreciation of the change issues and problems that need to be addressed. This conversation has three elements to it:

- It specifies the "*conditions of satisfaction*"[22] that are needed in order for the change to be deemed successful (e.g., "We need to ensure that there are no more than two customer complaints per thousand units produced.").
- It *enables participation* and involvement by those affected by the change.
- It *confirms the interpretations* that decision makers place on the change and enables confirmation and sharing of meanings and understandings.[23]

Conversations for performance focus on producing the actual change required. This is the action stage in which:

- *Promises* are made.
- *Obligations* are entered into.
- *Accountabilities* are established.
- *Deadlines* are set.[24]

Conversations for closure signal the completion of the change and may involve:

- *Acknowledgments*
- *Celebrations*
- *Rewards*

This conversation also facilitates the movement of people onto new projects and initiatives.[25] Breakdowns in change and the conversation process can occur when:[26]

- Initiative conversations are held with people who are not in a position to proceed with the change.
- There is a lack of shared understandings about the intended changes and the expectations for the "conditions of satisfaction."
- Shared understandings occur, but performance conversations are not entered into so that people do not know who is accountable for specific actions.
- Requests for action and performance are not rigorous and fail to specify intentions regarding results and deadlines.
- Closure conversations do not happen and people are left with the feeling that they are still involved with the change, often at the same time as being asked to move on to a new change process.

Ford and Ford recognize that not all change conversations occur in a linear manner; some stages may be skipped along the way.[27] The work of these authors is important in reinforcing the idea that change managers need skills and training in managing change conversations. At the same time, the authors acknowledge that their ideas are "speculative, not definitive."[28] We suggest that there are a number of issues to consider for practicing change managers:

- Where managers are engaged in multiple change processes, there will be issues relating to how smoothly they are able to transition themselves among different conversations.
- The stages of the conversations may be open to multiple interpretations among participants: Where managers assume that some conversations are complete and that it is appropriate to move on to another stage in the change conversations, others may have differing views.
- It is not clear that all managers are able to be trained or able to exhibit all conversation "skills" successfully: Some may have greater affinity, for example, with initiative conversations rather than performance conversations, and so forth.
- Change managers will need to confront the notion of power: The willingness of all participants to be involved meaningfully in each of the four change conversations

may be affected by significant power imbalances. This could mean, for example, that understandings may need to be not so much shared as enforced.

Talking Coherently

Sillince[29] supports the view that the use of language and change conversations is important. His focus is on the *coherence* of change conversations in achieving successful organizational transformation. Drawing on linguistic theory and political science theory, he outlines four dominant language forms used to convey organizational change conversations:

- *Ideals* (which express preferences).
- *Appeals* (which seek support).
- *Rules* (which seek to direct the behavior of individuals).
- *Deals* (which serve as a form of bargaining and exchange).[30]

Overreliance on one or another of these forms—such as a focus on deals rather than on ideals—can lead to problems such as the development of an individualist culture.[31] He argues "that motivating change during the early stage of organizational change requires the communication of appeals for support and statements of goals or ideals, and that the later stage of directing organizational change requires the communication of rules and the negotiation of deals."[32] He demonstrates this by focusing on the restructuring that occurred at AT&T during the 1970s and 1980s. His analysis is that despite the fact that there was no planned communication process, a logical sequence of language forms can be detected

> moving from attacking current ideals in 1973 (corresponding to the "unfreezing" stage in Lewin 1951), to supporting new ideals in 1973–1978, to attacking current rules or the lack of rules in 1979–1980, and increasingly supporting new ideals and new rules after 1981 (the "change" stage in Lewin 1951). The few deals referred to occur after 1981. Appeals tend to be promises and warning before change takes place and requests for support and exhortations to action during and after change.[33]

In comparing the successful changes at AT&T to the relatively unsuccessful changes at Chrysler, he notes that the former had a linguistic coherence that was lacking in the latter. He argues that, although this does not constitute definitive evidence, it does indicate that in successful organizational change there is found a linguistic coherence in the use of different forms of language during different parts of the change.[34] See Table 11.4 for an example of how IBM is attempting to manage linguistic coherence around moving high-cost programming jobs offshore.

Sillince's analysis operates at a macro level, characterizing large periods of time as fitting into different change phases. What remains intriguing is the way he has retained the sequential Lewinian model of change (unfreezing–changing–refreezing) as underpinning the way change occurs. However, as pointed out earlier in this book, if change is seen as chaotic or as nonsequential in the stages through which it passes, then this raises questions about whether change is as "orderly" as he portrays it—and whether language forms do progress through various stages that are coherent. Nevertheless, his work does alert managers to the differing linguistic modes open to them through which

TABLE 11.4 IBM's Change Language Script for "Offshoring" Jobs

Source: Adapted from Bulkeley, 2004. Reprinted with permission of the *Wall Street Journal*.

Internal IBM documents reported in *The Wall Street Journal* in January 2004 suggest that IBM is planning to move high-cost programming jobs offshore to countries such as Brazil, India, and China where labor costs are lower. For example, rather than paying $56 per hour in the United States, the documents indicate that a comparable programming job would cost only $12.50 per hour in China. The documents indicate that IBM is aware that this "offshoring" process is a sensitive change issue and provides managers with a draft change language "script" for how to present the information to affected employees.

One memo is reported to tell managers to ensure that any written communication to these employees is first "sanitized" by communications and human resources staff. It says: "Do not be transparent regarding the purpose/intent" and indicates that managers should not use terms such as "onshore" and "offshore."

Part of the "suggested script" for informing local staff that their jobs are being moved offshore is to say that "this is not a resource action"—an IBM euphemism for being laid off—and that the company will endeavor to find them jobs elsewhere. The draft change script also proposes that the news be conveyed to staff by saying: "This action is a statement about the rate and pace of change in this demanding industry. . . It is in no way a comment on the excellent work you have done over the years." and "For people whose jobs are affected by this consolidation, I understand this is difficult news."

they can communicate with staff during change. It points out to them the possibility of swapping from one linguistic mode to another when one is seen as not achieving the desired effect.

Aligning Your Language with the Desired Change

Marshak[35] maintains that one reason why change fails is because the imagery and metaphors that managers use are out of sync with the type of change that they desire. This leads to confusion among staff about what is really required. By way of example, he refers to a situation in which a large corporation needed to fundamentally reposition itself in its business because of declining access to government contracts that were the mainstay of the company. Unfortunately, when conveying this need for change to his middle managers, the CEO outlined it to them in terms of the need to build upon the company's past successes as a way of developing the company into the future. The result was that, rather than fundamentally shifting the company into new directions, middle managers based their actions on developing past practices. In this situation, the imagery of "developing" was out of sync with the "transformational" change that was required.[36]

To avoid such problems, Marshak urges managers to ensure that their language is aligned to the type of change they require. He identifies four different images of change and the language appropriate to each type:[37]

- *Machine imagery of change.* This is based on a "fix and maintain" view that depicts the organization as being "broken" and the change is designed to "fix" the problem. The change agent is depicted as a repairperson and words such as *repair*, *adjust*, and *correct* are aligned to this type of change.
- *Developmental imagery of change.* This is based on a "build and develop" view in which the organization needs to enhance its performance by building upon past and

current practices to make them even better. The change agent is viewed as a trainer or coach and words such as *nurturing*, *growing*, and *getting better* are aligned to this type of change.

- *Transitional imagery of change*. This is based on a "move and relocate" view in which the change is designed to alter how the organization operates, such as moving from manual to automated operational processes. The change agent acts as a guide or planner and words such as *moving forward*, *leaving the past behind*, and "moving from ________ to ________" are aligned to this type of change.
- *Transformational imagery of change*. This is based on a "liberate and re-create" view of the needed change such as reinventing itself or fundamentally changing the nature of the business or market in which the organization operates. The change agent acts as a visionary to help discover new possibilities and language appropriate to this type of change includes *reinventing*, *re-creating*, and *adopting* a new paradigm.

Marshak's insights about the need to align language and change are instructive in terms of identifying how managers can send out mixed signals to staff about what is required. They are also instructive in terms of getting managers of change to reflect upon the extent to which their metaphors for thinking about their organization and organizational change are "trapped" by a dominant or root metaphor that tends to influence their thinking. Adopting new metaphors and new language may produce new insights, actions, and unanticipated change directions.

At the same time, it needs to be recognized that managers may not always be able to introduce metaphors that will automatically "take"[38] with staff throughout the organization. Dominant logics; ingrained, embedded ways of operating and perceiving the organizational world; and even formal policies, procedures, and programs may act to inhibit new metaphors from taking hold and driving action toward desired change.[39] This means that change managers need to direct their attention to altering policies, systems, and processes in their organization that are in conflict with the language of the desired change (see Chapter 12). For example, if the language is about leaving the past behind, but the compensation and performance appraisal systems are still predicated on past practices, then these will serve as counteracting influences on the emergence of new, transformational change metaphors.

Creating a Common Change Language

For Hussey,[41] "Misused words and sentences can cause amusement, frustration and confusion." Managers often use terms and phrases in a way quite different from the meaning originators applied to the terms (see Table 11.5 for a humorous view of this). It is therefore important to not assume that different parties to a change share a common view of the change words and language that are in use.

A similar point has been made by Moosbruker and Lofton,[42] who argue that business process reengineering has often failed due to the different use of words and language when business process practitioners and organization development practitioners attempt to work together. For example:

- The word *system*. In *business process language*, this word is likely to refer to computer hardware; in *organization development language*, it is likely to refer to interconnections and relationships inside an organization as well as outside to its environment.

EXERCISE 11.3

Mixing Your Metaphors?

Marshak[40] argues that change managers need to ensure that their change "talk" is aligned to the type of change they desire. Think back to the change idea you identified in Exercise 11.1. Imagine that senior management has decided to run with your idea. They have come back to you for advice about the best way of describing it, compared to your organization's current operations.

1. Which metaphor "talk" will you use?
   - *Machine imagery*
   - *Developmental imagery*
   - *Transitional imagery*
   - *Transformational imagery*
2. Provide examples of three sentences, appropriate to the imagery that you have selected, that would fit in with your change idea, given your organization's current operations.
3. Now provide examples of three sentences (drawn from alternate imagery) that would be inappropriate to the type of change you envisage.
4. To what extent will your staff be open to this imagery: Is it likely to "take" (or resonate) with them? What modifications would you need to make to maximize the power of the language?
5. Are you more comfortable, as a change manager, with one type of change imagery or "talk"? To what extent do you tend to adopt this imagery regardless of the specific change? Are there any new skills you would need in consistently adopting differing change metaphors?

- The word *process*. In *business process language*, this word is likely to refer to a variety of sequential work steps; in *organization development language*, it is likely to refer to *how* to proceed.
- The word *function*. In *business process language*, this word is likely to refer to a set of operations related to business requirements; in *organization development language*, it may be used to indicate a series of tasks related to a specific organizational subunit.[43]

TABLE 11.5 Misused Management Terminology?

Source: Constructed from Hussey, 1998.

Term	Misused Meaning by Managers?
Emergent strategy	"Justifies a total lack of strategic thinking of any kind: after all, if a strategy will emerge, we do not have to do anything."
Learning organization	"Means that we were right after all to neglect training, as all we have to do is to tell employees that we like them to learn for themselves."
Empowerment	"Magic word that, if we say it enough, will make a downsized and delayered structure work without any further effort from us."
Culture	"Culture is what we say we will change when we cannot think of anything else to do."

Clearly, where the practitioners involved in implementing the change themselves fail to adopt a language with common meanings, then the change they are seeking to implement is likely to be problematic. Hence, checking the shared meaning of their concepts-in-use is important in terms of minimizing confusion about what is being attempted.

Lack of shared language and meaning among different parties has been used by Heracleous and Barrett[44] to explain the failed implementation in the London insurance market of an electronic risk-supporting system, a method whereby brokers seek insurance coverage from underwriters. They studied the language (discursive patterns) of the main stakeholders—market leaders, brokers, and underwriters—and how these changed over time. They differentiated between surface-level communication and the deeper discursive actions (interpretive schemes) that underpinned them. Deeper-level discursive structures include central themes, root metaphors, and rhetorical strategies.[45] Heracleous and Barrett suggest that one way of understanding the failure of the scheme and, in particular, the resistance of brokers and underwriters to it, is by focusing on the different discursive structures underlying these groups: "we saw stakeholder groups talking past each other, rather than to each other, because of their almost diametrically opposed discourses, at both the deeper structure levels and communicative action levels, and their lack of common ground on which to base a dialogue."[46]

They conclude that successful implementation of an electronic data interchange system requires change leaders to have skills in understanding the deeper discursive structures that underpin the discourses of different stakeholders. Even where agreement and synthesis occur at a surface communicative level, this may be tenuous where there is a lack of understanding and integration of deeper-level discursive structures that may act as a form of inertia on change actions. The authors acknowledge that simply understanding the deeper structures or schema of differing stakeholders will not guarantee change success. They maintain that "Uncovering and appreciating other stakeholders' deep structures, however, can be of help in avoiding dead ends and self-defeating compromises in change implementation."[47]

COMMUNICATING CHANGE WITH THE OUTSIDE WORLD

Much of the change communication literature focuses on *internally oriented* organizational communication processes, that is, how to communicate with staff about changes. In this section, we outline skills related to two types of *externally oriented* communication: one relates to communicating with external stakeholders about internal organizational changes; another relates to communication of change that results from crisis management.

Selling Internal Changes to External Stakeholders

Selling internal changes to external stakeholders is an important issue that can affect the impact of the change on organizational share performance. For instance, stock market performance is potentially under threat during transformational change due to the uncertainty associated with its outcomes. By way of example, and as outlined in Chapter 4, even where announced changes (e.g., downsizing) are initially well received by shareholders, stock performance may increase in the short term but plummet over the period of the change implementation.[48] This recognizes that an important, albeit often neglected, aspect of managing change is the management of its meaning for *external stakeholders*.

Arndt and Bigelow[49] looked at the impression management practices that were utilized by a group of not-for-profit hospitals in Massachusetts. These organizations moved from an institutionalized hospital structure to a diversified corporate structure.[50] Arndt and Bigelow point to how adopting the new structure sent a signal that the hospital was interested in nontraditional activities and, as a result, introduced uncertainty in terms of how this would be received by its stakeholders.[51] In studying annual reports of these innovating organizations, they identified four key defensive impression management practices that were used to protect themselves from negative reactions by their stakeholders:

- *Excuses* attributed the need for the change to forces beyond the actor, such as the external environment. The effect of these is to distance the actor from responsibility for any negative consequences of the corporate restructuring.
- *Justifications* took responsibility for the decision but presented it in a positive light without referring to any possible negative consequences.
- *Disclaimers* provided reassurance by pointing to careful planning, and the like, that preceded the restructuring decision.
- *Concealment* statements downplayed the innovative nature of the change and thereby decreased the perception of risk attached to it.[52]

Crisis Management and Corporate Reputation

Organizational crises are defined by Pearson and Clair[53] as being events that:

- Are highly ambiguous.
- Are low in probability but high in threat to organizational survival if they eventuate.
- Provide little time to react.
- Are often surprising to staff.
- Provide a dilemma about the type of change decisions that are needed.

Where these are triggered by situations external to the organization, then they serve to threaten the corporate reputation of the organization with external stakeholders. Corporate reputation is defined as "a collective representation of a firm's past actions and results that describes the firm's ability to deliver valued outcomes to multiple stakeholders."[54] It is an intangible[55] but important corporate asset, being positively correlated with organizational performance.[56] Maintaining, reestablishing, or legitimating corporate reputation during times of corporate crises is therefore a crucial part of managing these types of changes. A variety of communication strategies are on hand but, as the examples outlined below indicate, not all are successful in achieving their intent of repairing corporate reputation.

Hearit[57] analyzed how Chrysler, Toshiba, and Volvo went about presenting public apologies for crises associated with each company. The crisis for Chrysler related to reports that they were selling cars as new that were not—with Chrysler executives disconnecting odometers from their own vehicles and then later presenting them for sale as new cars. In the case of Toshiba, it was a result of making illegal sales of milling equipment to the Soviet Union. For Volvo, it was deceptive advertising in which Volvo cars were run over by "Monster" trucks without being crushed—but the cars that were used were internally reinforced compared to those normally for sale.[58] In each case there were three apology strategies used:

- *Persuasive accounts* of what had happened in order to provide a competing story to the publicly circulating one.
- *Statement of regret* about what had happened, but one that acknowledged only minimal responsibility.
- *Dissociation*, by which the company attempted to distance itself from the source of the wrongdoing, sometimes by scapegoating specific individuals or by maintaining that the source of the problem was peripheral to the mainstream operations of the company.[59]

Blaney et al.[60] report how Bridgestone-Firestone attempted to restore its public image in the wake of the August 2000 recall of over six million ATX and Wilderness AT tires because of "tread separation" in which the binding of the tire breaks down, causing blowouts. Eventually, 271 deaths were attributed to accidents resulting from this phenomenon.[61] Firestone used five crisis management change strategies:[62]

- *Mortification.* CEO Masatoshi Ono and his replacement, John Lampe, apologized to families who had suffered losses as a result of Firestone products.
- *Corrective action.* Defective tires were recalled and replaced with safe ones. However, this occurred at different times across the United States. Later the company also produced an advertising campaign titled "Making It Right," which implied that something had previously been wrong and this was being corrected.
- *Bolstering.* At the time of the recall of the tires, the company attempted to bolster its image as being concerned with safety by announcing that customer safety was paramount in the company; this strategy was later used through getting famous public car racing figures such as Michael Andretti to endorse Firestone's tires.
- *Denial.* Yoichiro Kaizaki, Bridgestone's president, suggested that fatal accidents were not caused by faulty Firestone tires.
- *Shifting the blame.* Underinflation was cited as the problem by Kaizaki and blame was shifted to Ford for not recommending appropriate tire pressures.

In evaluating their use of these communication techniques, Blaney et al. conclude that the "corrective action strategy was too little, too late, and too slow."[63] Apart from the recalls being staggered across different states at different times, they also had happened in other countries before being applied to the United States. In addition, the recalls were contradictory to the concurrent denial that the tires were not to blame, but, rather, underinflation was the problem. Ford claimed that Firestone was aware of the tire problem back in 1998 but had concealed this information and failed to act on it. Hence, shifting the blame to Ford apparently was not successful. This lack of success was apparently confirmed in a *CNN/USA Today* poll in June 2001 in which 56 percent of respondents reported an unfavorable view of Bridgestone-Firestone Inc.[64]

Quite apart from the ethical implications associated with the cases just discussed, what they highlight for change managers charged with handling externally oriented crises is that some strategies work well together while some are undermined by others. For example, in the Firestone case, mortification and bolstering were undermined by corrective action and denial.[65] Others may be undermined by a perceived lack of credibility or by the timing of their use; for example, corrective action being taken immediately rather than only when imminent pressure from external parties appears inevitable. For Chrysler, Toshiba, and Volvo, while the public apology strategy probably functioned to "deprive journalists of a continuing story and, thus, limit the damage done to corporate images,"[66] it did not stop eventual legal sanctions being applied to each of the three companies. It is worth pointing out that this literature is not well-integrated with the mainstream change literature, so there are many yet-to-be-researched questions in relation to it. For example, where change writers such as Ford and Ford and Sillince have focused on the role of change "conversations," these have been *internal* to the organization; what we do not yet know is whether similar or different change conversations should be directed to *external* stakeholders and, if so, the extent to which they need to vary at differing phases of a change or crisis management process.

Conclusion

Pettigrew et al. point out that "[t]he language of change can be a liberating intellectual force or an analytical prison."[67] By this they mean that the way change gets communicated influences what is seen, studied, and focused upon during a change effort. As outlined in Table 11.1, we also saw that what gets focused upon as key change communication skills is likely to be influenced by the images we hold of managing change. More generally, in this chapter, we have seen the range of linguistic and argumentation skills available to managers of changes, ones able to be oriented to communicating both inside and outside the organization. In particular, we suggest that the reflective change manager needs to consider issues such as differing change conversations at different phases of a change process, the linguistic coherence of these conversations, and the alignment of this talk with the type of change being attempted. As Karl Weick argues, "[t]he power of conversation, dialogue, and respectful interaction to reshape ongoing change has often been overlooked."[68] Communication, and language more specifically, is central not just to conveying or transmitting changes that are required; it is the medium through which change itself occurs. As Barrett et al.[69] point out, it is through changing organizational language and discourse that new possibilities and actions emerge: "Change . . . occurs when a new way of talking replaces an old way of talking." It is in and through everyday conversations in organizations that change occurs, with people trying out new ways of talking and acting and discarding old ways.[70] Change managers therefore need to reassess the appropriateness of their images of change and identify the range of communication skills available for them to draw upon and that can assist them in establishing new ways of talking throughout an organization. As outlined by Dervitsiotis, strategic change skills require "conversations-for-action, as opposed to idle talk."[71]

TABLE 11.6 Chapter Reflections for the Practicing Change Manager

- What are the key listening skills that you need to develop further?
- How important in your organization are toxic handlers? What recognition do they get? How important are they in moderating the change message?
- How successful have you been at "selling upward" your change ideas? How will you do things differently in the future?
- To what extent do you have different change conversations in different phases of a change process?
- How aligned is your change language with your desired change?
- What deeper, discursive structures exist among key stakeholders affected by the change process?
- What steps have you taken in terms of communicating externally to stakeholders about the internal changes occurring within your organization? What else would you do to facilitate this type of communication?

Supplemental Reading

Arndt, M., and Bigelow, B. 2000. Presenting structural innovation in an institutional environment: Hospitals' use of impression management. *Administrative Science Quarterly* 45(3):495–522.

Barrett, F. J., Thomas, G. F., and Hocevar, S. P. 1995. The central role of discourse in large-scale change: A social construction perspective. *Journal of Applied Behavioral Science* 31(3):352–72.

Boje, D. M. 1991. The storytelling organization: A study of story performance in an office-supply firm. *Administrative Science Quarterly* 36(1):106–26.

Dutton, J. E., Ashford, S. J., O'Neill, R. M., and Lawrence, K. A. 2001. Moves that matter: Issue selling and organizational change. *Academy of Management Journal* 44(4):716–36.

Ford, F. D., and Ford, L. W. 1995. The role of conversations in producing intentional change in organizations. *Academy of Management Review* 20(3):541–70.

Frost, P., and Robinson, S. 1999. The toxic handler: Organizational hero—and casualty. *Harvard Business Review* 77(4):96–106.

Gray, E. R., and Balmer, J. M. T. 1998. Managing corporate image and corporate reputation. *Long Range Planning* 31(5):695–702.

Heracleous, L., and Barrett, M. 2001. Organizational change as discourse: Communicative actions and deep structures in the context of information technology implementation. *Academy of Management Journal* 44(4):755–78.

Sillince, J. A. A. 1999. The role of political language forms and language coherence in the organizational change process. *Organization Studies* 20(3):485–518.

Tannen, D. 1995. The power of talk: Who gets heard and why. *Harvard Business Review* 73(5):138–48.

It's not impossible to pay $2,200 for a wastebasket and $6,000 for a shower curtain,[72] but when you claim them as company expenses, there will eventually be implications. This was precisely the situation that led to the misappropriation of $600 million that was allegedly stolen from Tyco and its shareholders,[73] a multinational corporation dealing in industries from hospital suppliers to fire sprinklers.[74] At the beginning of 2002, it was uncovered that the then-CEO Dennis Kozlowski and his associate, CFO Mark Swartz, were using the company's funds for inappropriate purposes. The official company stance on the scandal was reportedly, "Yes, they took the hundreds of millions—but the board let them do it."[75]

Within the organization morale was low. There was a sense of frustration among employees[76] and when the new CEO, Ed Breen, stepped in to the top role at Tyco in July 2002,[77] one of his major challenges was changing opinion of the corporation by communicating how the company was changing. The core business at Tyco was strong, so the focus of the change was never mediated by the possibility of bankruptcy.[78] In this sense, Breen was fortunate, heading up a corporation with a strong operational and financial basis on which to rebuild the company after the tarnished reputation that Kozlowski left behind.[79]

THE WAY TO INTEGRITY AND A CULTURE OF ACCOUNTABILITY

In order to change the organization's practices, Breen initiated a turnaround team to modify unethical behavior.[80] The first steps that were taken were symbolic gestures to show his determination to reinvent the company. Although he never openly commented on Kozlowski's past behavior, his immediate replacement of board members spoke louder than words.[81] By the end of 2002, there had been a complete overhaul of the executive team, with every member being replaced.[82] Without delay, Breen also made the move from Tyco's Manhattan office to a standard office in New Jersey—his office overlooked a car park instead of Central Park.[83] This symbolized that Breen was serious about changing the company and the leadership style of the past.

Through a letter to employees and shareholders, Breen stated that Tyco's most important commitment was to reinvent its credibility and integrity. A culture of accountability and good corporate citizenship was promoted by the company[84] and a change in the infrastructure of Tyco was of utmost importance. In order to flourish, it was crucial that the new management team re-create the way in which the organization functioned and the practices that they used.[85] This was reportedly initiated through a push to implement six-sigma training to increase the efficiency and quality of the company's services and products.[86] The dilemma was in how to communicate this change and the company's new ethical stance to the 260,000 employees worldwide.[87]

THE WAY CHANGE WAS COMMUNICATED

The main way in which Tyco planned to communicate its new policies in relation to ethical issues was through the development of a Guide to Ethical Conduct of Employees that outlines the regulations for the organization with regard to harassment, fraud, conflicts of interest, and compliance with laws.[88] An advisor from another company that had been through a similar process said, "if you want to change the hearts of the 260,000 people here as to the ethical climate they are working in, you need to bring to life this document."[89] In order to do this, the guide, which was launched worldwide using a mini–Web site,[90] illustrated problematic situations in this area using vignettes. These vignettes were dramatized by the use of six short videos.[91]

The new code of ethical conduct was implemented in meetings around the globe in May through June 2003[92]; more than 2,000 Tyco locations showed the videos alongside of corporate management making visits to Tyco sites.[93] In conjunction with this, a monthly newsletter provided employees worldwide with a column titled "A Matter of Principle" where they could submit questions on ethical issues, which were then answered and published.[94] Using this model, Tyco is creating a controllership guide[95] to accounting standards for the firm and hoping to gain more credibility within the community through reinforcing lawful organizationwide practices.

Questions

1. Describe how the turnaround team may have used Gerard and Teurfs' transformation skills to overcome the frustrations of employees.
2. Tyco used vignettes to communicate changes in ethical behavior. Write a vignette that could be used by Tyco to assist in overcoming the cultural change barriers that companies like Tyco faced.
3. Using Ford and Ford's four types of change conversations, describe how Tyco would go through the process of communicating change to its staff.
4. Imagine you are the CEO of Tyco. The former CEO is still on trial for fraud and you are trying to rebuild the company's corporate reputation. Write a script for your address to the shareholders after 18 months in the position. Pay attention to the appropriate use of metaphors in your "change conversation" to this group.
5. Role-play this script in class. What lessons emerge from this exercise?

TABLE 11.7 **Additional Case Studies**

Nestlé's Globe Program (A), (B), & (C) (Video and Case) Killing, P. (2000) *IMD Lausanne*
Sandy Weill and Citigroup Dutta, S., & Kamble, V. (2004) *ICFAI Knowledge Centre, India*
Coke's Changing Fortunes: The Need for Change Chowdary, N.V, & Kausiki, D. (2004) *ICFAI Business School Case Development Centre*

Bibliography

Anonymous. 2004. On trial. *BusinessWeek*, no. 3865 (January 12):80.

Arndt, M., and Bigelow, B. 2000. Presenting structural innovation in an institutional environment: Hospitals' use of impression management. *Administrative Science Quarterly* 45(3):495–522.

Barrett, F. J., Thomas, G. F., and Hocevar, S. P. 1995. The central role of discourse in large-scale change: A social construction perspective. *Journal of Applied Behavioral Science* 31(3):352–72.

Blaney, J. R., Benoit, W. L., and Brazeal, L. M. 2002. Blowout!: Firestone's image restoration campaign. *Public Relations Review* 28(4):379–92.

Boje, D. M. 1991. The storytelling organization: A study of story performance in an office-supply firm. *Administrative Science Quarterly* 36(1):106–26.

Bulkeley, W. M. IBM documents give rare look at sensitive plans on "offshoring." *The Wall Street Journal* 243(12) (January 19):A1.

Collins, D. 1998. *Organizational change: Sociological perspectives*. London: Routledge.

De Meuse, K. P., Vanderheiden, P. A., and Bergmann, T. J. 1994. Announced layoffs: Their effect on corporate financial performance. *Human Resource Management* 33(4):509–31.

Deephouse, D. L. 1997. The effect of financial and media reputations on performance. *Corporate Reputation Review* 1(1&2):68–72.

Dervitsiotis, K. N. 2002. The importance of conversations-for-action for effective strategic management. *Total Quality Management* 13(8):1087–98.

Dutton, J. E., Ashford, S. J., O'Neill, R. M., and Lawrence, K. A. 2001. Moves that matter: Issue selling and organizational change. *Academy of Management Journal* 44(4):716–36.

Fombrun, C., and van Riel, C. 1997. The reputational landscape. *Corporate Reputation Review* 1(1&2):5–13.

Ford, F. D., and Ford, L. W. 1995. The role of conversations in producing intentional change in organizations. *Academy of Management Review* 20(3):541–70.

Frost, P., and Robinson, S. 1999. The toxic handler: Organizational hero—and casualty. *Harvard Business Review* 77(4):96–106.

Gerard, G., and Teurfs, L. 1997. Dialogue and transformation. *Executive Excellence* 14(8) (August):16.

Hearit, K. M. 1994. Apologies and public relations crises at Chrysler, Toshiba, and Volvo. *Public Relations Review* 20(2):113–25.

Heracleous, L., and Barrett, M. 2001. Organizational change as discourse: Communicative actions and deep structures in the context of information technology implementation. *Academy of Management Journal* 44(4):755–78.

Hussey, D. E. 1998. Words, sentences and self delusion. *Strategic Change* 7(8):435–36.

Laing, J. R. 2003. The new Tyco. *Barron's* 83(50) (December 15):17.

Marshak, R. J. 1993. Managing the metaphors of change. *Organizational Dynamics* 22(1):44–56.

Moosbruker, J. B., and Loftin, R. D. 1998. Business process redesign and organization development: Enhancing success by removing the barriers. *Journal of Applied Behavioral Science* 34(3):286–304.

Palmer, I., and Dunford, R. 1996. Conflicting uses of metaphors: Reconceptualizing their use in the field of organizational change. *Academy of Management Review* 21(3):691–717.

Pearson, C. M., and Clair, J. A. 1998. Reframing crisis management. *Academy of Management Review* 23(1):59–76.

Pettigrew, A. M, Woodman, R. W., and Cameron, K. S. 2001. Studying organizational change and development: Challenges for future research. *Academy of Management Journal* 44(4):697–713.

Pillmore, E. 2003. How we're fixing up Tyco. *Harvard Business Review* 81(12):96–103.

Schweizer, T. S., and Wijnberg, N. M. 1999. Transferring reputation to the corporation in different cultures: Individuals, collectives, systems and the strategic management of corporate reputation. *Corporate Reputation Review* 2(3):249–66.

Sillince, J. A. A. 1999. The role of political language forms and language coherence in the organizational change process. *Organization Studies* 20(3):485–518.

Srivastva, S., and Barrett, F. J. 1988. The transforming nature of metaphors in group development: A study in group theory. *Human Relations* 41:31–64.

Tyco Web site. Governance changes. http://www.tyco.com

Useem, J. 2003. The biggest show no one's watching. *Fortune* 148(12) (December 8):156.

Vergin, R. C., and Qoronfleh, M. W. 1998. Corporate reputation and the stock market. *Business Horizons* 41(1):19–26.

Weick, K. E. 2000. Emergent change as a universal in organizations. In *Breaking the code of change*, ed. M. Beer and N. Nohria, 223–41. Boston: Harvard Business School Press.

Wolvin, A., and Coakley, C. G. 1996. *Listening.* 5th ed. Dubuque, IA: Brown & Benchmark.

Worrell, D. L., Davidson, W. N., and Sharma, V. M. 1991. Layoff announcements and stockholder wealth. *Academy of Management Journal* 34:662–78.

Notes

1. Collins, 1998:141.
2. Collins, 1998:153.
3. Wolvin and Coakley, 1996.
4. Gerard and Teurfs, 1997.
5. Gerard and Teurfs, 1997.
6. Gerard and Teurfs, 1997.
7. Boje, 1991:106. This and subsequent quotes copyright © 1991 Administrative Science Quarterly.
8. Boje, 1991:118.
9. Boje, 1991:125.
10. Boje, 1991:124.
11. Dutton et al., 2001:716. Copyright © 2001 Academy of Management Journal. Reproduced with permission through Copyright Clearance Center.

12. Dutton et al., 2001:716.
13. Dutton et al., 2001.
14. Dutton et al., 2001:721–28.
15. Dutton et al., 2001.
16. Frost and Robinson, 1999.
17. Frost and Robinson, 1999:100.
18. Frost and Robinson, 1999:98.
19. Ford and Ford, 1995.
20. Ford and Ford, 1995:566.
21. Paraphrased from Ford and Ford, 1995:546–52.
22. Ford and Ford, 1995:548.
23. Ford and Ford, 1995:548–49.
24. Ford and Ford, 1995:550–51.
25. Ford and Ford, 1995:551–52.
26. Paraphrased from Ford and Ford, 1995:556–60.
27. Ford and Ford, 1995:553.
28. Ford and Ford, 1995:543.
29. Sillince, 1999. Copyright © 1999 by Sage Publications. Reproduced with permission.
30. Sillince, 1999:487–90.
31. Sillince, 1999:491.
32. Sillince, 1999:492.
33. Sillince, 1999:499.
34. Sillince, 1999:508.
35. Marshak, 1993.
36. Marshak, 1993:53.
37. Adapted from Marshak, 1993:47–54.
38. Srivastva and Barrett, 1988:54.
39. See Palmer and Dunford, 1996:708.
40. Marshak, 1993.
41. Hussey, 1998:435.
42. Moosbruker and Loftin, 1998.
43. Moosbruker and Loftin, 1998:290.
44. Heracleous and Barrett, 2001:758. Copyright © 2001 Academy of Management Journal. Reproduced with permission of Copyright Clearance Center.
45. Heracleous and Barrett, 2001:758.
46. Heracleous and Barrett, 2001:774.
47. Heracleous and Barrett, 2001:774.
48. Worrell et al., 1991; De Meuse et al., 1994.
49. Arndt and Bigelow, 2000.
50. Arndt and Bigelow, 2000:497.
51. Arndt and Bigelow, 2000:500.
52. Arndt and Bigelow, 2000:504–11.
53. Pearson and Clair, 1998:60.

54. Fombrun and van Riel, 1997:10.
55. Schweizer and Wijnberg, 1999.
56. Deephouse, 1997; Vergin and Qoronfleh, 1998.
57. Hearit, 1994.
58. Hearit, 1994:114.
59. Hearit, 1994:119–21.
60. Blaney et al., 2002.
61. Blaney et al., 2002:379.
62. Blaney et al., 2002:383–86.
63. Blaney et al., 2002:386.
64. Blaney et al., 2002:388.
65. Blaney et al., 2002:389.
66. Hearit, 1994:122.
67. Pettigrew et al., 2001:700.
68. Weick, 2000:237.
69. Barrett et al., 1995:366.
70. Barrett et al., 1995:370.
71. Dervitsiotis, 2002:1088.
72. Pillmore, 2003. This case was prepared by El Feletto.
73. Anonymous, 2004.
74. Laing, 2003.
75. Useem, 2003.
76. Pillmore, 2003.
77. Laing, 2003.
78. Pillmore, 2003.
79. Laing, 2003.
80. Pillmore, 2003.
81. Laing, 2003.
82. Pillmore, 2003.
83. Laing, 2003.
84. Tyco Web site.
85. Pillmore, 2003.
86. Laing, 2003.
87. Pillmore, 2003.
88. Pillmore, 2003.
89. Pillmore, 2003.
90. Tyco Web site.
91. Pillmore, 2003.
92. Pillmore, 2003.
93. Pillmore, 2003.
94. Tyco Web site.
95. Pillmore, 2003.

Consolidating Change

Learning objectives

On completion of this chapter you should be able to:

- Recognize the difference between the appearance of change and change that has become consolidated within an organization.
- Identify a range of actions that can assist the consolidation of change.
- Be alert to a number of "pitfalls" that can be encountered when seeking to consolidate change.

The process of change in organizations can test the resources of an organization whether resources are conceived of in terms of capital, or time, or emotional resilience. One of the greatest challenges for those involved in managing change is to try to ensure that the change is not just a transitory phenomenon that "flames brightly" for a while before fading from the scene (see Table 12.1).

The focus of this chapter is specifically on this matter: What can be done to increase the probability that change initiatives do not falter and instead become embedded in the organization as normal practice? The treatment of the concept of consolidation that is provided in this chapter assumes that benefits can flow to the managers of change from an awareness of the issues that are covered. However, as with the topics of the previous chapters, what is considered to be achievable in terms of consolidation varies between the different images of change management (see Table 12.2).

CONSOLIDATION: WHAT ARE ITS SIGNS?

For a change to "stick," it must cease being seen as something separate from normal practice; it must become the new normality. It needs to become, in Nadler's terms, "baked in to the organization" or, in Kotter's terms, accepted by those in the organization as "the way we do things around here."[2] That is, it must become an integral part of the organizational culture, which ex-IBM CEO Lou Gerstner defines as "the mindset and instincts" of the people in the organization[3] (see Table 12.3). To be consolidated means that people no longer label the practices in question as "change," with all the emotional, political, and other connotations that come with that term.

TABLE 12.1 When the Momentum Goes Out of Change: The Case of the U.S. Postal Service[1]

Source: Reisner, 2002.

Robert Reisner joined the U.S. Postal Service in 1993 as vice-president for technology applications and in 1996 became vice president for strategic planning, a position he held until he left the organization in December 2001. During this period, the postal service went through a significant change process. The following is a summary of Reisner's commentary on this period.

In 1999, Lance Armstrong, sponsored by the U.S. Postal Service, won the Tour de France. This victory against the odds for the recent cancer survivor seemed to symbolize the changed fortunes for the Postal Service, which, during the late-90s, had transformed itself from the butt of sitcom jokes into an organization with an impressive record of improved performance.

It had generated more than $5 billion in net income from 1995 through 1998, locally mailed letters were being delivered within 24 hours 93 percent of the time (up from only 79 percent in the mid-1990s), and the public reported they were more satisfied with postal services than with those of any other government entity. Similarly, business customers such as magazine publishers, catalog companies, direct-mail advertisers, credit card companies, and utilities were pleased that there had been four years without a postage rate increase.

In parallel to these changes to its traditional businesses, the Postal Service was heavily investing in strategic and operational initiatives designed to provide the basis for its success in an age where electronic forms of communication were becoming increasingly the norm and to provide the basis for responding to the growing competition from companies such as FedEx and United Parcel Service.

However, by the beginning of 2001, the situation was very different. Revenue was falling and a $3 billion loss was being projected for the year; performance and morale were slipping.

"Turbocharging the Snail"

In the mid-1990s, the Postal Service was a nearly $70 billion enterprise with more than 800,000 employees serving 130 million delivery points six days a week.

Neither operational nor strategic change would be easy because of the nature of the Postal Service. Specifically, it has a legislative mandate to provide service to all citizens and it is one of the last regulated monopolies. The mandate to provide what is essentially a social service often conflicts with the demands of running a business. For example, 26,000 of the Postal Service's 40,000 post offices lose money, but federal law makes it extremely difficult to close them. Similarly, its monopoly status is accompanied by significant constraints; for example, the agency can't raise rates or offer new products or services without extensive hearings, it has limited control over labor costs (80 percent of its total costs) because a federal arbiter often must approve its contracts, and the agency is overseen by a plethora of officials and bodies.

The challenge that faced the postal service by the early-90s was, in Reisner's terms, to "turbocharge the snail." Digital technology posed a serious threat, not just in the form of e-mail but also because businesses and individuals would soon be able to receive and pay bills electronically, and digital signatures and electronic postmarks would enable the secure electronic transfer of sensitive documents. Direct marketing, bills, and bill payments together accounted for nearly half of the Postal Service's sales and a reduction of as little as 5 percent in this volume would threaten the agency's financial ability to maintain the infrastructure needed for the delivery of conventional mail.

In order to be able to meet the challenge that could come from the development of digital technologies, the Postal Service would need to itself become a provider of digitally based services. Unfortunately, this need coincided with deteriorating finances and declining performance in its conventional services. Net losses for 1992–1994 were $2.2 billion.

In 1994, postmaster general Marvin Runyon reorganized the agency's top-management team and charged it with improving financial performance through setting aggressive operational goals designed to improve efficiency and service. Because transforming the situation

TABLE 12.1 When the Momentum Goes Out of Change: The Case of the U.S. Postal Service[1]—*(concluded)*

would require more than just operational level, he also asked Congress to allow the Postal Service the freedom to manage "people, prices, and products."

The Postal Service launched www.usps.gov, which allowed customers to access useful information such as mailing tips, zip codes, and postal rates; created a system for issuing electronic postmarks and verifying digital signatures; experimented with Internet kiosks in post offices; and worked with Time Warner to develop an overnight shipping program for consumers ordering products through the company's pilot interactive cable service. They also "got lucky," benefiting from an increase in the price of stamps, a favorable labor settlement, and a strengthening economy.

At the end of 1995, the Postal Service was able to report a "nearly unheard-of" surplus revenue. By the time of a meeting of nearly 1,000 Postal Service executives in October 1996, finances and performance had continued to improve and the leadership team celebrated the beginning of a turnaround. At the meeting, a strategy was presented, the centerpiece of which was for the Postal Service to become a "twenty-first-century growth company" by offering competitive products and services.

Operational successes continued. The Postal Service had launched Customer Perfect, a performance management system, a key element of which was to focus attention on improving delivery times. By 1997, it had exceeded Runyon's thought-to-be-ambitious goal of accurately delivering first-class local mail within 24 hours 90 percent of the time. Improvements in efficiency helped generate a net income of $1.8 billion in 1995, $1.6 billion in 1996, and $1.3 billion in 1997.

This operational and financial performance had an effect on the way the Postal Service was viewed by its many constituencies, from customers to Congress to the media to employees. Most significantly, Postal Service employees began to think of their organization not as a lumbering bureaucracy but as a high-performing enterprise capable of dramatic change. In this regard, Reisner states:

> I was well aware that the particular characteristics of the Postal Service created serious impediments to launching bold, innovative initiatives. That's why the initial success of the agency's turnaround efforts was so exhilarating.[a]

Signs That All Is Not Well

By 1999, despite all the improved financial performance, many of the agency's managers were becoming indifferent, even resistant, to the change initiative efforts. A survey of senior managers found that most of them believed the Postal Service wouldn't be impacted by electronic commerce for another 10 to 15 years and were equally skeptical about other so-called competitive threats. As a result, some felt that efforts to address these threats—for example, the initiative to let people pay their bills electronically through the Postal Service—were a distraction that diverted them from their task of managing the growth in first-class mail volume. This de facto resistance within the management team was accompanied by explicit resistance from labor leaders.

A further problem that had emerged was the inability of the Postal Service to gain funding support for its new growth initiatives; the budget process continued to favor programs aimed at operational improvements. One half of the $3 billion capital-spending budget continued to be earmarked for the construction of plants and post offices, while the other half was allocated to automation and other initiatives largely designed to make mail handling more efficient.

By 2001, instead of the substantial surpluses of the late 1990s, the Postal Service reported a shortfall of $1.6 billion. The comptroller general, in testimony before the House Oversight Committee, warned that the strategic transformation of the Postal Service was at risk, while Senator Fred Thompson, chairman of the Senate Government Affairs Committee, having looked at the situation of the Postal Service, concluded: "The ox is clearly in the ditch. Big time.[b]"

[a]Reisner, 2002:46.
[b]Reisner, 2002:51.

TABLE 12.2 Images of Managing Change and Consolidation

Image of Managing Change	How Consolidation Is Viewed
Director	It is the responsibility of the change manager to design the change process and direct people to comply such that the change objective is achieved as planned.
Navigator	The change manager designs the change process so as to best fit the conditions faced, recognizing that modifications will almost certainly need to be made en route and that the final outcome may not be as originally envisaged.
Caretaker	To the extent to which intended outcomes are achieved, this is primarily the result of environmental factors, not management intervention.
Coach	If intended outcomes are achieved, it is because the change manager has been successful in helping organizational members develop within themselves the capabilities necessary for success.
Interpreter	The change manager plays a central role in the development of an understanding of the meaning of outcomes, in particular with regard to what is taken as a successful resolution of the change process.
Nurturer	Change processes will have outcomes, but these are in continual state of flux and are largely out of the hands of managers.

Unless this happens, that is, unless the change "seeps into the bloodstream of corporate life," the change may prove to be just a passing diversion, a temporary disruption to normal practice.[4]

However, organizational culture is not something that can be changed by edict or even by attempting to change it directly. Kotter explains:

> Culture is not something that you manipulate easily. Attempts to grab it and twist it into shape never work because you can't grab it. Culture changes only after you have successfully altered people's actions, after the new behavior produces some group benefit for a period of time, and after people see the connection between the new actions and the performance improvement.[5]

In a similar vein, Gerstner, commenting on his leadership of the transformation of IBM, states:

> What you can do is create the conditions for transformation. You can provide incentives. You can define the marketplace realities and goals. But then you have to trust. In fact, in the end, management doesn't change culture. Management invites the workforce itself to change the culture.[6]

TABLE 12.3 The Importance of Organizational Culture at IBM

Lou Gerstner presided over one of the major turnarounds in U.S. corporate history: the transformation of IBM from an organization widely predicted to be heading for extinction. For Gerstner, the importance of having the necessary changes become embedded in the culture of the organization was beyond dispute. In his words:

> I came to see, in my time at IBM, that culture isn't just one aspect of the game—it *is* the game . . . Vision, strategy, marketing, financial management—any management system, in fact—can set you on the right path and can carry you for a while. But no enterprise—whether in business, government, education, health care, or any area of human endeavor—will succeed over the long haul if those elements aren't part of the DNA.[a]

[a]Gerstner, 2002:182.

ACTIONS TO CONSOLIDATE CHANGE

In this section, the focus is on a range of actions that can help to consolidate a change. While no specific set of actions will guarantee success, if managers are alert to the capacity of various practices, the chances are that the odds of success can be improved (see Table 12.4).

Redesign Roles

The redesign of organizational roles is a common outcome of many organizational changes. However, role changes may be a critical element of the process of change, not just a product of change.

Beer et al. argue that most change programs don't work because they are guided by a theory of change that is "fundamentally flawed."[7] They argue that too much emphasis is placed on attempting to change people's behavior by changing their attitudes and beliefs through exposing them to new perspectives. It is an approach that treats change "like a conversion experience [in which] once people 'get religion,' changes in their behavior will surely follow."[8] However, they argue, the more significant direction of causality is that both behavior and attitudes are most influenced by the context of roles, relationships, and responsibilities in which people find themselves.

Redesign Reward System

According to Beer and Nohria, "there are virtually no fundamental changes in organizations that do not also involve some changes in the reward system."[9] Fisher cites the example of Integra Financial, a $14 billion (in assets) bank holding company that was formed through a merger. In order to reinforce the company's commitment to a teamwork initiative, it developed and implemented a carefully designed evaluation and reward system "to discourage hot-dogging, grandstanding, filibustering, and other ego games" and to ensure that "the best team players get the goodies."[10]

The rewards should include public recognition of those whose behaviors are consistent with the desired change; this both reinforces the behavior of the individual concerned and sends strong signals to others. The opposite also applies: failure to act in the face of behavior that is in direct opposition to the change undermines the

TABLE 12.4 Reflections on Change in the U.S. Postal Service

Source: Reisner, 2002.

Robert Reisner (see Table 12.1) has provided his views on the lessons to be taken from the stalled change in which he was involved at the U.S. Postal Service. While acknowledging the complexity of the Postal Service's situation, the effect of an economic downturn, the "bursting of the e-commerce bubble," and post-9/11 effects (e.g., security-related cost increases), he argues that there are lessons to be drawn that apply to any organization undertaking a major change initiative. He identifies "four hard lessons"[a]:

- **Don't miss your moment.**
  We missed numerous market opportunities that competitors such as UPS seized. Furthermore, we let pass at least two chances to capitalize on high morale and momentum within the Postal Service.
- **Connect change initiatives to your core business.**
  Most of the innovative programs we launched to boost revenue were "at the fringes" of the business. And we never established a path for them to migrate to the heart of our operations.
- **Don't mistake incremental improvements for strategic transformation.**
  [O]ur tremendous success in improving delivery times, which we enthusiastically celebrated, blinded us to the need for strategic change. For a time, we slipped into complacency, ignoring our competition and challenges and declaring ourselves the winner in a race with ourselves.
- **Be realistic about your limits and the pace of change.**
  [I]n a change initiative, it is important to identify which obstacles are in your control and which aren't. Some of what we wanted to do may simply not have been possible, at least at the time. . . While some of our constraints—our regulatory framework, if not our very size and complexity—are specific to us, every organization has limits of one kind or another. It may seem heretical to say so in the can-do environment of American business, but sometimes you need to accept those limits. A failure to acknowledge that you sometimes can't do certain things can breed discouragement and cynicism, ultimately undermining those change initiatives that are achievable.

[a]Reisner, 2002:51–52.

credibility of the program. In this regard, Nadler comments, "If you want to see change crumble before your eyes, this lack of action is the quickest way to let it happen."[11] Similarly, Lawler argues that changes in an organization's pay system "are often considered 'hot' change levers that potentially can derail as well as support organizational change effort."[12]

Link Selection Decisions to Change Objectives

Selection of staff constitutes "one of the most subtle yet potent ways through which cultural assumptions get embedded and perpetuated."[13] As with the allocation of rewards, who gets appointed to key positions can have a significant symbolic role in signaling whether the organization is "for real" in regard to the espoused change.

It is likely that some changes will occur in the top-management team before a major change is fully embedded in the organization. In this regard, "one bad succession decision at the top of an organization can undermine a decade of hard work."[14]

Act Consistently with Advocated Actions

Kanter et al. note that "organization members often wait for the signals from senior management that say 'we mean it' (or 'we don't really mean it')."[15] In this regard, what is required is action, not just words (or as Senge et al. put it, to "walk the talk" by making sure that there is "demonstration, not [just] articulation."[16] That is, it is "deeds, not words [that] are tangible."[17]

One indicator of this is whether key management practices have been changed to align with the espoused priorities. Fisher asks: "Who really gets the praise and recognition? Who gets promoted and why? Might you, for instance, be ballyhooing the wonderfulness of teamwork—while still rewarding me-first-and-damn-the-team behaviour?"[18] Similarly, Schein argues that one of the most powerful means for managers to communicate "what they believe in or care about is what they systematically pay attention to."[19] (See Table 12.5.)

Similarly, decisions about the allocation of resources (financial, staff/expertise, etc.) have symbolic as well directly tangible effects. This is especially so in the case of "credible commitments." A credible commitment is an action involving the allocation of resources to a project in such a way that to withdraw from the project would involve a real cost to the organization. By so doing, it conveys to those affected by the change that the architects of the change are prepared to "put their money where their mouth is."

In this regard, there is likely to be nothing more damaging to the credibility of a change program than for the actions of the change advocates to be inconsistent with what they espouse. While it may be tempting to dismiss the phrase "walk the talk" as a pop management cliché, it nonetheless highlights the dangers that can flow from an inconsistency between talk and action (see Table 12.6). "Unintentional hypocrisy" can be very damaging.[20]

Similarly, failing to act against those—particularly managers—who blatantly act inconsistently with core elements of the change must be brought into line. In regard to

TABLE 12.5 **Signals from Behavior**

Source: Schein, 1992.

Ed Schein tells the story of how the actions of a CEO communicated his commitment to espoused cultural values.

At an executive committee meeting, the treasurer reported on the state of the business. In doing so, he identified one product line as being in financial difficulty. Attention then turned to the vice president (VP) in charge of this area, who protested that he had not seen the treasurer's figure prior to the meeting and as such was not in a position to respond.

Executive members expected a rather strong response from the CEO. They got it, but it was not what they expected. Most expected that he would admonish the treasurer for "ambushing" the VP by failing to provide him with the figures prior to the meeting. However, the CEO targeted the VP, telling him that if he were "on top of" his business, he would have known the situation described by the treasurer and would have been able to respond to the questions raised.

The message in the CEO's response was clear: not being on top of the situation and not being able to respond to the treasurer was a "worse sin" than being in financial trouble. Schein comments: "The blowup at the line manager was a far clearer message than any amount of rhetoric about delegation and the like would have been."[a]

[a]Schein, 1992:235.

TABLE 12.6 Espoused Values and Actions at Falcon Computer

Source: Reynolds, 1987.

The senior management team of Falcon Computer created a document called "Falcon Values" that was intended to express the values central to the culture of the company. It dealt with such things as the manner in which customers and colleagues should be treated "respectful"), the preferred style of communication ("open"), and a commitment to quality ("Attention to detail is our trademark; . . . we intend to deliver defect-free products and services to our customers").

However, the statement of values had been created in a manner antithetical to open communication. The senior management team developed the first draft without consulting with middle management. Middle managers were subsequently asked to "discuss it," but as far as they were concerned this was a token gesture as they believed that it was fait accompli. The rest of the organization only found out about the affirmation of open communication after the "Falcon Values" had already been adopted by the company.

At the same time, while the public relations department was claiming that the company was shipping large numbers of computers to key clients, staff knew that the real situation was that a design flaw was almost requiring the handcrafting of each machine, with the result that manufacturing had slowed to a trickle.

Cynical humor emerged: The manufacturing division was referred to as "Research and Development" while one employee commented, "We do have a zero-defect program: don't test the product and you'll find zero defects."

The vice president of marketing was then fired one evening and by the morning "the company was abuzz with stories" fueled by the "no-comment" position taken by the senior management team—the advocates of open communication. One of the staff commented, "It makes you realize what bullshit Falcon Values are."

The Falcon senior management team may have genuinely believed in the values that the document espoused and also that these values constituted a basis for changing the organization for the better. However, the increasingly obvious disparity between their espoused position and their actions, as observed and experienced by the staff, led to a culture of cynicism. As far as staff were concerned, the Falcon Values were a rather sad joke in the face of a culture that was one in which secrecy and expediency were the values-in-practice.

this situation, Nadler comments that "if you want to see change crumble before your eyes, lack of action is the quickest way to let it happen."[21]

Encourage "Voluntary Acts of Initiative"

In a four-year study of organizational change in six corporations, Beer et al. found that the most effective senior managers specified the general direction in which they wished the company to move but left the details of specific changes to be determined "closer to the action," that is, lower down the organization.[22] Change was more likely to become embedded if those at the operational level were supported when they took action to develop the specific form of the general initiative that they believed appropriate for their local circumstance.

Measure Progress

A focus on measurement is important for two reasons. First, it is a means of monitoring the progress of the change. Second, what gets measured is likely to have a significant impact on how people act (see Table 12.7).

TABLE 12.7 Measures That Produced Change at Sears

Source: Rucci, Kirn, and Quinn, 1998; Hallowell, Cash, and Ibri, 1997, as discussed in Pfeffer and Sutton, 2000.

In 1992, Sears had revenue of $52 billion, a figure that was lower than that in each of the preceding three years and associated with a net loss of $3.9 billion. Arthur Martinez arrived in the fall of 1992 and began to oversee a transformation based on a change in measurement practice.

Historically, Sears had relied on very traditional accounting measures of performance. However, such measures failed to directly identify the existence of declining levels of both employee and customer satisfaction and were also lag, not lead, indicators. These were significant limitations given that these factors were directly linked to financial performance. A Sears model showed that a 5 percent improvement in employee attitudes produced a 1.3 percent increase in customer satisfaction and, in turn, a 0.5 percent growth in revenue.

Martinez oversaw the introduction of specific metrics in regard to the "3Cs" strategic intent of making Sears "a compelling place to shop, a compelling place to work and a compelling place to invest."[a] To assess the "3Cs," metrics were established for (1) customer satisfaction and customer retention, (2) attitudes about the job and the company, and (3) revenue growth, operating margins, asset utilization, and productivity.

Pfeffer and Sutton conclude:

> Just as one set of accounting measures had driven the company off course, a different set of measures, more embedded in the actual business model and operating processes of the retail business, helped the firm recover.[b]

[a]Pfeffer and Sutton, 2000:169.
[b]Pfeffer and Sutton, 2000:173.

Getting the metric right is important (see Table 12.8). Nadler argues that "at the very least, an organization should conduct a full-scale assessment within six months of the initiation of major change activities and then every year thereafter."[23] Recommended methods include quantitative performance measures, attitude surveys, focus groups, and individual interviews.[24] Kanter et al. argue that two kinds of measure are helpful: (1) results measures—"how we will know that we're 'there' and that we have 'done it' " and (2) process measures—"how we will know we are doing the things all along that will get us to 'it', or whether re-adjustments are in order."[25]

The Price Waterhouse Change Integration Team argue that a balanced set of performance measures will include:

- Leading and lagging measures.
- Internal and external measures.
- Cost and noncost measures.[26]

Leading measures are those that show the immediate results of a new initiative such as changes in processing time or time-to-market for new products. Lagging measures are those such as financial performance and company image that take some time to become apparent. Internal measures focus on intra-organizational processes; external measures are those that either give information on the perspective of stakeholders such as customers and suppliers or allow the performance of an organization to be compared with that of its competitors. Cost-based measures are directly financial; noncost-based

TABLE 12.8 Metrics at Continental Airlines

Source: Kurtzman, 1998.

When Gordon Bethune became chief executive of Continental Airlines in 1994, it had been losing money for most of the previous decade, had a debt-to-equity ratio of 50-to-one, and had served some time in Chapter 11 of the federal bankruptcy code.

During this period, Continental had emphasized competing on the basis of cheaper fares than its major competitors. However, although it achieved the lowest revenue per available seat mile (of the major airlines), it also had the lowest revenue per available seat mile and a loss overall.

Bethune reflects on this situation:

> I firmly believe that what you measure is what you get. This is an example of a company that said . . . that it couldn't compete with the big boys unless it was able to have cheaper fares . . . That set the culture and mind-set . . . So, we had a culture that said, "Cost is everything." That's the Holy Grail.
>
> We even had pilots turning down the air-conditioning and slowing down airplanes to save the cost of fuel . . . They made passengers hot, mad and late.
>
> That's a dysfunctional measure, a measure some accountant dreamed up who does not understand our business.[a]

Bethune responded by investigating what factors most influenced passengers' level of satisfaction with airlines. This revealed that on-time performance was the most significant factor. Unfortunately, at the time of Bethune's arrival, Continental ranked 10th of the 10 largest U.S. carriers on this criterion. Nonetheless, Bethune changed the core metric used inside Continental to on-time performance:

> We use that measure for two reasons. One because it is the single most vital sign of a functioning airline . . . and two, it's ranked by our Government and we can't screw the metrics.[b]

To reinforce the centrality of this factor, a new system of rewards was established in which bonuses were paid to all staff each month that Continental was ranked in the top five of the 10 largest U.S. carriers for on-time performance. The cost of the bonus payments was more than covered by the reduction in the amount—that had risen to $6 million per month—that. . . . Continental had been paying to put passengers on other airlines, put them up in hotels, bus them across town, and so forth.

> The next month, March 1995, we wound up in first place. We had never been in first place in 60 years. I mean, Continental, the worst company in America for the last 20 years, is first place in "on time" which is a metric everyone kind of understands.[c]

By 1996 (and again in 1997), Continental had won the J.D. Power & Associates award for customer satisfaction as the best airline for flights of 500 miles or more and was in the top three in terms of fewest customer complaints and lost baggage.

From 1995 to 1998, Continental's market capitalization rose from $230 million to $3 billion.

[a]Kurtzman, 1998:3–6.
[b]Kurtzman, 1998:3.
[c]Kurtzman, 1998:4.

measures may have financial implications but are not themselves directly financial, for example, market share and brand image (see Exercise 12.1).

Celebrate "En Route"

The outcomes of a change program may take some time, perhaps years, to become fully manifest. This can "test the patience" of organizational members as well as increasing the likelihood of skepticism as to the effectiveness of the program. Kotter notes:

> Zealous believers will often stay the course no matter what happens. Most of the rest of us expect to see convincing evidence that all the effort is paying off. Nonbelievers have even higher standards of proof. They want to see clear data indicating that the changes are working.[28]

In the terms used by the Pricewaterhouse Change Integration Team, "the need for quick results is real if for no other reason than to keep hope alive."[29] Similarly, Schaffer and Thomson argue that "there is no motivator more powerful than frequent successes."[30] In this regard, it is good if some tangible benefits can be identified relatively early in the program; that is, that there be some "short-term wins."[31]

EXERCISE 12.1

Testing for a Balanced Set of Measures[27]

For any given change, it is useful to consider what would be the appropriate measures of its success (or failure). List the proposed measure and note which type of measure it is by placing an "X" in the appropriate column.

Note: Any one measure is likely to be classifiable in more than one category. For example, brand image is likely to be lagging, external, and noncost.

If the proposed measures do not cover all six categories, you should be clear as to why it is not necessary to not have one (or more) category covered. If this cannot be clearly explained, it suggests that additional measures may be required.

	Type					
Measure	**Leading**	**Lagging**	**Internal**	**External**	**Cost**	**Noncost**
1.						
2.						
3.						
4.						

Where such "wins" are achieved, they should be acknowledged, even celebrated, because by so doing, they both reward those directly involved and more broadly enhance the credibility of the program (especially valuable where a level of skepticism exists).[32] The connection between changed actions/practices and organizational performance should not be left to employees to make on their own behalf. According to Kotter, when people are left to make their own connections, "they sometimes create very inaccurate links."[33] In a similar vein, Beer et al. argue that successes "can serve as catalysts for change only if others are aware of their existence and are encouraged to learn from them."[34]

One of the implications of this focus on celebrating en route is that there may be real benefits to be gained from identifying priority areas for the allocation of resources. Areas of the business needing the most urgent attention also may offer the opportunity for the demonstration of the clearest and most immediate improvements—the short-term wins—that can form the basis for celebration. The significance of establishing such priorities is such that failure to do so early in a change process (and failure to refine these priorities throughout the process) has been identified as a direct cause of project failure.[35]

Fine-Tune

It is unlikely that any change program will "get it all right" the first time, such that further modifications will not be required "down the track." Nadler argues that there are two main reasons for this.[36]

First, "smart" executives act on the basis of decisions that they consider to be substantially correct rather than waiting in the hope that, with the passage of time, a completely correct course of action will be revealed. This approach is based on the proposition that the timely application of a substantially correct change—with further modification added as a result of experience with the change—is a more effective form of managing than deferring change in the hope that, at some not-too-distant point in the future, the optimal intervention will become apparent.

Second, even if the change was absolutely ideal for the situation faced at the time of the change, circumstances can change rather rapidly, such that modification is required, not because of any flaw in the original blueprint for change but because of such changed circumstances (for example, the entry of a major new player into the market).

According to Nadler, one of the biggest challenges during the consolidation phase is to be able to adjust and refine elements of the change without this being interpreted by those affected as a sign of failure. He argues that the way to handle this situation is to communicate alterations in terms of their consistency with the original changes.[37] (See Table 12.9).

> It's up to leaders to help people make sense of what's going on, to shape and retell "The Story," and to explain that the core principles driving change remain intact.[38]

SOME WORDS OF CAUTION

Expect Some Unanticipated Outcomes

Unless one adopts a very mechanistic notion of the management of change—where the link between action and outcome is very controllable and predictable—there are likely

TABLE 12.9 Fine-Tuning at Ford

Source: Nadler, 1988.

In 1995, Ford Motor company introduced a series of changes to the way the company designed and manufactured its cars and trucks. This involved changing from the existing functional structure, consolidating activities into five vehicle centers, and using a reduced number of platforms for its vehicle range.

After a year and a half, senior management wished to make modifications in light of the initial experience. However, the initial changes had been viewed with some skepticism by some groups and individuals both inside the company and in the financial community. As a result, when the time came to announce the modifications (for example, consolidating further from five to three vehicle centers), the company paid a lot of attention to making sure that the further changes were presented as a refinement, that is, a logical adjustment completely in keeping with the spirit and intent of the original change.

TABLE 12.10 Unanticipated Consequences at FedEx

Source: Pascale et al., 2000.

Federal Express introduced a new aircraft routing system with the intention of increasing the productivity of its pilots. More powerful computers and developments in scheduling algorithms made this seem feasible, the estimated savings in the hundreds of millions certainly made it attractive, and the pilots had a record of supporting measures intended to improve competitive efficiencies.

However, things didn't work out as planned. The new system produced flight plans that required pilots to cross the time zones of two hemispheres, undertake back-to-back trans-Pacific and trans-Atlantic flights and spend hours traveling by land to change aircraft.[a] Efforts by FedEx to improve the working of the new system failed to produce any improvement, however the company persisted with the new system.

In response, the pilots' union, despite having a reputation for compliance with management requirements, threatened a work stoppage if the system was not abandoned. Then, having taken this stance, its demands extended to a substantial wage increase, fewer flying hours, and improved retirement benefits.

Faced with the prospect of a strike by the pilots—which would have been the first pilot strike in the company's history—the FedEx management relented and the new scheduling system was substantially abandoned.

[a]Blackmon, 1998, cited in Pascale et al., 2000.

to be, in the context of most change programs, some unanticipated consequences (see Table 12.10).[39]

Unanticipated consequences may be good, bad, or neutral in terms of the intended change. Their existence is not necessarily a sign of management failure; it is an expected characteristic of organizations.[40] Pascale et al. argue that organizations are living systems and that, as such, the outcomes of actions in organizations have a probabilistic effect, not a deterministic effect. Unlike machines where the outputs are predictable (save machine malfunction), living systems are beyond precise control.[41]

No amount of planning and establishing rules and procedures can ever remove the unexpected, placing a premium on "processes of resilience, intelligent reaction and improvisation."[42] The challenge for managers is how to respond to unexpected outcomes, especially as some may be warning signs of more serious problems. The first step is to face up to the outcome. Weick and Sutcliffe, in *Managing the Unexpected*,[43] warn that while "all of us tend to be awfully generous in what we treat as evidence that our expectations are confirmed," we are also prone to explaining away evidence that might be seen as disconfirming our expectations.[44]

Be Alert to Measurement Limitations

According to Senge et al., "assessing success of innovative practices is an inherently complex and ambiguous challenge."[45] One key reason for this is that the advantages that can flow from the new ways of doing things may not be picked up by traditional measures. This can make it very difficult for the virtues of the changes to be recognized where the credibility of the established measures is much more firmly embedded than that of the new practices.[46]

Another possible measurement problem to be alert to is that of "premature measurement." While it is good to have some "short-term wins," measuring the effects

TABLE 12.11 Gilbertson on the Timing of Measurement

Source: Senge et al., 1999:235.

> Even in the best cases, performance will decline at first because of the concentration of energy and effort you need with such a huge initiative. The board and top management need to understand this so you can manage it. The increased efficiencies will emerge over a longer period of time, while your costs increase at the beginning. You need to understand very clearly the time at which you expect to see cost savings and improved performance.
>
> Roger Gilbertson, CEO, Merit Health Care System

of change should be connected to the time frame over which expected benefits will become manifest. Beer et al. note that the "payoff" to organizational change will often come "from persistence over a long period of time as opposed to quick fixes [but that] this mind-set is difficult to maintain in an environment that presses for quarterly earnings."[47]

To complicate matters, organizational change does not necessarily flow in a linear fashion. Initiating change is likely to unleash many factors that interconnect—sometimes reinforcing, sometimes canceling out—in ways that mean that at various points change may seem to be proceeding at a great rate, while at other times it may seem to almost have stalled.

In fact, in some instances, things may get worse before they get better. As noted by Whittington et al., the benefits flowing from a change may conform to a "J curve," where the initial impact over time is negative (the curve turns down) for a period before it becomes positive (the curve turns upwards) (see Table 12.11).[48]

A key task for those involved in the management of change is to manage the expectations of others so that perceptions of the success of a change are not influenced (detrimentally) by unrealistic expectations as to the rate at which the positive effects of the change will become manifest.

Don't "Declare Victory" Too Soon

Because the embedding of change into the culture of the organization may take years in some cases, Kotter cautions against "declaring victory too soon."[49] He advises that "while celebrating a win is fine, declaring the war won can be catastrophic"[50] because until a change is firmly embedded in an organization's culture, there remains the real possibility of regression to prechange practices.

There may still be a significant number of people who are hoping that the change will fail and that things will return to "normal."[51] However, the existence of people who feel this way will not always be obvious. Fisher refers to "vicious compliance," whereby people exhibit apparent compliance ("they will nod and smile and agree with everything you say") but remain deeply resentful of the change and are simply biding their time until the time is right for the "old ways," to which they remain committed, to return.[52]

Beware Escalation of Commitment

Just as it is important to be aware of the potential for the premature labeling of a change as unsuccessful, it is also important to recognize that not all intended changes are a good idea. If a change is not producing the desired outcome, it may be that the wisdom of the proposed change needs reconsidering. In this regard, it is important to be alert to a tendency—at least on the behalf of the change's strongest advocates—to assume that the failure for the change to produce the intended outcomes is due to either the allocation of insufficient resources to the change or the change needing longer to "prove itself." This may lead to the further commitment of resources—an "escalation of commitment."[53] Unfortunately, such action may result in "throwing good money after bad."

Staw and Ross identify four factors ("determinants") that can lead to escalation:[54]

1. *Project determinants*. Commitment is likely to increase where the lack of progress is considered to be due to a temporary problem, or where additional funding is considered likely to be effective, or where the relative payoff to come from additional investment is considered to be large.
2. *Psychological determinants*. "Sunk costs are not sunk psychologically."[55] Escalation can result from self-justification biases in which having been personally responsible for a decision can lead to continued commitment in order to try to avoid being associated with losses.
3. *Social determinants*. Escalation may occur as those most closely identified with a project throw more resources at it in an attempt to revive it and thereby save face by not being associated with a failed project. This response is encouraged by the existence of "the hero effect"; that is, the "special praise and adoration for managers who 'stick to their guns' in the face of opposition and seemingly bleak odds."[56]
4. *Organizational determinants*. Organizational units are likely to resist the abandonment of a project that is seen as central to the organization's identity. Staw cites the example of Lockheed's L1011 Tri-Star Jet program, arguing that Lockheed persisted with the project for more than a decade, despite huge losses—and predictions that it was unlikely ever to earn a profit—because to abandon it would have meant admitting that they were simply a defense contractor and not, as they preferred to believe, a pioneer in commercial aircraft.[57]

Avoiding Escalation

The successful management of change is therefore assisted if actions are taken to reduce the prospects of escalation occurring. Keil and Montealegre identify seven practices that can help reduce escalation:[58]

1. Don't ignore negative feedback or external pressure.
2. Hire an external assessor to provide an independent view on progress.

3. Don't be afraid to withhold further resources/funding; as well as limiting losses, it has symbolic value in that it is a fairly emphatic signal that there is concern with progress.
4. Look for opportunities to redefine the problem and thereby generate ideas for courses of action other than the one being abandoned.
5. Manage impressions. Frame the "de-escalation" in a way that saves face.
6. Prepare your stakeholders because, if they shared the initial belief in the rationale for the change, their reaction to an announcement of the abandonment of the change may be to resist.
7. Look for opportunities to deinstitutionalize the project; that is, to make clear that the project is not a central defining feature of the organization, so that a "stepping back" from the project, should it occur, does not imply any weakening of commitment to the central mission of the organization.

Additional practices that can help to reduce escalation are identified by Ghosh:[59]

1. Unambiguous feedback on progress reduces escalation; where feedback is ambiguous, the tendency of people to selectively filter ambiguous information will lead to escalation by those already committed to the change.
2. Regular progress reports (including explanations for deviation from budget) reduce escalation; where they are not required, they will not necessarily be sought prior to further commitment of resources.
3. Information of the future benefits of incremental investment reduces escalation; without this specific information, decision making is too heavily influenced by historical costs.

Being aware of the phenomenon of escalation of commitment is the starting point for managers to be alert to its possible emergence. However, even where there is awareness, this is still a tricky situation to manage because "the line between an optimistic 'can-do' attitude and over-commitment is very thin and difficult to discern."[60]

Recognize "Productive Failure"

The failure of an intended change is not always a problem that we should seek to rectify. It may be failing because it is not an appropriate change. In this situation, the emphasis needs to be on the capacity of the organization to learn from the experience. Marks and Shaw refer to the value of "productive failure" through which an organization has the capacity to add to its store of knowledge.[61] A "learning organization" is one that treats a failed change as something to "own up to" and from which to learn, rather than as something necessitating a witch hunt so blame can be allocated.

A learning organization sees occasional failure as a natural rather than a deviant state and as an opportunity to develop an enhanced capacity for improved future performance. For Marks and Shaw, an organization may gain more in the long term from a "productive failure" than from an "unproductive success," *unproductive* in this context meaning that the change has gone well "but nobody quite knows how or why other than to say 'We must be doing something right!' "[62]

In a similar vein, Jick and Peiperl argue that, for many organizations, the success of a given change may be considerably less important than the creation of an organizational culture in which people "recognize and thrive on the continuing necessity of change."[63] That is, "what many companies really want is to institutionalize the *journey*, rather than the change."[64]

EXERCISE 12.2

Managing Risk

One of the implications of many of the images of managing change that are presented in this book is that change is a process where there is a complex, and not necessarily predictable, relationship between actions and outcomes. Nonetheless, it is still likely that certain action—or, taking the reverse, certain inaction—will affect the probability of certain outcomes.

Based on the material in this book, provide a range of actions that you believe are likely to enhance the prospect of a change process being successful. For each action, identify the effects/outcomes that you believe are more likely to occur if that action is *not* taken.

Action	Likely Effect of Inaction
1.	
2.	
3.	

EXERCISE 12.3

Reflection on Your Experience of Change: Profile of Managers in General

In Exercise 12.2, "Managing Risk," you provided a range of actions that you believed are likely to enhance the prospect of a change process being successful.

1. Repeat this list.
2. Based on your own experience of change, rate each action in terms of how well, in your view, managers "handle" this action. For example, if you believe that a particular action is almost always badly handled by management (bad handling could include rarely using the specified action), rate the handling as "very poor."
3. Which are the actions that you have identified as most in need of attention (those you rated poor or very poor)?
4. Where possible, discuss your ratings with others in the group/class. Are any particular actions most commonly nominated as needing attention? What could be done to improve managers' capacity in this regard?

	Quality of "Handling"				
Action	**Very Good**	**Good**	**Neutral**	**Poor**	**Very Poor**
1.					
2.					
3.					

EXERCISE 12.4

Reflection on Your Experience of Change: Profile of Yourself

In Exercise 12.2, "Managing Risk," you provided a range of actions that you believed are likely to enhance the prospect of a change process being successful.

1. Repeat this list.
2. Rate yourself in regard to each action.
3. Which are the actions that you have identified as most in need of attention (those you rated poor or very poor)?
4. Where possible, discuss your ratings with others in the group/class. Are any particular actions most commonly nominated as needing attention? What could be done to develop your capacity in this regard?

	Quality of "Handling"				
Action	**Very Good**	**Good**	**Neutral**	**Poor**	**Very Poor**
1.					
2.					
3.					

Conclusion

In this chapter, we have stressed the difference between the implementation of change and the consolidation of change. The former has an uncertain time frame—it may not be sustained—so in order to address this matter, attention should be given to actions that assist the change having a sustained effect. In this regard, a number of actions are identified and discussed: redesigning roles, redesigning reward systems, linking selection decisions to change objectives, acting consistently with advocated actions, encouraging "voluntary acts of initiative," measuring progress, celebrating "en route," and fine-tuning.

Consolidation also provides some special challenges that are addressed in the second half of the chapter. For example, even in the best-managed situation, not all outcomes are controllable or predictable. It is wise to expect some unanticipated outcomes and not necessarily see these as a sign of your (or some other person's) shortcomings. Measuring progress also produces its own set of challenges because of such matters as the potential of well-established metrics to not suit the new situation and the nonlinear path of change introducing uncertainty as to when the progress of a change is most appropriately measured. In the latter regard, an associated danger awaits in the form of "declaring victory" too soon. Finally, we deal with the need to be alert to the phenomenon of "escalation of commitment" where the advocates of change are blind to its shortcomings and instead believe that "all will be well" as long as more resources are committed to the implementation of the change.

TABLE 12.12 **Chapter Reflections for the Practicing Change Manager**

- If you have been involved previously as a manager of change, how would you rate yourself in terms of your handling of the need to take actions that consolidate change? What have you done well? What not so well?
- When you've been on the receiving end of the change initiatives of others, how well have they handled the need to take actions that consolidate change? What have they done well? What not so well?
- Of the various cases presented in this chapter, which one resonates best with you? What is it about this case that you can relate to? Are there any implications for how you would act in future?
- How good are you at handling unanticipated outcomes?
- If there was one main idea that you took away from this chapter that you believe can be of most use to you as a change manager, what would it be?
- If you were to add an idea to the treatment of consolidation provided in this chapter, what would be your contribution?

Supplemental Reading

Beer, M., Eisenstat, R. A., and Spector, B. 1990. Why change programs don't produce change. *Harvard Business Review*, November–December:158–66.

Bossidy, L., Charan, R., with Burck, C. 2002. *Execution: The discipline of getting things done*. London: Random House.

Gerstner, L. V. 2002. *Who says elephants can't dance? Inside IBM's historic turnaround*. New York: Harper Business.

Harris, L. C., and Ogbonna, E. 2002. The unintended consequences of culture interventions: A study of unexpected outcomes. *British Journal of Management*, 13:31–49.

Kotter, J. 1995. Leading change: Why transformation efforts fail. *Harvard Business Review*, March–April:59–67.

Kotter, J. 1996. Anchoring new approaches in the culture. In *Leading change*, chap. 10. Boston: Harvard Business School Press.

Nadler, D. A. 1988. Staying on course: Consolidating and sustaining change. In *Champions of change: How CEOs and their companies are mastering the skills of radical change*, chap. 12. San Francisco: Jossey-Bass.

Reisner, R. A. F. 2002. When a turnaround stalls. *Harvard Business Review* 80(2):45–52.

Senge, P., Kleiner, A., Roberts, C., Ross, R., Roth, G., and Smith, B. 1999. Assessment and measurement. In *The dance of change*, chap. 8. New York: Doubleday.

Weick, K. E., and Sutcliffe, K. M. 2001. Managing the unexpected: Assuring high performance in an age of complexity. San Francisco: Jossey-Bass.

THE *CHALLENGER* DISASTER[65]

On January 28, 1986, the space shuttle *Challenger* rose into the sky, its seven crew strapped into their padded seats while the 2,000-ton vehicle vibrated as it gained speed and altitude. The launch was going perfectly. Seventy seconds had passed since liftoff and the shuttle was already 50,000 feet above the earth. From Mission Control at Houston's Johnson Space Center, Spacecraft Communicator Richard Covey instructed "*Challenger* go at throttle up."

"Roger, go at throttle up," replied Commander Dick Scobee on board *Challenger*.

> But in the next few seconds *Challenger* slammed through increasingly violent manoeuvres. [Pilot] Mike Smith voiced sudden apprehension. "Uh-oh." In Mission Control, the pulsing digits on the screen abruptly stopped. . . Mission Control spokesman Steve Nesbitt sat above the four console tiers. For a long moment he stared around the silent, softly lit room. The red ascent trajectory line was stationary on the display screen across the room. Finally he spoke: "Flight controllers here looking very carefully at the situation. Obviously a major malfunction."[66]

The presidential commission, headed by former Secretary of State William Rogers, that was set up to investigate the cause of the disaster had little trouble identifying the physical cause. One of the joints on a booster rocket failed to seal. The "culprits" were the synthetic rubber O-rings that were designed to keep the rockets' superhot gases from escaping from the joints between the booster's four main segments. Resulting flames then burned through the shuttle's external fuel tank. Liquid hydrogen and liquid oxygen then mixed and ignited, causing the explosion that destroyed the *Challenger*.

However, "the Rogers Commission" investigations also revealed a lot about the internal workings of NASA. It was a geographically dispersed matrix organization. Its HQ was in Washington, D.C., where its most senior managers, including its head, NASA administrator James Begg, were mainly involved in lobbying activity reflecting the dependence on federal funds (and its subsequent vulnerability to fluctuations in funding). Mission Control was located at the Johnson Space Center in Houston, Texas; all propulsion aspects (main engines, rocket boosters, fuel tanks) were the responsibility of the Marshall Space Center in Huntsville, Alabama; while the assembly and launch took place at the Kennedy Space Center, Cape Canaveral, Florida.

The centers existed in an uneasy alliance of cooperation and competition. The Marshall Center in particular was known for its independent stance based on its proud tradition going right back through the *Apollo* program to the early days of rocketry with Werner von Braun. One manifestation of this pride, reinforced by its autocratic leader William Lucas, was that loyalty to Marshall came before all. Any problems that were identified were to be kept strictly "in-house," which at Marshall meant within Marshall. Those who failed to abide by this expectation—perhaps by talking too freely to other parts of NASA—could expect to receive a very public admonishment. Marshall was also at the center of a "can-do" attitude within NASA, the idea that great objectives are achievable if only the will is there. Born of the *Apollo* success, this took form in Marshall as a strong pride in the achievement of objectives and strongly held views that if a flight was to be delayed for any reason, it would not ever be because of something caused by Marshall.

The Commission also concluded that NASA was working with an unrealistic schedule for flights. The formal schedule was for 12 in 1984, 14 in 1985, 17 in 1986, 17 in 1987, and 24 in 1988. In practice it had managed five in 1984 and eight in 1985. Congressional critics had begun to question the appropriateness of continuing the current (high) level of funding to the program when NASA was falling so far short in meeting its own goals. However, rather than revise its schedules, these were retained and increased pressure to meet the schedules was placed by senior NASA managers on employees and contractors.

Most of the design and construction work in the shuttle program was contracted out. One of the contractors was Morton Thiokol, a Brigham City, Utah–based company that had won the contract to produce the solid rocket boosters. At the time of the *Challenger* launch, Thiokol and NASA were in the middle of contract negotiations that would determine whether or not Thiokol would be awarded a renewal of the contract.

The Commission revealed that there had been doubts about the reliability of the O-rings for some time. Since 1982 they had been labeled a "criticality 1" item, a label reserved for components whose failure would have a catastrophic result. However, despite evidence of O-ring erosion on many flights and requests from O-ring experts both inside NASA and inside Thiokol that flights be suspended until the problem was resolved, no action was taken. There was no reliable backup to the O-rings; this violated a long-standing NASA principle, but each time a flight was scheduled, this principle was formally waived.

A cold front hit Cape Canaveral the day before the scheduled launch; temperatures as low as 18°F were forecast for that night. Engineers from Thiokol expressed their serious reservations about the wisdom of launching in such conditions because the unusually cold conditions at the launch site would affect the O-rings' ability to seal. As a result, a teleconference was called for that evening.

At the teleconference, Roger Boisjoly, Thiokol's O-ring expert, argued that temperature was a factor in the performance of the rings and Robert Lund, Thiokol's vice president for engineering, stated that unless the temperature reached at least 53°F he did not want the launch to proceed. This position led to a strong reaction from NASA in the form of Lawrence Mulloy, Marshall's chief of the solid rocket booster program, and George Hardy, Marshall's deputy director of science and engineering. Hardy said that he was "appalled" at the reasoning behind Thiokol's recommendation to delay the launch and Mulloy argued that Thiokol had not proven the link between temperature and erosion of the O-rings, adding, "My God, Thiokol, when do you want me to launch, next April?" A view expressed at the Commission was that the Thiokol engineers had been put in a position where, in order for a delay to be approved, they were being required to prove that the O-rings would fail, rather than to prove that they would be safe at the low temperatures before a go-ahead was approved.

A break was taken in the teleconference to allow the Thiokol management team to consider their position. The Thiokol engineers were still unanimously opposed to a launch. Jerald Mason, Thiokol's senior vice president, asked Robert Lund to "take off his engineering hat and put on his management hat." Polling just the senior Thiokol managers present, not any of the engineers, Mason managed to get agreement to launch. The teleconference was then reconvened, the Thiokol approval was conveyed, no NASA managers expressed any reservations, and so the OK to launch was given.

POST-*CHALLENGER* CHANGES IN NASA

The Commission's recommendations included that NASA restructure its management to tighten control, set up a group dedicated to finding and tracking hazards in regard to shuttle safety, and review its critical items as well as submitting its redesign of the booster joint to a National Academy of Sciences group for verification. The official line within NASA was that the necessary changes had been successfully implemented. A NASA news release on January 22, 1988, stated that:

> In response to various reviews of NASA safety and quality programs conducted in the aftermath of the *Challenger* accident and associated recommendations for improvements, NASA has acted to elevate agency emphasis on safety and implement organizational changes to strengthen SRM&QA [Safety, Reliability, Management & Quality Assurance] programs. . . There has been a 30 percent increase in NASA personnel assigned to SRM&QA functions since January 1986.

THE *COLUMBIA* DISASTER[67]

On February 1, 2003, the space shuttle *Columbia*'s braking rockets were fired as the shuttle headed toward a landing at Kennedy Space Center. As it passed over the United States, observers spotted glowing pieces of debris falling from the shuttle. At 8:59:32 a.m. EST, commander Rick Husband replied to a call from Mission Control, but his acknowledgment ceased mid-transmission. About a minute later, *Columbia* broke up, killing its seven astronauts.

The *Columbia* Accident Investigation Board was formed to identify what had happened. In its August 2003 final report, it identified the physical cause of the accident. A 1.67-pound slab of insulating foam fell off the external fuel tank 81.7 seconds after *Columbia* was launched (January 16), hit the left wing, and caused a breach in the tiles designed to protect the aluminum wing from the heat of reentry. On reentry, the breach allowed superheated gas into the wing, which, as a result, melted in critical areas.

But the Board also addressed the nonphysical factors that contributed to the disaster. Because of no improvement in the level of NASA funding, NASA Administrator Daniel Goldin pushed a "Faster, Better, Cheaper" program that impacted on the shuttle program.

> The premium placed on maintaining an operational schedule, combined with ever-decreasing resources, gradually led Shuttle managers and engineers to miss signals of potential danger. Foam strikes on the Orbiter's Thermal Protection System, no matter what the size of the debris, were "normalized" and accepted as not being a "safety-of-flight risk."[68]

The shuttle workforce was downsized and various shuttle program responsibilities (including safety oversight) had been outsourced. Success was being measured through cost reduction and the meeting of schedules and the shuttle was still being mischaracterized as operational rather than developmental technology.

The Board particularly identified NASA's organizational culture as being as much to blame as the physical causes. According to the Board:

> Though NASA underwent many management reforms in the wake of the Challenger accident,...the agency's powerful human space flight culture remained intact, as did many practices...such as inadequate concern over deviations from expected performance, a silent safety program, and schedule pressure.[69]

Further, the Board stated:

> Cultural traits and organization practices detrimental to safety and reliability were allowed to develop, including: reliance on past success as a substitute for sound engineering practices (such as testing to understand why systems were not performing in accordance with requirements/specifications); organizational barriers which prevented effective communication of critical safety information and stifled professional differences of opinion; lack of integrated management across program elements, and the evolution of an informal chain of command and decision-making processes

that operated outside the organization's rules.[70]

According to the Board: "NASA's blind spot is that it believes it has a strong safety culture [when in fact it] has become reactive, complacent, and dominated by unjustified optimism."[71] The Board found that while NASA managers said that staff were encouraged to identify safety issues and bring these to the attention of management, there was evidence to the contrary, including insufficient deference to engineers and other technical experts. Also, while NASA's safety policy specified oversight at headquarters combined with decentralized execution of safety programs at the program and project levels, the Board found that the reality was that NASA had not been willing to give the latter the independent status for this to actually work.

The external tank of the shuttle was designed with a layer of insulation tiles that were designed to stick to the tank, not to be shed. Similarly, the shuttle's heat shield was not designed to be damaged (the tiles are very fragile, so much so that the shuttle isn't allowed to fly in rain or stay outside when it hails).

However, the experience of previous launches was that foam sometimes did fall off and tiles sometimes were damaged. But this was occurring without any noticeable negative effect on the functioning of the shuttle. Of 112 flights prior to the fatal Columbia flight, foam had been shed 70 times and tiles had come back damaged every time. Over time, NASA managers got used to the idea that such damage would occur and convinced themselves there was no safety-of-flight issue. The Board reported that "program management made erroneous assumptions about the robustness of a system based on prior success rather than on dependable engineering data and rigorous testing."[72]

The report cites eight separate "missed opportunities" by NASA during the 16-day flight to respond to expressions of concern or offers that could have assisted. For example, engineer Rodney Rocha's e-mail four days into the mission asking Johnson Space Center if the crew had been directed to inspect *Columbia*'s left wing for damage had been left unanswered. Also NASA had failed to accept the U.S. Defense Department's offer to obtain spy satellite imagery of the damaged shuttle.

The CAIB faulted NASA managers for assuming that there would be nothing that could be done if the foam strike had indeed caused serious damage to the TPS. After the accident, NASA engineers, working on the request of the CAIB, concluded that it might have been possible either to repair the wing using materials on board *Columbia* or to rescue the crew through a sped-up launch of the shuttle *Atlantis*.

The Board also criticized NASA managers for not taking steps to ensure that minority and dissenting voices were heard. It commented:

> all voices must be heard, which can be difficult when facing a hierarchy. An employees' location in the hierarchy can encourage silence. Organizations interested in safety must take steps to guarantee that all relevant information is presented to decision makers. This did not happen in the meetings during the Columbia mission....Program managers created huge barriers against dissenting opinions by stating preconceived conclusions based on subjective knowledge and experience, rather than on solid data.[73]

The NASA intercenter photo working group had recommended that the loss of foam be classified as an in-flight anomaly—a much more critical designation than it currently had—but this was not approved by the program requirements control board. The engineers were placed in the situation of having to prove that a safety-of-flight issue existed before the shuttle program management would take action to get images of the left wing. The Board found that this was just one example of a more general situation where those concerned with safety found themselves having to prove that a situation was unsafe, whereas it might be reasonably expected that the emphasis would be on proving that a high level of safety existed.

The Board also concluded that there was an unofficial hierarchy among NASA programs and directorates that hindered the flow of communications:

> Management decisions made during Columbia's final flight reflect missed opportunities, blocked or ineffective communication channels, flawed analysis, and ineffective leadership. Perhaps most striking is the fact that management... displayed no interest in understanding a problem and its implications. Because managers failed to avail themselves of the wide range of expertise and opinion necessary to achieve the best answer to the debris strike question—"*was this a safety-of-flight concern?*"—some Space Shuttle Program managers failed to fulfill the implicit contract to do whatever is possible to ensure the safety of the crew. In fact, their management techniques unknowingly imposed barriers that kept at bay both engineering concerns and dissenting views, and ultimately helped create "blind spots" that prevented them from seeing the danger the foam strike posed.[74]

The Board concluded that the post-Challenger changes "were undone over time by management actions"[75] and that "the pre-Challenger layers of processes, boards and panels that had produced a false sense of confidence in the system and its level of safety returned in full force prior to Columbia."[76]

Questions

1. What aspects of NASA practice revealed in the aftermath of the *Columbia* disaster suggest that the changes sought in the aftermath of the *Challenger* disaster were not consolidated?
2. This chapter provides a discussion of actions that can be taken to consolidate change. Which of the following do you see as most applicable to addressing the situation described in this case?

    - Redesign roles.
    - Redesign reward system.
    - Link selection decisions to change objectives.
    - Act consistently with advocated actions.
    - Encourage "voluntary acts of initiative."
    - Measure progress.
    - Celebrate en route.
    - Fine-tune.

3. This chapter provides some words of caution in terms of what to be alert to in regard to consolidation. Which of the following do you see as most applicable to addressing the situation described in this case?

    - Expect some unanticipated outcomes.
    - Be alert to measurement limitations.
    - Don't "declare victory" too soon.
    - Beware escalation of commitment.
    - Recognize "productive failures."

TABLE 12.13 **Additional Case Studies**

Lufthansa 2003: Energizing a Decade of Change
Bruch, H. (2004) *University of St Gallen, Switzerland*
GE's Two-Decade Transformation: Jack Welch's Leadership (Multimedia Case)
Bartlett, C. A., & Wozny, M. (2000) *Harvard Business School*
Citigroup 2003: Testing the Limits of Convergence (A)
Applegate, L. M. (2004) *Harvard Business School*
The New HP: The Clean Room and Beyond
Kind, L., & Perlow, L. A. (2004) *Harvard Business School*

Bibliography

Beer, M., Eisenstat, R. A., and Spector, B. 1990. Why change programs don't produce change. *Harvard Business Review*, November–December:158–66.

Beer, M., and Nohria, N. 2000. *Breaking the code of change*. Boston: Harvard Business School Press.

Berger, B. 2003. *Columbia* report faults NASA culture, government oversight. August 26. http://www.space.com/missionlaunches/caib_preview_030707-1.html

Blackmon, D. A. 1998. FedEx pilots trade their old loyalties for a tougher union. *The Wall Street Journal*, October 19:A1.

Brockner, J. 1992. The escalation of commitment to a failing course of action: Towards theoretical progress. *Academy of Management Review* 17:39–61.

Clarke, L. 1993. The disqualification heuristic: When do organizations misperceive risk? *Research in Social Problems and Public Policy* 5:289–312.

Columbia Accident Investigation Board (CAIB) (2003) *Report Volume 1*, Washington, DC: NASA.

Covault, C. 2003. Failure an option? NASA's shallow safety program put *Columbia* and her crew on same path as *Challenger*. *Aviation Week & Space Technology* 159(9):27–35.

Dodd-McCue, D., Matejka, J. K., and Ashworth, D. N. 1989. Deep waders in muddy waters: Rescuing organizational decision makers. In *Organizational behavior: Readings and exercises*, ed. J. W. Newstrom and K. Davis, 80–84. 8th ed. New York: McGraw-Hill.

Fisher, A. B. 1995. Making change stick. *Fortune*, April 17:121–24.

Gerstner, L. V. 2002. *Who says elephants can't dance? Inside IBM's historic turnaround*. New York: Harper Business.

Ghosh, D. 1997. De-escalation strategies: Some experimental evidence. *Behavioral Research in Accounting* 9:88–112.

Hallowell, R., Cash, J. I., and Ibri, S. 1997. Sears, Roebuck and Company (A): Turnaround. Case 9-898-007. Boston: Harvard Business School.

Harris, L. C., and Ogbonna, E. 2002. The unintended consequences of culture interventions: A study of unexpected outcomes. *British Journal of Management* 13:31–49.

Jick, T. D., and Peiperl, M. A. 2003. *Managing change: Cases and concepts*. 2nd ed. New York: McGraw-Hill/Irwin.

Kanter, R. M., Stein, B. A., and Jick, T. D. 1992. *The challenge of organizational change*, 375–81. New York: Free Press.

Keil, M., and Montealegre, R. 2000. Cutting your losses: Extricating your organization when a big project goes awry. *Sloan Management Review* 41(3):55–68.

Kotter, J. 1995. Leading change: Why transformation efforts fail. *Harvard Business Review*, March–April:59–67.

Kotter, J. 1996. *Leading change*. Boston: Harvard Business School Press.

Kurtzman, J. 1998. Paying attention to what really counts. *Art of Taking Charge* 3(1):1–12.

Lawler, E. E., III. 2000. Pay system change: Lag, lead, or both? In *Breaking the code of change*, ed. M. Beer and N. Nohria, 323–36. Boston: Harvard Business School Press.

Magnusson, E. 1986. A serious deficiency. *Time*, March 10:34–36.

Marks, M. L., and Shaw, R. B. 1995. Sustaining change: Creating the resilient organization. In *Discontinuous change: Leading organizational transformation*, ed. D. A. Nadler, R. B. Shaw, A. E. Walton, and Associates, 97–117. San Francisco: Jossey-Bass.

McConnell, M. 1987. Challenger*: A serious malfunction*. London: Simon & Schuster.

Morring, F., Jr. 2003. Culture shock. *Aviation Week & Space Technology* 159(9):31–34.

Nadler, D. A. 1988. *Champions of change: How CEOs and their companies are mastering the skills of radical change*. San Francisco: Jossey-Bass.

Olson, E. E., and Eoyang, G. H. 2001. *Facilitating organizational change: Lessons from complexity science*. San Francisco: Jossey-Bass/Pfeiffer.

Pascale, R. T., Millemann, M., and Gioja, L. 2000. *Surfing the edge of chaos*. New York: Crown Business.

Pfeffer, J., and Sutton, R. I. 2000. *The knowing-doing gap*. Boston: Harvard Business School Press.

Price Waterhouse Change Integration Team. 1995. *Better change: Best practices for transforming your organization*. New York: Irwin.

Price Waterhouse Change Integration Team. 1996. *The paradox principles: How high-performance companies manage chaos, complexity, and contradiction to achieve superior results*. New York: Irwin.

Reisner, R. A. F. 2002. When a turnaround stalls. *Harvard Business Review* 80(2):45–52.

Reynolds, P. C. 1987. Imposing a corporate culture. *Psychology Today*, March:33–38.

Rucci, A. J., Kirn, S. P., and Quinn, R. T. 1998. The employee-customer-profit chain at Sears. *Harvard Business Review*, January–February.

Schein, E. H. 1992. *Organizational culture and leadership*. 2nd ed. San Francisco: Jossey-Bass.

Schneider, B., Brief, A. P., and Guzzo, R. A. 1996. Creating a climate and culture for sustainable organizational change. *Organizational Dynamics*, Spring:7–19.

Senge, P., Kleiner, A., Roberts, C., Ross, R., Roth, G., and Smith, B. 1999. *The dance of change*. New York: Doubleday.

Shaffer, R. H., and Thomson, H. A. 1992. Successful change programs begin with results. *Harvard Business Review*, January–February:80–89.

Space.com Web site. http://www.space.com/columbiatragedy/

Staw, B. 1981. The escalation of commitment to a course of action. *Academy of Management Review* 6:577–87.

Staw, B. M., and Ross, J. 1987. Knowing when to pull the plug. *Harvard Business Review* 65 (March–April):68–74.

Staw, B. M., and Ross, J. 2004. Understanding behavior in escalation situations. In *Psychological dimensions of organizational behavior*, ed. B. M. Staw, 206–14. 3rd ed. Upper Saddle River, NJ Pearson Prentice Hall.

Weick, K. E., and Sutcliffe, K. M. 2001. *Managing the unexpected: Assuring high performance in an age of complexity*. San Francisco: Jossey-Bass.

Whittington, R., Pettigrew, A., and Ruigrok, W. 2000. New notions of organizational "fit." In *Mastering strategy*, ed. T. Dixon, 151–57. London: Financial Times/ Prentice-Hall.

Notes

1. The content of this case comes from Reisner (2002)
2. Nadler, 1988; Kotter, 1995.
3. Gerstner, 2002:177.
4. Kotter, 1995:67.
5. Kotter, 1996:156.
6. Gerstner, 2002:187.
7. Beer et al., 1990:159.

8. Beer et al., 1990:159.
9. Beer and Nohria, 2000:267.
10. Fisher, 1995:122.
11. Nadler, 1988:257.
12. Lawler, 2000:323.
13. Schein, 1992:243.
14. Kotter, 1995:67.
15. Kanter et al., 1992:513.
16. Senge et al., 1999:200.
17. Schneider, Brief, and Guzzo, 1996:12.
18. Fisher, 1995:122.
19. Schein, 1992:231.
20. Fisher, 1995. The term "unintentional hypocrisy" is attributed to Peter Scott-Morgan.
21. Nadler, 1998:257.
22. Beer et al., 1990.
23. Nadler, 1988:251.
24. Nadler, 1988:252.
25. Kanter et al., 1992:513.
26. Price Waterhouse Change Integration Team, 1996.
27. This exercise is based on the discussion of measures in Price Waterhouse Change Integration Team, 1996.
28. Kotter, 1996:119.
29. Price Waterhouse Change Integration Team, 1995:17.
30. Schaffer and Thomson, 1992:86.
31. Kotter, 1995; Nadler, 1988.
32. Kotter, 1995.
33. Kotter, 1995:67.
34. Beer et al., 1990:165.
35. Price Waterhouse Change Integration Team, 1995.
36. Nadler, 1988.
37. Nadler, 1988.
38. Nadler, 1988:254.
39. See also Harris and Ogbonna, 2002.
40. Pascale et al., 2000:6.
41. See also Olson and Eoyang, 2001.
42. Weick and Sutcliffe, 2001:67.
43. Weick and Sutcliffe, 2001.
44. Weick and Sutcliffe, 2001:34. See also Clarke, 1993.
45. Senge et al., 1999:282.
46. Senge et al., 1999:283.
47. Beer et al., 1990:166.
48. Whittington et al., 1999.

49. Kotter, 1995:66.
50. Kotter, 1995:66.
51. Nadler, 1988:255.
52. Fisher, 1995. The term “vicious compliance” is attributed to Michael Hammer.
53. Dodd-McCue et al., 1989; Staw, 1981; Staw and Ross, 1987; Brockner, 1992.
54. Staw and Ross, 2004.
55. Staw and Ross, 2004:208.
56. Staw and Ross, 2004:209.
57. Staw and Ross, 2004:210.
58. Keil and Montealegre, 2000.
59. Ghosh, 1997.
60. Keil and Montealegre, 2000:xx.
61. Marks and Shaw, 1995.
62. Marks and Shaw, 1995:116.
63. Jick and Peiperl, 2003:183.
64. Jick and Peiperl, 2003:183.
65. The information on the *Challenger* disaster is from the following sources: McConnell, 1987; Magnuson, 1986.
66. McConnell, 1987:xv.
67. The information on the *Columbia* disaster is from the following sources: http://www.space.com/columbiatragedy/ (in particular Berger, 2003; CAIB, 2003; Covault, 2003; Morring, 2003).
68. CAIB (2003):190.
69. CAIB (2003):101.
70. CAIB (2003):177.
71. CAIB (2003):203, 180.
72. CAIB (2003):184.
73. CAIB (2003):192.
74. CAIB (2003):170.
75. CAIB (2003):198.
76. CAIB (2003):199.

General Index

G

H

N

S

X

Y

Z